ATLAS OF ANCIENT EGYPT

Editor Graham Speake
Art editor Andrew Lawson
Map editor John-David Yule
Design Bernard Higton
Production Clive Sparling
Index Scott Glover

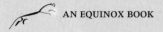 AN EQUINOX BOOK

Published in North America by
Facts on File, Inc., 460 Park Avenue South,
New York, N.Y. 10016, 1980;
reprinted 1982, 1984, 1985, 1986 (twice),
1987, 1988, 1989, 1990
Planned and produced by
Equinox (Oxford) Limited,
Musterlin House,
Jordan Hill Road,
Oxford, England, OX2 8DP
Copyright © Equinox (Oxford) Ltd 1980

Origination by Art Color Offset,
Rome, Italy; Chapman Brothers, Oxford;
M.B.A. Ltd, Chalfont St Peter, Bucks
Maps drawn and originated by
Lovell Johns Ltd, Oxford

Filmset by Keyspools Ltd,
Golborne, Lancs

Printed in Spain by Heraclio
Fournier SA, Vitoria

ISBN 0–87196–334–5

Frontispiece Ornamental titulary
of Ramesses VI (1151–1143), on
the pillars of a hall in his tomb
(No. 9) in the Valley of the Kings.
Adapted from the illustration in
Ippolito Rosellini, *I monumenti
dell'Egitto e della Nubia*, Vol. I:
Monumenti storici (Pisa, 1832).

ATLAS OF ANCIENT EGYPT

by John Baines
and Jaromír Málek

Facts On File®
New York • Oxford

CONTENTS

Part One – The Cultural Setting

Part Two – A Journey down the Nile

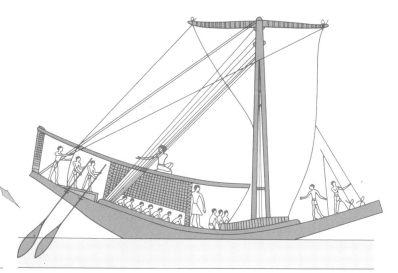

Part Three – Aspects of Egyptian Society

List of Maps

CHRONOLOGICAL TABLE

Dates marked * are absolute. All others are subject to margins of error. A full king list appears on pp. 36–37.

	BC 6500	4500	4000	3500	3000	2500
EGYPT	Late Paleolithic	Badarian (Nile valley) Merimda (delta) Faiyum	Naqada I (Nile valley)	Naqada II (Nile valley) Maʿadi el-ʿOmari (Memphite area)	**Foundation of the Egyptian state** (late Naqada II) **c. 3050** **Early Dynastic Period 2920–2575** 1st Dynasty 2920–2770 2nd Dynasty 2770–2649 3rd Dynasty 2649–2575	**Old Kingdom 2575–2134** 4th Dynasty 2575–2465 5th Dynasty 2465–2323 6th Dynasty 2323–2150 **1st Intermediate Period 2134–2040** 9th–10th Dynasties (Herakleopolis) 2134–2040 11th Dynasty (Thebes) 2134–2040

Painted terracotta figure of a dancing woman. Naqada I Period.

The Step Pyramid of Djoser at Saqqara. c. 2630.

Painting of geese from the tomb of Itet at Maidum. c. 2560.

	BC 6500	4500	4000	3500	3000	2500
LOWER NUBIA/ UPPER NUBIA	Late Paleolithic	Neolithic Abkan Post-Shamarkian Khartum Variant		Early A Group	Classic A Group Terminal A Group Little settled population	C Group *Kerma culture*
SYRIA/ PALESTINE	*Neolithic Jericho 8500*			Urban society: Habuba el-Kebira	Early Bronze Age *Egyptian contact with Palestine* Ebla	Egyptian contact with Byblos Destruction of Ebla Middle Bronze Age
MESOPOTAMIA/ IRAN	*Neolithic 6500* Neolithic 6000 Late Neolithic ʿUbaid 5000 Irrigation farming 5500			Urban society: Uruk Invention of writing *Proto-Elamite expansion (literacy)*	Jamdat Nasr Early Dynastic Period	Sargonid Dynasty 3rd Dynasty of Ur Isi
ANATOLIA	Neolithic Catal Hüyük 6500					
AEGEAN	Neolithic 6500				Early Bronze Age	Middle Bronze Age

2000	1500	1000	500	AD

Middle Kingdom 2040–1640
11th Dynasty (all Egypt) 2040–1991
12th Dynasty *1991–1783
13th Dynasty 1783–after 1640
2nd Intermediate Period 1640–1532
15th Dynasty (Hyksos) 1640–1532
17th Dynasty (Thebes) 1640–1550

New Kingdom 1550–1070
18th Dynasty 1550–1307
'Amarna Period 1352–1333
19th Dynasty 1307–1196
20th Dynasty 1196–1070
3rd Intermediate Period 1070–712
21st Dynasty 1070–945

22nd Dynasty 945–712
23rd Dynasty c.828–712
24th Dynasty 724–712
25th Dynasty (Nubia and Theban area) 770–712
Late Period 712–332
25th Dynasty (Nubia and all Egypt) 712–657
26th Dynasty *664–*525

27th Dynasty (Persian) *525–*404
28th Dynasty *404–*399
29th Dynasty *399–*380
30th Dynasty *380–*343
2nd Persian Period *343–*332
Greco-Roman Period *332–*395 AD
Macedonian Dynasty *332–*304
Ptolemaic Dynasty *304–*30 BC

Roman emperors *30 BC–395 AD
Byzantine Period *395–*640

Head of Ma'ya, relief in the Theban tomb of Ra'mose No. 55. c.1360.

Detail of facade of the Great Temple of Abu Simbel. c.1270.

The "Berlin Green Head," from a private statue of schist. c.75 BC (?).

Inlaid gold funerary mask of Tut'ankhamun. c.1325.

Inlaid bronze figure of the Divine Adoratrice Karomama. c.850.

Facade of the temple of Hathor at Dendara. Construction dedicated 17 November 34 AD (the decoration is later).

Egyptian occupation
Kerma state
Kerma conquest
Pan-grave culture

Egyptian conquest (Upper and Lower)

Depopulation
Egyptian withdrawal

Rise of Napata-Meroë (the later 25th Dynasty)
25th Dynasty
Napata-Meroë state —4th century AD

Meroïtic-Egyptian condominium in Dodekaschoinos
Meroïtic writing

Meroïtic settlement
Fall of Meroë
X Group

Egyptian contact with Byblos   Hittite incursions

Late Bronze Age: city states
Egyptian occupation c.1530–1200
Mitanni 1520–1330
Hittite domination
Neo-Hittite states
Joshua and Judges

United Israelite monarchy
Kingdoms of Israel and Judah
Assyrian expansion
Babylonian captivity
Jews in Egypt

Persian rule
Revolt of Satraps
Alexander the Great
Seleucid Empire
Ptolemies

Roman Empire
Byzantine Empire

1st Dynasty of Babylon
Old Elamite Kingdom
Fall of Babylon (1595 or 1531)
Kassite Dynasty

Independence of Assur c.1380
Elamite expansion
2nd Dynasty of Isin

Assyrian Empire
Fall of Nineveh
Neo-Babylonian Empire
Medes

Persian conquest
Alexander the Great
Seleucid Empire
Parthian Dynasty

Parthian Dynasty
Sasanid Dynasty

Hittite Old Kingdom

Hittite Empire
Fall of Hittite Empire

Urartu
SW Anatolian states
Gyges of Lydia

Persian rule
Alexander the Great
Seleucid Empire
Ptolemies

Roman Empire
Byzantine Empire

Late Bronze Age

Linear B
Cretan destruction
Mycenaean destruction
Sub-Mycenaean

Protogeometric
Geometric
Orientalizing Period
Greeks in Egypt
Archaic Period

Classical Period
Wars with Persia; aid to Egypt
Alexander the Great *336–*323
Macedon
Seleucid Empire
Ptolemies

Roman Empire
Byzantine Empire

INTRODUCTION

The monuments – pyramids, temples and tombs, statues and stelae – represent the most valuable source for our knowledge of ancient Egypt. A study of Egyptian monuments, either those still at various sites all over Egypt, or those in their new locations in museums and collections, is a happy meeting-ground of specialists and non-specialists. No special knowledge is required in order to be impressed by the grandeur and technical accomplishment of the Great Pyramid at Giza, to be enchanted by paintings in the Ramessid private tombs at Deir el-Medina, or be left dumbfounded by the opulence and – rather erratic – taste shown in the objects from the tomb of Tut'ankhamun in the Valley of the Kings, and now in the Cairo Museum. Nonetheless, knowledge may add to our appreciation and enjoyment.

So the aim of this book is easily defined: to provide a systematic survey of the most important sites with ancient Egyptian monuments, an assessment of their historical and cultural importance and a brief description of their salient features, based on the most up-to-date Egyptological knowledge. Further chapters and special features deal with general aspects of Egyptian civilization. These enable the reader quickly to find his bearings in the initially bewildering mass of names of places, kings and gods, and at the same time help him to understand the broader issues in the development of Egyptian society, and provide a background to the fluctuating fortunes of Egyptian towns and temples.

Geographically, the basic limits of the book are set by the frontiers of Egypt along the Nile, at the first cataract of the Nile and at the sea; the main exception is Egypt's traditional imperial extension of Lower Nubia. The maps present much of the book's content topographically, and supplement the information in the text at many points. Those in Parts One and Three are organized by theme and period. In Part Two the maps for each section present a detailed, large-scale view of the successive stages of our journey, including both ancient and modern features.

The period covered by the native Egyptian dynasties of kings (with the brief interruptions of foreign rule), about 2920 BC to 332 BC, provides the temporal setting. But some knowledge of the Predynastic Period is essential for understanding the earliest stages of Egyptian dynastic history, while for centuries the culture of the Greco-Roman Period remained largely Egyptian; these two phases, sometimes treated as separate units, are referred to and discussed where appropriate.

In writing this book we have envisaged our "typical reader" as anybody interested in ancient Egypt. We hope we have succeeded in eliminating the technical Egyptological jargon of our everyday work. The book is arranged in such a way that there is no need to read it straight through for its individual sections to remain comprehensible. There is a firm geographical framework, and the sites are discussed proceeding from south to north. The ancient Egyptians themselves used this scheme, and began their systematic lists at Elephantine (Aswan). Many modern books are arranged from north to south, which was the approach experienced by a traveler of the last century who arrived by boat at Alexandria, went from there to Cairo and, provided he was adventurous and prepared to accept some discomfort, further south. We have decided instead to follow the Egyptians, so that we can see the country as far as possible from their own viewpoint. The reader is, of course, free to begin his personal journey wherever he wishes. One of our aims has been to help those intending to visit Egypt by pointing out sites of interest to them and "briefing" them in advance. Those who have already seen that fascinating country might like to refresh their memory, and perhaps broaden their understanding of it, while those who simply like reading about civilizations of long ago may enjoy a new approach to one of the greatest. We hope that students in related disciplines will find this book useful when seeking reliable information about ancient Egypt.

Last, and most important, we hope that we shall communicate to our readers some of the enjoyment that brought us to the subject in the first place.

Part One is largely the work of John Baines and Part Two of Jaromír Málek; Part Three has been shared between us. We are particularly grateful to Helen Whitehouse for contributing "Egypt in Western Art," in which she is a leading expert. We should also like to thank Revel Coles, John Rea and John Tait for help with topics in their special fields.

PART ONE
THE CULTURAL SETTING

THE GEOGRAPHY OF ANCIENT EGYPT

Ancient Egypt was exceptional in its setting and unique in its continuity. The setting is the extreme case among several cultural and physical oases which were the great states of antiquity. It is almost impossible for us to recapture a feeling for this situation, with its mixture of geographical and human elements, just as we find it difficult to comprehend the time-span involved, half as long again as the Christian era. The position of the designer of the first pyramid, who created the earliest stone building on its scale in the world and lived in the only large, united state of the time, can never be recaptured. Any understanding of ancient Egypt must include an awareness of these and other enormous differences between antiquity and our own times. Yet mankind is the same everywhere, and much of our detailed knowledge of other civilizations will include material as ordinary as anything in our own lives. When approaching an alien civilization we need knowledge about both the ordinary and the exotic. Both are affected by the constraints of the environment. One exploits it in a routine fashion, the other more creatively; neither is independent of it.

In its geographical context Egypt is part of the larger area of northeastern Africa, and within this wider region its proximity to the heartlands of agricultural development in western Asia was initially of great significance. Dynastic Egypt was largely self-contained at most periods, but this was only because its economy was very heavily agricultural; for many important raw materials and for the requirements of high civilization foreign trade or travel into the desert was necessary, so that the perspective of the wider region is essential for understanding Egyptian culture. The same is true of the population of the country, which probably came from all the surrounding areas, and was always racially heterogeneous.

The boundaries of ancient Egypt

A definition of the boundaries of Egypt in antiquity – a theme of which the ancient texts are very fond and which reflects the Egyptian obsession with demarcations in general – is not simple. The basic areas of the country, the Nile valley, the delta and the Faiyum, were supplemented by parts of the surrounding regions over which the Egyptians exerted particular rights, such as those of mining. The southern frontier, traditionally at the first cataract of the Nile just south of Aswan, moved further south in some periods; in the New Kingdom, texts sometimes use words for Egypt to refer also to parts of Nubia, which were then incorporated into the state. Apart from these extensions of Egyptian territory, the line of oases that runs from Siwa in the north to el-Kharga in the south, approximately parallel to the Nile and about 200 kilometers west of it, was settled and governed by Egyptians during most of the Dynastic Period, reaching the peak of its prosperity in Roman times.

The main areas of Egypt form a river oasis in the desert. As such, the country was isolated from its neighbors to a greater extent than the other major states of antiquity, and its exceptional stability was due in large measure to this isolation, a striking indication of which is the complete absence of mention of Egypt in texts of the third millennium BC from Mesopotamia and Syria. Egypt was a magnet for settlers, but not for a concerted invasion, until perhaps the 13th century BC, and immigrants were always absorbed quickly into the population. But while much of Egyptian history is internal history, this is less true of the broader, imperfectly known changes of prehistory. Although the oasis of Egypt was fully formed by the end of the third millennium, it is necessary to relate this stage of climatic evolution to the more extensive alterations in earlier periods.

In the millennia after the end of the last Ice Age (about 10,000 BC) the Nile valley was one of the areas that attracted population from the Sahara and much of North Africa. During the Pleistocene era the valley was for much of the time impassable swamp, and river levels were very much higher than now. As the Sahara dried out at the end of this phase, it became progressively more inhospitable to the nomadic bands which had originally spread over much of its area. From as early as 15,000 BC there is a concentration of Paleolithic sites on the desert plateau on the edge of the valley, and one detail of the cultures may indicate that they were already feeling the effects of shortages and population pressure. Some of the flint blades from sites in both Egypt and Nubia show traces of use for gathering grasses, most probably wild grasses that could yield cereal grains. This is perhaps the earliest indication of cereal consumption known in the world, rivaled only by the site of Hayonim Terrace in Palestine. It is not evidence for a settled, agricultural life, but rather for an intensified use of resources by a still nomadic population.

This isolated instance of "progress" in Egypt seems not to have had any long-term influence. In the years from about 10,000 to 5000 BC there was a continuation of late and epi-Paleolithic modes of life, and there is no clear continuity between remains of this period and of the succeeding cultures. These are normally termed "Predynastic" by Egyptologists, and are Neolithic (with some use of metal), agricultural and settled; some stimuli in their development probably came from western Asia. They date from perhaps 4500 BC to the beginning of the Dynastic Period. The Egyptian setting of the Predynastic Period offered opportunities for exploitation not fundamentally different from those found at the beginning of the 19th century AD. The analogy is important, because most settlement has always been within the Nile valley and the delta, not on the desert edges (all areas not reached by the inundation are desert, or at best desert savanna, unless irrigated). It is likely that the

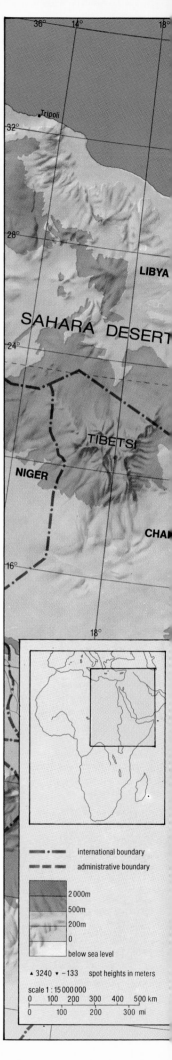

LIBYA

SAHARA DESERT

TIBETSI

NIGER

CHAI

Tripoli

international boundary

administrative boundary

2 000m
500m
200m
0
below sea level

▲ 3240 ▼ -133   spot heights in meters

scale 1 : 15 000 000
0   100   200   300   400   500 km
0   100   200   300 mi

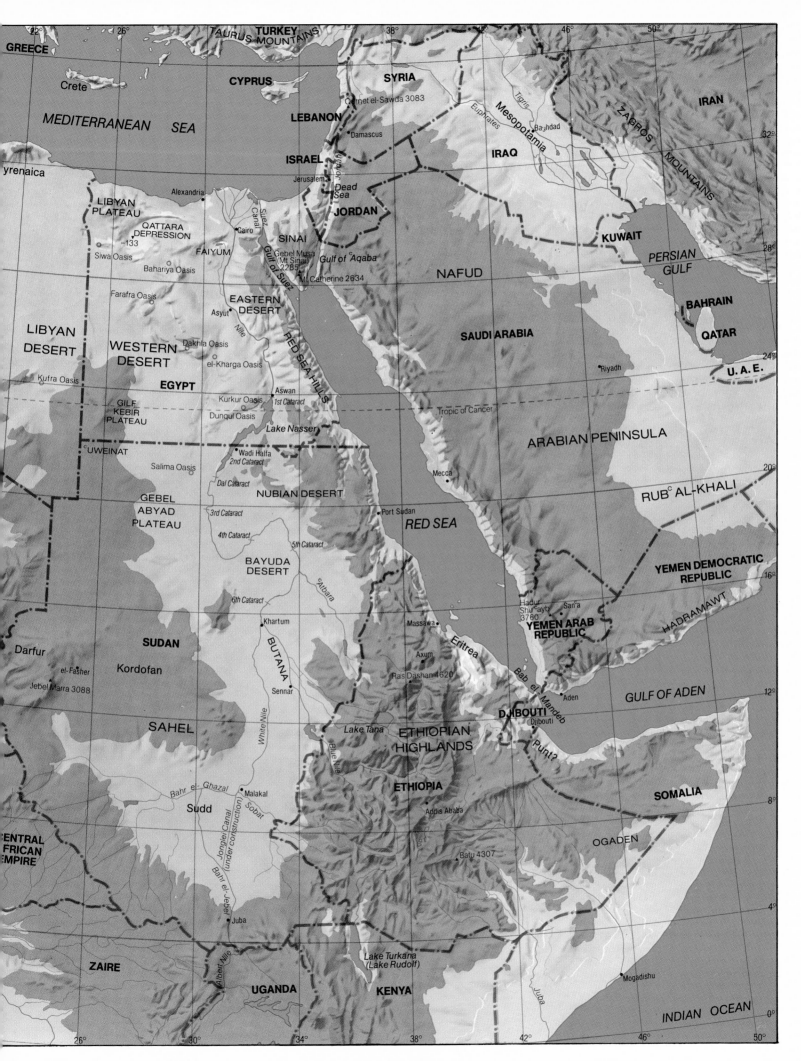

GREECE

MEDITERRANEAN SEA

Crete

TURKEY
TAURUS MOUNTAINS

CYPRUS

SYRIA

Qurnet el-Sawda 3083

LEBANON

Damascus

ISRAEL

Jerusalem

Dead Sea

JORDAN

Tigris

Euphrates

Mesopotamia

Baghdad

IRAQ

ZAGROS MOUNTAINS

IRAN

KUWAIT

PERSIAN GULF

Cyrenaica

Alexandria

LIBYAN PLATEAU

QATTARA DEPRESSION

-133

Siwa Oasis

Bahariya Oasis

Cairo

Suez Canal

FAIYUM

SINAI

Gebel Musa (Mt Sinai) 2285

Gulf of Suez

Mt. Catherine 2634

Gulf of 'Aqaba

NAFUD

BAHRAIN

QATAR

Farafra Oasis

EASTERN DESERT

Asyut

SAUDI ARABIA

U.A.E.

LIBYAN DESERT

WESTERN DESERT

Dakhla Oasis

Nile

RED SEA HILLS

Riyadh

el-Kharga Oasis

Kufra Oasis

EGYPT

Aswan

Kurkur Oasis

1st Cataract

GILF KEBIR PLATEAU

Dunqul Oasis

Tropic of Cancer

ARABIAN PENINSULA

UWEINAT

Lake Nasser

Wadi Halfa
2nd Cataract

Mecca

RUB' AL-KHALI

Salima Oasis

Dal Cataract

NUBIAN DESERT

GEBEL ABYAD PLATEAU

3rd Cataract

Port Sudan

RED SEA

4th Cataract

5th Cataract

YEMEN DEMOCRATIC REPUBLIC

BAYUDA DESERT

HADRAMAWT

6th Cataract

'Atbara

Hadur Shu'ayb 3760

San'a

Khartum

Massawa

YEMEN ARAB REPUBLIC

SUDAN

BUTANA

Eritrea

Darfur

Axum

el-Fasher

Kordofan

Ras Dashan 4620

Bab el Mandeb

Aden

GULF OF ADEN

Jebel Marra 3088

Sennar

White Nile

Blue Nile

DJIBOUTI

Djibouti

SAHEL

Lake Tana

ETHIOPIAN HIGHLANDS

Punt?

Bahr el- Ghazal

Malakal

Sobat

ETHIOPIA

SOMALIA

Sudd

Jonglei Canal (under construction)

Addis Ababa

CENTRAL AFRICAN EMPIRE

Bahr el-Jebel

OGADEN

Batu 4307

Juba

Albert Nile

Lake Turkana (Lake Rudolf)

Juba

ZAIRE

UGANDA

KENYA

Mogadishu

INDIAN OCEAN

13

precise location of settlements has not changed much, as there is the advantage in building on an earlier site that any accumulation of debris will raise a village above the valley floor and the danger of high floods. Both because earlier sites will be buried under modern ones and because 3 or more meters of silt have been deposited over the whole valley since 3000 BC, the archaeological record of settlement within the inundated and cultivated area is almost nil. Much of Egyptian archaeology is therefore very hypothetical.

The Nile valley of the Predynastic and later periods was a focal point in northern Africa for the development of agriculture and, later, urban society (agriculture is found at an earlier date further west along the Mediterranean coast). The whole region from the confluence of the Blue and White Niles to the delta may originally have been culturally similar, but the differences became marked by the beginning of the 1st Dynasty in Egypt proper. The concentration of population from various sources brought innovation from different directions, with the main stimulus perhaps coming from the Near East. It is a striking feature of native Egyptian culture at all periods that it is not technically innovative. Possibly the very prodigality of the land and its water has not encouraged invention.

In these formative periods contact between Egypt and neighboring areas was easier than it is now, as the desiccation of the Sahara was not yet complete, and the desert to the west, and especially the east, of the Nile valley supported a wider variety of flora and fauna and perhaps a larger nomadic population than now. Even for the inhabitants of the Nile valley these regions had some significance. During the later fourth and third millennia the desert became progressively more arid, a development that may be significant for the formation of the Egyptian state. The political collapse at the end of this climatic phase (c. 2150 BC) may have been triggered off by low inundations, which could be a symptom of a dry phase over the whole of northern Africa, rather like the drought in the Sahel in the early 1970s, another time of low floods.

Climate and geography played an important part in these developments. It is not possible to say that they determined their direction, for different results can be imagined, but they did rule out a continuation of previous subsistence patterns. The Nile and its flooding were dominant factors in the organization of the newly formed Egyptian state.

The Nile valley

Rainfall in the Nile valley is negligible, and it is no more than 100–200 millimeters per year in the delta; without the Nile, agriculture would be impossible in Egypt, except perhaps on the Mediterranean coast. It is a more regular and predictable source of water than any other of the world's great rivers whose valleys are used for irrigation farming. In antiquity its annual inundation between July and October covered most of the land in the Nile valley and the delta, and with careful management the water deposited was adequate to produce a crop. The pattern of the inundation can no longer be seen in operation, because the river has been checked by a whole series of dams and sluices built since 1830. These provide regulation of water levels from Sennar on the Blue Nile to the apex of the delta

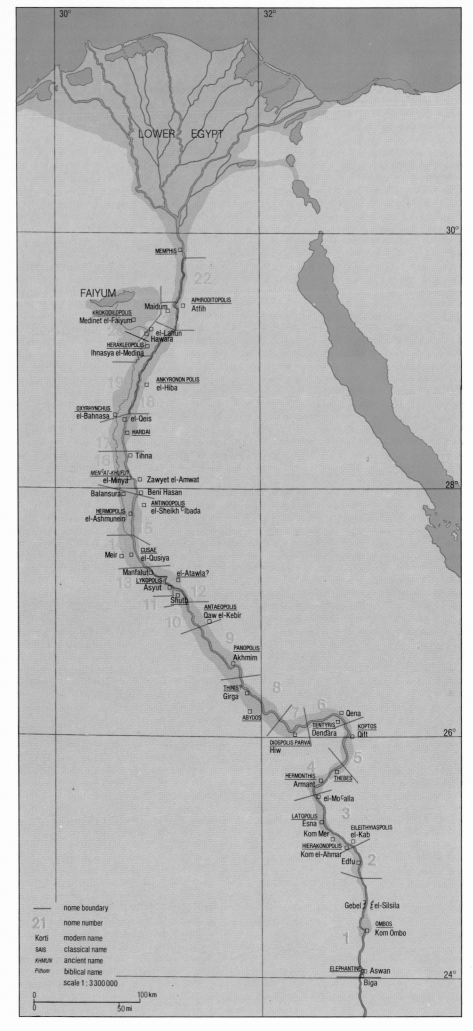

Left: The nomes of Upper Egypt
The nomes were the administrative divisions of Egypt, whose origins go back to the Early Dynastic Period. The 22 nomes of Upper Egypt were fixed by the 5th Dynasty, and their lengths along the river are recorded in the kiosk of Senwosret I at Karnak. The divisions on this map are based on the interpretation of these measurements, and are not valid for all periods. For Lower Egypt, the definitive number of 20 nomes was not established until the Greco-Roman Period. The Faiyum and the oases were not part of the scheme.

The total number of 42 had a symbolic value: there were 42 judges of the dead, and the early Christian writer, Clement of Alexandria (2nd century AD), states that the Egyptians had 42 sacred books.

Names underlined are those of ancient nome capitals. Where more than one is given, the capital shifted or the nome division changed at some period; where none is given, the capital is uncertain.

Right: The nomes of Lower Egypt
This arrangement of the 20 nomes of the Greco-Roman Period is based on lists in the temples of Edfu and Dendara. Many nome boundaries run along waterways whose reconstructed position is tentative. The names of known nome capitals are underlined.

Nomes had ensigns, which are worn on the heads of rows of nome personifications that decorate the base areas of temples. The ensigns of Upper and Lower Egypt are:

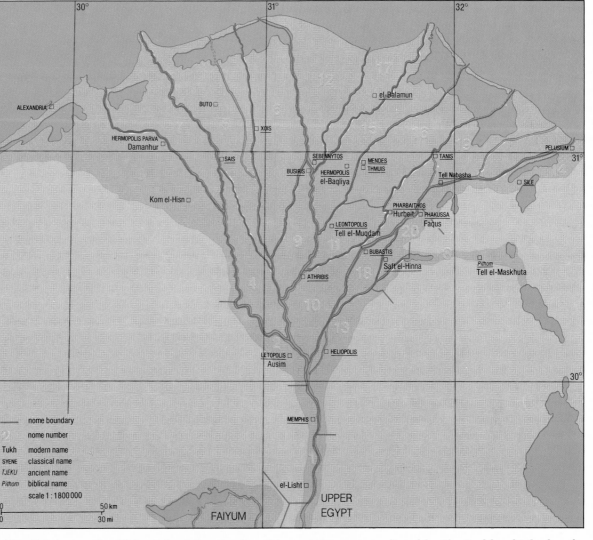

north of Cairo, and will be joined by the Jonglei canal on the White Nile in southern Sudan, between the Bahr el-Jebel and the Sobat river. Instead of observing modern conditions we must rely on earlier sources, from pharaonic documents to the *Description de l'Égypte* produced by Napoleon's expedition, and the writings of 19th-century irrigation engineers. In order to establish the precise area cultivated at any time in the past it is necessary to make detailed local studies. An estimate for early periods is shown in the map on p. 31.

The waters of the Nile come from the Blue Nile, which rises in the Ethiopian highlands, and the White Nile, which divides into a bewildering variety of smaller rivers in southern Sudan and reaches as far as Lake Victoria in central Africa. The White Nile is fed by the rains of the tropical belt, and provides a relatively constant supply through-

out the year, mediated by the Sudd, which absorbs much of the water in the rainy season. The Blue Nile and the ʿAtbara, which flows into the Nile some way north of Khartum, bring vast quantities of water from the Ethiopian summer monsoon, and provide almost all the water in the river from July to October (earlier in Sudan itself). This period corresponds to the time of the rains on the savanna in central Sudan. In Egypt the water in the river was at its lowest point from April to June. In July the level rose, and the flood normally began in August, covering most of the valley floor approximately from mid-August to late September, washing the salts out of the soil and depositing a layer of silt, which built up at the rate of several centimeters per century. After the water level fell, the main crops were sown in October and November, ripening from January to April according to variety. In antiquity

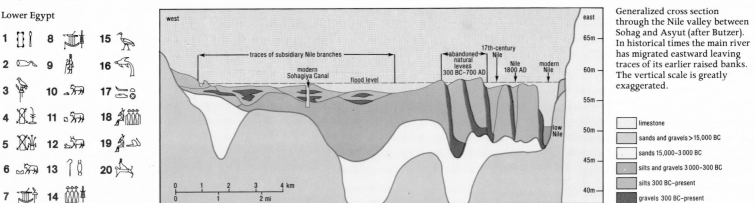

Generalized cross section through the Nile valley between Sohag and Asyut (after Butzer). In historical times the main river has migrated eastward leaving traces of its earlier raised banks. The vertical scale is greatly exaggerated.

limestone
sands and gravels > 15,000 BC
sands 15,000–3 000 BC
silts and gravels 3 000–300 BC
silts 300 BC–present
gravels 300 BC–present

agriculture was possible over much of the Nile valley and in large parts of the delta, the chief exceptions being tracts of swamp.

The valley and delta together form an area of about 34,000 square kilometers (1949–50 figures). Over long periods the valley area has varied considerably, but there has been no fundamental change in the last 5,000 years. The accumulation of silt and the management of water by man have, however, led to a gradual increase in useful land as the swamps that used to lie at the desert edge have been reclaimed for cultivation and flat stretches of desert have been incorporated in the flood plain. The profile of the valley and the detailed pattern of the flooding are relevant to this process. The water in the channel itself tended to erode the bed, and the deposition of silt during the flood raised the level of the land nearest the river, where the flow was strongest. So the profile of the valley is convex, and land near the river was drier and more readily settled than that further away. The flood was not a general overflowing of the bank, but ran through overflow channels on to the lower-lying land behind the banks. The flood crest ran more or less in parallel on the main area of the plain and in the river.

Agriculture involved controlling this flow pattern as far as possible. The areas of the plain were leveled to some extent, and formed into a series of basins of considerable size that "terraced" the land for irrigation in stages both down river and away from the banks (each terrace was only imperceptibly lower than the last, as the drop in river level from Aswan to the sea is no more than 85 meters). Because of the large size of the irrigated units a certain degree of central organization must have been needed for efficient exploitation of the land. Effective units would have been as large as the ancient provinces or nomes, of which there were just over 20 from the first cataract to south of Memphis. In the Dynastic Period the irrigated area in the valley increased gradually, with occasional setbacks, especially around 2100 BC, partly through improved technology (most imported), and partly through the reclamation of low-lying and swampy land. In early periods the areas of swamp provided a refuge for wild life that was hunted by the rich, and were the source of papyrus, which was made into a writing material and used for making mats, boats and utensils. These resources were replaced by those of intensive agriculture, and papyrus died out in the Middle Ages.

The main crops were cereals, emmer (*Triticum dicoccum*) for bread, and barley for beer (wheat was introduced in the Greco-Roman Period). In addition to these there were pulses, like lentils and chickpeas; vegetables – lettuces, onions and garlic; fruit, especially dates; an uncertain amount of fodder crops for animals, which were important for hides as well as meat; and plants grown for oil, such as sesame. Little is known about herbs, spices and seasonings. Honey was the chief sweetener, and bee keeping must have been an important activity. Meat was a luxury. Herds were probably grazed on swampy, marginal land, especially in the delta. The most prestigious meat was beef, but mutton, pork and goat were probably also eaten, as was the flesh of various species of antelope. Fowl was the food of the rich. Pigeon, which is very common in Egypt today, was eaten, probably the birds being raised in

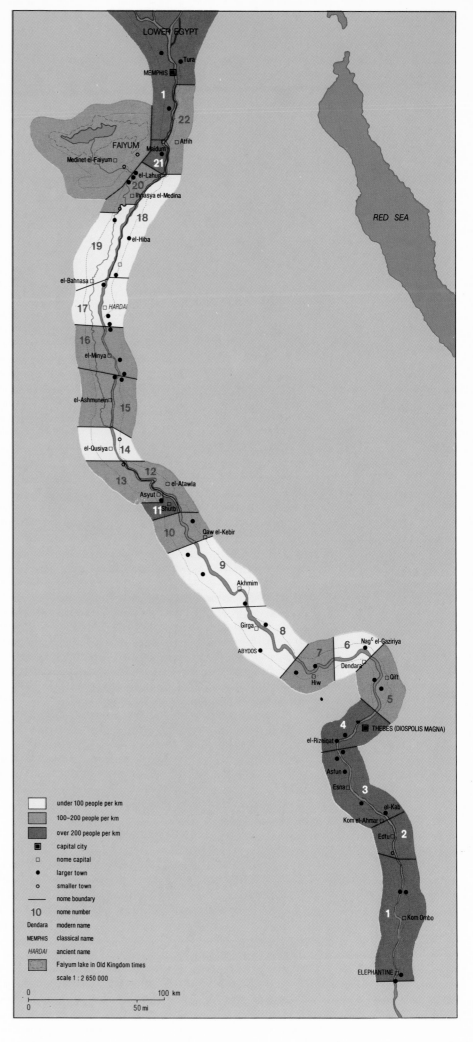

	under 100 people per km
	100–200 people per km
	over 200 people per km
▣	capital city
▫	nome capital
●	larger town
○	smaller town
——	nome boundary
10	nome number
Dendara	modern name
MEMPHIS	classical name
HARDAI	ancient name
	Faiyum lake in Old Kingdom times
	scale 1 : 2 650 000

Population density in the Nile valley
Estimated population densities in the nomes of the Nile valley in dynastic times (after Butzer). The densities are higher in narrow parts of the valley and near the capital, probably because these areas were fully settled at an earlier date, and may have been easier to exploit. The evidence does, however, favor them, since sites are preserved more easily where the desert is closer to the river; the result may therefore be a little exaggerated. The population of the delta, where there is no basis for a detailed estimate, probably overtook that of the valley in the New Kingdom.
    Large settlements are indicated according to approximate size, giving a rough supplementary guide; all are attested from Dynastic sources. Villages are not shown.

dovecotes, as were ducks, geese and various game birds. Chickens were not known before the New Kingdom, and probably became common only in the Greco-Roman Period. Grapes were grown chiefly in the western delta and in the oases, and made into wine, which was a luxury product; red wines are well attested, and white ones are known from Greek sources. The normal alcoholic drink was a coarse barley beer, which was made in the home; pomegranate and date wines are also known. Finally, two very important plant crops were papyrus and flax, which was used for almost all clothing and for sails and ropes (and possibly linseed oil), and also exported. The date palm was an additional important source of fiber.

The delta

The delta presents a generally similar picture to the Nile valley, but must have been a more difficult challenge for reclamation for agriculture. Even now large areas remain unsuitable for cultivation, but some of these may be swamps and lagoons created by later incursion of the sea. Because of the conditions, land reclamation was probably significant for the development of the area at all times. This was true already by the 4th Dynasty, when the delta is prominent in the lists of estates in Memphite tombs. Through its agricultural strength it dominated Egyptian political and economic life to an increasing extent from about 1400 BC on. The amount of land available in the delta was double that in the Nile valley, and the delta was closer to the Near East, contacts with which played an increasing part in later Egyptian history.

The delta was created by an interplay between the sea, in periods of high sea levels in earlier geological ages, and the mud deposited by the Nile. The areas suitable for permanent settlement were

Early photograph of a Nile boat with a cargo of water pots. Because of the ease of river transport, cheap and bulky objects are sent great distances and probably always have been. These pots are made near Qena, where there are suitable clays for porous jars that keep water cool by evaporation.

Old photograph of a pair of *shaduf*s – weight arms with buckets – being used to lift water for irrigation (the women in the foreground are collecting it for domestic purposes). The *shaduf*, which was introduced in the New Kingdom, could lift water as much as 3 meters, or more when used in tandem, as here, but it is so labor-intensive that its value is limited to garden crops or to topping up the water level of inundated areas.

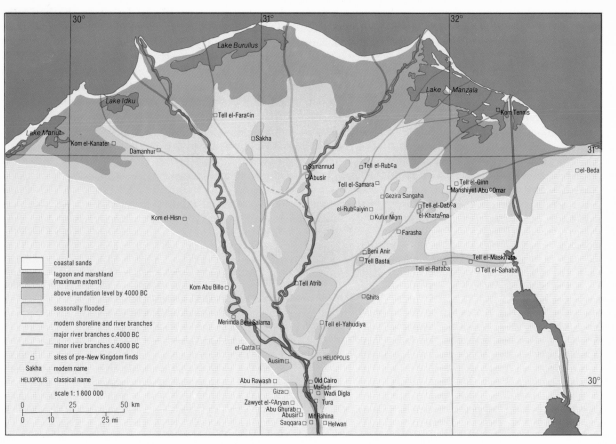

Map legend:

- coastal sands
- lagoon and marshland (maximum extent)
- above inundation level by 4000 BC
- seasonally flooded
- modern shoreline and river branches
- major river branches c.4000 BC
- minor river branches c.4000 BC
- □ sites of pre-New Kingdom finds
- Sakha — modern name
- HELIOPOLIS — classical name

scale 1:1 800 000

0   25   50 km
0   10   25 mi

Delta topography
The topography of the delta reconstructed for c.4000 BC (after Butzer), and compared with the modern situation.

The northern delta was formerly lagoon and swamp, and was gradually coated with layers of Nile mud, slowly increasing the area of land that was only seasonally flooded. The northernmost margin may, however, have been more attractive for early settlement than this might imply; there are early sites in the northeast and a nome around Lake Burullus. As is suggested by submerged sites on the coastline, this area may later have warped downwards in relation to the southern delta, roughly on the axis of the Wadi Tumilat.

The general development of the river branches – probably much influenced by man – has been to reduce their number and to shift the main discharge westward.

Areas above inundation by 4000 BC are composed of sand and mud, and are often known by the Arabic word *gezira*, "island." Their edges are particularly favorable for settlement. The sites shown have produced significant pre-New Kingdom finds. A number of further place names are known from texts, but these are omitted.

sandy ridges between the Nile branches and other water channels. Some of these were probably occupied from the beginning of the Predynastic Period; the general pattern of expansion was probably northwards. The land around the ridges could be used for crops or, if wetter, for grazing, and the swamps, like those in the Nile valley, contained wild life, fish and papyrus. Because of the different characters of the two main regions, their agricultural uses will have been substantially different, and there is evidence for trade between them. No large cities of the earlier periods have been found in the delta. This apparent lack of centers of population may be due in part to the relative proximity of Memphis, south of the delta apex, but it may also be illusory, as ancient sites in the delta are far less accessible even than those in the Nile valley. It is not surprising that the archaeological material from the delta is only a small fraction of that from Upper Egypt, and does not reflect the area's true importance.

The Faiyum

The third sizable area of ancient settlement was the Faiyum. This is a lakeside oasis west of the Nile valley and south of Memphis, which is fed by the Bahr Yusuf, a branch of the Nile that diverges westward north of Asyut and terminates in the Birket Qarun or Lake Moeris of antiquity. The lake has dwindled gradually from its Neolithic extent, which was little less than that of the entire Faiyum. The lake was already a focus for settlement in the late Paleolithic (about 7000 BC) and Neolithic periods, and is also attested for the Old Kingdom. The earlier cultures were of hunters and gatherers, but by the Old Kingdom agriculture had no doubt been introduced. Intensive exploitation of the area depended on lowering the water level in the lake to reclaim land, and using the water that would

otherwise have filled it to irrigate both above and below the natural lake level. Major works were undertaken by 12th-Dynasty kings, who must, to judge by the siting of some of their monuments, have reduced the lake considerably and won back about 450 square kilometers for cultivation. Later the Ptolemies made it into one of the most prosperous and heavily populated parts of the country, with about 1,200 square kilometers of agricultural land; much of the area irrigated then is now desert. A different form of irrigation is required in the Faiyum from the rest of Egypt, relying on large amounts of labor rather than any very advanced techniques. In the lower-lying areas it will have been possible to produce two crops per year, and this may have been true of most of the region in the Ptolemaic Period.

An area analogous to the Faiyum but very much less significant is the Wadi el-Natrun, a natural oasis close to the delta, northwest of Cairo and south of Alexandria. The word "Natrun" in its name refers to the salt lakes there. These were the chief ancient source of natron, which was used for cleaning, ritual purposes including mummification, and the manufacture of Egyptian faience and of glass. The oasis is poor in agricultural resources; in the Byzantine Period it became a refuge for Christian ascetics.

The western desert

The remaining areas to be discussed were more peripheral to Egypt, and could be held only when there was a strong government.

The oases of the western desert produced some valuable crops like grapes and the best dates, and were also important as links in trade with more remote areas. From north to south four main oases were governed by Egypt: Bahariya, Farafra, el-Dakhla and el-Kharga (east of el-Dakhla), of which the last two were by far the most significant. In addition, the more remote westerly oasis of Siwa was incorporated into Egypt in the Late Period; it acquired world renown through the abortive mission of Cambyses to it in 525 BC (it has recently been reported that remains of Cambyses' army have been found in the desert) and Alexander the Great's subsequent consultation of the oracle there. There are also smaller oases west of the Nile and further south, Kurkur, Dunqul and Salima, which are staging posts on long-distance caravan routes, but have not produced any ancient remains.

There is Middle and New Kingdom evidence for people fleeing from justice or from persecution to el-Kharga and el-Dakhla oases, while in the 21st Dynasty political exiles were banished there. In this respect the area was one facet of the Egyptian Siberia, the other being forced labor in appalling conditions, with great loss of life, in the mines of the eastern desert.

The entire area west of the Nile valley was called Libya in antiquity. The coastal region west of Alexandria as far as Cyrenaica probably contained the majority of the Libyan population, and was less inhospitable than it now seems. Almost all the Egyptian evidence from here dates to the reign of Ramesses II, who built forts along the coast as far as Zawyet Umm el-Rakham, 340 kilometers west of Alexandria, and to the Greco-Roman Period, when the Ptolemies built in both Greek and Egyptian style at Tolmeita in Cyrenaica, about 1,000 kilometers from Alexandria.

For most of Egyptian history the oases were an Egyptian outpost against the Libyans, who tried to infiltrate at many periods. In the reigns of Merenre' and Pepy II the expedition leader Harkhuf made several journeys to Yam, a country probably in the region of modern Kerma and Dongola south of the third cataract of the Nile. On one occasion he took the "desert road," leaving the Nile valley near Abydos and no doubt passing through el-Dakhla. When he arrived he found that the ruler of Yam had gone to "smite the ruler of the Libyan land to the western corner of the sky" – a discovery probably related to the western route used for this expedition. This detail shows that "Libya" for Egyptians extended 1,500 kilometers or so south from the sea. Remains from the Fezzan, probably dating to around the time of Christ, show the possibilities of settlement in southern Libya in antiquity, while the 'Uweinat area was settled in the third millennium BC. In early periods the Libyans were culturally similar to the Egyptians and may have spoken a dialect of the same language, but contacts during the Dynastic Period were mostly hostile.

From the western oases a trail now called the Darb el-Arba'in ("40-day track") leads to el-Fasher, the capital of Darfur province in western Sudan. Harkhuf used the first part of this, but it is possible that its entire length was opened up to trade in antiquity. Harkhuf traveled with donkeys, but effective exploitation of such routes may have depended on the camel, apparently introduced to Egypt in the 6th–5th centuries BC.

The eastern desert
To the east of Egypt were a number of important sources of minerals. The northernmost is Sinai, which supplied turquoise, mined by the Egyptians from the 3rd Dynasty to the end of the New King-

The only ancient Egyptian map. A fragment of a sketch map that probably shows the central area of the Wadi Hammamat, where there are graywacke quarries and gold mines. Further fragments (not shown) give a long track with few topographical details. The hieratic captions describe man-made and natural features, and the whole is related to the extraction of a half-worked statue that was taken to the Theban West Bank in year 6, perhaps of Ramesses IV. Turin, Museo Egizio.

dom, but not later (finds dating to the beginning of the Dynastic Period have recently been reported from the area). The main sites with Egyptian remains are in western Sinai at Wadi Maghara and Serabit el-Khadim, and there was at times semi-permanent Egyptian settlement there. Sinai is also a source of copper, and copper mines contemporary with the Egyptian 18th–20th Dynasties have been excavated at Timna near Eilat. These were probably worked by the local population under Egyptian control; there is no evidence that the Egyptians

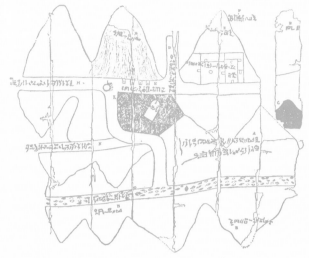

themselves mined copper anywhere in Sinai. It is possible that, as with Egyptian trade in grain with the Near East, the Egyptians did mine copper but did not consider the activity prestigious enough to record. Otherwise they may have employed local labor, as at Timna, or traded with the local population for copper, or acquired most of their supplies from elsewhere.

The eastern desert of Egypt yielded a number of building and semiprecious stones, and was the route to the Red Sea. Some quarries were near the Nile valley, like Gebel Ahmar for quartzite and Hatnub for Egyptian alabaster, but others, especially the sources of graywacke (a hard, blackish stone) in the Wadi Hammamat and the gold mines, most of which are south of the latitude of Koptos, required large-scale expeditions. They could not have been exploited without Egyptian domination of, or collaboration with, the local nomadic population. The Egyptians also needed control in order to use the three main routes to the Red Sea. These run by way of the Wadi Gasus to Safaga, the Wadi Hammamat to Quseir, and the Wadi 'Abbad to Berenike; there is also a minor route from about 80 kilometers south of Cairo to the Gulf of Suez, attested from the reign of Ramesses II. The earliest evidence for their use is from the end of the Predynastic Period (Wadi el-Qash, leading from Koptos to Berenike); this may relate to Red Sea trade or to mining. The northerly routes are attested for all the main periods of Egyptian history, and the southernmost from the New Kingdom on.

At the termination of the Wadi Gasus was a temple of the 12th Dynasty, and in 1976 remains from the nearby Egyptian port of the same date were discovered. There is renewed evidence in the 25th and 26th Dynasties (700–525 BC), and the pattern probably continued in the Persian Period (6th–5th century BC), when there were links with Iran around the Arabian coast. The Roman Period is represented at the sites of Quseir and Berenike, which were ports for trade with East Africa and India. Although we have no evidence that the Egyptians had contacts so far afield, such ports were probably used for trade with the semimythical land of Punt, which is mentioned in texts from the Old Kingdom on. The location of Punt is not firmly established, and the country had a number of idealized associations for the Egyptians, but it is most likely to have been in the region of modern Eritrea or Somalia, where finds of the Hellenistic and Roman Periods have recently been reported. The articles obtained from Punt were all exotic or luxury goods, the most important being incense. Whether the Punt trade was the only reason for navigation on the Red Sea, apart from access to some areas of Sinai, is quite uncertain. There is a report of Egyptian 18th-Dynasty beads found on the coast south of the river Juba near the Equator; but this does not mean that the Egyptians themselves penetrated this far.

Nubia

The political boundary of Egypt at the first cataract was probably established in the late Predynastic or Early Dynastic Period, replacing an earlier natural frontier at Gebel el-Silsila, where the limestone hills to either side of the Nile give way to sandstone, which is the basic element in the rock as far south as the Butana in central Sudan. At Gebel el-Silsila the sandstone comes down to the river on either side, and the site was the Egyptians' main quarry for building stone from the New Kingdom on. Limestone has allowed the Nile to carve a relatively broad floodplain, whereas the useful area of land beside the sandstone reaches is very small.

South of Gebel el-Silsila was the first Egyptian nome or province, whose main towns were Aswan and Kom Ombo. Its early separate status was recorded in its name "Nubia." Between the first and second cataracts lay Lower Nubia, which was always the prime target for incorporation into Egypt. Early Dynastic rock inscriptions and reliefs in the second cataract area show Egyptian interest in it at that date. In the 4th and 5th Dynasties there was almost no settled population in Lower Nubia. An Egyptian settlement at Buhen north of the second cataract implies hegemony, if not rule. In the 6th Dynasty the Egyptians yielded to local inhabitants, but control was regained in the 11th Dynasty and again at the end of the 17th. The 18th-Dynasty kings extended Egyptian rule as far as Kurgus, south of the caravan route across the desert from Korosko to Abu Hamed. This acquisition of territory was very important for later history, as an Egyptian-influenced culture became established at Napata, the capital of Upper Nubia, and eventually produced the 25th Egyptian Dynasty and the kingdom of Napata-Meroë, which survived into the 4th century AD.

Lower Nubia seems to have been regarded almost as being Egyptian by right, and was significant for access to raw materials, principally hard stones and gold, in the desert to either side of the Nile. At an early period it was used as a source of wood, but it can never have been agriculturally important, as the cultivable area is no more than a narrow strip on either side of the river. It was also, however, the route through which came many of the African products prized by the Egyptians. These included spices, ivory, ebony, ostrich feathers and certain species of baboon; pygmies were also traded occasionally, and figured in the stereotyped landscape of the Nile in Classical antiquity. It is not known what the Egyptians paid in return for all this, and virtually no archaeological evidence for ancient trade with Egypt has so far been found in sub-Saharan Africa. The ultimate provenance of many of the goods is unknown – pygmies probably never spread north of the Nile–Congo divide, while some other commodities must have come from the rain forest – and they may have passed through a number of intermediaries before reaching Egypt. It is difficult for us to evaluate the importance of these products for the Egyptians, which was often religious, but they were made into a focus for prestige comparable to precious stones today.

Palestine and Syria

The last major area that needs to be mentioned here is the coastal region of Palestine and Syria. Contacts between Egypt and the Near East are attested already in the Predynastic Period, and the name of Na'rmer, the latest Predynastic king, has been found at Tel Gat and Tel 'Arad in Palestine. Trade in lapis lazuli, whose main ancient source was Badakshan in Afghanistan, was flourishing at that time, and Egypt may already have been importing metal from Asia. Connections between Egypt and Byblos in the Lebanon are attested in the Old Kingdom, and the funerary boat of Khufu, the builder of the Great Pyramid, was made of Lebanese cedar. There are few trees in Egypt, and their wood is of poor quality, so that good timber always had to be imported from the Near East. The Middle Kingdom saw an intensification of these links, while in the New Kingdom Egyptian kings conquered large parts of the area and held them for more than two centuries, exploiting subject peoples and trading with neighbors. During resurgences of Egyptian power in the 22nd and 26th Dynasties parts of Palestine were again conquered, and the pattern was repeated in the Ptolemaic Period. The possession of part of Syria-Palestine was a natural goal for a strong regime in Egypt, but its achievement was far more difficult than in Nubia.

Many advances in Egyptian material culture came from the Near East. In return for these "invisible" imports and for wood, copper, possibly tin, silver, precious stones, wine and oil, the Egyptians could offer four main resources: gold, food surpluses, linen and, particularly in later periods, papyrus. Trade in gold and the bartering of African goods imported into Egypt are well known, but exports of food and other non-prestige products can be proved only in exceptional cases. They leave little mark in the archaeological record and are almost never mentioned in texts, the best-known textual allusion being a gift of grain by Merneptah to the Hittites during a famine, which is not trade. But Egyptian agriculture was far more secure and productive than any in the Near East, and just as Rome's granary in imperial times was Egypt, so may the Near East's have been in earlier periods. Grain was very important in Late Period foreign policy.

A number of areas more remote from Egypt played a part in Egyptian history at different times, among them Mesopotamia, Hittite Anatolia, Crete and Cyprus; these cannot be surveyed here.

Below Granite outcrop near Aswan with quarry marks. The rows of tooth-like indentations are where slots were cut before inserting wooden wedges. The wedges were wetted and swelled to split the stone. The scorings on some surfaces were probably made with iron tools, and thus date after c. 700 BC.

Bottom Landscape in the southern part of the eastern desert. Although this area is somewhat less arid than the western desert, the organization of expeditions to mine or collect minerals in it must have posed formidable problems. Even so, exploration was very thorough; few significant mineral deposits have been found that were not exploited in antiquity.

Natural resources of ancient Egypt
The sites indicated are places where there are ancient workings of the minerals named. It is often impossible to date these workings precisely, but several are exclusively Greco-Roman, such as the sources of emerald or beryl, porphyry and the granite of Mons Claudianus.

Further semiprecious stones and minerals are found scattered over the eastern desert: agate; breccia; calcite (for 140 km north of Asyut); carnelian; chalcedony; felspar; garnet; iron; jasper; rock crystal (quartz); serpentine.

Gypsum is found west of the Nile for 100 km south from Cairo, and flint is widespread on either side of the valley, especially from Luxor to el-Kab. The hills near the Nile are composed of limestone as far south as Gebel el-Silsila; only quarries of good-quality building stone are marked.

Commodities imported from further afield included incense and myrrh from Punt (northern Somalia ?) and Yemen (?), obsidian from southern Ethiopia, silver from Syria and lapis lazuli from Badakshan in northeastern Afghanistan. Most of these were luxury products; the normal Egyptian lived as a subsistence farmer and had little economic contact with the outside world.

The area under cultivation fluctuated, while the land available for grazing varied with long-term climatic changes.

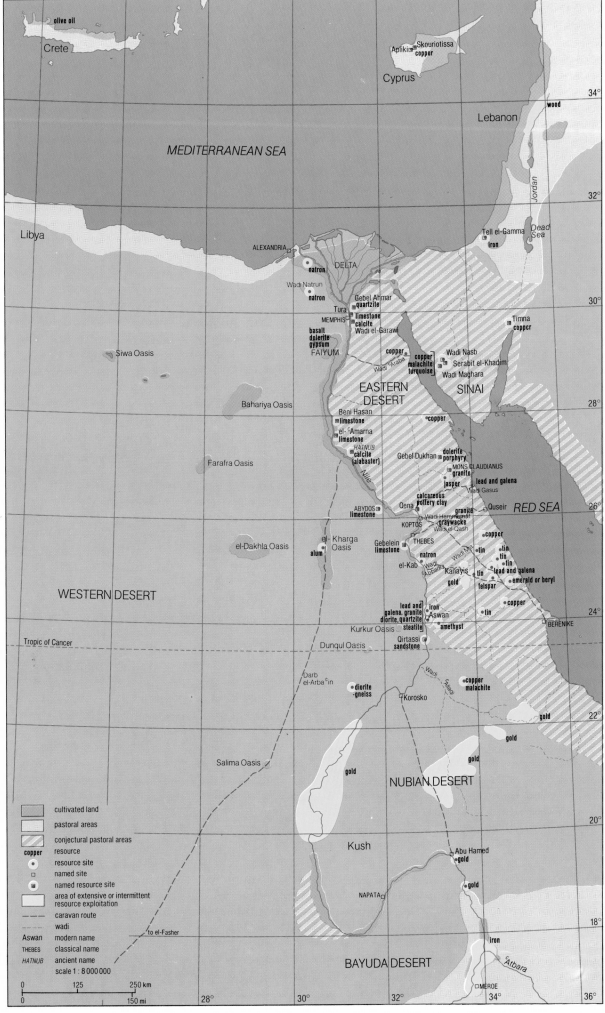

cultivated land

pastoral areas

conjectural pastoral areas

copper   resource

○   resource site

□   named site

▣   named resource site

area of extensive or intermittent resource exploitation

— — —   caravan route

- - - -   wadi

Aswan   modern name

THEBES   classical name

HATNUB   ancient name

scale 1 : 8 000 000

0   125   250 km

0   150 mi

THE STUDY OF ANCIENT EGYPT

Egypt has been of almost continual interest to Europeans, and has been written about by authors from the Greek Hekataios of Miletos in the 6th century BC (whose book is lost) to today. When ancient Egyptian civilization became extinct in the later Roman Period it could no longer be an object of contemporary study, but it continued to be remembered throughout the Middle Ages for its monuments, most notably the pyramids. A number of medieval pilgrims to the Holy Land visited Egypt, mostly to see the sites associated with Christ's stay there, and even the pyramids were believed to relate to the biblical story, being the "granaries of Joseph."

The first stages
Interest in antiquity and knowledge of it revived in the Renaissance, and among the first Classical texts to be brought to light in the 15th century was the *Hieroglyphica* of Horapollo, a work of the 4th century AD, which purports to be Egyptian in origin and gives symbolic explanations of the meaning of a number of signs in the hieroglyphic script, and the Hermetic Corpus, a set of philosophical tracts of the early centuries AD, which were probably written in Egypt and contain genuine Egyptian ideas interspersed with Neoplatonist and other material. Texts of the latter type tended to support the assumption, which goes back to early Greek philosophers, that Egypt was the fount of wisdom. The same is true of the *Hieroglyphica*, which was held to describe a method of encapsulating profound truths in pictorial signs.

In the 16th century antiquarians studied more than before the physical remains of antiquity, and in Rome, the chief center of their researches, they were immediately confronted with Egyptian objects, most of which had been imported for the popular Isis cult in the early empire. These are found in early publications of antiquities, and formed, with the obelisks that are still such a striking element in the Roman scene, a nucleus for study that was mostly recognized as being Egyptian, and interpreted with the aid of writings about Egypt by Classical authors. Illustrators of the time had no conception of the differences in character between their own methods of representation and those of ancient Egypt, so that many of their reproductions resemble the originals only very remotely.

The late 16th and early 17th centuries were the time of the first visits to Egypt in search of antiquities. Pietro della Valle (1586–1652) traveled all over the eastern Mediterranean, staying in the east from 1614 to 1626, and brought Egyptian mummies and important Coptic manuscripts back with him to Italy. The manuscripts were in the latest form of the Egyptian language, written in Greek letters, and this language was regularly learned by priests in the Coptic Church in Egypt, where it is used for liturgical purposes to this day. They could therefore be studied by those who knew Arabic, the

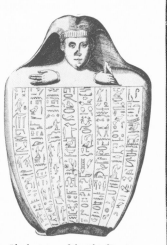

Block statue of the Chief Lector-Priest Petamenope: engraving in G. Herwart von Hohenburg, *Thesaurus Hieroglyphicorum* (1620), the earliest published collection of hieroglyphic inscriptions. Herwart shows the same object as two different ones, using two 16th-century manuscript sources. From Rome (?), originally from Thebes; c.650 BC. Paris, Musée du Louvre.

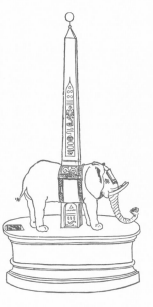

Obelisk and elephant: illustration of a mausoleum from Francesco Colonna, *Hypnerotomachia Polifili* (Venice, 1499). The "hieroglyphic" inscription is mostly after a Roman temple frieze that was believed to contain Egyptian hieroglyphs.

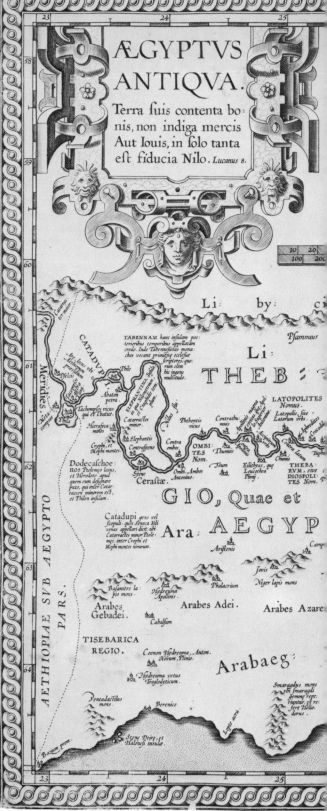

Map of ancient Egypt by Abraham Ortelius, Amsterdam, 1595. The motto reads "Rich in natural resources, Egypt places all her trust in the Nile, and so has no need of either foreign trade or the rain of heaven" (Lucan, *Civil War* 8. 446–47). As on many other pre-1800 maps, north is placed on the right in order to give a "landscape" of the Nile. The map is a remarkable achievement, showing most towns and nomes in their correct relative positions, including Thebes 125 years before its site was identified on the ground. The information is almost all from Classical sources, the only ones then available for ancient Egypt, so that, for example, the Classical river mouths are shown. Note the list of unidentified places. The topography is not based on a survey and is very inaccurate. London, British Library.

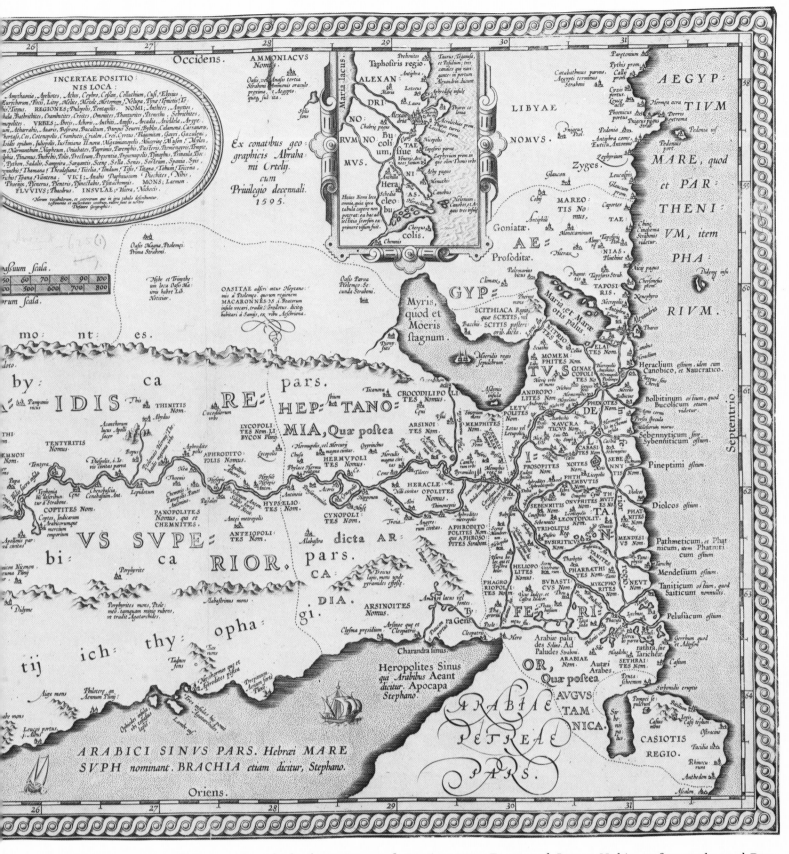

language in which the primers of Coptic were written. Two centuries later Coptic was to form the basis of the decipherment of the hieroglyphic script. It was also the initial study of the great polymath Athanasius Kircher (1602–80), who wrote numerous works about ancient Egypt, and was one of the first to attempt a decipherment.

A fascinating byway in the development of European knowledge of Egypt is revealed by a manuscript recording the visit of an anonymous Venetian in 1589, who traveled through Upper Egypt and Lower Nubia as far south as el-Derr. The author says he "did not travel for any useful purpose, but only to see so many superb edifices, churches, statues, colossi, obelisks and columns." But "even though I went a great distance, none of the buildings I saw was worthy of admiration, except for one, which is called Ochsur [Luxor, within which he includes Karnak] by the Moors." His judgment was to be fashionable about 250 years later, when Luxor became a center of tourism, and here he shows himself especially prophetic. Of

Karnak he says: "Judge whether this tremendous building is superior to the seven wonders of the world. One of them still exists, one of the pyramids of the pharaohs; in comparison with this construction it is a small thing. I am not sending anyone who wishes to see the monument to the end of the world; it is only ten days' journey from Cairo, and one can go there quite cheaply." This amazing work was not published until the 20th century, and seems to have had no influence on other writers.

In the next century the most nearly comparable text, known from secondary publications, is a narrative of the visit of two Capuchin friars to Luxor and Esna in 1668 where, they say, "in the memory of man no Frenchman had ever been." Like their predecessor, they were pressed for time, but they succeeded in crossing to the west bank at Thebes and seeing the Valley of the Kings, the prime tourist attraction that had eluded the Venetian.

Travelers and archaeologists

Explorations like those just mentioned cannot be termed archaeological. The word can, however, be used for the work of John Greaves (1602–52), an English astronomer who published his *Pyramidographia, or a Discourse of the Pyramids in Aegypt* in 1646. Greaves visited Giza on two occasions in 1638–39, measured and examined the pyramids thoroughly, and made a critical analysis of ancient writings about them; he also went to Saqqara. The resulting work was more penetrating than any other of its time on ancient Egypt; a notable feature is the citation of medieval Arabic sources. Essentially Greaves followed the example of humanist scholarship of the Renaissance, but his application of the methods to Egypt was scarcely imitated by others.

From the later 17th century the number of travelers to Egypt increased gradually, and their writings started to incorporate usable drawings of the monuments. The most significant advance in knowledge was made by the Jesuit Claude Sicard (1677–1726), who was commissioned by the French regent to investigate ancient monuments in Egypt. Only some of his letters on the subject are now preserved. He visited Upper Egypt four times, and was the first modern traveler to identify the site of Thebes, and to ascribe correctly the colossi of Memnon and the Valley of the Kings – all on the basis of Classical descriptions. His most important successor was the Dane Frederik Ludwig Norden (1708–42), who visited Egypt in 1737–38, and whose posthumously published volume of travels, magnificently illustrated with his own drawings, appeared in various editions from 1751 to the end of the 18th century.

The increase in the numbers of visitors to Egypt went together with an improvement in the treatment of Egyptian matters – and of antiquity and exotic cultures as a whole – in the more famous works of the 18th century, of which the most important are the multi-volume compilations of Bernard de Montfaucon (published in 1719–24) and the Baron de Caylus (1752–64). Both give a surprising amount of space to Egyptian objects, while also assigning to Egypt much that came from elsewhere. Considerable collections of antiquities already existed, and some, like the small group that belonged to Archbishop Laud in the 1630s, even included forgeries.

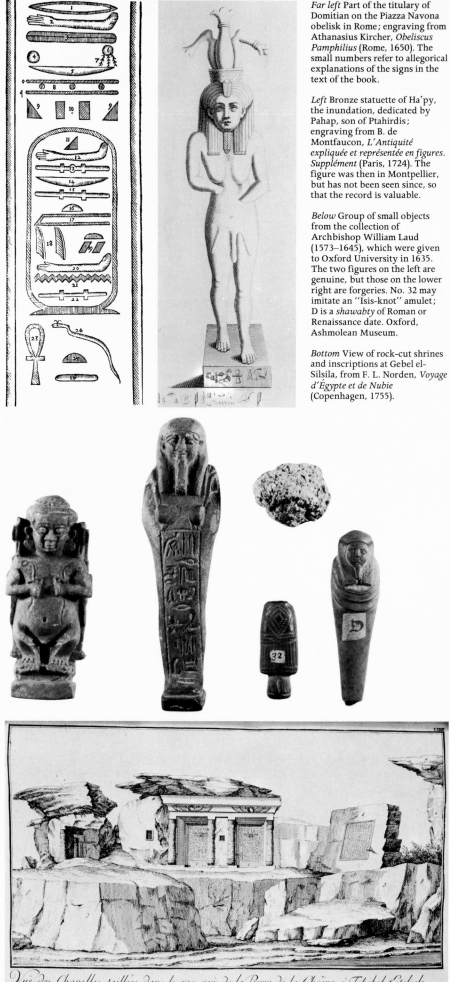

Far left Part of the titulary of Domitian on the Piazza Navona obelisk in Rome; engraving from Athanasius Kircher, *Obeliscus Pamphilius* (Rome, 1650). The small numbers refer to allegorical explanations of the signs in the text of the book.

Left Bronze statuette of Ha'py, the inundation, dedicated by Pahap, son of Ptahirdis; engraving from B. de Montfaucon, *L'Antiquité expliquée et représentée en figures. Supplément* (Paris, 1724). The figure was then in Montpellier, but has not been seen since, so that the record is valuable.

Below Group of small objects from the collection of Archbishop William Laud (1573–1645), which were given to Oxford University in 1635. The two figures on the left are genuine, but those on the lower right are forgeries. No. 32 may imitate an "Isis-knot" amulet; D is a *shawabty* of Roman or Renaissance date. Oxford, Ashmolean Museum.

Bottom View of rock-cut shrines and inscriptions at Gebel el-Silsila, from F. L. Norden, *Voyage d'Égypte et de Nubie* (Copenhagen, 1755).

Travelers to Egypt and Sudan before 1800
The towns and sites marked are prominent in the records of travelers before Napoleon's expedition of 1798. Some of their names and the dates of their visits are given in bold type.

Also shown are:
+ Egyptian sites visited principally for their Christian associations.
———— the conventional itinerary of medieval pilgrims to the Holy Land who also went to Sinai and Egypt
———— the route of Felix Fabri through Sinai in 1483
———— a caravan route to the Red Sea on the 15th-century map *Egyptus novelo*
◇ sites visited by the anonymous Italian of 1589
———— the itinerary followed by a group of Franciscans (including Theodor Krump), French Jesuits, and the doctor Poncet towards the Funj capital Sennar and Gondar in Ethiopia in 1698–1710.
———— the route by which the Scot, James Bruce, returned to Aswan from Gondar in 1771–72.

Inset Excerpts from the books of less important travelers, published on their return to Europe. There are more than 200 accounts of travelers whose journeys included Egypt between 1400 and 1700.

Top Christoph Fürer von Haimendorf, aged 69, dated 1610; from *Itinerarium Aegypti, Arabiae, Syriae, aliumque regionum orientalium* (Nuremberg, 1610).

Center Jean de Thevenot (1633–67), frontispiece of *Voyages de M. de Thevenot en Europe, Asie & Afrique* (Amsterdam, 1727; originally Paris, 1665). The inscription says "Friend, you may know the author from this portrait;/you could not find a traveler more perfect."

Bottom Obelisk of Senwosret I at Heliopolis; the hieroglyphs are legible but quite un-Egyptian, and the landscape is European. From Gemelli Careri, *Voyage du tour du monde* (Paris, 1729), who implies that the obelisk was at Alexandria.

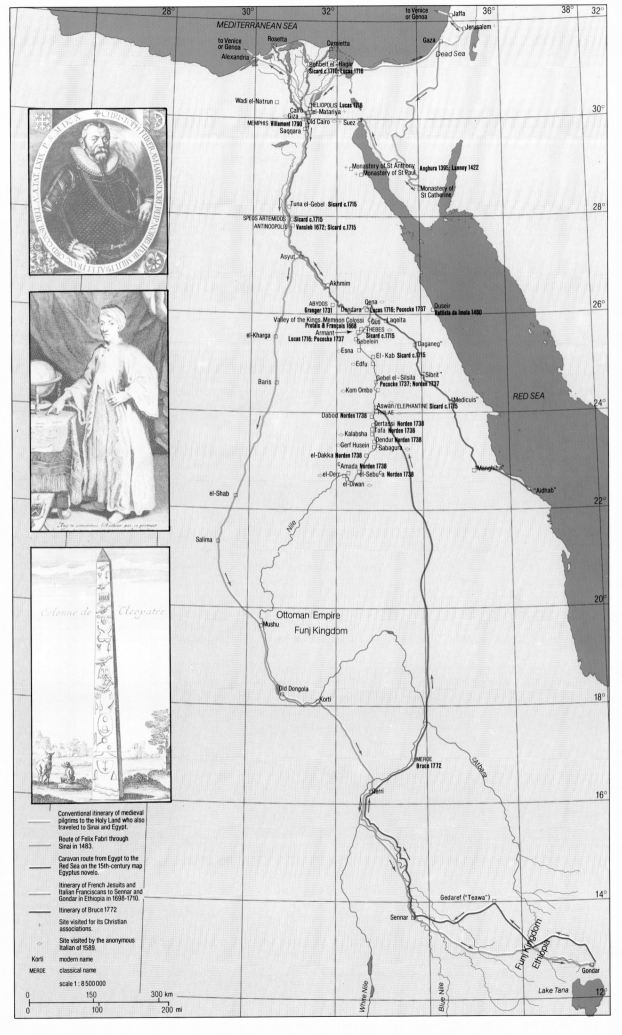

Conventional itinerary of medieval pilgrims to the Holy Land who also traveled to Sinai and Egypt.

Route of Felix Fabri through Sinai in 1483.

Caravan route from Egypt to the Red Sea on the 15th-century map Egyptus novelo.

Itinerary of French Jesuits and Italian Franciscans to Sennar and Gondar in Ethiopia in 1698-1710.

Itinerary of Bruce 1772

+ Site visited for its Christian associations.

◇ Site visited by the anonymous Italian of 1589.

Korti   modern name

MEROE   classical name

scale 1 : 8 500 000

0   150   300 km

0   100   200 mi

Decipherment of the hieroglyphic script

Throughout the 18th century the hieroglyphic script continued to be studied, although little progress was made towards a decipherment. Both the antiquarian and the linguistic interest in Egypt culminated in Georg Zoëga (1755–1809), whose two major works, a treatise on obelisks, which includes a section on the hieroglyphic script, and a catalog of Coptic manuscripts in the Vatican collections, are of lasting value. The date of the work on obelisks, 1797, is symbolic as the culmination of Egyptian studies before Napoleon's expedition in 1798. Although the script could, and no doubt would, have been deciphered without the discovery of bilingual inscriptions, Egyptology as we know it is a product of the expedition, the unearthing of the Rosetta stone, the associated surge of enthusiasm for Egypt, and of gradual changes in the intellectual climate of western Europe.

The campaign was accompanied by a team of scholars who were to study and record all aspects of Egypt, ancient and modern. The Rosetta stone soon passed into English hands, but the team produced a fundamental multi-volume work, the *Description de l'Égypte*, first published in 1809–30. This was the last, and much the most important, such work produced before the decipherment of the script by Jean François Champollion le Jeune (1790–1832) in 1822–24, which is the beginning of Egyptology as a separate subject. Champollion and Ippolito Rosellini (1800–43), an Italian from Pisa, mounted a joint expedition to record monuments in Egypt in the 1820s, but by that time they were latecomers in the field. In the previous 20 years numerous travelers had visited Egyptian and Lower Nubian sites and had rifled them for antiquities, written books about them, or both. Prominent among them were the consuls Anastasi, d'Athanasi, Drovetti and Salt, the Italian strong man Belzoni, the French sculptor Rifaud, and the Swiss travelers Gau and Burckhardt. The collections gathered by some of these men formed the nuclei of the Egyptian

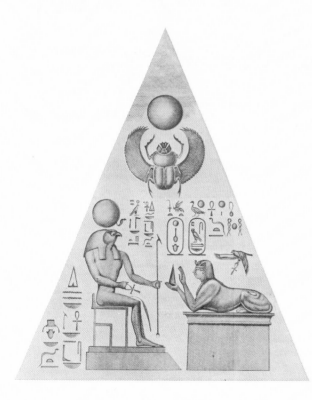

sections of the British Museum, the Louvre in Paris, the Rijksmuseum van Oudheden in Leiden and the Museo Egizio in Turin (there was no Egyptian Museum in Cairo until the late 1850s). In the first half of the 19th century digging in Egypt was primarily for objects. The recovery of information, as opposed to objects, came a very poor second.

Before his death in 1832 Champollion had already made great progress in understanding the Egyptian language and in reconstructing Egyptian history and civilization, but this work had little impact, both because of delays in publication and because of its strictly academic nature. By 1840 the first generation of Egyptologists was already dead, and the subject retained a precarious existence in France, with Vicomte Emmanuel de Rougé (1811–

Above Frontispiece of F. L. Norden, *Voyage d'Égypte et de Nubie* (Copenhagen, 1755). The central allegory shows: Fame; Ancient Egypt displaying her treasures; a lion with the arms of ancient kings of Denmark; and the Nile. There is also a Classical figure of Isis, and Egyptian monuments and other motifs.

Left Pyramidion of the obelisk of Psammetichus II by the Palazzo di Montecitorio in Rome; from G. Zoëga, *De origine et usu obeliscorum* (Rome, 1797). The copy is accurate and legible, but its style is un-Egyptian.

72), in Holland with Conrad Leemans (1809–93), and especially in Prussia with Carl Richard Lepsius (1810–84). Lepsius's 12-volume *Denkmaeler aus Aegypten und Aethiopien* (1849–59), the result of an expedition up the Nile as far as Meroë in 1842–45, is the earliest reliable publication of a large selection of monuments, and is still of fundamental importance. The English pioneer Wilkinson is treated in detail below on pages 106–07.

The growth of Egyptology

In the middle of the century Lepsius, his younger contemporary Heinrich Brugsch (1827–94) and a handful of other scholars continued to advance the subject, while work in Egypt was placed on a permanent footing by Auguste Mariette (1821–81), a Frenchman who was originally sent to acquire Coptic manuscripts for the Louvre in 1850. Mariette entered the service of the Khedive Saïd in 1858, excavated a large number of sites before and after that date, and founded the Egyptian Museum and Antiquities Service. The aims of the latter were to preserve and record the monuments, to excavate, and to administer the museum. Until the Egyptian Revolution of 1952 its directors were European, the most famous of them being Mariette's successor Gaston Maspero (1846–1916).

The aims of scientific excavation in Egypt were first stated in 1862 by the Scot Alexander Rhind (1833–63), but they were not realized on any scale until the work of W. M. F. Petrie (1853–1942). Petrie first went to Egypt in 1880 to make measurements of the Great Pyramid for pyramidological purposes. He later excavated at sites all over Egypt, publishing a volume almost every year on the results of the preceding winter. Among his excavations were some spectacular discoveries, but his work was far more important in providing a framework of information about the different areas and periods, often resulting from a reworking of sites that had

already been excavated summarily by others. During his own lifetime Petrie's standards were overtaken, notably by the American G. A. Reisner (1867–1942), but Reisner published little of his results, thereby lessening their value.

From about 1880 to 1914 there was a great deal of archaeological work in Egypt, and sites in Nubia came into prominence with the building and subsequent raising of the first Aswan dam (1902 and 1907). The end of the 19th century also saw major advances in the understanding of Egyptian language and chronology, made in Berlin by Adolf Erman (1854–1937) and Eduard Meyer (1855–1930) respectively, and the discovery of remains of all historical periods, and of Predynastic times from Naqada I on. Egyptological work since then has developed knowledge greatly in all areas, but in few of them has it changed the outlines fundamentally. In comparison, the 19th century was a time of continuous change. Up till about 1870 most Egyptological knowledge related to the latest stages of the civilization, while there was no proper division of the physical remains or of the language into periods. As this changed, interest tended to focus on the earlier, more "classical" phases of both.

Excavation in the 20th century

Excavation in this century has been dominated by a few spectacular discoveries and by the salvage campaigns in Nubia occasioned by the second raising of the first Aswan dam and the construction of the High Dam. There has been no systematic survey, but increasing numbers of sites have nonetheless been explored. Complementary to excavation, and at least as important, is the recording and publication of standing monuments, which first reached adequate standards around 1900. This does not have the glamor of excavation, and has seldom attracted the same public interest or support.

Foremost in the attention it has received has been

Palestinian temple of the Middle Bronze Age at Tell el-Dabʿa in the delta, excavated by an Austrian mission in the late 1960s. Techniques of European archaeology have been used. The site is dug in 10-meter squares, with grid sections left as a check on stratification.

exploration in the Valley of the Kings at Thebes. The first find of royalty was the discovery in the 1870s by the 'Abd el-Rasul family of Qurna of the pit containing the mummies of a majority of the New Kingdom kings. They had been removed from their original tombs early in the 21st Dynasty and reburied in the area of Deir el-Bahri for greater security. Like so many of the most important discoveries, this was the result of the search by local inhabitants for marketable antiquities, not of systematic excavation. While Egyptologists rightly deplore the loss of valuable information that goes with these discoveries, many of them would never have been made by orthodox expeditions.

In 1898 the tomb of Amenophis II was discovered by Victor Loret (1859–1946) in the Valley of the Kings, and proved to contain the mummies of most of the kings missing from the earlier find. Work on the valley continued almost without interruption until 1932. The most methodical of these examinations was by Howard Carter (1874–1939), mostly working for the Earl of Carnarvon. Carter's main discovery was, of course, the tomb of Tut'ankhamun, which he found in 1922 and worked on almost continuously for ten years. Although other largely intact royal burials have been found in the Near East, it is the richest single find of the sort, and contained many unique objects.

Several other royal burials or cemeteries have been excavated in Egypt in this century. Reisner's discovery of the tomb of Hetepheres at Giza in 1925 is the only major find of jewelry and furniture of the Old Kingdom; the recovery of the forms of the objects, whose wood was completely decayed, was a triumph of painstaking recording. In the 1940s Pierre Montet (1885–1966) excavated a set of intact tombs of the 21st- and 22nd-Dynasty kings and royal family at Tanis, which provide rare examples of art in precious materials from a period that has left few significant remains.

The most important excavated settlement sites, el-'Amarna and Deir el-Medina, have both been the objects of different expeditions and numerous campaigns. After the clandestine discovery of the el-'Amarna cuneiform tablets in the 1880s Urbain Bouriant (1849–1903) worked there, and produced a volume with the memorable title *Two Days' Excavation at Tell el Amarna*. He was followed by Petrie (1891–92), whose brief stay produced much of value, but was overshadowed by a German expedition in 1913–14 under Ludwig Borchardt (1863–1938), during which the house of the sculptor Thutmose was found. This contained the world-famous bust of Nefertiti, and a number of other masterpieces. In the 1920s and 1930s there were several seasons of British excavation, which contributed both to the history of the later 18th Dynasty and to the understanding of the short-lived capital; work has recently resumed on the site. Deir el-Medina was a source of finds throughout the 19th century, and was excavated by an Italian expedition at the turn of the century and a German one under Georg Möller (1876–1921) in 1911 and 1913. In 1917 the Institut Français d'Archéologie Orientale in Cairo began excavations at the site which have continued, with interruptions, up till now, and have almost completely uncovered the workmen's village and adjacent necropolis.

It is fitting to mention here the activities of the

Egyptian Antiquities Service and of Egyptian Egyptologists. After the foundation of the Service under Mariette the first Egyptian official in it was Ahmed Kamal (1849–1932), who worked in the Cairo Museum and excavated at a number of sites. From the beginning of this century an increasing proportion of the staff of the Service was Egyptian, and Egyptians taught Egyptology at Cairo University. Since 1952 both sectors have been completely Egyptian. The Service has excavated more than any other body, and much of the material in the Cairo Museum, as well as in Alexandria, Minya, Mallawi, Luxor and Aswan, comes from its excavations. The most striking Egyptian discoveries are probably those at Tuna el-Gebel, where an animal necropolis and a Greco-Egyptian city of the dead have been excavated, and the pioneer work of Ahmed Fakhry (1905–73) in the oases of the western desert.

Surveys and publications

There have been exhaustive surveys of Nubia as far as the Dal cataract, and in archaeological terms Lower Nubia is now perhaps the most studied area in the world. Only the fortress site of Qasr Ibrim remains above water, and this is still being excavated. The expansion in Nubian studies, and the wide spread of finds from the Paleolithic to the 19th century AD, have led to the creation of a virtually separate field of study.

The recording of complete monuments in Egypt was initiated by Maxence de Rochemonteix (1849–91) and Johannes Dümichen (1833–94), but neither lived to complete his work. In the years after their deaths the Egypt Exploration Fund (later Society) began an "Archaeological Survey of Egypt," which was to record standing monuments, while Jacques de Morgan (1857–1924) started a *Catalogue des monuments*, which published the temple of Kom Ombo in its entirety. Both these projects were too ambitiously conceived, but the Archaeological Survey initiated the work of N. de G. Davies (1865–

Group of foreign captives – a Libyan, a man from Punt (?), an Asiatic and another Libyan – on a relief from the causeway of the mortuary complex of Sahure' at Abusir. The superbly accurate drawing is from L. Borchardt, *Das Grabdenkmal des Königs Śa3ḥu-Re'*, Vol. II (Leipzig, 1913).

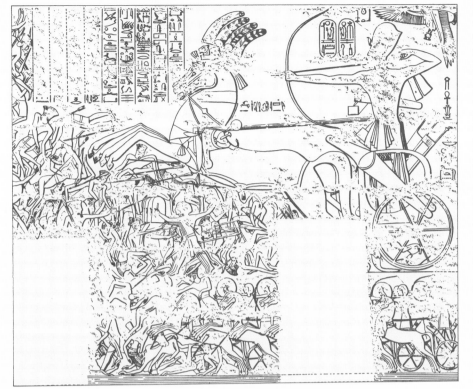

Relief of Ramesses III in battle against the ''sea peoples''; in his temple at Medinet Habu, north exterior wall. From *Medinet Habu*, the definitive publication by the Oriental Institute of the University of Chicago.

1941), the greatest copyist of Egyptian tombs. He published more than 25 volumes on tombs alone, almost always presenting a complete record of the decoration in them, and his wife Nina and others made colored reproductions of selected scenes. There have not been complete publications of monuments in color photographs until recently, and even these are not fully satisfactory; really effective presentation of the unique and fast-vanishing legacy of color on Egyptian monuments has yet to be achieved.

The most important epigraphic venture to follow Davies was the foundation of Chicago House, a field station of the Oriental Institute of the University of Chicago at Luxor, in 1924. The Oriental Institute itself was the creation of James H. Breasted (1865–1935), who was effectively the founder of American Egyptology, and a major scholar in his own right. For Chicago House he gained the support of John D. Rockefeller. The Chicago expedition has produced the only exhaustive record of a large Egyptian temple in facsimile (*Medinet Habu*, 1930–70) and a number of other volumes. Another work that set comparable standards, also funded by Rockefeller, was the publication of the inner parts of the temple of Sethos I at Abydos by A. M. Calverley (1896–1959) and M. F. Broome. After a lull the flow of publications has increased recently.

Egyptology outside Egypt

Indispensable though it is, activity in Egypt is a small part of the total work of Egyptologists, and there is often surprisingly little contact between the field and the study. It is far more difficult to select names from the list of mainly armchair Egyptologists than it is for fieldworkers, but it is necessary in order to provide a balance.

The first objective of Egyptologists has always been to understand the language. Early in this century F. Ll. Griffith (1862–1934) and Wilhelm Spiegelberg (1870–1930) advanced enormously the knowledge of demotic, the cursive script and

language of the Late and Greco-Roman Periods, while Adolf Erman continued to make discoveries in the earlier phases of Egyptian. In 1927 Sir Alan Gardiner (1879–1963) produced a grammar of Middle Egyptian which incorporated discoveries of his own and of Battiscombe Gunn (1883–1950), and has yet to be superseded. In 1944 H. J. Polotsky, the grand old man of Egyptology today, published a revolutionary study of some aspects of Egyptian and Coptic grammar, and over the last 30 years he has transformed our understanding of much of the language of all periods. The day when all our difficulties with Egyptian will have been solved is, however, nowhere in sight. Similarly, the 11-volume dictionary edited by Adolf Erman and Hermann Grapow (1885–1967), which was published between 1926 and 1953, marked a great advance on the pioneer work of Heinrich Brugsch, but is still the beginning rather than the end of the study of the meaning of Egyptian words.

For his work away from the monuments the Egyptologist needs publications of the monuments, more detailed studies on texts – hieroglyphic and hieratic and demotic – and numerous other types of aid. In these areas Kurt Sethe (1869–1934) was perhaps the leading scholar. He started as a grammarian, but later made contributions in almost all areas of the subject, and was the most prolific of all editors of texts, whose work will remain indispensable for generations. Sir Alan Gardiner was the most important editor of papyrus texts, who set new standards in the treatment of the papyri themselves and in their presentation. His collaborator Jaroslav Černý (1898–1970) was the outstanding worker on the ostraca and other cursive documents from Deir el-Medina in particular.

As examples of more general Egyptological studies it is worth singling out, more or less arbitrarily, the work of two writers who have changed whole areas of the subject; further important names may be found in the bibliography. Heinrich Schäfer (1868–1957) published the fundamental work on Egyptian art, which analyzes how the Egyptians depict objects and figures in the natural world (see pp. 60–61). Gerhard Fecht has similarly transformed our way of looking at the organization of Egyptian texts. He has shown that the majority of them are written in a kind of meter; it seems that writing was more normally in ''verse'' than in ''prose,'' so that in order to compose texts it was necessary to become a versifier, if not a poet. Both these scholars have illuminated areas that are very alien to modern eyes, and both have demonstrated features that are a prerequisite to a true comprehension of the ancient sources. Everywhere in Egyptology what has been done is a prelude to what might be done.

Today Egyptology is a conventional academic discipline, whose study is centered on universities, museums and national archaeological institutes; there are more than 20 countries where the subject is represented. The 300 or so Egyptologists cover fields such as language, literature, history, religion, art, which for the modern world would be separate. This has advantages in forcing one to maintain a general perspective, but drawbacks for detailed work or for major projects like dictionaries. Sadly, original work in Egyptology has become an almost exclusively academic pursuit.

THE HISTORICAL BACKGROUND

Predynastic Egypt

The culture of northern Africa was very uniform as late as the end of the last Ice Age (c. 10,000 BC), and the gradual formation of Egypt was a separation from this background, much affected by changes in climate. The most striking features of this process are the rapid acceleration of change in the centuries before the beginning of the Dynastic Period, and the lack of resemblance between the Egyptian state of the 4th Dynasty and its Predynastic antecedents, perhaps half a millennium earlier. Egyptian culture did not then become static, but there was never again such a surge of growth, and there is a continuity discernible from the Old Kingdom to the Roman Period, which cannot be found between Predynastic and Dynastic Egypt.

The earlier Predynastic cultures were not uniform over the country, and the two main areas cannot easily be related in their development. In the Nile valley the earliest Neolithic, settled, food-producing cultures are the Tasian and the Badarian (named for the sites at which they were first identified, as are those mentioned below), which may not in fact be separate (c. 4500 BC). These are confined to an area south of Asyut, and consist mainly of modest cemetery sites, probably near settlements that are now lost. In the Faiyum, cultures of an approximately similar date are known from the shore of the lake at its level of the time, but there is little evidence that these people were farmers; they may have lived largely by hunting and gathering. On the delta margins the large site of Merimda may be older than Badari, and there was probably also settlement of the central delta at that time. Several further Neolithic cultures are known from the second cataract area.

Naqada I (sometimes called Amratian) is, like its predecessors, a local, small-scale village culture, which shows little sign of social stratification. It is, however, known from a rather wider area, and is a prelude to the more expansive phase of Naqada II (or Gerzean); it shows no trace of foreign influence.

Naqada II forms the turning point in the development of Predynastic Egypt. It is the first culture to have contacts with other countries, while it spread over the entire Nile valley north of Gebel el-Silsila and into the delta. There is also social stratification and a development of significant population centers, notably Hierakonpolis (Kom el-Ahmar), Koptos (Qift), Naqada and Abydos. It is, on the other hand, the last period during which there was some cultural uniformity extending south of the first cataract. The Nubian cultures of this period, which are found as far south as Khartum, are not sharply distinct from those of Egypt. There was probably exchange over the whole area, and no central political authority. The cultural demarcation with the Nubian A group, which becomes noticeable south of Gebel el-Silsila in Naqada II, probably accompanies the beginnings of state organization in Egypt and the definition of a political frontier. This process leads into the Early Dynastic Period, in which Egypt is united, within boundaries comparable to those of later periods, under a single ruler. There is no sharp cultural break between Naqada II and the Early Dynastic Period, even though the transformation over the centuries is almost total.

During Naqada II some motifs in art and items of technology demonstrate cultural contact with Mesopotamia. Egyptian writing may have been invented in response to stimulus from Mesopotamia, but the systems of the two countries are not closely similar. The most likely method of

Predynastic and Early Dynastic Egypt
Egyptian-type sites are marked in black and numbered according to cultures attested:
1 from Tasian/Badarian
2 from Naqada I
3 from Naqada II
4 Lower Egyptian and delta cultures (contemporary with Badarian to mid-Naqada II, but not uniform)
5 Faiyum Predynastic culture
6 late Naqada II and Early Dynastic
Categories 1–5 are listed much more comprehensively than category 6. Many Predynastic sites ceased to be used in the Early Dynastic Period, probably because their inhabitants no longer exploited the desert margins so much, and moved further into the valley.

Rock drawings of very varying dates are common in all areas of the desert, many of them probably carved by nomads. Most often they are close to tracks; in Lower Nubia they are also frequent near the Nile. Their style continues to be un-Egyptian in the Dynastic Period. The hard stones of the eastern desert were used by the valley dwellers throughout the Predynastic and Early Dynastic Periods.

The precise political status of the capital cities marked, with the exceptions of Abydos and Memphis, is unknown.

Nubian-type sites are marked in brown. Those of the A group are distinguished as:
● from early A group (contemporary with late Naqada I and early Naqada II)
○ Classic and Terminal A group (contemporary with late Naqada II and 1st Dynasty respectively)
Nubian-type sites of the second cataract area include:
◌ Khartum Variant, c.4500–3500 BC
▽ Post-Shamarkian, c.3500 BC
◌ Abkan, c.4000–3200 BC and overlapping with Classic A group. Favorable conditions and extensive surveys have led to the identification of numerous sites of all these types, which are much better known than their Egyptian counterparts.

Far right: The second cataract area in Predynastic times

Left Objects from tombs of the Naqada I period. Left: mud statuette of a woman with her right hand under her left breast, with exaggerated thighs and legs. Center: fine black-topped red-ware pot with an incised design of uncertain meaning. Right: elaborately worked flint knife, probably a ceremonial object. Oxford, Ashmolean Museum.

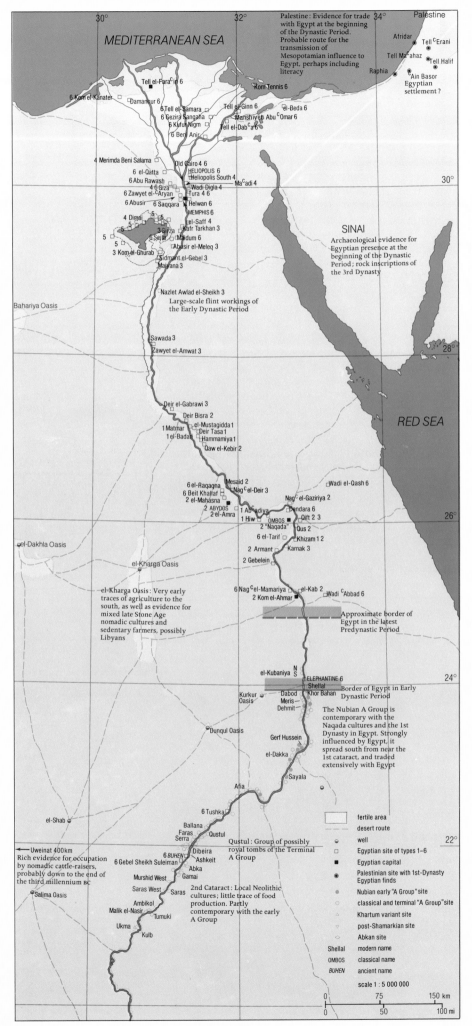

Palestine: Evidence for trade with Egypt at the beginning of the Dynastic Period. Probable route for the transmission of Mesopotamian influence to Egypt, perhaps including literacy

MEDITERRANEAN SEA

SINAI
Archaeological evidence for Egyptian presence at the beginning of the Dynastic Period; rock inscriptions of the 3rd Dynasty

RED SEA

Baharia Oasis

el-Dakhla Oasis

el-Kharga Oasis: Very early traces of agriculture to the south, as well as evidence for mixed late Stone Age nomadic cultures and sedentary farmers, possibly Libyans

Approximate border of Egypt in the latest Predynastic Period

Border of Egypt in Early Dynastic Period

The Nubian A Group is contemporary with the Naqada cultures and the 1st Dynasty in Egypt. Strongly influenced by Egypt, it spread south from near the 1st cataract, and traded extensively with Egypt

Qustul: Group of possibly royal tombs of the Terminal A Group

Uweinat 400km
Rich evidence for occupation by nomadic cattle-raisers, probably down to the end of the third millennium BC

2nd Cataract: Local Neolithic cultures; little trace of food production. Partly contemporary with the early A Group

fertile area
desert route
○ well
□ Egyptian site of types 1–6
■ Egyptian capital
● Palestinian site with 1st-Dynasty Egyptian finds
○ Nubian early "A Group" site
○ classical and terminal "A Group" site
△ Khartum variant site
▽ post-Shamarkian site
▽ Abkan site
Shellal modern name
OMBOS classical name
BUHEN ancient name
scale 1 : 5 000 000

0   75   150 km
0   50   100 mi

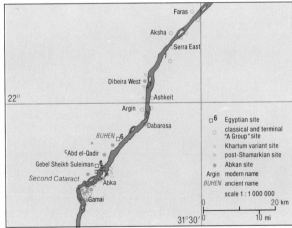

□ 6 Egyptian site
○ classical and terminal "A Group" site
△ Khartum variant site
▽ post-Shamarkian site
● Abkan site
Argin modern name
BUHEN ancient name
scale 1 : 1 000 000

0   20 km
0   10 mi

cultural transmission between the countries is trade, which was already far-flung. Evidence for trade between Egypt and Sinai and southern Palestine in the Early Dynastic Period has been found, but it is an open question whether this trade was accompanied by immigrants or by invasions. It is possible for a small nomadic group to conquer a large sedentary one; a takeover of this sort in late Naqada II cannot be ruled out, and would have left virtually no archaeological trace.

Our later written sources suggest that there were rulers of all Egypt before the beginning of the 1st Dynasty, and that they succeeded earlier dynasties of rulers of the two lands of Upper and Lower Egypt. But the idea of two Predynastic kingdoms may be a projection of the pervasive dualism of Egyptian ideology, not a record of a true historical situation. More probably there was a gradual unification of a previously uncentralized society, reflected in the cultural uniformity of the country in later Naqada II, and in objects bearing early versions of the later royal emblem of the *serekh*. This is a brick facade whose developed form is the king's Horus name, consisting of a hawk surmounting a *serekh* with a space for a name. Motifs of this sort have been found in Upper Egypt, in the area around Memphis and in the delta. The appearance of the motif is roughly contemporary with a cemetery at Abydos, near the later tombs of the 1st-Dynasty kings, which may contain Predynastic royal tombs. If so, there were rulers in later Naqada II, centered on Abydos, who controlled most of the country.

The monumental slate palettes and mace heads of the latest Predynastic kings, especially Na'rmer, are similar in type to later royal reliefs, and appear to record victories over places in the delta and in Libya, and agricultural and ritual events. At later periods, however, most scenes of this sort convey no precise historical information; these reliefs are significant rather in showing that the king's role was defined and given a visual formulation by this early date. The historical events in question were probably earlier in date.

Early Dynastic Period

Two main changes appear to mark the beginning of the 1st Dynasty: a spread in the use of writing, and the founding of Memphis, which may have been the political capital from that time on. There may also have been a change of ruling family, as is suggested by differences in the naming of the kings. Writing was used notably for year names, which recorded a salient event for each year for dating purposes. Lists of these year names later formed the first annals.

The 1st Dynasty begins with the legendary Menes, whose name is known from later Egyptian king lists and from Classical sources. In their own time these kings were mostly known by their Horus names, the official royal element in the titulary, and not by their birth names, which are those used in the lists. As a result both the identification and the existence of Menes are disputed, but he is most probably the same as King 'Aha, to whose reign dates the earliest tomb at Saqqara. The two main centers of power at this time were Abydos and Memphis, while Hierakonpolis, a very old site, also has substantial Early Dynastic remains. The two guardian deities of the Egyptian king, Nekhbet and Wadjit, belong to Hierakonpolis and to Buto (Tell el-Fara'in) in the delta, and it is probable that Buto too was important from an early period. The duration of the 1st Dynasty is estimated at about 150 years. Large cemeteries of the period, with rich burials, have been found in many parts of the country, including the delta; the finest of these date to the long reign of Den. Their spread implies that there was less centralization of wealth than in the central Old Kingdom, when provincial cemeteries of importance disappear.

Little direct evidence of Egyptian relations with the Near East or with Libya is preserved for the 1st Dynasty, but this may be due to chance. In Nubia a graffito of roughly this period has been found in the second cataract area, and shows a king triumphing over enemies, indicating that the Egyptians did not simply come to trade.

The kings were buried at Abydos in a cemetery set well back in the desert, while areas near the cultivation appear to have been marked out for the royal mortuary cult, and may have contained ceremonial buildings of flimsy materials which were renewed as the need arose. The royal tombs themselves were modest in size, and were thoroughly ransacked in later periods, but what little remains from them is of superb workmanship.

While the kings and their court were buried at Abydos, a group of high officials had imposing mud-brick tombs of a different design on the edge of the desert escarpment at north Saqqara (similar tombs have also been found at other sites). There were probably no more than one or two of these officials at one time, since the number of tombs is only slightly greater than that of the kings, with more tombs dating to the reigns of the longer-lived kings. The contents of some of the storage chambers in the superstructures of these tombs have been preserved, and include a remarkable array of objects in copper and, most striking of all, huge quantities of stone vessels in a wide variety of materials and shapes. The genre of stone vessels originated in Predynastic times, and they were the principal luxury product of the country until the 3rd Dynasty.

At the beginning of the 2nd Dynasty the royal necropolis moved to Saqqara. After the third king of the dynasty, Ninetjer, the record is very uncertain; there were probably rival claimants to the throne, and later traditions include names from both sides. The first king of the dynasty whose name has been found at Abydos is Peribsen, the only king in Egyptian history to bear the title Seth instead of Horus. Peribsen apparently altered his name from a

Horus name, Sekhemib. Horus and Seth are the two warring gods of Egyptian myth, who struggle to gain the inheritance of the land – but this myth could have been formulated after the 2nd Dynasty – and the change in title might refer to a belief in the triumph of Seth, or to a difference in local loyalties, among other possibilities. Peribsen's actions seem to have provoked opposition from a king Kha'sekhem, of whom objects are known only from Hierakonpolis in the south. The next king, Kha'sekhemwy, was probably the same person as Kha'sekhem; his name has been found over the whole country on objects that presumably date from after Peribsen's death. The name Kha'sekhem alludes to a "power" (sekhem), which means Horus, while Kha'sekhemwy refers to two "powers" – Horus and Seth – and is surmounted by figures of both gods. It is accompanied by a sentence, "the two lords are at rest in him." The whole is therefore an announcement that the struggle is over. Kha'sekhemwy's reign looks forward to the 3rd Dynasty. His queen, Nima'athapi, is associated with its first two kings, and architecture of his time shows great advances.

The first king of the 3rd Dynasty, Zanakht (2649–2630), is a shadowy figure who was probably the same as a king Nebka. His successor, Djoser (2630–2611), is known above all as the builder of the Step Pyramid at Saqqara, the oldest stone building of its size in the world. In addition to this, fragments of a shrine from Heliopolis of his reign show a fully developed Egyptian style and iconography. The Step Pyramid is in many ways a tentative structure, and shows many changes of plan, but it is evidence of astonishing technical mastery and economic power.

The time of Djoser was later looked back upon as a golden age of achievement and wisdom. The name of Imhotep, the probable architect of the Step Pyramid – he held the titles of a master sculptor among others – came to be especially venerated, and in the Greco-Roman Period he was a popular deity, associated particularly with healing. His name is also found as a graffito on a stretch of the enclosure wall of the pyramid of Djoser's successor, which was buried almost at once in a modification of the original plan. Perhaps he was a hero among the workmen of his own time.

Djoser's buildings stood out from the group of massive mud-brick mastabas of his reign at north Saqqara; not until the next dynasty did other men have stone tombs. But the perfection of relief work extended beyond the royal monument, and the wooden reliefs from the contemporary tomb of Hezyre' are among the finest ancient sculpture in the material. Although they were made for a private person, they may be from a royal workshop.

The still more grandiose monument of Djoser's successor Sekhemkhet (2611–2603) scarcely progressed beyond ground level, and his reign is followed by an obscure period. This interlude before the 4th Dynasty is an illustration of how the rulers predominate in the record and hence in our view of the history. Where the king and his organization were strong the country's resources could be harnessed in a most impressive way, probably through corvée labor. When he was weak the normal subsistence pattern continued without harming the economic fabric of the country, but without dedicating its potential to the same enduring end.

Historical maps: sites and topography
The maps in this chapter show all sites for which remains of the relevant periods are noted in Part Two, as well as a number of additional places. They do not give a complete coverage of sites by period, and it must be remembered that most settlements have been occupied continuously, so that ancient remains are destroyed or deeply buried. The distribution shown is therefore indicative of important finds rather than of settlement patterns. There is proportionally heavier indication of Nubian, desert and oasis sites, because of better conditions for preservation and less stringent criteria for inclusion.

These maps show hypothetical reconstructions of ancient topography. This differs from the modern in the smaller cultivated area in the Nile valley (pp. 31–33 only); the more westerly meander axis of the Nile in the Nile valley (after Butzer); the fluctuating size of the Faiyum lake; the delta waterways (after Butzer and Bietak); and the possible greater size of the Gulf of Suez.

Symbols in black and brown give locations. Symbols in blue placed by names qualify the names but are *not* locations.

Some features of ancient topography are too hypothetical to be included. Among these are possible fluctuations in the delta coastline (e.g. the land was about 2·5 meters higher in relation to the sea in the Greco-Roman Period); and the "eastern canal," of very uncertain purpose and date (Middle Kingdom or Late Period), traces of which can be seen on air photographs of the area between Lake Timsah and near Tell el-Farama.

Egypt in the Old Kingdom and First Intermediate Period
◇ Sites that have yielded papyri. There are very few papyri preserved from the Old Kingdom; unlike those of later periods, the provenance of all of them is known.
▽ Provincial sites with decorated tombs, mainly of the end of the Old Kingdom and the First Intermediate Period. The proliferation of these tombs reflects the decentralization of the period, and perhaps a leveling of wealth.
● Graffiti of Old Kingdom expeditions abroad, principally for minerals, but in Nubia also for trade and raiding. Most of the texts are of the 6th Dynasty.

Wawat, Irtjet and Zatju are Nubian states of the late Old Kingdom that were united at the beginning of the reign of Pepy II (boundaries after Edel).

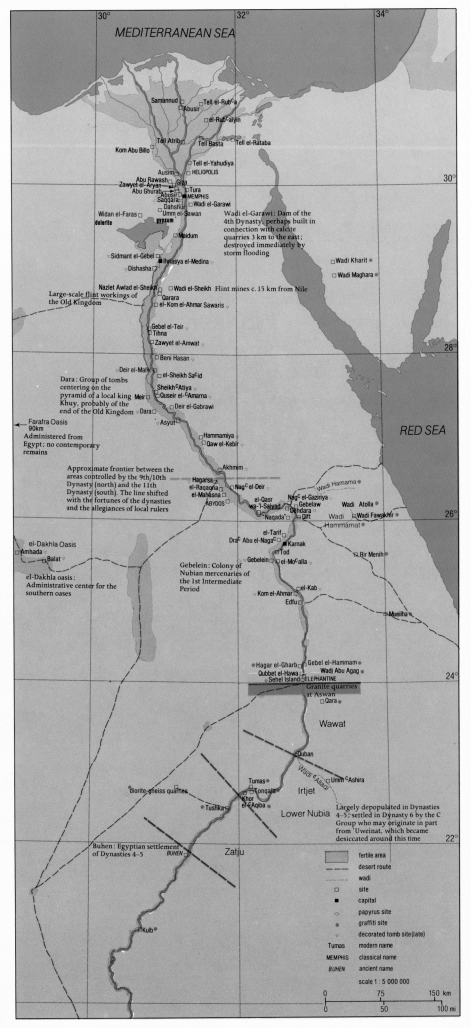

By the end of the Early Dynastic Period Egypt had acquired its classical southern frontier at the first cataract, while its script, administration and technical and artistic capabilities had evolved virtually into their classic forms. There had been a progressive centralization of power which cannot be seen in the record, except in the decline of provincial cemeteries. This was the precondition for the exploits of the 4th-Dynasty rulers.

Old Kingdom

The 4th Dynasty is the time of the great pyramids, but it would be wrong to allow our view of it to be dominated by their massive durability. No less than any other, it is a period of change and of political conflict.

Snofru (2575–2551), the first ruler of the dynasty, built the two pyramids at Dahshur and completed – or possibly built – the Maidum pyramid. This building program is as vast as those of his successors, and implies the same level of efficiency in the economy and in organization. In addition to the pyramids there are mastabas of his reign at Maidum and Saqqara. The reliefs and paintings in these contain the earliest examples of the repertory of subjects found in later Old Kingdom tombs (mid-4th-Dynasty tombs are largely undecorated).

Some details of the administration of the time are known, especially from the inscriptions in the tomb of Metjen from Saqqara. Widely separated estates were given to high officials, possibly in order to discourage the creation of baronial areas. Metjen's estates were mostly in the delta, perhaps on previously uncultivated land. Unlike the very highest officials of the time, Metjen was not a member of the royal family, which dominates our other records.

During the reign of Snofru there was a major campaign or campaigns to Nubia, which is recorded in the fragmentary royal annals (the Palermo Stone) and may be linked with rock inscriptions in Nubia itself. This led to the foundation of an Egyptian settlement at Buhen, which lasted for centuries and was probably used as a base for mining expeditions and for trade. Between the 1st and 4th Dynasties Egyptian activities, perhaps combined with a worsening of the climate, seem to have eliminated the settled Nubian A group, which is followed by a gap before the arrival of the C group about 2250 BC.

A major factor in 4th- and 5th-Dynasty history is solar religion. The true pyramid is most probably a solar symbol, so that Snofru himself was a solar innovator. But the compounding of royal names with the sun god Reʿ and the use of the royal epithet "Son of Reʿ" are not found until the reign of Raʿdjedef (the name of Reʿneb of the 2nd Dynasty is probably irrelevant in this respect). It seems that the influence and importance of the sun god grew continuously until the mid-5th Dynasty, and that the different political factions were united in their adherence to Reʿ.

Of the remaining rulers of the 4th Dynasty Khufu (2551–2528) and Khephren (2520–2494) stand out through their buildings; Menkaureʿ (2490–2472) comes a considerable way behind. The placing of their monuments in a close group at Giza may show factional solidarity, while the pyramid of Raʿdjedef (2528–2520) at Abu Rawash, the excavation for a pyramid at Zawyet el-ʿAryan (whose builder's name is uncertain) and the tomb of Shepseskaf (2472–2467) at south Saqqara perhaps belonged to more ephemeral rival factions. The centralization of rule and the authority of the two main kings can be read off the rigidly ordered groups of tombs around the pyramids. This concentration of power is not, however, the cause of power, since Snofru was as strong as his successors, but did not use the same methods. It may be no coincidence that he later had a good reputation and was deified, whereas Khufu and Khephren were said in folklore to be tyrants.

In addition to buildings, the 4th Dynasty produced much of the finest sculpture of the Old Kingdom, and the scanty surviving reliefs, inscriptions and tomb furniture are of the same quality. In terms of material culture it is the high point of the period, but of its intellectual culture and daily life we know almost nothing.

Shepseskaf built himself a massive mastaba instead of a pyramid, and this almost unique departure may be reflected in the practice of the 5th-Dynasty kings. The first of these, Userkaf (2465–2458), built a small pyramid at Saqqara, east of the Step Pyramid, and a sun temple near Abusir, the idea for which was copied by five of his successors. The temples were separate institutions from the pyramids, but were closely associated with the kings who built them, and probably had a mortuary significance for them.

The architectural continuity which may be posited between the two dynasties has a parallel in the ruling families. In both respects Shepseskaf forms the turning point as much as Userkaf. Khentkaus, the mother of Userkaf and Sahure' (2458–2446), was a member of the 4th-Dynasty royal family. The father of the kings is unknown, but he may have been from another branch of the same very large group. Despite this continuity, the internal policies of the 5th Dynasty were very different from those of the 4th. The reduction in the size of pyramids was not accompanied by a compensating increase in other construction, and the change must reflect either economic decline or an increase in the consumption of things that leave no trace. While there is clear evidence of decline in the late 6th Dynasty, the level of activity in the two preceding centuries was roughly constant. There is no simple explanation for this pattern, and we should perhaps ask instead what provoked the departure from convention in the extraordinary phase of building in the 4th Dynasty.

In the 5th Dynasty private tombs are no longer regimented into rows or confined on a single site, and the amount of decoration in them increases continually. This is evidence for greater freedom of expression – within close limits – for the elite, but not necessarily for any increase in their wealth. A further significant change is the location of some tombs in the provinces towards the end of the dynasty. The provincial administrators, originally central appointees, turned slowly into local ruling families. By the end of the Old Kingdom there are large provincial cemeteries, and this development marks a loosening of royal power. It is seen rather earlier in the holders of high office, who are no longer members of the royal family, although they may marry into it. An administration based on autocracy and kinship gives way to something like a fixed bureaucracy.

The latest royal name found at the Egyptian settlement of Buhen is that of Neuserre' (2416–2392), and Egypt probably lost control of Nubia soon after. Some generations later there are records of trading expeditions to the south from Egypt, which presumably replaced the permanent depot.

The last kings of the 5th Dynasty did not build sun temples, which implies a lessening in the importance of solar religion. Wenis (2356–2323) appears to be a transitional figure, heralding the 6th Dynasty. His pyramid complex, with its remarkably small pyramid, is of great interest both for the reliefs on its causeway and for the texts on the walls of the internal chambers. The texts had probably been used for earlier kings, so that they do not necessarily point to a change in belief. The practice of inscribing them is continuous from Wenis to the 8th Dynasty, but the selection in the different pyramids varies greatly.

We know more of the political history of the 6th Dynasty than we do for earlier periods, but it is still a random selection of information; much of what we regard as typical of it could have happened at other times too. This applies particularly to military campaigns, like those to the east of Egypt recorded by the high official Weni. The location of the area attacked is uncertain – immediately east of the delta or in southern Palestine – and the nature of the enemy is not clear. But even if the import of these campaigns is unknown, their existence is certain. Campaigns recorded in royal mortuary reliefs have no simple relationship with fact. A campaign to Libya shown in the complex of Sahure' (2458–2446)

Statue of an Asiatic (?) captive, perhaps from the mortuary complex of Djedkare' Izezi at Saqqara. There were large numbers of these statues depicting various different nationalities, in 5th- and 6th-Dynasty complexes, but the sites have been so ransacked that we do not know how they were arranged. They are the counterpart of relief scenes of the defeat of enemies. New York, Metropolitan Museum of Art.

Roughly worked funerary stela of the Nubian Senu, from el-Rizeiqat near Gebelein. The texts state that the owner and his son, who is shown directly under him, are Nubian; both wear a distinctive, sporran-like garment. They were probably mercenaries. Height 37 cm. First Intermediate Period. Boston, Museum of Fine Arts.

is repeated by Neuserreʿ (2416–2392), Pepy I (2289–2255), Pepy II (2246–2152) and finally Taharqa (690–664); this is a ritual event, which probably corresponds with a real campaign earlier than the reign of Sahureʿ, but with no other specific happening.

Occasional archaeological evidence highlights our ignorance of Egyptian relations with the Near East. Pieces of 5th-Dynasty goldwork have appeared in Anatolia, and stone vases of Khephren and Pepy I have recently been excavated at Tell Mardikh in Syria, the capital of the important state of Ebla that fell around 2250 BC. We can only guess at the degree of contact implied by these finds. As in the Middle Kingdom, the main channel of communication must have been Byblos, where a number of Old Kingdom objects have been found.

The inscriptions of the expedition leaders in their tombs at Aswan give much information about trade to the south in the 6th Dynasty, some of it through the oases of el-Kharga and el-Dakhla. Among other events, they show the settling of the C group in Lower Nubia, first in three princedoms, and later in a single political unit, with which Egypt's relations gradually deteriorated.

This deterioration is probably an aspect of Egypt's declining power during the immense reign of Pepy II (2246–2152, of which the latter part is not attested from contemporary sources). The decline can be seen in private tombs in the Memphite area, whose decoration is much more modest than hitherto, and sometimes all underground, perhaps for reasons of security. But even though we can point to details of this sort, nothing prepares for the eclipse of royal power and the poverty that come after Pepy II. The numerous kings of the next 20 years (late 6th and 7th–8th Dynasties) were nominally accepted in the whole country, but there was no real central control. Provincial officials had become hereditary holders of their posts, and treated their nomes virtually as their property, whose interests they defended, often by force, against their neighbors. Famine was common and

may be the key to understanding the period, since it has been suggested that the political collapse was due primarily to a series of disastrous low inundations. This would explain why there is relatively little indication of decline before the catastrophe, but the human elements of a line of weak kings and failing administration should also be taken into account. The reality of disaster is confirmed by an analysis of death rates in cemeteries, which show a marked increase at this time.

First Intermediate Period and the 11th-Dynasty reunification

The 1st Intermediate Period (2134–2040) is the time during which Egypt was divided, being ruled by the 9th/10th Dynasty from Herakleopolis (Ihnasya el-Medina) and another from Thebes (the 11th); at its beginning the Herakleopolitans may have had control of the whole country for some years. The new dynasties were started by nomarchs who proclaimed themselves kings, and were able to gain acceptance among their neighbors. At first the change to dual sovereignty probably made little difference to the running of the country, since the dynasties were too weak to exert much influence on local politics. Their power gradually increased, however, and there were frequent clashes at the border, which was mostly north of Abydos. The presence of considerable numbers of Nubian mercenaries in Upper Egypt is an indication of how violent the times were. Despite general poverty, there are relatively large numbers of modest, and frequently crude, monuments of the period, made for lower strata of society than hitherto.

The Herakleopolitan Dynasty suffered frequent changes of ruler, and produced no outstanding kings. The most important king of the more stable Theban Dynasty was the fourth, Nebhepetreʿ Mentuhotpe (called I or II by different writers, 2061–2010), who defeated the northern dynasty and reunited the country. Mentuhotpe began with a programmatic Horus name, "Who gives heart to the Two Lands," which was replaced first by "Divine of the White Crown" (the crown of Upper Egypt) and later by "Uniter of the Two Lands." These changes may correspond to stages in the reunification, the second indicating that he had united all of Upper Egypt and the third – a traditional epithet which was given a new iconographic formulation by Mentuhotpe – that he had accomplished the conquest of the whole country. His reign also includes activity in Lower Nubia (possibly building on campaigns of his predecessors), and the construction of a novel and impressive mortuary complex at Deir el-Bahri, from which reliefs and sculpture have been recovered. The artistic style is a refined version of 1st Intermediate Period work rather than a resumption of Old Kingdom traditions, and emphasizes, as does the Theban location of the complex, the local base of the king's power. Mentuhotpe was held in later periods to be one of the founders of Egypt; part of this prestige may go back to his own self-glorification, for he was shown in relief in a form more nearly divine than that of most Egyptian kings. This was probably intended also to enhance the status of the kingship at an important juncture; it continued under his successor.

Kings of Egypt

The list on these pages contains the names and *approximate* dates of most of the important kings of Egypt, with the names of queens regnant designated Q.

A king's full titulary consisted of five main elements, of which the first three were given in their order of origin. These are (1) Horus, (2) Two Ladies, (3) Golden Horus, all of which are epithets that seem to refer to aspects of the king's being as a manifestation of a deity. The fourth, the first cartouche name, is prefaced by two words for king, which came to be identified with the two halves of the country, and usually contains a statement about the sun god Reʿ in relation to the king. The fifth, the second cartouche, is normally the king's own birth name, and is preceded by the designation "Son of Reʿ."

Since the pronunciation of names is often unknown, Greek forms, from the history of Manetho (3rd century BC), are used for many kings. In the list the birth name is normally given first, followed by the first cartouche, which is always in *italics*. The kings of the 20th Dynasty used Ramesses as a dynastic name in their second cartouches, and Ptolemaic kings were similarly called Ptolemy.

Overlapping dates within dynasties indicate coregencies. Where two or more dynasties overlap they were mostly accepted in different parts of the country.

Dates that are known with precision are marked *.

The dates are computed from ancient lists, especially the Turin royal papyrus, and various other sources, including a few pieces of astronomical evidence. The margin of error rises from about a decade in the New Kingdom and 3rd Intermediate Period to as much as 150 years for the beginning of the 1st Dynasty. Most 12th-Dynasty dates are fixed precisely, and 18th- and 19th-Dynasty ones must fit one of three astronomically determined alternatives; here a combination of the middle and lowest ones is used. All dates from 664 BC are precise. All native rulers mentioned in Part Two are included in the list.

Above A typical full titulary. "Horus: Mighty bull, perfect of glorious appearances; Two Ladies: Enduring of kingship like Atum [the aging sun god]; Golden Horus: Strong of arm, oppressor of the Nine Bows [traditional enemies]; *Nisut* and *bity* [terms for king]: Menkheprureʿ [Reʿ is enduring of manifestations]; Son of Reʿ: Tuthmosis [IV], greatly appearing one; beloved of Amon-Reʿ, giver of [or: given] life like Reʿ."

Right Typical hieroglyphic writings of selected kings' names; those in the first line are Horus names. Most of the rest are pairs of throne names, by which the kings' contemporaries knew them, and birth names, by which we now know them.

LATE PREDYNASTIC c. 3000
Zekhen; Naʿrmer

EARLY DYNASTIC PERIOD 2920–2575

1st Dynasty 2920–2770
Menes (= ʿAha?); Djer; Wadj;
Den; ʿAdjib; Semerkhet; Qaʿa

2nd Dynasty 2770–2649
Hetepsekhemwy; Reʿneb;
Ninetjer; Peribsen;
Khaʿsekhem(wy)

3rd Dynasty 2649–2575
Zanakht (= Nebka?) 2649–2630
Djoser (Netjerykhet) 2630–2611
Sekhemkhet 2611–2603
Khaʿba 2603–2599
Huni(?) 2599–2575

OLD KINGDOM 2575–2134

4th Dynasty 2575–2465
Snofru 2575–2551
Khufu (Cheops) 2551–2528
Raʿdjedef 2528–2520
Khephren (Raʿkhaʿef) 2520–2494
Menkaure 2490–2472
(Mycerinus)
Shepseskaf 2472–2467

5th Dynasty 2465–2323
Userkaf 2465–2458
Sahureʿ 2458–2446
Neferirkareʿ Kakai 2446–2426
Shepseskareʿ Ini 2426–2419
Raʿneferef 2419–2416
Neuserreʿ Izi 2416–2392
Menkauhor 2396–2388
Djedkareʿ Izezi 2388–2356
Wenis 2356–2323

6th Dynasty 2323–2150
Teti 2323–2291
Pepy I (*Meryre*ʿ) 2289–2255
Merenreʿ Nemtyemzaf 2255–2246
Pepy II (*Neferkare*ʿ) 2246–2152

7th/8th Dynasty 2150–2134
Numerous ephemeral kings,
including Neferkareʿ

**1st INTERMEDIATE
PERIOD** 2134–2040

9th/10th Dynasty 2134–2040
(Herakleopolitan)
Several kings called Khety;
Merykareʿ; Ity

11th Dynasty (Theban)
2134–2040
Inyotef I (Sehertawy) 2134–2118
Inyotef II (Wahʿankh) 2118–2069
Inyotef III 2069–2061
(Nakhtnebtepnufer)
Nebhepetreʿ 2061–2010
Mentuhotpe

MIDDLE KINGDOM 2040–1640

11th Dynasty 2040–1991
(all Egypt)
Nebhepetreʿ 2061–2010
Mentuhotpe
Sʿankhkareʿ 2010–1998
Mentuhotpe
Nebtawyreʿ 1998–1991
Mentuhotpe

12th Dynasty *1991–1783
Amenemhet I *1991–1962
(*Sehetepibre*ʿ)
Senwosret I *1971–1926
(*Kheperkare*ʿ)
Amenemhet II *1929–1892
(*Nubkaure*ʿ)
Senwosret II *1897–1878
(*Khaʿkheperre*ʿ)
Senwosret III *1878–1841?
(*Khaʿkaure*ʿ)
Amenemhet III 1844–1797
(*Nima*ʿatreʿ)
Amenemhet IV 1799–1787
(*Maʿakherure*ʿ)
Nefrusobk 1787–1783
(*Sebekkare*ʿ) Q

13th Dynasty 1783–after 1640
About 70 kings. Better-known ones are listed; the numbers are their positions in the complete list
Wegaf (*Khutawyre*ʿ) 1 1783–1779
Amenemhet V (*Sekhemkare*ʿ) 4
Harnedjheriotef (*Hetepibre*ʿ) 9
Amenyqemau 11b
Sebekhotpe I c. 1750
(*Khaʿankhre*ʿ) 12
Hor (*Awibre*ʿ) 14; Amenemhet
VII (*Sedjefakare*ʿ) 15; Sebekhotpe
II (*Sekhemre*ʿ-*khutawy*) 16;
Khendjer (*Userkare*ʿ) 17
Sebekhotpe III c. 1745
(*Sekhemre*ʿ-*swadjtawy*) 21
Neferhotep I c. 1741–1730
(*Khaʿsekhmre*ʿ) 22
Sebekhotpe IV c. 1730–1720
(*Khaʿneferre*ʿ) 24
Sebekhotpe V c. 1720–1715
(*Khaʿhotepre*ʿ) 25
Aya c. 1704–1690
(*Merneferre*ʿ) 27
Mentuemzaf (*Djedʿankhre*ʿ) 32c;
Dedumose II (*Djedneferre*ʿ) 37;
Neferhotep II (*Sekhemre*ʿ-
sʿankhtawy) 41a

14th Dynasty
A group of minor kings who were probably all contemporary with the 13th or 15th Dynasty

**2nd INTERMEDIATE
PERIOD** 1640–1532

15th Dynasty (Hyksos)
Salitis; Sheshi;
Khian (*Swoserenre*ʿ)
Apophis c. 1585–1542
(*Awoserre*ʿ and others)
Khamudi c. 1542–1532

16th Dynasty
Minor Hyksos rulers, contemporary with the 15th Dynasty

17th Dynasty 1640–1550
Numerous Theban kings;
numbers give positions in the complete list
Inyotef V c. 1640–1635
(*Nubkheperre*ʿ) 1
Sebekemzaf I (*Sekhemre*ʿ-
*wadjkha*ʿu) 3; Nebireyeraw
(*Swadjenre*ʿ) 6; Sebekamzaf II
(*Sekhemre*ʿ-*shedtawy*) 10; Taʿo (or
Djehutiʿo) I (*Senakhtenre*ʿ) 13;
Taʿo (or Djehutiʿo) II (*Seqenenre*ʿ)
14
Kamose c. 1555–1550
(*Wadjkheperre*ʿ) 15

NEW KINGDOM 1550–1070

18th Dynasty 1550–1307
ʿAhmose (*Nebpehtire*ʿ) 1550–1525
Amenophis I 1525–1504
(*Djeserkare*ʿ)
Tuthmosis I 1504–1492
(ʿ*Akheperkare*ʿ)
Tuthmosis II 1492–1479
(ʿ*Akheperenre*ʿ)
Tuthmosis III 1479–1425
(*Menkheperre*ʿ)
Hatshepsut 1473–1458
(*Maʿatkare*ʿ) Q
Amenophis II 1427–1401
(ʿ*Akheprure*ʿ)
Tuthmosis IV 1401–1391
(*Menkheprure*ʿ)
Amenophis III 1391–1353
(*Nebma*ʿatreʿ)
Amenophis IV/Akhenaten
(*Neferkheprure*ʿ *wa*ʿenre)
1353–1335
Smenkhkareʿ 1335–1333
(ʿ*Ankhkheprure*ʿ) (= Nefertiti Q?)
Tutʿankhamun 1333–1323
(*Nebkheprure*ʿ)
Aya 1323–1319
(*Kheperkheprure*ʿ)
Haremhab 1319–1307
(*Djeserkheprure*ʿ)

19th Dynasty 1307–1196
Ramesses I 1307–1306
(*Menpehtire*ʿ)
Sethos I 1306–1290
(*Menma*ʿatreʿ)
Ramesses II 1290–1224
(*Userma*ʿatreʿ *setepenre*ʿ)
Merneptah 1224–1214
(*Baenre*ʿ *hotephirma*ʿat)
Sethos II 1214–1204
(*Userkheprure*ʿ *setepenre*ʿ)
Amenmesse (*Menmire*ʿ),
usurper during reign of Sethos II
Siptah 1204–1198
(*Akhenre*ʿ *setepenre*ʿ)
Twosre 1198–1196
(*Sitre*ʿ *meritamun*) Q

20th Dynasty 1196–1070
Sethnakhte 1196–1194
(*Userkha*ʿureʿ *meryamun*)
Ramesses III 1194–1163
(*Userma*ʿatreʿ *meryamun*)
Ramesses IV 1163–1156
(*Heqama*ʿatreʿ *setepenamun*)
Ramesses V 1156–1151
(*Userma*ʿatreʿ *sekheperenre*ʿ)
Ramesses VI 1151–1143
(*Nebma*ʿatreʿ *meryamun*)
Ramesses VII 1143–1136
(*Userma*ʿatreʿ *setepenre*ʿ
meryamun)
Ramesses VIII 1136–1131
(*Userma*ʿatreʿ *akhenamun*)
Ramesses IX 1131–1112
(*Neferkare*ʿ *setepenre*ʿ)
Ramesses X 1112–1100
(*Kheperma*ʿatreʿ *setepenre*ʿ)
Ramesses XI 1100–1070
(*Menma*ʿatreʿ *setepenptah*)

**3rd INTERMEDIATE
PERIOD** 1070–712

21st Dynasty 1070–945
Smendes 1070–1044
(*Hedjkheperre*ʿ *setepenre*ʿ)

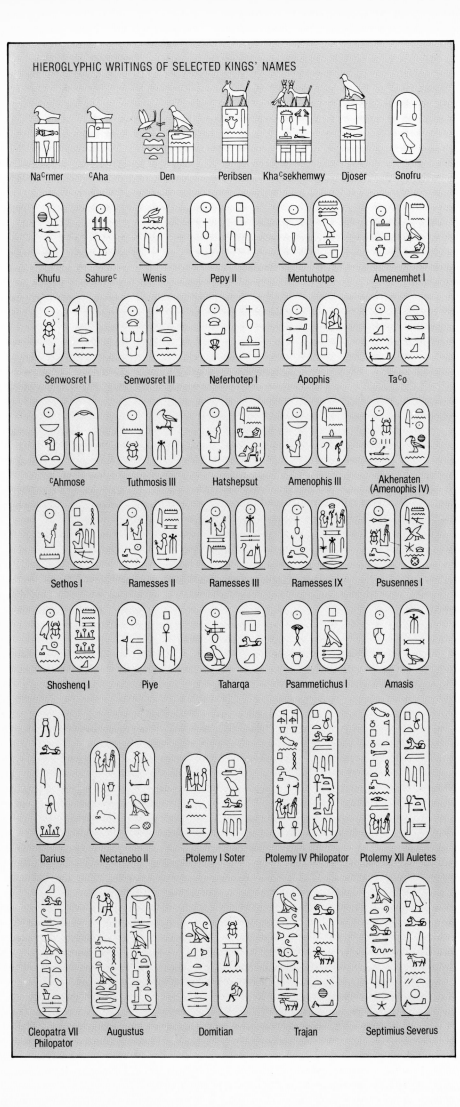

HIEROGLYPHIC WRITINGS OF SELECTED KINGS' NAMES

Na°rmer °Aha Den Peribsen Kha°sekhemwy Djoser Snofru

Khufu Sahure° Wenis Pepy II Mentuhotpe Amenemhet I

Senwosret I Senwosret III Neferhotep I Apophis Ta°o

°Ahmose Tuthmosis III Hatshepsut Amenophis III Akhenaten (Amenophis IV)

Sethos I Ramesses II Ramesses III Ramesses IX Psusennes I

Shoshenq I Piye Taharqa Psammetichus I Amasis

Darius Nectanebo II Ptolemy I Soter Ptolemy IV Philopator Ptolemy XII Auletes

Cleopatra VII Philopator Augustus Domitian Trajan Septimius Severus

Amenemnisu (Neferkare')	1044–1040
Psusennes I ('Akheperre' setepenamun)	1040–992
Amenemope (Userma'atre' setepenamun)	993–984
Osorkon I ('Akheperre' setepenre')	984–978
Siamun (Netjerkheperre' setepenamun)	978–959
Psusennes II (Titkheprure' setepenre')	959–945

22nd Dynasty **945–712**

Shoshenq I (Hedjkheperre' setepenre')	945–924
Osorkon II (Sekhemkheperre' setepenre')	924–909
Takelot I (Userma'atre' setepenamun)	909–
Shoshenq II (Heqakheperre' setepenre')	–883
Osorkon III (Userma'atre' setepenre')	883–855
Takelot II (Hedjkheperre' setepenre')	860–835
Shoshenq III (Userma'atre' setepenre'/amun)	835–783
Pami (Userma'atre' setepenre'/amun)	783–773
Shoshenq V ('Akheperre')	773–735
Osorkon V ('Akheperre' setepenamun)	735–712

23rd Dynasty **c.828–712**
Various contemporary lines of kings recognized in Thebes, Hermopolis, Herakleopolis, Leontopolis and Tanis; precise arrangement and order are still disputed

Pedubaste I	828–803
Osorkon IV	777–749
Peftjau'awybast (Neferkare')	740–725

24th Dynasty (Sais) **724–712**

(Tefnakhte (Shepsesre'?)	724–717)
Bocchoris (Wahkare')	717–712

25th Dynasty **770–712**
(Nubia and Theban area)

Kashta (Nima'atre')	770–750
Piye (Userma'atre' and others)	750–712

LATE PERIOD **712–332**

25th Dynasty **712–657**
(Nubia and all Egypt)

Shabaka (Neferkare')	712–698
Shebitku (Djedkaure')	698–690
Taharqa (Khure'nefertem)	690–664
Tantamani (Bakare')	664–657
(possibly later in Nubia)	

26th Dynasty ***664–525**

(Necho I	*672–664)
Psammetichus I (Wahibre')	*664–610
Necho II (Wehemibre')	*610–595
Psammetichus II (Neferibre')	*595–589
Apries (Ha'a'ibre')	*589–570
Amasis (Khnemibre')	*570–526
Psammetichus III ('Ankhkaenre')	*526–525

27th Dynasty ***525–404**
(Persian)

Cambyses	*525–522
Darius I	*521–486
Xerxes I	*486–466
Artaxerxes I	*465–424
Darius II	*424–404

28th Dynasty ***404–399**

Amyrtaios	*404–399

29th Dynasty ***399–380**

Nepherites I (Baenre' merynetjeru)	*399–393
Psammuthis (Userre' setepenptah)	*393
Hakoris (Khnemma'atre')	*393–380
Nepherites II	*380

30th Dynasty ***380–343**

Nectanebo I (Kheperkare')	*380–362
Teos (Irma'atenre')	*365–360
Nectanebo II (Senedjemibre' setepenanhur)	*360–343

2nd Persian Period ***343–332**

Artaxerxes III Ochus	*343–338
Arses	*338–336
Darius III Codoman	*335–332

Period interrupted by a native ruler Khababash (Senentanen setepenptah)

GRECO-ROMAN PERIOD
*332 BC–395 AD

Macedonian Dynasty ***332–304**

Alexander III the Great	*332–323
Philip Arrhidaeus	*323–316
Alexander IV	*316–304

Ptolemaic Dynasty ***304–330**

Ptolemy I Soter I	*304–284
Ptolemy II Philadelphus	*285–246
Ptolemy III Euergetes I	*246–221
Ptolemy IV Philopator	*221–205
Ptolemy V Epiphanes	*205–180
Ptolemy VI Philometor	*180–164, *163–145
Ptolemy VIII Euergetes II (Physkon)	*170–163, *145–116
Ptolemy VII Neos Philopator	*145
Cleopatra III Q and Ptolemy IX Soter II (Lathyros)	*116–107
Cleopatra III Q and Ptolemy X Alexander I	*107–88
Ptolemy IX Soter II	*88–81
Cleopatra Berenice Q	*81–80
Ptolemy XI Alexander II	*80
Ptolemy XII Neos Dionysos (Auletes)	*80–58, *55–51
Berenice IV Q	*58–55
Cleopatra VII Q	*51–30
Ptolemy XIII	*51–47
Ptolemy XIV	*47–44
Ptolemy XV Caesarion	*44–30

There were further coregencies with queens called Arsinoe, Berenice and Cleopatra, who had no independent reigns. Native usurpers: Harwennofre (205–199), 'Ankhwennofre (199–186), Harsiese (131)

Roman emperors ***30 BC–395 AD**
(names found in hieroglyphic and demotic texts, down to the tetrarchy)

Augustus	*30 BC–14 AD
Tiberius	*14–37
Gaius (Caligula)	*37–41
Claudius	*41–54
Nero	*54–68
Galba	*68–69
Otho	*69
Vespasian	*69–79
Titus	*79–81
Domitian	*81–96
Nerva	*96–98
Trajan	*98–117
Hadrian	*117–138
Antoninus Pius	*138–161
Marcus Aurelius	*161–180
Lucius Verus	*161–169
Commodus	*180–192
Septimius Severus	*193–211
Caracalla	*198–217
Geta	*209–212
Macrinus	*217–218
Diadumenianus	*218
Severus Alexander	*222–235
Gordian III	*238–244
Philip	*244–249
Decius	*249–251
Gallus and Volusianus	*251–253
Valerian	*253–260
Gallienus	*253–268
Macrianus and Quietus	*260–261
Aurelian	*270–275
Probus	*276–282
Diocletian	*284–305
Maximian	*286–305
Galerius	*293–311

Gallery of Kings

The image of an Egyptian king is more a statement of an ideal than a portrait. Of those shown, only Amenophis IV and Ptolemy IV depart from the norm, one highly stylized, the other influenced by Hellenistic portraiture.

Faces may depict general qualities. Some early figures convey an impressive strength, which becomes greatly refined. Neferhotep I follows the 12th-Dynasty tradition of the "suffering king." The later heads are mostly rather blander.

Kings normally wear a crown, uraeus (cobra on the forehead) and false beard. The most important of the many crowns are the tall white crown, the primary symbol of kingship in early periods, associated with *nisut* (the normal word for king) and with Upper Egypt; and the squat blue crown – blue is the most prestigious color – from the 18th Dynasty on. Further crowns on these figures are the *nemes* headcloth, typical of the Middle Kingdom; a flat cap; and a skull cap. Merenre' is youthful and bareheaded.

Palette of Na'rmer, late Predynastic (c.2950). Schist.

1st-Dynasty king, c.2850. Ivory.

Kha'sekhem, 2nd Dynasty (c.2670). Limestone.

3rd-Dynasty king, c.2600. Pink granite.

Shepseskaf, 2472–2467 (?). Diorite.

Merenre' Nemtyemzaf, c.2255. Copper.

Neferhotep I, c.1741–1730. Black basalt.

Amenophis IV (Akhenaten), c.1350. Sandstone.

Tut'ankhamun, 1333–1323. Wood and gesso.

Ramesses II, 1290–1224.
Black granite.

Sethos I, 1305–1290. Black
basalt.

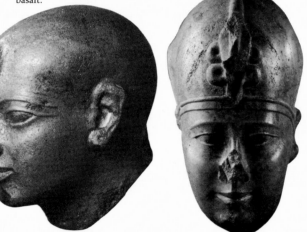

King of the 3rd Intermediate
Period, c.1000–800. Quartzite.

Amasis, 570–526 (?). Quartzite.

Ptolemy IV Philopator,
221–205 (?). Schist.

Middle Kingdom

The last two kings of the 11th Dynasty retained Thebes as the capital. The second, Nebtawyre' Mentuhotpe, is ignored by later lists, probably being seen as an illegitimate ruler. During their reigns there was building activity in much of the country. Quarries were opened up, most notably in the Wadi Hammamat, and the Red Sea route was revived. All this indicates that Egypt was strong, but the political order did not last. The vizier under Nebtawyre' Mentuhotpe, Amenemhet, was also the first king of the 12th Dynasty, but the mode of transfer of power to him is unknown; he came from a prominent family in Elephantine.

The most important political act of Amenemhet I (1991–1962) was to move the royal residence from Thebes to near Memphis, where he founded a city called Itjtawy, "[Amenemhet is] seizer of the Two Lands." The site itself was probably an administrative area, including the pyramids of Amenemhet I and Senwosret I, while the main city remained at Memphis. The capital was both an innovation and a return to Old Kingdom traditions, which were also taken up in art.

In foreign policy Amenemhet I built on the work of Nebhepetre' Mentuhotpe in Nubia, and in several campaigns in the last years of his reign, in which he did not take part himself, conquered the whole area as far as the second cataract. The leader of these campaigns was Senwosret I (1971–1926), and the ten-year overlap between their reigns was another innovation, setting the institutional pattern for coregencies. Senwosret I was the more active partner for the joint years. Amenemhet I was apparently murdered while his son was on a campaign to Libya, but, perhaps because of the coregency, there was no resulting disorder.

During the reigns of Amenemhet I and Senwosret I there was much building in Egypt, and the great series of forts in Lower Nubia was begun. At the same time a number of important works of literature were written, and the material and intellectual achievements of the dynasty made it classical in later Egyptian and in modern eyes. An instance of this is the relief carving of the chapel of Senwosret I at Karnak, which served as a model for early 18th-Dynasty artists. But despite these achievements of its first rulers, far more archaeological material is preserved for the reigns of Senwosret III (1878–1841), Amenemhet III (1844–1797), and later, than there is for the years 2000–1900 BC.

The 12th-Dynasty king with the most lasting reputation was Senwosret III. He is noted especially for his Nubian campaigns, in which the frontier was moved south to Semna, at the southern end of the second cataract, for the establishment of new forts and for the extension of others. In later times he was worshiped there as a god, and the temple of Tuthmosis III at Semna is dedicated to him and to Dedwen, a local deity. The main purpose of this military activity may have been to counter the increasing influence of the Kerma rulers to the south. During his reign there was also a campaign to Palestine, which was apparently not intended to conquer the area, but which came at the beginning of a period of considerable Egyptian influence there. The region was then seminomadic, and did not become settled until the end of the 12th Dynasty. Senwosret III worked with a sizable standing army, whose organization has only recently begun to be understood.

Senwosret III made important reforms in the administration of Egypt, which seem to have completed the removal of power from provincial governors. The country was organized into four "regions," each of which corresponded to roughly half the Nile valley or the delta. From documents of the late 12th and 13th Dynasties, principally from el-Lahun, we gain an impression of a pervasive bureaucratic organization, which came to run the country under its own momentum.

Within Egypt the most striking visible legacy of Senwosret III is his royal sculpture, which breaks earlier conventions in showing an aging, careworn face, perhaps symbolizing the burdens of kingship, as depicted in the literature of the period. The same style was used in statues of his successor Amenemhet III, whose long reign was apparently peaceful. Amenemhet III was deified later in the Faiyum, where he built one of his two pyramids and a number of other monuments, and where he may have begun a land reclamation scheme. His predecessors had, however, also taken an interest in the area, and he may have reaped the glory of a long enterprise.

In the reigns of Amenemhet IV (1799–1787) and Queen Nefrusobk (1787–1783) there was no loss of prosperity in the country, but the presence of a woman on the throne indicates that the ruling family was dying out. There is a complete continuity in the archaeological record between the 12th and 13th Dynasties, even though the nature of

Right: Egypt in the Middle Kingdom and Second Intermediate Period
● Sites with finds of the Palestinian Middle Bronze culture of the 18th–17th century BC.
▿ Selected sites of the "pan-grave" culture of the Second Intermediate Period. These people were nomads of the eastern desert, many of them mercenaries in the service of various rulers. Pottery similar to theirs has been found in the Red Sea hills and at Kassala in southeastern Sudan. By the New Kingdom they were completely assimilated in Egypt, giving their name, *Medjay*, to the police force.

Far right: The second cataract forts of the Middle Kingdom
The cataract area is a largely unnavigable stretch of rapids 30 km long. The chain of 12th-Dynasty frontier forts was the largest surviving ancient group in the world until it was submerged in Lake Nasser. The northern forts were begun under Senwosret I; Semna and Kumma were added by Senwosret III.

Below Reliefs in the chapel of Senwosret I at Karnak, reconstructed from blocks found in the 3rd pylon. The scene shows Atum leading the king before Amon-Re' Kamutef. The elaborate, refined style inspired artists of the early 18th Dynasty.

the kingship seems to have changed considerably.

In about 150 years some 70 kings of the 13th Dynasty came and went. While at times there were no doubt rival claimants to the throne, this was not the rule. The country seems to have remained stable, even though there was no official means of replacing kings in rapid succession, but the kings themselves must have been of relatively little account. The most important people in the country seem instead to have been the viziers, the highest officials, of whom a family is known that spanned a large part of the 18th century. Official titles of all ranks proliferated at this time, quite possibly because of an increase in the size of the bureaucracy, a phenomenon with parallels elsewhere in the world in periods of slow decline.

As late as 1720 Egypt appears to have lost little power or prestige at home or abroad. If we use the number of private monuments as a measure, there seems even to have been an increase in prosperity in the country, and a leveling of wealth, since there are few royal monuments. There were many immigrants from Palestine, apparently peaceful arrivals, who were absorbed into the lowest levels of Egyptian society, but at least one of whom, Khendjer, became king of Egypt. They probably came as a result of shifts of population in the Near East after 1800, and were forerunners of the movement that was to bring foreign rule in the 2nd Intermediate Period. In the later 13th Dynasty the eastern delta was heavily settled by Asiatics, including areas that had been completely Egyptian in the 12th Dynasty, such as that around

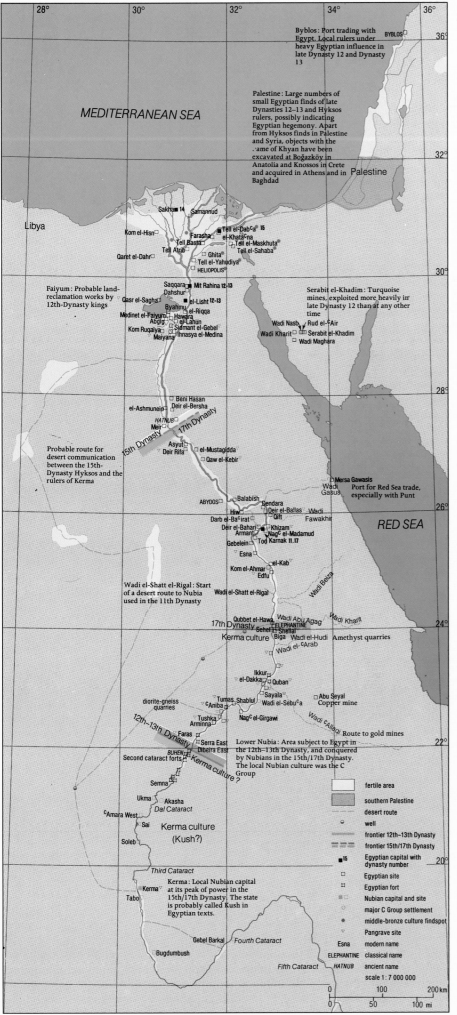

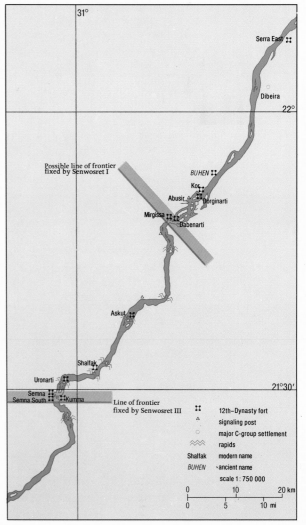

Qantir, which became the Hyksos and later the Ramessid capital of Egypt. Egypt retained control of Lower Nubia, probably until near the end of the 13th Dynasty, but the local army contingents became increasingly independent, and settled as permanent inhabitants, some of whom stayed behind after the area was overrun from the south at the beginning of the 15th/17th Dynasties.

Second Intermediate Period

Around 1640 the position of the 13th Dynasty was usurped by a foreign group conventionally called the Hyksos, a Greek form derived from an Egyptian phrase meaning "ruler of foreign lands"; the method of takeover is uncertain. The Hyksos, the 15th Egyptian Dynasty, seem to have been recognized as the chief line of kings in the whole country, but they tolerated other contenders. The 13th Dynasty may have continued in existence, as may also the 14th, a line of rulers in the north-western delta (whose existence has been doubted).

There was also a parallel group of Hyksos rulers known as the 16th Dynasty, a term which may simply cover other Asiatic rulers who proclaimed themselves king, wherever they may have been. The most important of these dynasties was the 17th, a line of native Egyptians who ruled from Thebes, holding the Nile valley from the first cataract north as far as Cusae (el-Qusiya). In the south Lower Nubia was conquered by the Nubian rulers of Kerma. There were therefore three main divisions of the area that had been held by the 12th–13th Dynasties. For almost a century there appears to have been peace among them.

The names of 15th-Dynasty kings have been found on small objects from widely separated sites in the Near East, showing that they had diplomatic or trading relations over a very large area. Contact abroad brought with it a number of primarily technical innovations which were to be important in later periods. Some of the novelties probably came with Asiatic immigrants, while other specifically military ones may have been acquired during campaigns, in some cases in the early 18th Dynasty. Until this time Egypt had been technologically backward in comparison with the Near East; during the New Kingdom the two were roughly on a par. Among the new techniques were bronzeworking, which replaced the importation of ready-alloyed bronze and the use of arsenic copper; an improved potter's wheel and the vertical loom; hump-backed cattle (zebu) and new vegetable and fruit crops; the horse and chariot, composite bows, and new shapes of scimitar and other weapons. On a different plane new musical instruments came into fashion, and 18th-Dynasty dances are different from those of earlier periods.

With Seqenenre' Ta'o II of the 17th Dynasty the Thebans began their struggle to expel the Hyksos. The first episode of the battle is known only from a New Kingdom story, the "Quarrel of Apophis [the Hyksos king] and Seqenenre'," but Seqenenre''s

mummy shows that he died violently, possibly in battle. Two stelae of his successor Kamose describe extensive skirmishes between Thebes and the Hyksos, who were allied with the Nubian kings. Kamose nearly reached Avaris, the Hyksos capital, and campaigned as far south as Buhen, but we hear nothing of him after his third year.

New Kingdom

Kamose's successor 'Ahmose (1550–1525) finally drove out the Hyksos rulers around 1532 – many years after Kamose's attempts. The course of the expulsion is recorded very briefly by 'Ahmose, son of Ebana, a soldier from el-Kab. After his victory 'Ahmose continued his thrust into Palestine, where the Hyksos may have had allies or some measure of control, and campaigned there for some years. In Nubia he fought as far south as the island of Sai, near the third cataract, while he also apparently had to deal with a rebellion in Egypt. His reign has left a number of inscriptions from different parts of the country, including one showing family piety to his grandmother in Abydos; there is a notable emphasis on the women of the royal family at this time.

'Ahmose left behind him a unified state with a much-improved economy. It stretched from south of the second cataract to somewhere in Palestine, and was the chief power in the Near East of the time. His son Amenophis I (1525–1504) may have extended Egyptian influence still further south; nothing is known of Asian affairs during his reign. In the late 18th–20th Dynasties Amenophis and his mother 'Ahmose-Nofretari were revered by the inhabitants of Deir el-Medina, possibly because he had founded the institutional complex to which they belonged, which built the royal tombs. The first burial in the Valley of the Kings and the foundation of the village itself appear, however, to date to the next reign.

Tuthmosis I (1504–1492) was a relative by marriage of his predecessor, who had probably left no male heir. His military exploits were the most extraordinary of any Egyptian king. In the first years of his reign he reached the Euphrates in the north and Kurgus, upstream of the fourth cataract of the Nile, in the south. These feats define the limits of territory ever conquered by Egypt, but may not have been such a leap forward as they seem. In Syria-Palestine there may have been preparatory battles in the previous reigns, and it seems that the Egyptians laid claim to the area when there was no other major power there. During the reign of Amenophis I the kingdom of Mitanni, Egypt's chief rival for a century, was formed in northern Syria, and this was Tuthmosis I's adversary on the Euphrates.

The petty states of Syria and Palestine that formed the Egyptian "empire" were bound to the Egyptian king by oaths of allegiance and paid him tribute, but remained self-governing and pursued their own local political ends. Egyptian presence was maintained by relatively small army detachments and a few high officials. Nubia, however, was treated as a colonial land and administered directly by Egyptians under a viceroy who was responsible to the Egyptian king. Both areas included territories that formed part of the endowment of Egyptian institutions such as temples, but the harsher terms of the Nubian system seem to have contributed to widespread depopulation in the 19th–20th

Right: Egypt in the New Kingdom and Third Intermediate Period
The political divisions shown are those of the Third Intermediate Period, when the area including el-Hiba and stretching south to Aswan was ruled by the high priests in Thebes, who were only nominally subject to the northern kings of Dynasties 21–23. North of el-Hiba the kings of Dynasties 21–22 ruled directly, their territory being later subdivided into virtually autonomous areas (see map p. 47).

Left Two name scarabs and a cowroid of the Second Intermediate period. These are typical of the time, and our main source for its history and administration.
a The Eldest King's Son Ipeq, who is known from more than 40 scarabs; 15th Dynasty.
b The Ruler of Foreign Countries ("Hyksos") Khian, 4th ruler of the 15th Dynasty.
c Cowroid of King Nikare', an obscure ruler, perhaps of the 16th Dynasty. Steatite. Maximum height 17·5 mm. Frazer – von Bissing Collection, University of Basel.

Below Dagger handle of the reign of Nebkhopeshre' Apophis (probably the same as 'Awoserre') of the 15th Dynasty. The man hunting antelopes is the "servant of his lord [Apophis], Nahman" (a Semitic name). From Saqqara. Length of handle 11·4 cm. Cairo, Egyptian Museum.

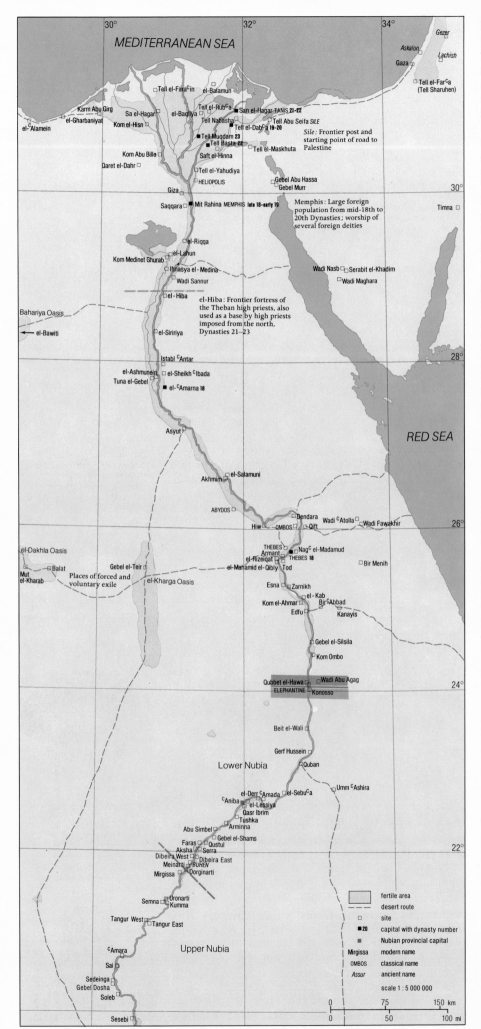

Dynasties. Both in the Near East and in Nubia a prime motive for Egyptian presence was to secure the routes for long-distance trade and access to raw materials; defense was probably a secondary consideration. Trade and Nubian gold produced much of the country's wealth and power in international relations.

Within Egypt the corollary of the continued wars of expansion was an enlarged standing army. In effect there were two new forces in the internal politics of the country, the priesthood and the army. These became ever more important in later Egyptian history, but even in the 18th Dynasty the role of religion may be seen in royal donations to the temples – particularly that of Amun at Karnak – in gratitude for success in war, and in the oracular choice of some kings by gods. On the military side a number of the most important men of the period were former army officers, and the army itself was drafted for constructional work.

Tuthmosis II (1492–1479), whose reign has left little trace, was succeeded by his young son by a minor wife, Tuthmosis III (1479–1425), for whom Hatshepsut, Tuthmosis II's widow, acted initially as regent. During the first 20 years of Tuthmosis III's reign there was little military activity, and Egypt seems to have lost ground considerably in Asia. In Tuthmosis III's seventh year Hatshepsut proclaimed herself female "king" (there was no place in Egyptian ideology for a queen regnant), and ruled as the dominant partner and personality in a co-regency with her nephew until her death around his year 22. Tuthmosis III clearly acquiesced in the situation to some extent, since for much of the time he was old enough to have organized resistance to his aunt if he had wished.

Under Hatshepsut there flourished one of Egypt's few great commoners, Senenmut, who was tutor and steward to her daughter. About 20 statues of Senenmut have been recovered from sites in the Theban area, and he was uniquely privileged in having himself depicted among the reliefs in the temple of Deir el-Bahri. His charge, Nefrure', who is also very prominent in the record, may have been intended to be the future coregent or wife of Tuthmosis III, but died shortly after he assumed sole rule.

There is no record of campaigns to Asia under Hatshepsut. A curious inscription in the temple of Speos Artemidos near Beni Hasan details her hatred for the Hyksos, stating that she restored good order – a strange assertion two generations after their expulsion. It is as if her rejection of the Hyksos, who had not previously come in for such vilification, justified her not following her predecessors' policy in Asia. At her death Tuthmosis III launched a long series of Near Eastern campaigns, in which he began by reconquering territory in Palestine that had recently fallen away from allegiance to Egypt. In the next 20 years the Egyptians fought mainly in Syria, where the Mitanni resisted successfully, and Tuthmosis had to renounce his furthest points of expansion on the Euphrates. This conflict was to last for another generation. Tuthmosis III also campaigned in Nubia late in his reign, and established the provincial capital of Napata near the fourth cataract.

Tuthmosis III built at many sites, and important private tombs date to his reign. All this activity is a

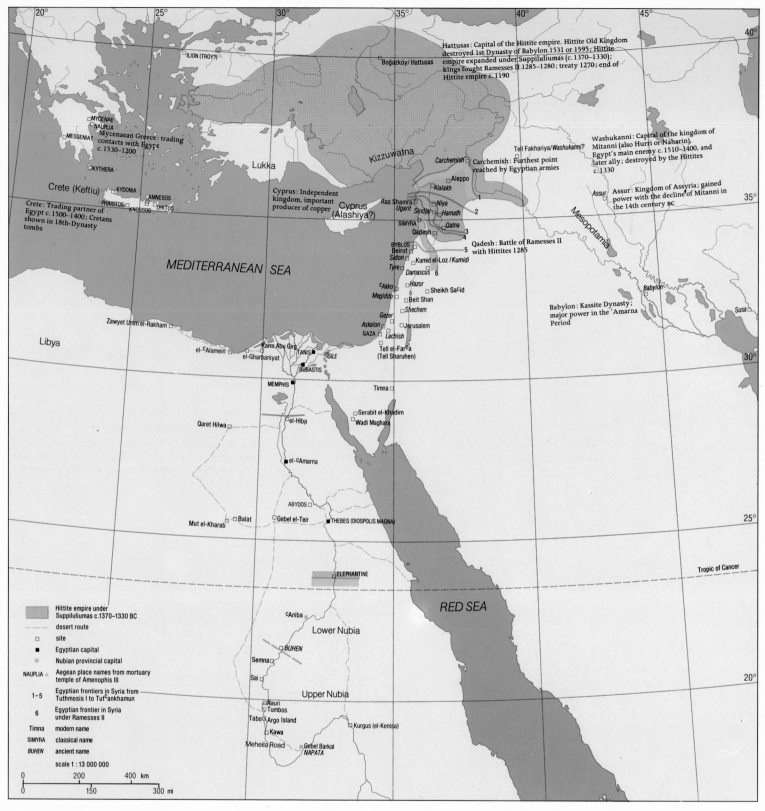

Egypt and the Near East (c.1530–1190 BC)
The successive frontiers of Egyptian possessions in Syria-Palestine, from north to south and in chronological order, are (after Helck):
——— the limit of Egyptian expansion under Tuthmosis I
——— late in the reign of Tuthmosis III
——— year 7 of Amenophis II
——— under Tuthmosis IV
——— under Tut'ankhamun
– – – under Ramesses II
△ places in the Aegean area identified in a list from the mortuary temple of Amenophis III

sign of the economic benefits of expansion. Late in his reign he turned against the memory of Hatshepsut, ordering that her images in relief be erased and replaced with figures of himself and his two predecessors, and that statues of her be smashed. This change of heart may have been due as much to the internal politics of the time when it was done as to actions of Hatshepsut herself.

In his last years Tuthmosis III took his son Amenophis II (1427–1401) as his coregent. Amenophis fought campaigns both before and after his father's death, and, like other kings, was faced with the problem that petty rulers owed allegiance to and had respect for a king rather than for Egypt in general. New kings often needed to assert their authority afresh. His military exploits were parades of strength as far as Syria – he presented himself as a formidable athlete – not campaigns of strategic significance. The parades had a message for foreign powers; at the end of the campaign of year 9 Amenophis received presentations of gifts (the normal mode of diplomatic contact) from the three major powers of the time, the Hittites, Mitanni and Babylon. The Hittites and Babylon were emerging from a period of relative weakness, while Mitanni was at the peak of its power.

Both abroad and at home the reigns of Tuthmosis IV (1401–1391) and Amenophis III (1391–1353) form a single phase. Egypt lost more ground to Mitanni under Tuthmosis IV, but the two powers made a peace before his death and sealed it with the marriage of a Mitanni princess as a minor wife of Tuthmosis IV. The one-way traffic in women shows either that Egypt was acknowledged to be the superior power or simply that, in the words of Amenophis III to the king of Babylon, "since antiquity, a daughter of the king of Egypt has not been given to anybody." In his turn Amenophis III married more than one Mitanni princess.

Peace brought with it a further upsurge in the country's wealth. For the number and size of buildings erected the reign of Amenophis III can be compared only with the much longer one of Ramesses II, while royal and private sculpture was produced on a greater scale than at any other time. Much of this work is of a very high quality. New approaches were exploited in the planning of the whole Theban area (and probably Memphis), with processional ways lined with sphinxes linking the main temples. An enormous artificial lake on the west bank, the Birket Habu, acted as the focus of a new quarter that included a royal palace at el-Malqata and the king's massive mortuary temple. In a significant ideological shift, the king deified himself in his own lifetime. The most important private individual of the reign, Amenhotpe son of Hapu, was a retired military official who directed much of the building work and was honored with a mortuary temple of his own. In later periods he was deified, his reputation in death building on his status in life.

Amenophis IV (1353–1335) became crown prince after the death of a prince Thutmose. He started his reign by giving himself the title of high priest of the sun god, a role which was traditional for Egyptian kings but was not incorporated into their titulary. He then formulated a new dogmatic name for the sun god, "Reʿ-Harakhty who rejoices on the horizon in his name of Shu [or 'light'] which is the sun disk [Aten]." This was soon incorporated into a pair of cartouches, giving the god the character of a king, and a new representation of the god was devised, which shows a disk with rays ending in hands that hold out the hieroglyph for "life" to the king and queen. The development of this cult, which left almost no place for any of the traditional deities except the sun god, became, with self-glorification, the king's main purpose in life. His chief wife, Nefertiti, played an almost equally prominent role in the changes. There was a vast building program at Karnak in the first six years of the reign, in addition to structures in a number of other towns. All were decorated with reliefs in a radically new artistic style and iconography. One of the Karnak shrines contained a series of colossal royal statues, of which perhaps a quarter were of the queen; pictures of temple decoration at el-ʿAmarna from later in the reign show equal numbers of colossi of king and queen.

Probably in his fifth year of reign Amenophis IV changed his name to Akhenaten ("beneficial to the disk") and began a new capital on a virgin site at el-ʿAmarna. The remains of the city were very thoroughly dismantled in the following period, but have nevertheless produced much valuable evidence. Akhenaten's great sun hymn was inscribed in the tomb of his chief official, Aya, and other reliefs and small objects demonstrate the development of his religion. Around year 9 the god's dogmatic name was changed to the more purist "Reʿ, horizon ruler, who rejoices on the horizon in his name of Reʿ the father, who has returned as the sun disk," but after this there was little further development, and the number of monuments from the latest years of the reign is small. Probably at the time of the introduction of the second dogmatic name Akhenaten closed temples for other gods throughout the country, and had the word Amun, and occasionally "gods" in the plural, hacked out wherever they occurred – a vast undertaking, which must have had military support. There was probably little popular enthusiasm for these changes.

Akhenaten had six daughters but no sons by Nefertiti; his second successor Tutʿankhamun was probably the son of a secondary wife, Kiya, whose memory was persecuted late in the reign. At about the same time as this a coregent appeared on the monuments who seems to have been Nefertiti, using her second name Nefernefruaten with additional elements and wearing the attributes of kingship – like Hatshepsut earlier in the dynasty. The titulary of Nefernefruaten changed rapidly; in the final version Smenkhkareʿ displaced the original name – a stage which may correspond to a brief reign by the former Nefertiti after Akhenaten's death. Tutʿankhaten, later Tutʿankhamun, a boy of about seven, then succeeded (1333–1323). Early in his reign the new religion was abandoned, although its complete exclusion and persecution date rather later, and Memphis, which had long been the chief city, became the capital.

While Tutʿankhamun was king, power was in the hands of Aya and the general Haremhab. Tutʿankhamun's inscriptions record the restoration

Above Cuneiform letter from Tushratta of Mitanni to Amenophis III. At the bottom of the tablet is an Egyptian hieratic filing note of year 36 of Amenophis, in ink. The letter accompanied a statue of Ishtar of Nineveh that was sent to Egypt as a healing deity. The statue had been in Egypt once before in the time of Tushratta's predecessor Suttarna II. From el-ʿAmarna. London, British Museum.

Above Cartouches of the sun god of Amenophis IV/Akhenaten. The left pair is the early form and the right the late form; translations in the text.

Right Squatting statue of Amenhotpe, son of Hapu, shown as a corpulent, elderly man (he lived more than 80 years); found by the 7th pylon at Karnak. The statue was later venerated, and its nose was recut in antiquity. Height 1·42 m. Reign of Amenophis III. Cairo, Egyptian Museum.

of the temples, but no details of foreign policy; Egyptian possessions in the Near East were in disarray after the campaigns of the Hittite king Suppiluliumas. Aya (1323–1319) occupied the throne briefly, and was succeeded by Haremhab (1319–1307), who is normally placed in the 18th Dynasty, but was considered by Egyptians of the next century to be the first king of their era, which we call the 19th Dynasty.

Haremhab dismantled the temples of Amenophis IV at Karnak and built there extensively himself. He also annexed most of Tut'ankhamun's inscriptions, perhaps from a feeling that they recorded his own exploits. His second successor, Sethos I (1305–1290), carried his restoration work to fruition, repairing countless monuments, persecuting the memory of Akhenaten, and removing his name and those of his three successors from the official record. He also built extensively himself. In the Near East he fought several campaigns, succeeding, during a period of Hittite weakness, in regaining temporarily some Egyptian possessions in Syria. The main records of the campaigns are impressive battle reliefs of a new, more realistic type.

Late in his reign Sethos I associated his son Ramesses II (1290–1224) with him on the throne. The new king inherited his father's problems in Syria. After a success in year 4 he confronted the Hittite army for the first time in year 5 in an indecisive battle at Qadesh, which Ramesses presented as a great victory and recorded in many temple reliefs. After further engagements in the next few years there was a truce, followed by a formal treaty in year 21. The text of this is preserved in Egyptian in temple reliefs of Ramesses II, and in Akkadian on cuneiform tablets from the Hittite capital Boğazköy (ancient Hattusas). Peace continued for more than 50 years, confirmed by marriages between Ramesses II and Hittite princesses.

Ramesses II built more buildings and had more colossal statues than any other Egyptian king, also having his name carved or reliefs cut on many older monuments. Like Amenophis III, he was deified in his own lifetime, and by his projection of his personality he made the name Ramesses synonymous with kingship for centuries. But the official building program was not accompanied by as many works for private individuals as that of Amenophis III. Many projects date to early in his reign, while the later buildings show a fall-off in craftsmanship. It seems that there was considerable economic decline in his later years.

One of the most important undertakings of Ramesses II was the removal of the capital to a new site in the delta called Pi-Ri'amsese ("Domain of Ramesses"), probably at modern el-Khata'na and Qantir. The royal family came from this area, but the main reason for the move was probably that the international and economic center of the country had shifted into the delta proper. This change is one reason why we know less of the history of the Late Period than we do of the New Kingdom.

Ramesses II survived many of his enormous family, and was succeeded by his 13th son Merneptah (1224–1214). Early in his reign Merneptah was confronted with Libyan aggression, which had already been resisted by Sethos I and had led to Ramesses II's construction of forts westwards along the Mediterranean coast. A battle was fought in the western delta against invading Libyans and "sea peoples" – a group of tribes with names that suggest Mediterranean origin. The invaders had intended to settle, and brought their wives and children with them. The battle went against them, however, and some fled, while others were forcibly settled as prisoners of war.

After the death of Merneptah there was a period of dynastic struggles which ended in the brief sole rule of a queen, Twosre (1198–1196), the widow of the short-lived Sethos II (1214–1204). During this time the true power in the land seems to have been a high official, Bay, perhaps of Syrian origin, who may be mentioned under an alias in a later document that presents such a person as the evil genius of the period.

The first king of the 20th Dynasty, Sethnakhte (1196–1194), refers in an inscription to a period of civil war which lasted into the second and last year of his own reign, and ended with his defeat of the rebels. He implies that disorder was widespread in the country before his arrival, but there were officials who lived from the reign of Merneptah into that of Ramesses III, so the violence was probably limited to court and military circles. Ramesses III (1194–1163) inherited a stable internal situation, and exploited it in a number of building works, but was severely pressed from the north by two attempted Libyan invasions and by a renewed attack of the "sea peoples" that came in the gap between them. All of these were defeated, and Egypt also retained control of Sinai and southern Palestine.

Ramesses III's titulary was almost identical to that of Ramesses II, and his mortuary complex at Medinet Habu was modeled closely on Ramesses II's Ramesseum. He and the other 20th-Dynasty kings were unusually conservative in their presentation of themselves, as if they did not have the confidence to be self-sufficient. But whereas the achievements of Ramesses III were considerable, this is not true of his successors. In 90 years there were eight more kings called Ramesses, a name they adopted in addition to their birth names on becoming king. All were apparently descended from Ramesses III, but the throne was the center of much rivalry, beginning with the death of Ramesses III himself, before which there was a conspiracy among his wives to place one of his sons on the throne. Abroad Egypt lost control of Palestine during the dynasty, while Nubia fell away at its end. Its only major monuments after the reign of Ramesses III are the royal tombs and the temple of Khons at Karnak, which was not completed until the Ptolemaic Period.

It is possible to reconstruct much of the administration of the country in the 19th and especially the 20th Dynasty from papyrus documents and ostraca. The most important long-term change was that a high proportion of land passed to temples, in particular that of Amun at Karnak. State and temple were interlocked in the management of the country, but the temple of Amun eventually acquired virtual control of Upper Egypt. The major priestly offices became hereditary, and thus largely independent of the king, so that the high priests formed a dynasty that came to rival him. Another significant practice was the settling of prisoners of

Egypt in the late Third Intermediate Period

This map shows the political divisions of Egypt about the time of the campaign of Piye (c.730).

■ cities ruled by a king, with dynasty number if appropriate

◈ cities listed with their rulers in the victory stela of Piye; several further cities cannot be located. Compare Assurbanipal's list marked on map p. 49.

The frontiers of the areas ruled by Hermopolis and Herakleopolis are very hypothetical.

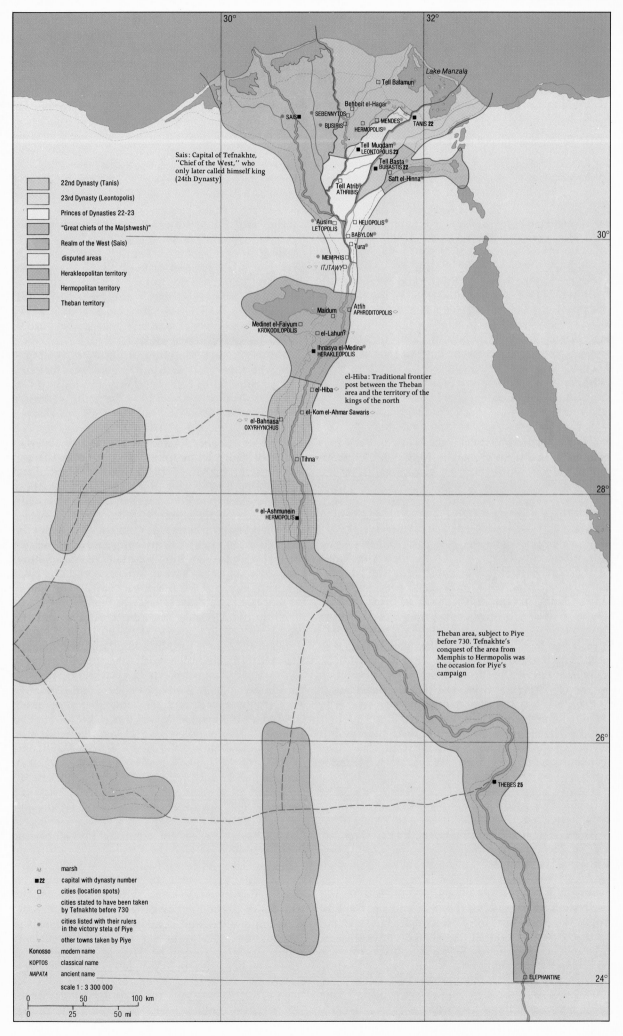

Legend:

- 22nd Dynasty (Tanis)
- 23rd Dynasty (Leontopolis)
- Princes of Dynasties 22-23
- "Great chiefs of the Ma(shwesh)"
- Realm of the West (Sais)
- disputed areas
- Herakleopolitan territory
- Hermopolitan territory
- Theban territory

Sais: Capital of Tefnakhte, "Chief of the West," who only later called himself king (24th Dynasty)

el-Hiba: Traditional frontier post between the Theban area and the territory of the kings of the north

Theban area, subject to Piye before 730. Tefnakhte's conquest of the area from Memphis to Hermopolis was the occasion for Piye's campaign

Map labels:

Tell Balamun
Lake Manzala
Behbeit el-Hagar
SAIS
SEBENNYTOS
MENDES
TANIS 22
BUSIRIS
HERMOPOLIS
Tell Muqdam
LEONTOPOLIS 23
Tell Basta
BUBASTIS 22
Tell Atrib
ATHRIBIS
Saft el-Hinna
Ausim
LETOPOLIS
HELIOPOLIS
BABYLON
Tura
MEMPHIS
ITJTAWY
Maidum
Atfih
APHRODITOPOLIS
Medinet el-Faiyum
KROKODILOPOLIS
el-Lahun?
Ihnasya el-Medina
HERAKLEOPOLIS
el-Hiba
el-Kom el-Ahmar Sawaris
el-Bahnasa
OXYRHYNCHUS
Tihna
el-Ashmunein
HERMOPOLIS
THEBES 25
ELEPHANTINE

Symbols legend:

- marsh
- ■22 capital with dynasty number
- □ cities (location spots)
- ◇ cities stated to have been taken by Tefnakhte before 730
- ◈ cities listed with their rulers in the victory stela of Piye
- ▽ other towns taken by Piye

Konosso — modern name
KOPTOS — classical name
NAPATA — ancient name

scale 1 : 3 300 000

0   50   100 km
0   25   50 mi

war in military colonies. The Libyans were the most important of these groups. Although they were soon completely Egyptian, they kept a separate identity, marked by the tribal name Meshwesh (often abbreviated to Ma), and in time became the main political force in the country.

While these elements were splitting Egypt into a loose-knit, almost feudal society, the movements of peoples in the Near East at the beginning of the dynasty introduced the Iron Age there, but not in Egypt. The entire eastern Mediterranean entered a twilight period, from which Egypt suffered less than other countries, but the Near East emerged technologically more advanced, and Egypt lost its preeminent position for good.

In the reign of Ramesses XI (1100–1070) the viceroy of Nubia, Panehsy, fought a battle for the Theban area which he ultimately lost, retiring to 'Aniba in Lower Nubia, where he was buried. After his intervention the previous line of high priests disappeared from office, and a military man called Herihor replaced them in Ramesses' year 19. Priest and officer made a powerful combination, and Herihor enhanced his status beyond that of any of his predecessors, having himself portrayed as king and using an alternative dating system, which probably alludes to the presence of two "kings" in the country. After only five years he died. His successor Pi'ankh also predeceased Ramesses XI, but by then the virtual partition of the country was established, although later high priests only occasionally claimed the titles of king. The pattern had been set for the next period.

Third Intermediate Period

Ramesses XI was succeeded by Smendes (1070–1044), the first king of the 21st Dynasty, and Pi'ankh by Pinudjem I. The kings ruled from Tanis in the northeastern delta, controlling the country north of el-Hiba. They may have been collateral descendants of the 20th-Dynasty royal family. Their capital city had not previously been an important center, and its monuments were mostly transferred from other sites in the delta. It was close to the Ramessid capital, and the move to it may have been dictated by the silting-up of waterways.

The Nile valley from el-Hiba to Aswan was controlled by the Theban high priests, who acknowledged the Tanite kings, dated by their regnal years, and married into their family, but were effectively rulers of a separate state. The Thebans harked back to their military origins, and it is clear from the names of many of them that the "Libyan" element among them was strong. The Libyans were also active in the north of the country – their chief area of settlement – and Osorkon I (984–978), the obscure fifth king of the Tanite Dynasty, was a member of their group. The last king, Psusennes II (959–945), was probably also high priest of Amun, uniting the two realms in his person, but not turning them into a single unit.

Shoshenq I (945–924), the first king of the 22nd Dynasty, belonged to a "Libyan" family from Bubastis (Tell Basta) that had been prominent for at least a generation before he gained power. He took advantage of the simultaneous extinction of the line of high priests to install his son in Thebes, thus attempting to centralize Egypt once again. This precedent was followed by some of his successors.

But, although there was never a fully independent ruler of Thebes, the area was not integrated into the country for another 300 years.

Shoshenq I fought a campaign in Palestine, which is recorded in reliefs at Karnak, where he began extensive building works. In Asia he may have followed an initiative of Siamun (978–959), but his undertaking was more ambitious. He also revived relations with Byblos, Egypt's traditional trading partner on the Phoenician coast, which were maintained for several generations. The basis for Shoshenq I's activities was an increase in prosperity which can be seen in renewed building activity early in the dynasty.

After nearly a century of peace the 22nd Dynasty from the reign of Takelot II (860–835) was a period of conflict and decline. The first major cause of unrest was the appointment of Takelot's son and heir, Osorkon, as high priest of Amun, an office which he combined with military functions. Osorkon was rejected by the Thebans, and a long civil war followed, which he recorded in an enormous inscription at Karnak.

Beginning with the reign of Shoshenq III (835–783), who apparently usurped the throne which had been destined for his brother, the high priest Osorkon, the kingship became split between different claimants. The first rival was Pedubaste I (828–803) of the 23rd Dynasty, who was recognized alongside Shoshenq III. From this time on the way was open for any minor potentate to call himself king, and to be accepted wherever this suited the local population. By the end of the 8th century there were therefore numerous kings in the country, with the 22nd–25th Dynasties all ruling simultaneously, quite apart from other kings who are ignored by the official list. In about 770 an important force joined the melee. A Nubian king Kashta (770–750), whose capital was at Gebel Barkal, was accepted as a ruler in Upper Egypt as far north as Thebes, and marks the arrival of the 25th Dynasty in Egypt.

While the kingship weakened, so also did the high priesthood of Amun. Osorkon IV of the 23rd Dynasty (777–749) installed his daughter Shepen-wepet in an old office with the title of "divine adoratrice of Amun" in Thebes. From this time on the adoratrice, who could not marry, and passed on her office by "adoption," was a member of the royal family and the chief religious figure in the Theban area. For later periods we know that the real power lay with nominally subordinate male officials, but in the case of Shepenwepet this is not clear. The 23rd-Dynasty control of the office was short-lived. Shepenwepet soon adopted Amenirdis I, a sister of Kashta, who had presumably been forced on her by the more powerful Nubians. The instigator of this was Kashta's brother and successor Piye (formerly read Pi'ankhi, 750–712).

In the later 8th century the most important factions in Egypt were the ancestors of the 24th Dynasty, who were local rulers in Sais in the western delta, and the 25th Dynasty. Around 730 they came into conflict, perhaps because of the expansion of Saite influence into the Nile valley, which was the traditional Theban preserve, and therefore part of the area to which the 25th Dynasty were the chief claimants. Piye set out from Napata on a campaign through Egypt as far as Memphis to claim submission from local rulers,

Egypt in the Late Period, with the state of Napata-Meroë (712 BC-4th century AD)
Egyptian sites are marked in black.
○ cities whose "kings" are listed in Assurbanipal's annals (several further Assyrian names cannot be identified in Egypt). Compare those of the campaign of Piye on map p. 47.
● sites where texts in Aramaic, the official language of the Persian empire, have been found; these include papyri, ostraca and rock graffiti. The route of the Nubian campaign sent by Psammetichus II in 591 BC is conjectural; its soldiers left Greek and Carian graffiti at Buhen and Abu Simbel, and probably at Gebel el-Silsila.

The canal from the Nile to the Red Sea appears on this map. This was begun by Necho II, completed by Darius I, who set up stelae c.490 at locations marked ▲, and later restored by Ptolemy II Philadelphus, Trajan and Hadrian, and Amr ibn el-'Asi, the Muslim conqueror of Egypt. Its length from Tell el-Maskhuta to Suez was about 85 km.
Sites of the Napata-Meroë state are marked in brown.

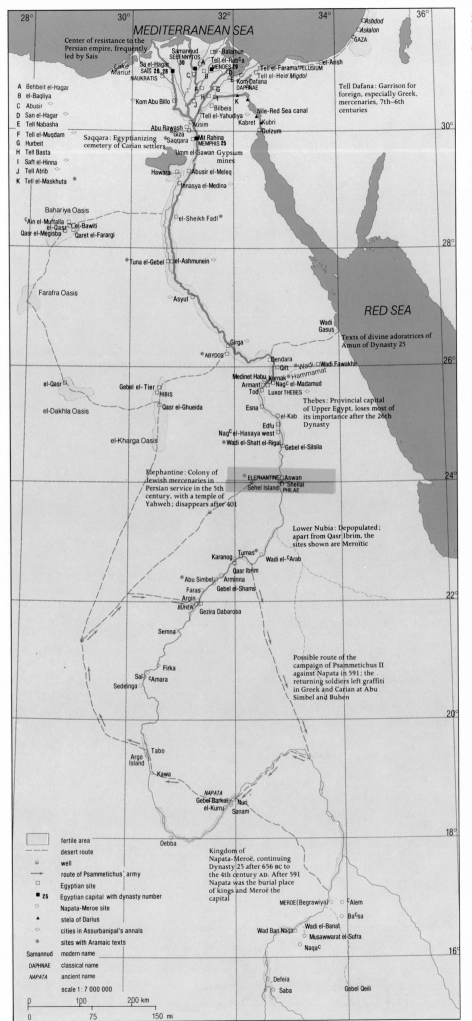

A Behbeit el-Hagar
B el-Baqliya
C Abusir
D San el-Hagar
E Tell Nabasha
F Tell el-Muqdam
G Hurbeit
H Tell Basta
I Saft el-Hinna
J Tell Atrib
K Tell el-Maskhuta

Saqqara: Egyptianizing cemetery of Carian settlers

Tell Dafana: Garrison for foreign, especially Greek, mercenaries, 7th–6th centuries

Texts of divine adoratrices of Amun of Dynasty 25

Thebes: Provincial capital of Upper Egypt, loses most of its importance after the 26th Dynasty

Elephantine: Colony of Jewish mercenaries in Persian service in the 5th century, with a temple of Yahweh; disappears after 401

Lower Nubia: Depopulated; apart from Qasr Ibrim, the sites shown are Meroïtic

Possible route of the campaign of Psammetichus II against Napata in 591; the returning soldiers left graffiti in Greek and Carian at Abu Simbel and Buhen

Center of resistance to the Persian empire, frequently led by Sais

Kingdom of Napata-Meroë, continuing Dynasty 25 after 656 bc to the 4th century AD. After 591 Napata was the burial place of kings and Meroë the capital

Legend:
- fertile area
- desert route
- well
- route of Psammetichus' army
- □ Egyptian site
- ■ 25 Egyptian capital with dynasty number
- ○ Napata-Meroe site
- ▲ stela of Darius
- • cities in Assurbanipal's annals
- * sites with Aramaic texts
- Samanud modern name
- DAPHNAE classical name
- NAPATA ancient name
- scale 1 : 7 000 000

0 100 200 km
0 75 150 mi

in particular Tefnakhte of Sais. The episode was recorded on an enormous stela set up in the temple of Amun at Napata, which is of outstanding interest both for its text and for its relief showing four kings, whose names are written in cartouches, doing obeisance to Piye. Tefnakhte (who did not call himself king) was in theory forced to submit, but he did not come to Piye in person. The affair had little immediate impact, since Piye was content to establish his claim, and returned to Napata without making himself the sole king of Egypt. In his inscription he is presented as being more Egyptian than the Egyptians, while the campaign is almost a holy mission to right the evils of the land. Napata was an old center of the worship of Amun, so that this may be true, but Piye could have been providing a religious justification for a political act.

Late Period

Shabaka (712–698) marks the beginning of the Late Period in Egypt. In his first year of reign the conflict between Napata and Sais was renewed, and the 24th-Dynasty King Bocchoris (717–712) was killed in battle between the two powers. Shabaka's action finally disposed of all the other kings in the country. From his reign on the Nubians took a far greater interest in Egypt as a whole, making Memphis their capital, and residing in Egypt for some of the time. The elimination of other kings did not, however, alter the political structure much, since local rulers remained largely independent, and were indeed called "kings" in the Assyrian records of the invasion of Egypt 40 years later. Nonetheless, the economic gains from the change were considerable. The half-century of Nubian rule produced as many monuments in Upper Egypt as the previous two and saw a notable artistic revival, which looked to earlier periods for its inspiration.

Under Shebitku (698–690) and Taharqa (690–664) economic improvement continued. Taharqa left monuments over much of Egypt and Nubia, where his name has been found at the later capital of Meroë. Several inscriptions recount the beneficial effects of a high inundation in his year 6, which is also documented by records of water levels on the quay at Karnak. There may have been a general increase in inundation levels at the time, which would have contributed to prosperity.

In Thebes Shebitku's sister Shepenwepet II was adopted by Amenirdis I, and members of the Nubian royal family held high offices in the cult. Under Taharqa Shepenwepet II adopted Amenirdis II. The real power in the area lay, however, with one or two local families. The most important person in Thebes was Montemhet, the fourth priest of Amun and "prince of the city," who was the effective ruler of much of Upper Egypt, and survived well into the 26th Dynasty. His tomb, statues and inscriptions are the first great private monuments of the Late Period, on a grander scale than New Kingdom tombs and displaying much learning and technical accomplishment.

The unified Egyptian and Nubian state was a major power, whose only rival in the Near East was Assyria, which had been expanding since the 9th century. The furthest southwestern extension of the Assyrian empire was Palestine, whose small states were constantly attempting to throw off Assyrian rule, and looked to Egypt for assistance.

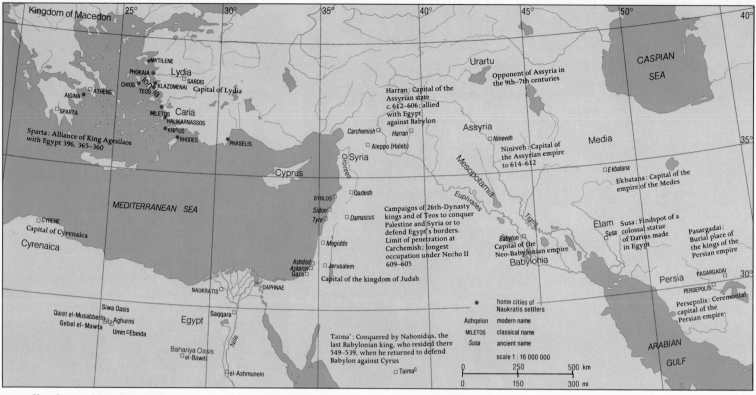

Initially the Nubian kings did not respond to these approaches, but in 701 an Egyptian force fought the Assyrian King Sennacherib (704–681) in Palestine on the side of the kings of Judah. The engagement was inconclusive, and for 30 years the two main powers kept a buffer of small states between each other.

The Assyrian King Esarhaddon (681–669) attempted to conquer Egypt in 674, but was defeated at the frontier post of Sile. A renewed attack in 671 was successful; Memphis was taken and the whole country forced to pay tribute. Taharqa fled south, but returned within two years to retake Memphis. Esarhaddon died on the way to Egypt for a counterattack, and the next campaign was sent by his son Assurbanipal (669–627) in about 667. Assurbanipal used the ruler of Sais, Necho I (672–664), who now styled himself king, and his son Psamtik (later Psammetichus I) as his chief allies in reestablishing Assyrian rule. In 664 Tantamani (664–657 in Egypt, possibly later in Nubia) succeeded Taharqa and immediately mounted a campaign through Egypt as far as the delta (in his account of this he does not even mention the Assyrians). The main opponent of the Nubians was Necho I, who appears to have died in the fighting. The remaining local rulers accepted Tantamani fairly readily.

Sometime between 663 and 657 Assurbanipal led a campaign of reprisal in person, and plundered the whole country, while Tantamani fled to Nubia. This was the last phase of the Assyrian occupation; Assurbanipal had to combat a rebellion in Babylon, and Psammetichus I (664–610) was able to make himself independent from him before 653. These events mark the end of Egypt's isolation in the world; it was involved with all the empires of antiquity.

Between 664 and 657 Psammetichus I eliminated all the local rulers in Lower Egypt, and in 656 he had his daughter Nitocris adopted by Shepenwepet II as the next divine adoratrice in Thebes, bypassing

Amenirdis II. Until the previous year dating in Thebes had been by Tantamani's years of reign.

Psammetichus I's campaigns of unification were of significance in another way. He was the first king to employ Greek and Carian mercenaries, setting the pattern for 300 years. By the 4th century all the major powers used Greek troops, who were a prerequisite for engaging in international conflict, and often determined its course. Some of them settled in Egypt, building up a nucleus of foreigners in the country who played a disproportionate part in history because of their specialization in trade and warfare. The Greeks also influence our view of the history of this time, because native Egyptian sources are sparser than Classical ones.

In the Late Period the Egyptian economy was less self-sufficient than before, since the most important metal, iron, was imported, apparently from the Near East rather than Nubia. Egypt had exports to offer in return – notably grain and papyrus – but, unlike Greece and Anatolia, did not have coinage, and was forced back on more cumbersome systems of exchange.

The reunification of Egypt and the imposition of a central administration in place of local rulers brought a continuation of the 25th-Dynasty increase in prosperity, culminating in the later 26th Dynasty, but relatively little of this wealth can now be seen, because it was concentrated in the delta. The chief exception is the small group of grandiose private tombs of the later 7th century in Thebes. The artistic revival also continued, and there is an archaizing flavor in the use of some titles and religious texts, but in most respects this is a superficial phenomenon. The kings of the period may have wished to bypass the importance of temples in the country's politics and reach back towards earlier, more secular periods, but in this they failed.

There were two main features of 26th-Dynasty policy in the Near East: maintenance of a balance of power by supporting the rivals of whichever power

Right Figures of an Egyptian and a Persian, from the base of a statue of Darius I found at Susa. The base has 24 figures representing provinces of the Persian empire. They kneel with their hands raised in adoration of the king; their names are written in ovals beneath. The statue was made in Egypt, but the figures were carved according to a foreign model. The statue as a whole seems to be an attempt at an international style for the whole empire. Tehran, Museum Iran Bastan.

Left: Egypt, the Aegean and the Near East in the Late Period

Assyrian empire Expanded from the 9th century; occupied Syria and Palestine in the 8th; held Egypt 671–c.657. Destroyed by the Medes and Babylonians 614–612.

Kingdom of Judah Principal local enemy of Assyria and Babylon in Palestine until the captivity of 586; looked to Egypt for help, usually without success.

Lydia Allied with Psammetichus I against the Assyrians; defeated by the Kimmerians c.653.

Caria and Ionia Homelands of many of the foreign soldiers employed in Egypt from the reign of Psammetichus I on.

Neo-Babylonian empire (612–539) Defeated the Assyrian successor state before 605 and attacked Egypt 591 and 567; destroyed by Cyrus of Persia 539.

Persian empire Expanded in succession to the Medes from 549; at its maximum extent included Sind, Anatolia, Cyrenaica and Egypt. Destroyed 336–323 by Alexander the Great, who inherited the same area and held in addition Macedonia and Greece.

Athens Frequent ally of Egypt against the Persians; expedition of 200 ships to help Egyptian rebels in the western delta sent in 460, finally annihilated in 454. In 385–c.375 and 360 the Athenian general Chabrias commanded Egyptian resistance to Persia. Egypt paid in grain for Athenian help.

Cyrenaica Settled by Greek colonists who founded a local dynasty c.630; internal wars in 570 led to Amasis' seizure of the Egyptian throne. Subsequently allied with Amasis; incorporated in the Persian empire c.515.

Cyprus Held by Amasis c.567–526. King Euagoras allied with Egypt against Persia 389–380.

Naukratis Greek trading settlement founded late 7th century and made into the exclusive Greek community in Egypt by Amasis. The original Greek settlers came from the cities marked

was dominant, and attempts to repeat New Kingdom conquests in Palestine and Syria. Thus Psammetichus I supported Lydia and later Babylon against Assyria until the Assyrian decline after 620, when he changed his allegiance to Assyria; in the 6th century Egypt continued to support the enemies of Babylon until Persia had become the main power. Necho II (610–595), Psammetichus II (595–589) and Apries (589–570) built on the work of Psammetichus I and moved into attack. Necho II, possibly following an initiative of Psammetichus, campaigned in Syria from 610 to 605, but was forced to withdraw. In 601 he repulsed an attack by the Babylonian King Nebuchadnezzar II (604–562) on Egypt. He also fitted out Egyptian fleets with triremes in both the Mediterranean and the Red Sea, attempting at the same time to link the Nile and the Red Sea with a canal. In the 5th century this sea route was to become of international importance. There is evidence for a later persecution of Necho's memory, which may account for the small number of monuments with his name.

Psammetichus II made a single campaign to Asia, with no apparent long-term effects. His most significant political act, however, was a major campaign to Nubia in 591, which brought an end to 60 years' peaceful relations. The invading army, which included Egyptians, Greeks and Carians, apparently reached Napata, but no conquest seems to have been intended. On the return journey the foreign soldiers left graffiti at Buhen and Abu Simbel in Lower Nubia, from which the course of the campaign has been reconstructed. After 591 the memory of the 25th-Dynasty kings was persecuted in Egypt.

In 595 the divine adoratrice of Amun, Nitocris, who must have been in her seventies, adopted Psammetichus II's daughter 'Ankhnesneferibre' as her successor. 'Ankhnesneferibre' took office in 586, and was still alive in 525. Thus only two women acted as the representatives of the royal family in Thebes for 130 years.

Like his predecessors, Apries supported the Palestinian states against Babylon. The Babylonian captivity of the Jews occurred during his reign, and many Jews fled to Egypt. From the next century we have records of a Jewish colony in Elephantine. Some of those in the rest of the country may have

been ancestors of the Jewish population of Alexandria.

In 570 Apries supported a local Libyan ruler in Cyrene against Greek colonists. An all-Egyptian army was sent, which was defeated and then mutinied. Apries sent a general, Amasis, to quell the revolt, but Amasis joined it, declared himself king (570–526), and drove Apries into exile. In 567 Apries returned with a Babylonian invading force sent by Nebuchadnezzar II, but was defeated and killed. Amasis then buried him with royal honors and recorded the whole episode on a stela, in terms that disguise his seizure of power.

From the point of view of the Greeks, who are our sources, Amasis' most notable policy was his treatment of the Greeks, whose trading activities were confined to the delta town of Naukratis, while foreign soldiers were kept in garrisons in Memphis only. The Greeks felt that the special status of Naukratis was a favor to them, yet the policy reduced the possibilities of friction between Egyptians and Greeks by restricting contact of any sort. Amasis was also remembered as a drinker and a philanderer; both Herodotus and later Egyptian sources tell stories to illustrate these characteristics.

The end of Amasis' reign was overshadowed by the growing power of Persia, but it was his short-lived successor Psammetichus III (526–525) who had to face the Persian invasion, which was immediately successful. Cambyses (525–522), the first ruler of the 27th Dynasty, was also the first outsider, whose main interest was not Egypt, to become king of Egypt. He undertook campaigns through Egypt to Nubia and to the western oasis of Siwa, but both failed. His rule was later resented bitterly, partly because of an attempt to reduce the incomes of the politically influential temples. Darius I (521–486) followed a more conciliatory line, commissioning temple buildings, including the temple of Hibis in el-Kharga oasis, the only substantially complete temple that remains from the period 1100–300. The importance of the oases at this time may be connected with the momentous Persian introduction of the camel. In a similar vein Darius completed Necho II's Nile–Red Sea canal, adorning it with monumental stelae in a mixture of Egyptian and Near Eastern style. Until it silted up, the canal provided a direct sea link between Persia and Egypt. The mixed style, which was first used in statues of Darius, proclaimed the cosmopolitan character of Darius' empire.

The reign of Darius was prosperous, but Persian rule was tolerated in Egypt only so long as there was no real chance of escaping from it. The Persian defeat at the battle of Marathon in 490 signaled the beginning of 80 years of Egyptian resistance, in which Egyptian rebels traded grain with Greek states in return for military aid. The western delta was the center of resistance; Persian rule was more easily maintained in the Nile valley, which could be reached by the Red Sea route. Foreign troops were also used by the Persians, in whose employ was the Jewish frontier garrison at Elephantine. A number of papyri in Aramaic, the administrative language of the Persian empire, have been found there and at other sites. There are scarcely any Egyptian documents or monuments from the period 480–400. This reflects insecurity, hatred of the Persians, and the impoverishment of the country.

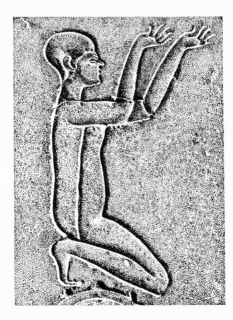

In 404 Amyrtaios of Sais freed the delta from Persian rule, and by 400 the entire country was in his hands. Like some earlier rebels against the Persians he styled himself king, but unlike them he became part of the official listing as the sole ruler of the 28th Dynasty. In 399 Nepherites I of Mendes (399–393) usurped the throne, founding the 29th Dynasty. He and Psammuthis (393) and Hakoris (393–380) built at numerous sites and warded off a Persian attack in 385–383. In these battles the Egyptians relied on Greek mercenaries. The 4th-century generations of them had no intention of settling in Egypt, and their loyalty was variable – as proved fatal more than once.

Nectanebo I (380–362), a general from Sebennytos in the delta, usurped the throne from Nepherites II (380) and founded the 30th Dynasty. In his inscriptions he was quite frank about his non-royal origins. He began a period of great prosperity, in which there was building all over the country, and artistic traditions of the 26th Dynasty were taken up again and developed. In 373 a Persian invasion was defeated, and in the 360s Nectanebo I joined a defensive alliance of Persian provinces. His successor Teos (365–360 with a coregency) moved into the offensive in Palestine, but was betrayed by a rebellion in Egypt, in which a cousin, Nectanebo II (360–343), was placed on the throne, and by the defection of his Spartan ally to the new king.

Nectanebo II withstood an invasion attempt by the Persian Artaxerxes III Ochus in 350, but the attack of 343 was successful. The ten-year Second Persian Period (also called the 31st Dynasty) was itself interrupted for about two years by a native king Khababash, whose memory lived on for many years; he appears to have controlled all of Lower Egypt. Renewed Persian rule was oppressive and predisposed the country towards almost any alternative.

Greco-Roman Period

In 332 Alexander the Great took possession of Egypt without a struggle. During his brief stay the plan was made to build Alexandria, and he sacrificed to the Egyptian gods, and consulted the oracle of Ammon (probably not the Egyptian Amun) in the oasis of Siwa. At his death Ptolemy, son of Lagus, succeeded in acquiring Egypt as his satrapy, and buried his king in Memphis (the body was later moved to Alexandria). In late 305 or early 304 he followed the lead of other satraps and made himself the independent king of Egypt.

For the next 250 years Egypt was ruled by Greeks, but as a separate country with its own interests to pursue, even if they were not always those of the native population. Ptolemaic rule was oppressive in some ways – possibly no more than its native forerunners – and provoked nationalistic uprisings, but, unlike its predecessor and successor, it was centered on Egypt. An indication of this is that the Ptolemies sought to enlarge Egyptian possessions in a traditional way, by annexing Palestine and later moving a short distance into Lower Nubia, where there was some sort of condominium with the Meroïtic state. In addition, Cyrene, Cyprus (already held briefly by Amasis), parts of Anatolia and some Aegean islands came under Ptolemaic control for a time.

The reigns of the first three Ptolemies were a period of development for Egypt, in which the country was brought into the Hellenistic world in terms of agriculture, commerce and, for the Greek population, education. The most important agricultural innovation was the widespread introduction of two crops per year. Many economic changes were managed by state monopolies; it is uncertain whether the Ptolemies followed earlier Egyptian kings in this. There was also a policy of settling foreign soldiers on crown land, which they

Greco-Egyptian terracotta statuettes. *Left*: the Egyptian god Bes holding a knife and a Roman shield. *Above*: a high relief of Herakles-Harpokrates (Horus the Child) holding a cornucopia and seated on a phoenix. The whole genre of terracotta is Greek rather than Egyptian; but while the former is close to Egyptian style, the latter is almost wholly Classical. Roman Period. Cairo, Egyptian Musuem.

Left Over-life-size diorite head of an Egyptian of the 1st century BC, from Mit Rahina (Memphis). This commanding piece continues the traditions of Late Period portraiture; only the rendering of the hair shows Greek influence. Brooklyn Museum.

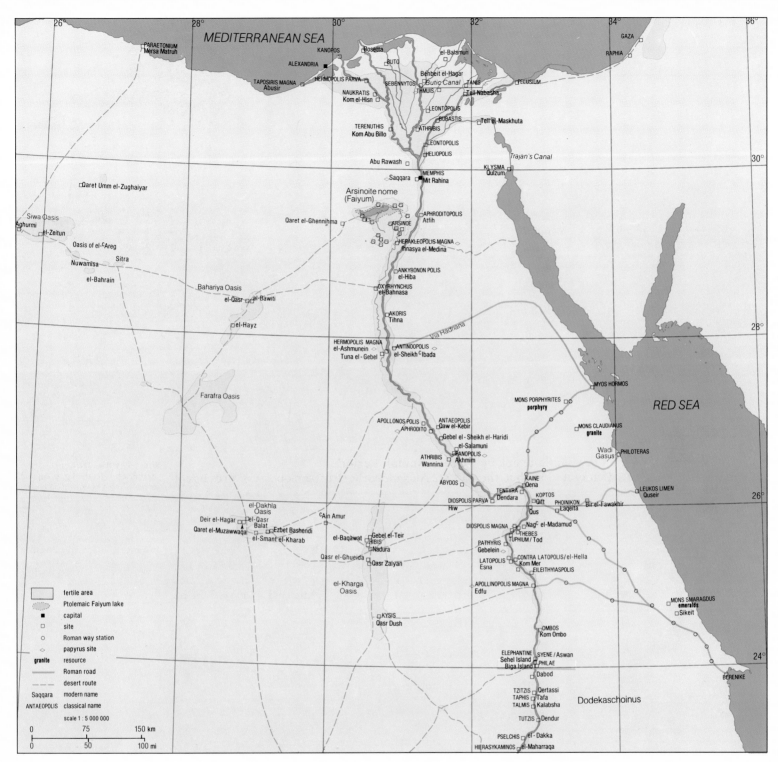

Above: Egypt in the Greco-Roman Period

The map shows numerous sites across Egypt including: PARAETONIUM Mersa Matruh, Siwa Oasis, Aghurmi, el-Zeitun, Oasis of el-ᶜAreg, Sitra, Nuwamisa, el-Bahrain, Bahariya Oasis, el-Qasr, el-Bawiti, el-Hayz, Farafra Oasis, el-Dakhla Oasis, Deir el-Hagar, Qaret el-Muzawwaqa, el-Qasr, Balat, Ezbet Bashendi, el-Smant el-Kharab, Qaret Umm el-Zughaiyar, Qaret el-Ghennihma.

MEDITERRANEAN SEA, KANOPOS, Rosetta, BUTO, el-Balamun, GAZA, RAPHIA, ALEXANDRIA, HERMOPOLIS PARVA, TAPOSIRIS MAGNA Abusir, SEBENNYTOS, Butic Canal, Behbeit el-Hagar, TANIS, PELUSIUM, NAUKRATIS Kom el-Hisn, THMUIS, Tell Nabasha, LEONTOPOLIS, BUBASTIS, Tell el-Maskhuta, TERENUTHIS Kom Abu Billo, ATHRIBIS, LEONTOPOLIS, HELIOPOLIS, Abu Rawash, MEMPHIS Mit Rahina, Saqqara, KLYSMA Quizum, Trajan's Canal, Arsinoite nome (Faiyum), ARSINOE, APHRODITOPOLIS Atfih, HERAKLEOPOLIS MAGNA Ihnasya el-Medina, ANKYRONON POLIS el-Hiba, OXYRHYNCHUS el-Bahnasa, AKORIS Tihna, HERMOPOLIS MAGNA el-Ashmunein, Tuna el-Gebel, ANTINOOPOLIS el-Sheikh ᶜIbada, Via Hadriana, MYOS HORMOS, RED SEA, MONS PORPHYRITES porphyry, APOLLONOS POLIS, ANTAEOPOLIS Qaw el-Kebir, APHRODITO, Gebel el-Sheikh el-Haridi, el-Salamuni, MONS CLAUDIANUS granite, Wadi Gasus, PHILOTERAS, ATHRIBIS Wannina, PANOPOLIS Akhmim, ABYDOS, KAINE Qena, LEUKOS LIMEN Quseir, DIOSPOLIS PARVA Hiw, TENTYRA Dendara, KOPTOS Qift, PHOINIKON Laqeita, Bir el-Fawakhir, DIOSPOLIS MAGNA, Nagᶜ el-Madamud, THEBES, TUPHIUM/Tod, PATHYRIS Gebelein, LATOPOLIS Esna, CONTRA LATOPOLIS/el-Hella, Kom Mer, EILEITHYIASPOLIS, APOLLINOPOLIS MAGNA Edfu, MONS SMARAGDUS emeralds, Sikeit, KYSIS Qasr Dush, OMBOS Kom Ombo, ELEPHANTINE, SYENE/Aswan, Sehel Island, PHILAE, Biga Island, Dabod, BERENIKE, TZITZIS Qertassi, TAPHIS Tafa, TALMIS Kalabsha, Dodekaschoinus, TUTZIS Dendur, PSELCHIS el-Dakka, HIERASYKAMINOS el-Maharraqa.

el-Baqawat, Gebel el-Teir, HIBIS, Nadura, Qasr el-Ghueida, Qasr Zaiyan, el-Kharga Oasis, ᶜAin Amur.

Above: Egypt in the Greco-Roman Period

◇ important finds of Greek papyri and ostraca

○ Roman way-stations, sited at regular intervals along roads in the eastern desert; these normally had a well. The roads led to four Red Sea ports, which traded with East Africa and India throughout the period.

Right: The Faiyum in the Greco-Roman Period

Land reclamation from Lake Moeris and desert irrigation made the Faiyum (the Arsinoite nome) into the most prosperous area of Greek agricultural settlement.

◇ important finds of Greek papyri. Many of the sites are now in the desert, where papyrus is easily preserved.

Legend:
- fertile area
- Ptolemaic Faiyum lake
- ■ capital
- □ site
- ○ Roman way station
- ◇ papyrus site
- **granite** resource
- Roman road
- desert route
- Saqqara modern name
- ANTAEOPOLIS classical name

scale 1 : 5 000 000

0   75   150 km
0   50   100 mi

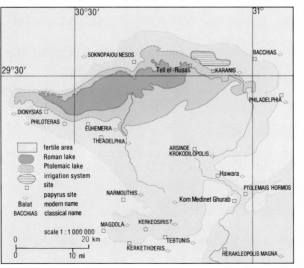

SOKNOPAIOU NESOS, BACCHIAS, Tell el-Rusas, KARANIS, DIONYSIAS, PHILOTERAS, EUHEMERIA, THEADELPHIA, PHILADELPHIA, ARSINOE KROKODILOPOLIS, Hawara, NARMOUTHIS, PTOLEMAIS HORMOS, Kom Medinet Ghurab, MAGDOLA, KERKEOSIRIS?, TEBTUNIS, KERKETHOERIS, HERAKLEOPOLIS MAGNA.

Legend:
- fertile area
- Roman lake
- Ptolemaic lake
- irrigation system
- site
- papyrus site
- Balat modern name
- BACCHIAS classical name

scale 1 : 1 000 000

0   20 km
0   10 mi

cultivated in return for a liability for military service. Greek settlements grew up in many areas, especially where, as in the Faiyum, there were land reclamation schemes. Although contact between native and Greek was limited, this new activity, and the increase in the area of cultivated land, generated wealth for the country as a whole. The chief development was, however, foreign: the building of Alexandria, which became the leading city in the Greek world. In later parlance Alexandria was "adjoining," not "in" Egypt. By acting as a magnet for the country's wealth and as the kings' chief concern it restricted expansion in other areas, especially because of its location in the extreme northwest.

The 2nd century was a time of decline in the economy and of political strife. Within the ruling family there were conspiracies, while native revolts

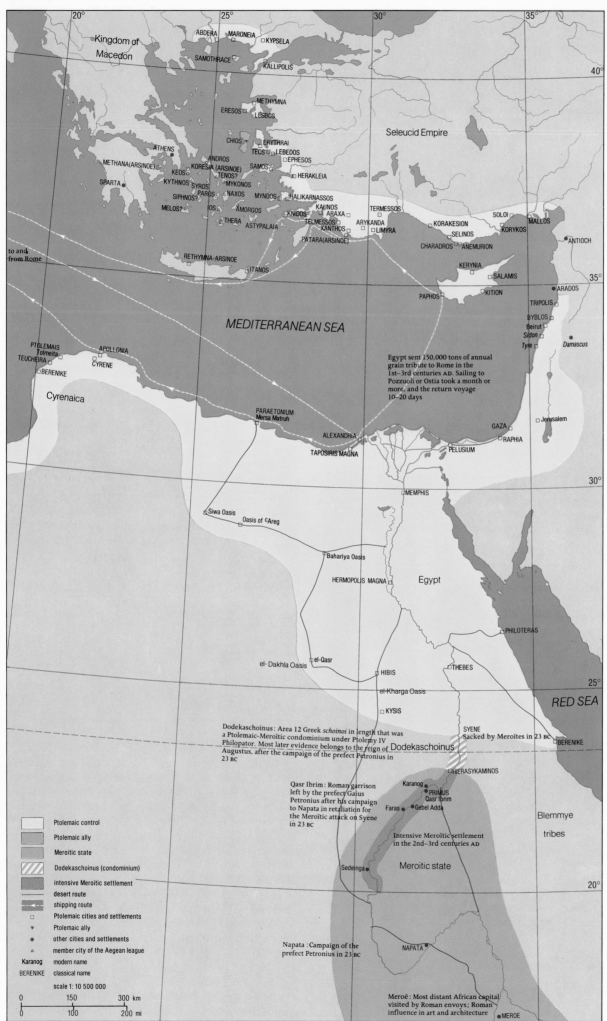

Egypt and the east Mediterranean in the Greco-Roman Period
In the 3rd century BC the principal powers in the Near East were the kingdom of Macedon, the Seleucid empire and the Ptolemaic kingdom. This map shows the approximate maximum extent of Ptolemaic possessions in the reigns of Ptolemy III Euergetes I and IV Philopator. Almost all were lost before 30 BC, when the entire Mediterranean area shown was incorporated in the Roman empire.

□ cities through which the Ptolemies exercised control. The kingdom was one of cities, not regions; the edge of the colored area indicates the approximate limit of their control, but is not a political frontier.

△ names of islands belonging to the Aegean league of the 3rd century BC; probable members are queried. This league was formed under Ptolemaic influence. Chios, an independent state, was a Ptolemaic ally.

Egypt sent 150,000 tons of annual grain tribute to Rome in the 1st–3rd centuries AD. Sailing to Pozzuoli or Ostia took a month or more, and the return voyage 10–20 days

Dodekaschoinus: Area 12 Greek *schoinoi* in length that was a Ptolemaic-Meroïtic condominium under Ptolemy IV Philopator. Most later evidence belongs to the reign of Augustus, after the campaign of the prefect Petronius in 23 BC

Qasr Ibrim: Roman garrison left by the prefect Gaius Petronius after his campaign to Napata in retaliation for the Meroïtic attack on Syene in 23 BC

Syene Sacked by Meroïtes in 23 BC

Intensive Meroïtic settlement in the 2nd–3rd centuries AD

Napata: Campaign of the prefect Petronius in 23 BC

Meroë: Most distant African capital visited by Roman envoys; Roman influence in art and architecture

Legend
- Ptolemaic control
- Ptolemaic ally
- Meroitic state
- Dodekaschoinus (condominium)
- intensive Meroitic settlement
- desert route
- shipping route
- □ Ptolemaic cities and settlements
- ▼ Ptolemaic ally
- ● other cities and settlements
- △ member city of the Aegean league
- Karanog modern name
- BERENIKE classical name

scale 1: 10 500 000

0   150   300 km
0   100   200 mi

Right Pair of over-life-size statues of Ptolemy II Philadelphus and his queen Arsinoe II Philadelphus, who holds a necklace counterpoise in her left hand. The style and iconography are wholly Egyptian; even the "smile" occurs in native works. Found in 1710; from the imperial pavilion in the Gardens of Sallust on the Monte Pincio in Rome, where they were set up under Domitian or Hadrian; originally from Heliopolis. Highly polished pink granite. Rome, Città del Vaticano, Museo Gregoriano Egizio.

Below Coffin of Artemidorus with portrait, from Hawara in the Faiyum. The coffin goes back to Late Period models. Top register: Anubis embalms the mummy; center: Horus and Thoth protect an emblem of Osiris; bottom: the resurrecting Osiris with Isis hovering over him in the form of a kite. The portrait is one of many hundreds, very few of which are still with their coffins. They are the only substantial legacy of Classical painted portraiture. 2nd century AD. London, British Museum.

in Upper Egypt were common from the reign of Ptolemy IV Philopator (221–205); the most serious was put down as late as 85. Egypt lost most of its foreign dependencies, and was even conquered by Antiochus IV Epiphanes of Syria, who proclaimed himself king for a short time in 168. In the 1st century the weakness of government continued, working in some ways to the native population's advantage. But the overshadowing force of Rome doomed Egyptian independence.

The Ptolemies and the Roman emperors appeared on the native monuments as traditional Egyptian kings, and the earlier ones set up inscriptions in Egyptian with accounts of such of their deeds as were intended to benefit the native population. Public announcements that were for all were set up in three scripts, hieroglyphic Egyptian, demotic Egyptian and Greek. The most famous of these is the decree preserved on the Rosetta stone, which was promulgated in 196 by Ptolemy V Epiphanes (205–180).

Throughout the dynasty traditional Egyptian temples were built. It seems that the temple lands, which produced the everyday income of temples, were more or less unchanged from earlier periods, so that the additional resources for building programs probably came from the kings. The benefactions for building temples were not greatly affected by the ebb and flow of the economy, but may have been a consistent royal policy aimed at attracting native support – and, perhaps, pleasing the native gods. Within the temples, however, the king who performed the traditional cult was a completely artificial figure. In times of confusion images of kings continued to be carved in temple reliefs but the cartouches for their names were left blank.

There was a rich development of traditional private sculpture in the period, showing the continuing vitality and wealth of the native elite, even though their sphere of action was curtailed, as is reflected in the tone of pietism and resignation in temple and private inscriptions. Only in the 1st century is there clear evidence in their monuments of receptiveness to Greek influence. The Greek population was itself influenced by Egyptian religion, in increasing measure as the Greco-Roman Period progressed.

The Ptolemaic Period saw the greatest development of animal worship in Egyptian religion. The cults attracted both Egyptians and Greeks, and created mortuary towns for the mummification of animals, pilgrimage and oracular consultations.

Under Roman rule (after 30 BC) there was an initial increase in prosperity. But the improved administration was aimed at securing wealth for Rome, not at developing Egypt for its own sake, and by the later 1st century AD problems of excessive taxation and official coercion were serious. Some emperors, most notably Hadrian (117–138 AD), showed a special regard for Egypt, but there was never any fundamental change in policies to the benefit of the local Greek population, let alone the Egyptian. Unlike other provinces of the empire, Egypt was not granted any degree of local autonomy, but was administered by a prefect under the jurisdiction of the emperor.

In terms of Egypt's later fame the Greco-Roman Period was very important. Egyptian cults spread into the Mediterranean world under the Ptolemies, but their greatest popularity was in early imperial times, when native Egyptian priests, as well as many Egyptian objects, came to Rome, while the cults traveled to much of the empire. Prominent among them was that of Sarapis, a Greco-Egyptian god created as a deliberate hybrid at the beginning of the Ptolemaic Dynasty. Egypt was also the exotic land *par excellence*, whose landscape was shown in a fanciful form in Roman paintings and mosaics.

Native-style temples were built in Egypt in the Roman Period, and the native religion continued to function. Very few new structures were erected after the 1st century AD, perhaps because of the general impoverishment of the country, but the decoration of existing ones continued, even keeping up with the struggles for the imperial throne in the names used in cartouches. The latest inscription in hieroglyphs dates to 394 AD, while Egyptian demotic documents and literary texts are common as late as the 3rd century.

The force that eventually destroyed traditional Egyptian culture and led to the mutilation of the monuments was not Roman rule but Christianity, whose success was due in large measure to its not being Roman. Native Egypt may, however, have contributed also to Christianity: the role of the Virgin Mary and the iconography of Virgin and Child resemble strikingly the myth and representation of Isis and the infant Horus. The notional end of ancient Egyptian history in 395 AD is the date of the final separation of the Roman Empire, by then strongly Christian, into east (Byzantine) and west; Egypt belonged with the east.

ART AND ARCHITECTURE

Egyptian representational art forms – sculpture in the round, relief and painting – acquired a distinctive character around the beginning of the Dynastic Period. At the same time the level of work in decorative and functional art forms, such as painted pattern work, stone vase manufacture, ivory carving, furniture making and metalwork, was very high, while architecture evolved rapidly from then on, continuing to develop with the mastery of new materials and the introduction of new forms. From the beginning, works of art in a wide range of genres are the most important single legacy from ancient Egypt, and one that is remarkably homogeneous. Changes in art through the different periods reflect changes in society and throw light on them, although art seeks its inspiration more in other art than in the world. Egyptian art is superficially approachable, but at another level very alien from western art.

Very few Egyptian works were produced as "art for art's sake." They all had a function, either as everyday objects or, more commonly among those preserved, in a religious or funerary context. It has sometimes been said that they should not be called "art," but there is no necessary contradiction between an object's artistic character and its function. One might say that the artistic quality of an object is the aesthetic element that is additional to its functional character. The status of Egyptian art as "art" in the minds of Egyptians was different in degree from that of western art for western viewers, but there is no fundamental difference in kind. Indeed, Egyptian and western genres resemble each other strikingly. In Egypt as in western society art was an important focus of prestige.

Relief and painting

Relief achieves its effect through modeling, light and shade, while painting works with line and color, but the techniques of representation in both are basically the same; both were also colored. Relief can be raised or sunk. In raised relief the surface surrounding the figures is removed to the depth of perhaps 5 millimeters, so that they stand out against it; in sunk relief the outlines of the figures are incised in the surface, which is then left, and the figures are modeled within it. Raised relief was generally used indoors, and sunk relief, which shows up better in the sun, out of doors. There were, however, variations in fashion in different periods; sunk relief was also cheaper. Major religious buildings and the better private tombs were decorated in relief. Painting was used in private tombs where poor rock made relief impossible, or in order to save expense, or where the work was not permanent and the surface to be covered was not suitable for relief, as in mud-brick private houses and royal palaces. Although painting was second best, there are many magnificent works in paint, whose techniques encouraged artists to work more freely than in relief.

A third, very rare type is representation in inlay. A small group of 4th-Dynasty tomb scenes at Maidum was made of colored paste set in the stone, while in later times glass and colored stones were used in the same way, chiefly on small objects, and to supply details in elaborate reliefs, a method typical of the ʿAmarna Period.

In Egypt writing and representation are very closely linked. The hieroglyphic signs are themselves pictures, whose conventions, apart from the linguistic and ornamental ones that govern their juxtaposition, are not very different from those of representation. Conversely, most pictures contain hieroglyphic texts, which may comment on the scene, supplying non-pictorial information, or may completely dominate the visual component, as they do in some temple reliefs. In tomb reliefs the main figure is a greatly magnified hieroglyph, replacing a sign that is omitted from the text caption, which supplies the person's name. Figure and text are mutually dependent.

Methods of representation

In contrast with western art and with the optical devices of photography and motion pictures, Egyptian representation is not based on either of the two main principles of perspective, the use of foreshortening and the adoption of a single, unified viewpoint for an entire picture. Instead, figures are rather like diagrams of what they show, whose aim is to convey information. The picture surface is mostly treated as a neutral element, not as an illusionistic space; spatial features are commonest in small groups of figures. These characteristics are universal in the world; perspective became the norm of representation only very slowly, and its adoption seems almost everywhere to have been the result of direct or indirect Greek influence.

In order to understand Egyptian "diagrams" it is necessary to become familiar with their conventions, rather as we do when we learn to read a map. In theory the conventions could be as arbitrary as in a map, but in fact they are not, and

Right Schist statue of Amenopemhat kneeling to present an emblem of Hathor to Ptah. The momentarily flexed calf muscle is clearly visible (the forearm is also tensed); a comparable treatment occurs already in the Old Kingdom. c.630 BC. Height 64 cm. New York, Metropolitan Museum of Art.

Above Statue of Metjetjy, carved from a single block of wood. The medium is exploited in a subtle composition that departs from conventional standing types. Note the detail of the right hand holding the kilt. Height 61·5 cm. Reign of Wenis, from Saqqara. Brooklyn Museum.

Left Inlay relief from the tomb of Itet at Maidum. Most of the inlay is restored, but the man's kilt and right leg retain substantial areas of the original paste. Early 4th Dynasty. Oxford, Ashmolean Museum.

Below Raised and sunk relief, after Schäfer. A Stages in carving raised relief. B Stages in carving sunk relief. C Sunk relief with beveled incisions. D Raised relief with two thicknesses and with one thickness.

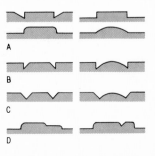

A

B

C

D

their very resemblance to perspective images often seduces the modern viewer into reading whole works in perspective. Among non-perspective representational systems the Egyptian is one of the closest to the visual image. It allows objective and mathematically precise depiction, as in the human figure, and it is relatively simple to transmit and to understand, unlike the highly elaborate conventions of early Chinese or Central American art. There must be further reasons for this visual character, which have not so far been identified. It has been suggested that the Egyptians' belief in the recreative force of representation was its origin, but the strength of this belief has probably been exaggerated, and in its extreme form such an idea would imply that they were more literal-minded than is easily credible. On a different plane, the conventions of artistic representation are, as we shall see, a repository of Egyptian values.

The Egyptians typically depicted an object by means of an assembly of its most characteristic aspects, which was contained within an outline that itself conveyed much of the necessary information. The various aspects were shown without foreshortening, which means that rectilinear forms were rendered precisely. In such a scheme the front and side of a box, for example, might well be next to each other. With objects with curved surfaces the method is more paradoxical, and very occasional foreshortenings are found, although they are not significant for the system as a whole (in true perspective, too, such objects cause the greatest difficulty). There are many further conventions that stem from the basic principles. Thus a part of an object that would not be visible in reality may be shown in a "false transparency," or the contents of something may be shown above it. The number of parts shown and the choice of them depend on the information that is to be conveyed rather than on visual considerations.

The representation of single objects is best exemplified by the human form, which is an elaborate composite. The description here is of the standing figure at rest; there are many possible variations of pose and of detail. The basic type faces to the right. The head is a profile, into which a half-mouth is set, which may be less than half the width of a mouth in full view. A full-view eye and eyebrow are placed within the profile. The shoulders are shown at their full width, but on the forward side of the body the line from armpit to waist is a profile which includes the nipple. The expanse of the chest may show details of clothing, most commonly necklaces and the shoulder straps of dresses, but, except in occasional figures that are turning or in other unusual poses, does not depict any specific part of the body. The line from the back armpit to the waist appears similarly to be no more than a connecting line. The waist is in profile, as are the legs and feet. The navel is placed near the front line of the waist, which often bulges slightly at that point (it could not be shown in the profile). The rendering of the feet is an instance of how the form is an assembly rather than a view. Until the mid-18th Dynasty, and often after that, both feet were shown from the inside, with a single toe and the arches indicated. Since arches cannot otherwise be shown without indication of depth, the whole foot leaves the ground to form them. This feature

acquires a life of its own, and the second foot may be seen through the gap of the arch, so that the drawing convention has been interpreted visually. This is one of countless self-generating elaborations of the system.

In the Egyptian language color, skin and nature are related words. A colorless figure would not be complete, and the intentional absence of color is rare. The color is as diagrammatic as the figures to which it is applied. Since they do not render views, light and shade are irrelevant. The color is uniform over the whole figure. It may be a single tone or a texture or pattern, such as are used for wood grain or for the skins of some animals. The basic repertory of colors is small: black, white, red, yellow, blue, green. From the 18th Dynasty on the range becomes wider, but is still simple and clear. Colors are not mixed, and there are few transitions from one to another. Despite the ubiquitousness of color, it is dominated by line, and is never the only means of conveying information. Outlines are picked out in contrasting colors, chiefly black.

There are two main approaches to composing scenes and whole walls: arranging the elements on a neutral surface, or using the surface as a depicted flat area, as we do in maps. The former is almost universal, the latter being used only for specialized purposes and during particular periods.

The basis of articulation according to the first approach is the register. The figures stand on horizontal lines called base lines, which may represent the ground but more often do not, and are spaced at intervals up the wall. Thematically related scenes may be next to one another in a single register, may be read in sequences up or down a wall, or may follow both principles. Two different versions of the same set of scenes – for example, a sequence from plowing to reaping – may be organized in opposite fashion, showing that the position on the wall does not in itself convey information.

Examples of the alternative, "map" method of composition are plans of houses and areas of desert. In either case the outline that defines the map – which seldom shows a specific location – may also serve as a base line for figures depicted in registers. Very occasionally a group of figures in a "map" composition is rendered in a set of vertical layers which coincides strikingly with images of recession in the optical field. This is, however, virtually the only feature that tends towards the assumption of a unifying viewpoint, as in perspective. Such an assumption is contradicted by other features.

A vital characteristic of all Egyptian representation is the treatment of scale, which forms, with iconography, the main means of ideological expression. Within a figure the parts are shown in their natural proportions, and this is often true also of whole scenes, but entire compositions are organized by scale around their chief figures. The larger the figure, the more important it is. In private tombs a single figure of the owner is often the height of the entire relief area of a wall, as many as six registers, whose scenes he is "viewing" as he faces them. He may also be several times the size of figures of his wife and children, who have their arms around his calves. The king towers similarly above his subjects. In New Kingdom battle reliefs an enormous figure of the king and his chariot may

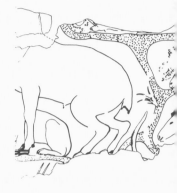

Detail of hunting scene in the tomb of Qenamun at Thebes (No. 93). The speckled picture surface shows the desert, and is both ground and background. Blank areas adapt to the animals' forms and make lairs for some; the outlines are base lines and perhaps paths. Reign of Amenophis II.

False transparency. The man is dipping a ladle into a cooking cauldron. Ladle and contents are visible inside the cauldron, but could not be seen in reality. Tomb of Ramesses III.

Contents above an object. A man lifts the lid of a jewel box; within is another box in the form of two royal cartouches, which is shown on the rim. Theban Tomb 181. Reign of Amenophis III.

Internal elaboration of the system. The arches of the feet are shown as a curve above the base line. The dogs' paws are visible through the non-existent "hole." 12th-Dynasty stela. Berlin (East) Museum.

occupy almost half the area, the rest being filled with Egyptian soldiers, defeated enemies, and an enemy fort on a hilltop, containing tiny people whom the king reaches out to grasp. The internal visual logic and the ideological message win over verisimilitude. The main reliefs in which there are few variations in scale are in temples, where only the king and deities are normally shown, all being of comparable rank within the context. Scaling may also be adjusted for reasons of style. Thus offering bearers of all periods often lead minute animals that overlap their legs in an arrangement that economizes on space and produces a neat grouping. At the opposite extreme, 4th-century bearers sometimes carry strangely colossal geese around their shoulders; here the reason seems to be stylistic exuberance.

A further ideological feature of Egyptian art is not representational, but is almost as fundamental as if it were. In most preserved works there is a pervasive idealization; things are shown as they should be, not as they are. The idealization is, however, as selective as the treatment of scale. Major figures are in ideal form, mostly shown in youthful maturity, while the women are all young and slim. They are normally at rest. Subordinate figures, on the other hand, may be depicted as wrinkled, balding and deformed, and they may argue and fight. Details of this sort are commonest in the finest Old Kingdom tombs, where they may be added partly in order to give interest and individuality to the scenes. They are absent from temple reliefs, which show a timeless, abstract world.

Sculpture in the round

The obvious stylistic similarity between sculpture in the round and relief and painting is based in part on techniques that are common to both. There may be more fundamental reasons for the rigid axes of sculpture, since the characteristic is nearly as widely distributed in the world as non-perspective representation in two dimensions, but it is not clear what they are. Whatever the answer to this wider question may be, the continuity and parallels in development between the two forms are remarkable.

Almost all major statues show a figure that looks straight ahead in a line at right angles to the plane of the shoulders, and whose limbs are constrained within the same planes. Mostly it stands at rest or is seated, and is not engaged in any activity. The organic interplay of the parts of the body is scarcely indicated, so that statues resemble the two-dimensional "diagram" in being an assembly of discrete parts. The analogy suggests that this may be a basic feature of representation, not an element of style. Part of the similarity between the genres is due to sculpture's dependence on drawings in a modified version of normal Egyptian two-dimensional representation.

The chief exceptions to rigid geometry are heads that look up, perhaps in order to see the sun, or down, in scribe statues, to look at a papyrus unrolled across the lap. Kneeling figures sometimes have flexed calf muscles, presumably showing that their pose is a momentary gesture of deference. Details of this sort, and slight indications of the organic coherence of the body, are restricted to the

finest works, in which the normal rigidity is taken for granted and softened, probably for aesthetic reasons. There are also some small works, principally in wood and of the later 18th Dynasty, that depart from the rules in showing turns and contrapposto, and retaining no more than traces of the normal defining sets of axes. These are important in showing that the strict forms were not the only ones the Egyptians had at their disposal.

Techniques in painting, relief and sculpture

In two and in three dimensions the basis of the artist's work was the preparatory drawing. Squared grids or sets of guide lines were used in order to ensure accurate representation. For the human body the grids were founded, until the 26th Dynasty, on a square the size of the fist of the figure being drawn, which is related proportionally to all the other parts of the body. In theory the grid had to be redrawn for each figure of a different size, but in practice the less important ones may often have been drawn freehand. The preliminary drawings were inscribed within the grids, and were then turned into the finished product in a multi-stage process of correction and elaboration. Artists evidently worked in groups, and were probably specialized in the tasks they performed.

Paintings were produced by this process, using a prepared background of stone or mud plaster with a fine gypsum plaster wash. Reliefs were carved and then painted. This involved the initial drawing, carving, and then fresh drawings which served as the basis for painting.

Works of sculpture started as squared blocks, the main sides of which served as surfaces for grids and drawings. The stone was then removed, with the drawing acting as a guide. As work progressed the drawings were renewed again and again; there are almost completely finished works that have the line

Boxwood statuette of a servant girl carrying an unguent jar. The equilibrium of a body carrying a weight is well rendered; the figure is almost free from the axial constraints of most Egyptian sculpture. Height 15 cm. Reign of Amenophis III. Durham, Gulbenkian Museum of Oriental Art.

Block statue of Petemihos. The sloping line of the arms balances the raised head. Gray granite. From Tell el-Muqdam. Height 46·3 cm. Brooklyn Museum.

Conventions of Representation

Egyptian representation is rooted in Egyptian culture. Unlike perspective, it is not based on scientific laws, but it does respect a "lowest common denominator" of ease of recognition. Where what is shown is familiar to us, we have little difficulty in understanding it, although it is easy to be misled. Where the object or scene is unfamiliar, it may be impossible to identify it, or we may fail to apply a rule that explains a puzzling feature. On this page different methods of representation are illustrated, all of them operating within the basic rules.

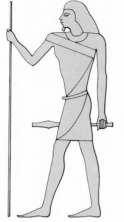

Orientation
Figures are designed to face right, and the relationship between right and left is symbolically important. Where a figure faces left, it sometimes retains the "correct" hands for the insignia it holds. Here the staff is held by a left hand, on what looks like a right arm, and the scepter is in a right hand. Probably because of the visual incongruity of this, there are several different solutions to this problem in left-facing figures.

Oxen with artificially deformed horns illustrate the same point. Their left horns are bent down, but where the ox faces left, the bent horn is the apparent "right" one. The effect is so natural that it is very easy to misunderstand the detail.

Assembly of parts: depiction of turns and occasional views
Statues of women show that they wore dresses whose shoulder straps covered their breasts.

In relief such figures show a bare breast, because the forward line of the body is a chest profile at this point. The shoulder straps are within the torso.

When a figure is turning, the normal scheme may be modified. Occasional nude figures show both breasts from the front and on the profile. These are often musicians, whose bodily attractions were important. Very rare figures in complex groups are shown full face, but they too are composites.

In the freest pictures, such as this sketch of a woman blowing into an oven, figures can be in almost pure profile (except for the eye). The indication of breath is an unusual detail. A broken hieratic text states that her "head is towards the chamber (opening?)," and she is "blowing into the oven."

Some statues of lions have crossed paws, with the head at 90° to the body. In a painting, the lion appears to face straight ahead; there is no means of deducing the form of the statue from the painting.

Relationship of parts; materials
Furniture is particularly difficult to depict clearly, because it is both three-dimensional and rectilinear.

This early painting shows two-legged couches whose surfaces slope to the ground. They are in a side profile both with and without indication of the surface, which ceases to be right-angled. There seem to be two couches, but these may be two pictures of the same one.

When two people sit on a chair, their ranking is shown. The man is ahead of the woman, who is on his left, inferior side. But in this position it is impossible to show her right arm around his shoulder, or her left arm over the chair arm. The apparent depth of the chair is probably its width, while the man is placed arbitrarily so that his body is not obscured by the chair's arm.

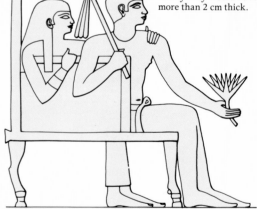

The material of which an object is made may be indicated in unexpected ways. This man's shelter is made of fresh reed matting (painted green) and his chair is on a mat. The thickness of the "walls" is enough to show that they are of matting; in reality they would have been no more than 2 cm thick.

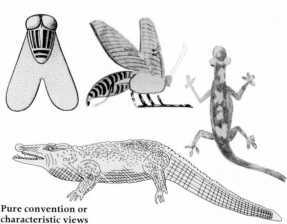

Pure convention or characteristic views
In some cases arbitrary rules help to distinguish similar forms. Crocodiles are always in a side profile, while lizards are shown from above. This takes into account the size of the creatures, and hence the angle from which they are normally seen. But with flies and bees the difference is simply a convention.

The production of a relief

Reliefs and paintings depended heavily on preliminary drawings, which were prepared according to guidelines, or from the Middle Kingdom within squared grids. Grids were also drawn over existing works to facilitate copying.

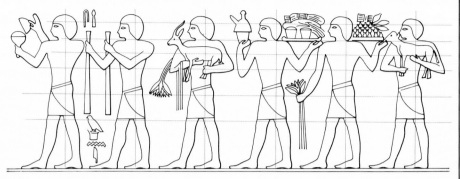

In the early scheme six horizontal guidelines intersected with the vertical median lines of the body to define its proportions. The horizontal lines were often continued through long processions of figures. For the human figure both the guidelines and the grids worked according to the canon of proportion, which was closely related to normal Egyptian measures of length. When these changed in the Late Period, the canon was modified too. Existing lines are shown in red, conjectural ones in yellow.

The earlier grid is based on 18 squares from the ground to the hair line (the part above is variable in size according to the type of headdress worn). Although it relates only to figures at one scale at a time, it sometimes covers the whole area that is to be filled with a scene; the design may then have been enlarged mechanically from a smaller draft. Occasionally the grid is subdivided.

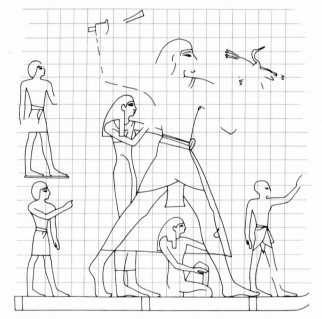

The later grid has 21 squares up to a new, lower measuring point at the eyes. Differences in proportions between the two systems are infinitesimal.

Grids were also used for animals. In this example the squares are preserved above the ox, but the figure itself has been modeled in the stone, removing the original surface and the drawing.

of the vertical axis marked down the middle of the face. As in relief, the final stages involved smoothing the surface, obliterating tool marks and applying paint.

The technical difficulty of sculpture varied greatly with the different materials, but the Egyptians mastered with the simplest tools even the hardest substances available to them. Unstinting labor was the chief component of success, but cannot account by itself for the artistry and sophistication of its products.

All the basic techniques had been acquired by the beginning of the Dynastic Period, so that artistic development was chiefly in the elaboration of representational forms and in iconography and composition. The main equipment consisted of copper (later bronze) saws, drills and chisels, all used with wet sand as the abrasive that did most of the actual cutting, and hammers of very hard stone. The latter could have various forms; one example from the Great Pyramid is about the size and shape of a tennis ball. For wooden sculpture the tools and techniques were those of carpentry. Iron tools appeared around 650.

For large works of sculpture technical problems turned into ones of engineering. The first stages of work on a colossal statue had more in common with quarrying than with art. Such statues were probably transported in a state of near completion, in order to make them as light as possible, and finished off at their destination. Moving them involved specially constructed roads and ships, and extensive earthworks for the final siting.

Architecture

Religious buildings form the vast majority of surviving works of architecture. Virtually all of them were symbolic as well as narrowly functional. The precise nature of the symbolism in mortuary buildings – pyramids, mastabas and rock-cut tombs – is not well established, but with temples the matter is relatively clear. The principles are, however, probably similar for both types: they recreate the cosmos or part of it. This cosmos is an ideal one, purified and set apart from the everyday world, and its relationship with the latter is one of analogy, not of direct representation. Its aim is to make the inhabitant of the temple (or tomb) partake symbolically in the process of creation itself or in the cosmic cycles, in particular that of the sun.

This symbolism is expressed in the siting and design of temples and in the decoration of the walls and ceilings. All of this is most easily observed in the temples of the Greco-Roman Period, which are probably little different in meaning from their New Kingdom forerunners. The structure is set apart from the outside world by a massive mud-brick enclosure wall, which may mimic the watery state of the cosmos at creation. Within this is the main pylon or entrance wall, decorated on the outside with scenes of the king slaughtering enemies; these ensure magically that disorder should not enter the temple behind. The pylon is the largest element in the temple; viewed in section, it encloses the area behind it within its height. At the same time its two massifs with the gap between them resemble the hieroglyph for "horizon" ⌂. The theoretical orientation of most temples is east–west (since this is based on the Nile and not on the cardinal points

Tomb Stelae

The tomb stela (gravestone) and the coffin with the mummy were the most important elements of Egyptian tombs (as opposed to simple graves).

The stela usually identified the deceased by his name and titles (the Egyptians said that it "made his name live"), and showed him seated at a table laden with offerings or receiving offerings from members of his family. On later stelae, the deceased was represented in the company of gods. This was the ideal state of affairs which everyone wished for his *ka*; the stela therefore helped to perpetuate it eternally. In early periods a list or representations of the provisions the *ka* needed for its existence was an important element of the stela. The *hotep-di-nesu* formula, which was a constant feature, ensured that these commodities were forthcoming: "A boon which the king gives to Osiris, so that he may give invocation-offerings of bread, beer, oxen, fowl, alabaster, clothing, and all things good and pure on which a god lives, to the *ka* of the deceased." The ancient formula shows how the provisioning of the tomb was thought to have been done: the king presented offerings to Osiris, the ruler of the underworld, and it was through him that the *ka* of the deceased received its share. Visitors and passers-by were asked to recite the formula and thus make the wish contained in it come true.

Unlike the burial chamber, the tomb stela was usually publicly accessible. It was the focus of the funerary cult of the deceased, and offerings were brought and placed on offering-tables in front of it on prescribed days.

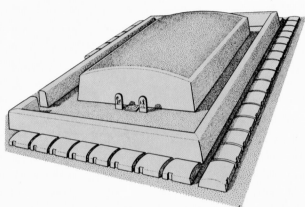

Royal stelae of the 1st Dynasty (*right*) are known from Abydos. Two of them, round topped, symmetrically designed and free standing, were set up against one of the faces of the mastaba (*below*). They contained only the name of the king.

The false door (*left*) was the typical stela of the Old Kingdom, which developed from the earlier "palace facade" and its niche stela. While the stela can still be recognized in the false door's panel, the "palace facade" was transformed into a complex system of jambs and lintels designed along the lines of real doorways (*below*). This dummy "door" connected the world of the living with the world of the dead, and the *ka* was believed to pass freely through it. The false door was usually made of stone, less often of wood, and formed part of the western wall of the tomb chapel.

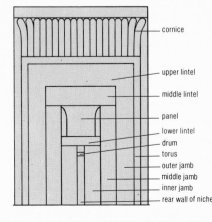

- cornice
- upper lintel
- middle lintel
- panel
- lower lintel
- drum
- torus
- outer jamb
- middle jamb
- inner jamb
- rear wall of niche

Provincial stelae of the 1st Inter-mediate Period (*left*) gave up the elaborate design of the false door in favor of flat rectangular forms and simple decoration, as if looking back to the tradition of niche stelae. Their representations were often crude and the writing of their inscriptions poor, but these features enable us to ascribe stelae to specific areas of Egypt with remarkable accuracy.

Stelae of the Middle Kingdom (*left and right*) developed from those of the 1st Intermediate Period, and can be either rectangular or round topped. They varied enormously in their subject matter and texts, but many criteria have been established by which they can be dated (e.g. the type of the *hotep-di-nesu* formula) and ascribed to a particular necropolis (e.g. the selection of the deities invoked).

Brick-built superstructures of private tombs of the first three dynasties had a "palace facade," an elaborate design of recesses (niches) (*above*). In the rear wall of one of these, near the south-eastern corner of the mastaba, was a stone or wooden *niche stela* (*left*). The "palace facade" was occasionally used in the chapel inside the mastaba; the number of niche stelae was then increased.

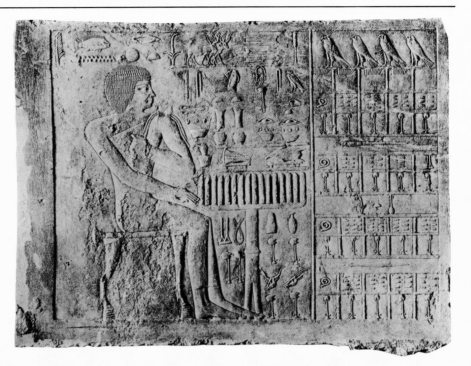

Slab stelae (*above*) were characteristic of the earliest mastabas with stone super-structures built at Giza during the 4th Dynasty. Positioned in the eastern face of the mastabas, they were, like the tombs them-selves, presented by the king, and made by the best craftsmen.

Despite the enormous variety in form and decoration, designers employed simple constructional procedures. These, rather than mysterious "systems," are responsible for the interplay of proportions, as shown here on a *Late Period stela*.

Apart from some new forms, the most striking feature of *New Kingdom stelae* (*above*) was the appearance of gods (in particular Osiris) in their main scenes.

there is in fact considerable variation), so that the sun "rises" in the pylon gateway, sending its rays into the sanctuary, which is placed directly in the axis, and runs its course through the temple.

The most imposing part of the main temple is the hypostyle or columned hall, which conveniently summarizes the decorative scheme of the whole. The column capitals show aquatic plants, and the lowest register of the walls has similar plants in relief; symbolically the hall is the marsh of creation. The architraves and ceiling have reliefs of the sky, so that the decoration encompasses the whole world. What is shown on the walls is the activity of this world. Instead of marsh, the lowest register may contain offering bearers who do duty for the king in bringing the produce of the land to provide for the temple. Neither is part of the more abstract main scheme, which consists of several registers of scenes, arranged like a checkerboard, showing the king, who faces in towards the sanctuary, making offerings to and performing rituals for the god. The god, who takes up residence in the temple, faces outwards; the deities shown in the reliefs are a wider range than that worshiped in any one temple. Many scenes show rituals performed in the temple, but others have a less specific meaning. In terms of the temple, the give and take between king and god is the focus of the world's activities. Most of the reliefs in the temple are of the same character.

The inner areas have a raised floor level and lower ceiling than the hypostyle hall. They are therefore contained within the protection of the outer area, and are more sacred. There are a number of relatively small rooms around the sanctuary, whose outside wall mimics the outside of a temple, forming a structure within a structure. The sanctuary represents the mound of creation, and relates to the marsh of the hypostyle hall; in passing towards the sanctuary a procession goes through the stages of creation.

Techniques

Egyptian stone working produced rock-cut structures with techniques akin to those of quarrying, solid mounds – the pyramids – and more conventional free-standing structures. Here work on the latter is described.

We know very little of how the planning and surveying of sites was done; most reconstructions of the processes are almost entirely speculative. However it was achieved, there was enormous expertise in maintaining an accurate plan and elevation for a large pyramid, or in constructing the sloping walls of a pylon.

The foundations of Egyptian buildings were often surprisingly meager, consisting of a trench filled with sand and topped with a few courses of rough stonework (the sand may even have had a symbolic as much as a functional purpose). Only in the Greco-Roman Period were there regularly massive foundations of proper masonry, much of it constructed from earlier buildings demolished to make way for the new ones.

In masonry mortar was used very sparingly. The technique was to lay a course of blocks, level it along the top, coat the surface with a thin layer of mortar whose prime purpose was to act as a lubricant, and slide the next course into position. The under surfaces and probably the rising joints of the blocks were dressed before they were used. Each block was fitted individually to the next, since the rising joints were not always vertical, or at right angles to the surface. A single block could even form an internal corner, and the levels of the horizontal courses might be maintained only for a short distance. Wooden cramps were often set into the horizontal joints behind the surface in order to provide extra rigidity or to prevent slippage while the mortar was setting. The main purpose of the complex jointing techniques was probably to minimize waste and to use the largest practicable size of block. The edges of the blocks were cut to size when they were mounted, but the main surface was left rough.

The Egyptians probably worked without mechanical lifting devices; the basic method of raising weights was to bury the wall that was being built behind a rubble ramp. This was added to continually until the walls reached their full height. The stones were then dressed smooth, either from the ramps as they were dismantled, or from wooden scaffolding, which was probably used at a later stage for carving the relief decoration. The various stages of work on a building often proceeded at once, so that stonemasons, draftsmen, plasterers, relief carvers and painters could all be employed together. Something of this can be seen in the private tombs at el-'Amarna and in the tomb of Haremhab (1319–1307) in the Valley of the Kings. Since few Egyptian tombs or temples were ever completely finished, the resulting confusion may have seemed the natural state of affairs.

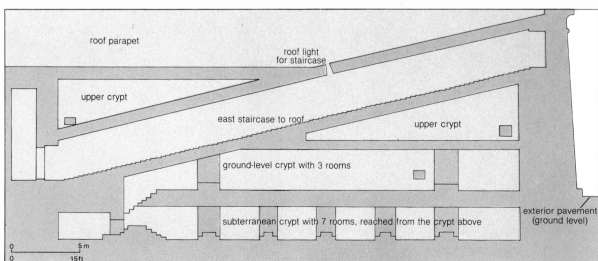

roof parapet

roof light for staircase

upper crypt

east staircase to roof

upper crypt

ground-level crypt with 3 rooms

subterranean crypt with 7 rooms, reached from the crypt above

exterior pavement (ground level)

0   5 m
0   15 ft

Temple of Dendara, section of east wall. The massive wall accommodates suites of rooms, called crypts, and a staircase within its thickness. The lowest set of crypts is below ground, contained within foundations about 10 meters deep. The roof area is similarly lavish; above the ceiling line on the left the outside wall forms a parapet 8·5 meters high. The blue squares in the ground-level and upper crypts are access holes from within the temple. Those in the upper crypts are 4 meters above ground level. All were concealed within the decoration of the rooms that contained them. 1st century BC.

PART TWO

A JOURNEY DOWN THE NILE

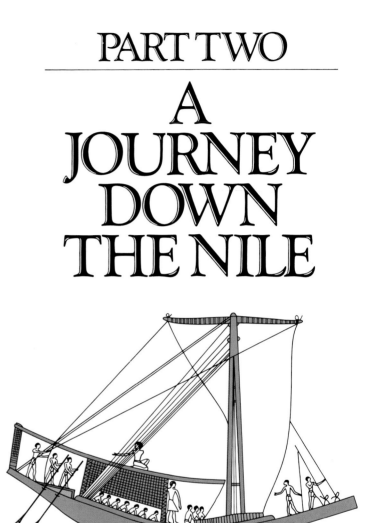

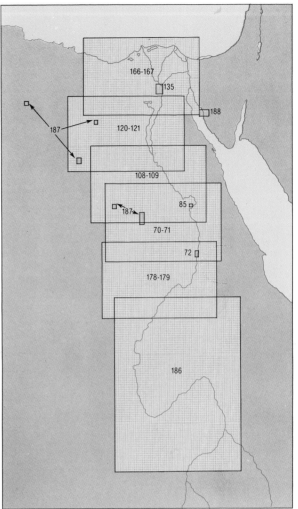

The land of Egypt has been likened to a lotus, with the heavy flower of the delta on the very long and thin stalk of the Nile valley, and the bud of the Faiyum nestling close to it. The surrounding areas, with the exception of the chain of oases running parallel to the river on the west, were arid and inhospitable, and thus unsuitable for settled habitation.

Two cities played key roles in Egyptian history until the scene shifted northwards during the 19th Dynasty: Memphis, close to the apex of the delta, and Thebes, its counterbalance in the south. These provide two of the points at which we break our imaginary boat journey down the Nile through ancient Egypt. The first Nile cataract in the south is our logical point of departure.

Nubia, the oases and Sinai, though never described as parts of Egypt, were colonized, in the case of the first two, and frequented, in the case of the third, to such an extent that their inclusion is essential. Going upstream into Nubia is, however, a different proposition from sailing gently down the Nile, and a donkey must replace our boat for the journeys into the oases and Sinai.

Boats on the Nile

The simple raft, made of bundles of papyrus stalks lashed together with ropes, was the earliest boat on the Nile. It was of limited life and use, but cheap and easily replaceable, a necessity for some, such as herdsmen who had to cross crocodile-infested waters while grazing cattle in the delta, and a means of pleasure for hunters fowling in the swamps.

The word *sepy*, "to bind," was later also used for the building of wooden boats.

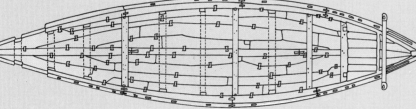

Geographically, it is hard to imagine a more absurd form than that of ancient Egypt: long and narrow, it reminds one of a sprawling town bestriding a motorway. Indeed, the main advantage of this was ease of communication, because the Nile (the motorway) connected all important localities. The boat was the most important means of transport.

The construction of the hull of smaller boats reflected the lack of local quality wood. The shipbuilder had to use fairly short planks which were tenoned and mortised or secured to each other by binding; wood for larger craft and seagoing boats was imported. At least until the New Kingdom the most conspicuous constructional feature of Egyptian boats was the absence of the keel.

Northerly winds, favorable to sailing up the river, prevailed in the Nile valley, but downstream traffic depended on oars. This was reflected in the hieroglyphic writing to such an extent that in the words for "to travel northwards" ("to fare downstream") and "to travel southwards" ("to sail upstream") the appropriate boat-sign was used even when describing an overland journey.

A simple but effective stepping of the mast was required by the frequent changes from sailing to rowing.

The main element of the steering gear was a massive rudder oar attached to a rudder post and the boat's stern. The boat was steered by moving the tiller sideways and thus rotating the stock of the rudder oar and its blade.

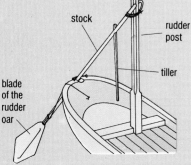

stock

rudder post

tiller

blade of the rudder oar

Our knowledge of ancient Egyptian shipping derives from representational evidence (reliefs and paintings), model boats found in tombs, and isolated discoveries of buried funerary boats (at Giza and Dahshur). Textual sources are scarce and not very informative. Ancient Egyptian Nile boats varied greatly according to their purpose (traveling boats, cargo boats, ceremonial barks etc.), but a fairly reliable guide to their dating is provided by (1) the appearance of the hull, (2) the method of steering, (3) the type of the mast and sail, (4) the vessel's paddles or oars, (5) the disposition of the deckhouses, and (6) unusual features.

Predynastic Period: (1) sometimes, though not always, sharply upturned prow and stern (even large Nile craft were made mostly of papyrus or similar material); (2) one or more large steering oars; (3) rectangular sail; (4) and (5) paddles in two groups (interrupted by central deckhouse); (6) prow decoration of tree branches (?); standard close to deckhouse.
Old Kingdom: (1) "classical" Egyptian hull shape (wood now the main building material), often with animal-head prow; (2) several large steering oars, but from 6th Dynasty special steering gear; (3) usually bipod mast; probably trapezoidal sail, usually more tall than wide; (4) from 5th

Dynasty oars.
Middle Kingdom: (1) higher stern; (2) steering gear operated by a helmsman standing between the massive rudder post and the usually single large rudder oar; (3) single mast, lowered and supported on a forked stanchion when sailing downstream; (5) deckhouse forward of the rudder post.
New Kingdom (large range of specialized types): (2) steering gear with usually two rudder oars, operated by a helmsman standing in front of the rudder post; (3) sail more wide than tall; (5) castles forward and aft, with centrally placed deckhouse.
Late Period: (1) tendency towards a higher stern.

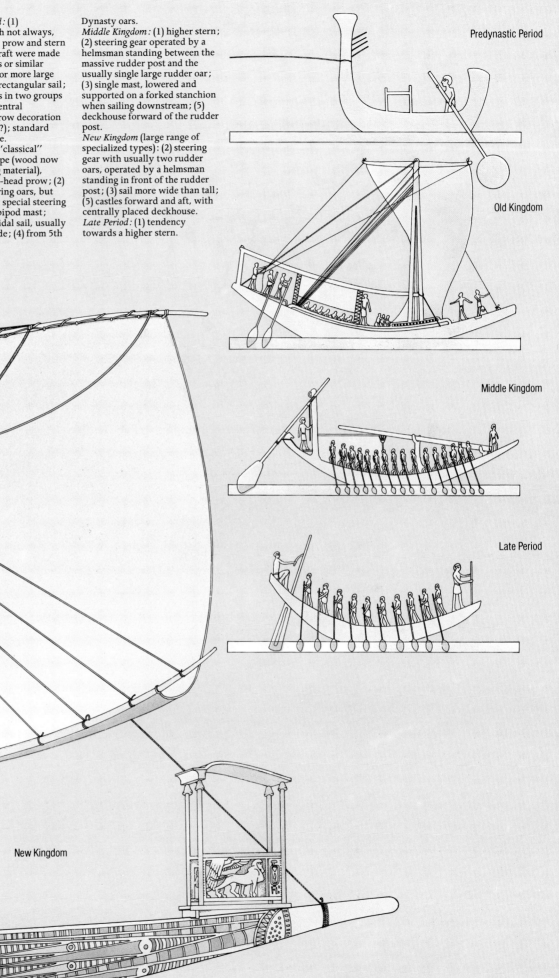

Predynastic Period

Old Kingdom

Middle Kingdom

Late Period

New Kingdom

SOUTHERN UPPER EGYPT

Because the Egyptians oriented towards the south, Aswan was the "first" town in the country north of the actual frontier at Biga island.

The southernmost part of the country falls into the natural divisions of the 1st Upper Egyptian nome, from Biga to north of Gebel el-Silsila, and the 2nd–4th nomes as far as Thebes. The two are roughly equal in length along the river, but the former belongs to the sandstone belt of Nubia, and is forbidding, infertile country, dominated by the desert and rich in minerals. To this day its character is strongly Nubian.

Kom el-Ahmar was one of the earliest urban centers, but declined in importance during the historical period. Probably because of the dominant position of Thebes, the districts to the south were included in the Viceroy of Nubia's territory during the New Kingdom. In this stretch of the river the

valley is relatively narrow, and could not support as large a population as the Theban area. There are, however, desert routes for trade and mining expeditions to east and west that were significant at most periods.

As befits its early importance, there are numerous Predynastic and Early Dynastic sites in Southern Upper Egypt. The best-represented later periods are the late Old Kingdom and 1st Intermediate Period, early New Kingdom and Greco-Roman Period. These were all times when government was not very strongly centralized, so that an outlying area could benefit. Apart from the magnificent landscape, best seen from the river, the most impressive monuments are now probably the chapels and shrines of Gebel el-Silsila, with their reminder of the importance of the inundation for Egypt, and the major Greco-Roman temples, Philae, Kom Ombo, Edfu and Esna.

Top left Elephantine island from the east bank of the river. In the foreground are restored Roman walls near the Nilometer.

Above left Kiosk of Trajan at Philae, with foundations of a small chapel in the foreground; photographed in 1964 before the building of the High Dam.

Top right Colossal gray granite hawk at the entrance to the hypostyle hall of the temple of Edfu; probably Ptolemaic.

Above right Tomb complex of Pepynakht and others at Qubbet el-Hawa, north of Aswan; late 6th Dynasty. The entrance court, columns and stairways are cut in the sandstone cliff.

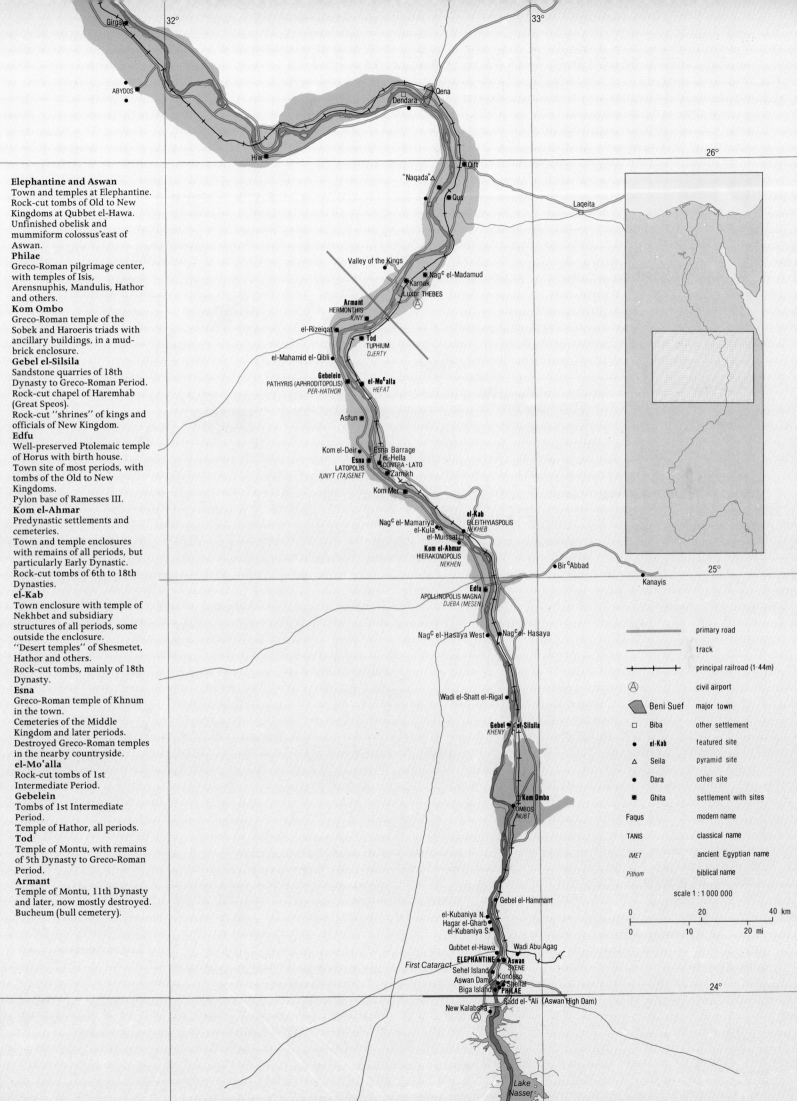

Elephantine and Aswan
Town and temples at Elephantine.
Rock-cut tombs of Old to New
Kingdoms at Qubbet el-Hawa.
Unfinished obelisk and
mummiform colossus east of
Aswan.

Philae
Greco-Roman pilgrimage center,
with temples of Isis,
Arensnuphis, Mandulis, Hathor
and others.

Kom Ombo
Greco-Roman temple of the
Sobek and Haroeris triads with
ancillary buildings, in a mud-
brick enclosure.

Gebel el-Silsila
Sandstone quarries of 18th
Dynasty to Greco-Roman Period.
Rock-cut chapel of Haremhab
(Great Speos).
Rock-cut ''shrines'' of kings and
officials of New Kingdom.

Edfu
Well-preserved Ptolemaic temple
of Horus with birth house.
Town site of most periods, with
tombs of the Old to New
Kingdoms.
Pylon base of Ramesses III.

Kom el-Ahmar
Predynastic settlements and
cemeteries.
Town and temple enclosures
with remains of all periods, but
particularly Early Dynastic.
Rock-cut tombs of 6th to 18th
Dynasties.

el-Kab
Town enclosure with temple of
Nekhbet and subsidiary
structures of all periods, some
outside the enclosure.
''Desert temples'' of Shesmetet,
Hathor and others.
Rock-cut tombs, mainly of 18th
Dynasty.

Esna
Greco-Roman temple of Khnum
in the town.
Cemeteries of the Middle
Kingdom and later periods.
Destroyed Greco-Roman temples
in the nearby countryside.

el-Mo'alla
Rock-cut tombs of 1st
Intermediate Period.

Gebelein
Tombs of 1st Intermediate
Period.
Temple of Hathor, all periods.

Tod
Temple of Montu, with remains
of 5th Dynasty to Greco-Roman
Period.

Armant
Temple of Montu, 11th Dynasty
and later, now mostly destroyed.
Bucheum (bull cemetery).

Girga   32°

ABYDOS

Qena

Dendara

Hiw

Qift   26°

"Naqada"△

Qus

Laqeita   33°

Valley of the Kings

Nag^c el-Madamud

Karnak
Luxor THEBES

Armant
HERMONTHIS
IUNY

el-Rizeiqat

Tod
TUPHIUM
DJERTY

el-Mahamid el-Qibli

Gebelein
PATHYRIS (APHRODITOPOLIS)
PER-HATHOR

el-Mo^calla
HEFAT

Asfun

Kom el-Deir

Esna Barrage
el-Hella

Esna   CONTRA - LATO
LATOPOLIS
IUNYT (TA)SENET   Zarnikh

Kom Mer

Nag^c el-Mamariya   **el-Kab**
el-Kula△   EILEITHYIASPOLIS
el-Muissat□   NEKHEB

Kom el-Ahmar
HIERAKONOPOLIS
NEKHEN

Bir ^cAbbad   25°

Kanayis

Edfu
APOLLINOPOLIS MAGNA
DJEBA (MESEN)

Nag^c el-Hasaya West   Nag^c el- Hasaya

Wadi el-Shatt el-Rigal

Gebel el-Silsila
KHENY

Kom Ombo
OMBOS
NUBT

Gebel el-Hammam

el-Kubaniya N.
Hagar el-Gharb
el-Kubaniya S.

Qubbet el-Hawa   Wadi Abu Agag

ELEPHANTINE ■ **Aswan**
SYENE
First Cataract   Sehel Island
Aswan Dam   Konosso
Biga Island   Shellal
PHILAE   24°

New Kalabsha

Sadd el-^cAli (Aswan High Dam)

Lake
Nasser

---

primary road

track

principal railroad (1·44m)

Ⓐ   civil airport

Beni Suef   major town

□   Biba   other settlement

●   **el-Kab**   featured site

△   Seila   pyramid site

●   Dara   other site

■   Ghita   settlement with sites

Faqus   modern name

TANIS   classical name

IMET   ancient Egyptian name

Pithom   biblical name

scale 1 : 1 000 000

0   20   40 km

0   10   20 mi

Elephantine and Aswan

Elephantine was the capital of the 1st Upper Egyptian nome, which was probably annexed to Egypt at the beginning of the Dynastic Period. The site is strategically important because of the natural barrier of the first cataract immediately to the south, and because of the large number of nearby mineral deposits, but it is in an almost barren area, and the town may always have relied on food brought from further north. It made its living as a garrison and by trade. The common meaning of the ancient Egyptian word *swenet* from which the name Aswan was derived is "trade."

The main town and temple area were at the southern end of Elephantine island. This was inhabited almost continuously from the Early Dynastic Period. So far little can be said of the town, which is now the subject of a long-term excavation

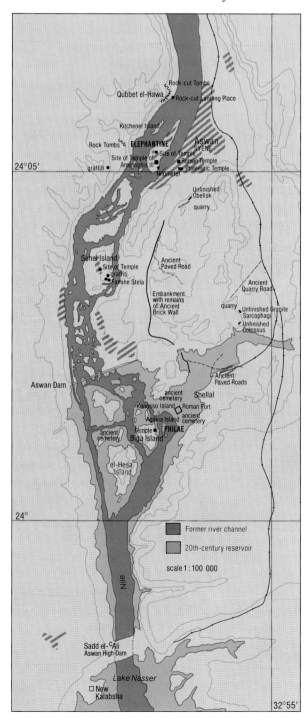

program. The expedition has found an important deposit of Early Dynastic votive figurines, similar to those from Kom el-Ahmar (Hierakonpolis), showing indirectly that there was already a temple at that time. From the late Old Kingdom has come unique wooden relief paneling, which clad the entrance to a memorial chapel for one of the notables of the 6th Dynasty, whose tombs are across the river. A monument of rather similar character was the shrine of Heqaib, a 6th-Dynasty official who was deified after his death and remained the subject of a local cult into the Middle Kingdom. From most later periods down to the Roman come fragments of relief from the temples of Khnum, Satis and Anukis, the local triad of deities, but there are no complete structures, and few elements *in situ*. A small colonnaded temple of Amenophis III was, however, virtually complete as late as 1820, as was a building

Above left Remains of the sacred area on Elephantine island, looking northwest, with the modern village in the background. The stone walls that are visible date to many different periods (the standing gateway is restored).

Left Mummiform colossus abandoned in the granite quarries east of Aswan; possibly 19th Dynasty. The rock outcrops are characteristic of the cataract area, while the boulder by the statue shows clear marks of quarrying. The figure itself has been much eroded, and its face polished by generations of visitors.

Above Decorated pillar in the tomb of Setka at Qubbet el-Hawa; late 6th Dynasty. This is perhaps the finest of the Old Kingdom relief work at Aswan. The figure of the deceased has the leopard skin, full kilt and cropped hairstyle of an elderly priest; he is described as the "Count, Overseer of the Phyles [groups of priests] of Upper Egypt." Setka confronts visitors to the tomb; just visible on the left face of the pillar are registers of animals and offering figures moving towards him.

of Tuthmosis III. In the area of a temple of Alexander IV burials of sacred rams of Khnum have been excavated, dating to the Greco-Roman Period. The mummies were given elaborate gilt cartonnage headpieces, some of which are now in the nearby museum, and were placed in stone sarcophagi that have been left where they were found. The best-known monument now visible on the island is the Nilometer, a staircase with cubit markings beside it for measuring the height of the river, on the east. The inundation levels recorded on it are of the Roman Period.

On the west bank north of the town, at Qubbet el-Hawa, "windy dome" in Arabic, are the rock-cut tombs of the Old Kingdom expedition leaders, Middle Kingdom nomarchs and some New Kingdom officials. The 6th-Dynasty tombs, some of which form linked family complexes, contain important biographical texts, but the decoration is sparse and provincial. The 12th-Dynasty tomb of the elder Sarenput is much more impressive both in architecture and in decoration, although it too has reliefs only in a few areas.

The granite rocks of the cataract south of Elephantine have quarrying marks in many places, and the quarry area also extends some 6 km east of the town center. The most striking remains are an abandoned obelisk and an almost complete mummiform colossus. The obelisk developed faults, but it is not clear why the colossus was never moved. Both in the river and on land there are numerous ancient graffiti, either commemorating quarrying expeditions or having a more general purpose. The greatest single body of them is on the island of Sehel, 3 km south of Elephantine.

Aswan town contains few visible remains, probably because they have been continuously built over. The two tiny Greco-Roman Period temples probably formed only a small proportion of the original sacred area.

Philae

In its grandiose setting in the first cataract, the lush island of Philae was the most romantic tourist attraction in 19th-century Egypt, but with the raising of the first Aswan dam it became submerged for most of each year. Now, as a result of the building of the High Dam, the temples have been dismantled and reerected on the nearby island of Agilkia.

The earliest monuments on the site are of the reign of Nectanebo I, but blocks discovered in foundations take the island's history back to the reign of Taharqa. Philae is the site of the latest hieroglyphic inscription (394 AD) and still later demotic graffiti (the latest of 452 AD).

The Egyptians gave an etymology to the name of

Philae, "island of the time [of Reʿ]," which implies that the site recreated the primeval world when the sun god ruled on earth. On the neighboring island of Biga was the Abaton or "pure mound," one of many tombs of Osiris in the country. This was approached by way of the small temple of Biga, which faces Philae. The temple of Isis was the architectural climax of Philae, so that the most important pair of

Top The temple area at Philae, seen from nearby Biga; watercolor by David Roberts (published 1846). The temple of Biga, partly converted into a church, is visible in the foreground. The rear wall of the west colonnade forms the edge of Philae; to the left it continues into a landing stage and the entrance to the gate of Hadrian. Behind can be seen (right to left): the 1st east colonnade: kiosk of Trajan; 1st pylon; birth house and 2nd east colonnade; 2nd pylon and temple of Isis. There are remains of modern houses on the roof of the Isis temple (removed in the 19th century).

Above Sistrum figure of the reign of Ptolemy VI Philometor in the entrance to the main hall of the temple of Hathor at Philae. The motif, often a column capital, comprises a Hathor head on the sign for gold (the metal of Hathor), flanked by a pair of uraei, with a naos shape above (the actual sistrum).

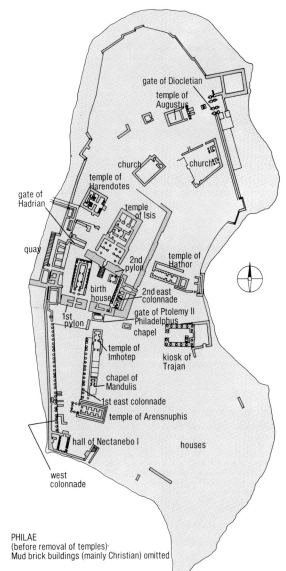

PHILAE
(before removal of temples)·
Mud brick buildings (mainly Christian) omitted

gate of Diocletian
temple of Augustus
church
church
temple of Harendotes
gate of Hadrian
temple of Isis
quay
2nd pylon
temple of Hathor
birth house
2nd east colonnade
gate of Ptolemy II Philadelphus
1st pylon
chapel
temple of Imhotep
kiosk of Trajan
chapel of Mandulis
1st east colonnade
temple of Arensnuphis
hall of Nectanebo I
houses
west colonnade

Below Gate of Hadrian at Philae: relief of Isis (cow-headed) pouring milk over the sacred grove of trees on Biga, with the resurrected "soul" of Osiris above. Behind is the rocky "landscape" of Biga with a figure of the inundation in the cave from which it emerges, and a hawk and a vulture above.

Right Temple of Sobek and Haroeris at Kom Ombo, from the east. The mud brick outer wall is in the foreground, with the outer and inner enclosure walls beyond; the colossal relief figures are Roman.

deities of the period had an island each. Isis was much the more popular, and had devotees to north and south. In the Ptolemaic Period there was a short condominium between Egypt and the Meroïtic kings. This has left traces in the decoration of the temple of Arensnuphis, which was done in the names of Ptolemy IV Philopator and of the Meroïtic Arqamani (c. 220–200 BC); there are also Meroïtic graffiti dating from the 3rd century BC to the 3rd century AD. Nonetheless, the buildings are completely Egyptian, and were presumably built with Egyptian resources.

The southeast portions of the island probably contained dwelling quarters. Pilgrims landed near the hall of Nectanebo I on the south, and proceeded into the open space bounded by the monumental west colonnade and first east colonnade. These are probably later structures added to round off the group of buildings; they may be inspired by the planning of public spaces in the Classical world. The decoration of the west colonnade is mainly of Roman date.

On the east were temples dedicated to the Nubian gods Arensnuphis and Mandulis, and a temple of Imhotep, the deified official of the reign of Djoser, who is also mentioned in a Ptolemaic rock stela on the island of Sehel to the north. In the gap north of the first east colonnade is a gate of Ptolemy II Philadelphus, leading to a small chapel and to the much later kiosk of Trajan by the eastern shore of the island.

The first part of the temple of Isis is composed of isolated elements. Behind the first pylon a courtyard is formed by the birth house, which is unconventionally placed parallel with the temple axis, and the second east colonnade with a set of rooms leading off it. The decoration of these areas is late Ptolemaic and early Roman. The main temple behind, whose earliest decoration dates to Ptolemy II Philadelphus, contains an abbreviated version of the full pylon, court and hypostyle hall, and is on a smaller scale than the other great temples of the period. On the roof are chapels dedicated to Osiris.

The most notable of the remaining temples is that of Hathor, who was here the angry goddess of myth,

who went south into Nubia spreading devastation, and had to be pacified by Thoth before she would return. The columns of the temple's entrance courtyard contain figures of musicians, including the god Bes, who held performances in order to placate the goddess.

At the northern end of the island were a temple of Augustus and a gate known as the "Gate of Diocletian" (284–305 AD). Between these and the temple of Isis were two churches; from the mid-4th century AD these coexisted with the pagan cults, which were finally suppressed under the Byzantine Emperor Justinian (527–565 AD). The hypostyle hall of the temple of Isis was turned into a church, and, as on many other sites, the flesh areas of all accessible figures of kings and gods in the temple were defaced.

Kom Ombo

Kom Ombo stands on a promontory at a bend in the Nile, at the northern end of the largest area of agricultural land south of Gebel el-Silsila. Because of improved agricultural techniques it was prominent in the Ptolemaic Period, to which almost all the monuments date. An 18th-Dynasty gateway was, however, seen by Champollion in the southern enclosure wall, and scattered New Kingdom blocks have been found on the site. Part of the temple forecourt has been eroded by the river, while the

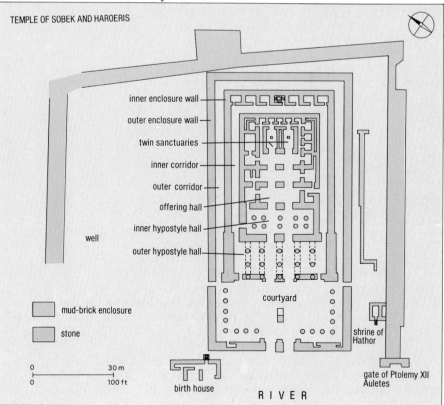

TEMPLE OF SOBEK AND HAROERIS

inner enclosure wall
outer enclosure wall
twin sanctuaries
inner corridor
outer corridor
offering hall
inner hypostyle hall
outer hypostyle hall
well
courtyard
shrine of Hathor

mud-brick enclosure
stone

0   30 m
0   100 ft

birth house
gate of Ptolemy XII Auletes

RIVER

Seated figure of a god with offerings in front, including a tall box of possibly surgical instruments that is placed on a stand; outer corridor, Roman Period.

Well-preserved colored detail of the king on a column in the forecourt; reign of Tiberius. The crown relates the king to Onuris-Shu; the sign behind him symbolizes protection.

encloses the entire inner part of the temple and has within its width a number of small chambers at the back. This is enclosed in its turn by a second wall and corridor, which take in the courtyard. Thus the double axis goes together with other dual features. Some of the reliefs in the inner corridor and its small rooms are unfinished, giving valuable insight into artists' methods in this period. On the inner face of the outer corridor there are some unique and bizarre scenes, and a representation of a set of instruments that have traditionally been assumed to be those of a surgeon.

A figure of Haroeris in the first hypostyle hall revives an ancient technique of relief embellishment: it has a hole instead of an eye; this must have been inlaid in order to give special opulence and liveliness to the figure of the god.

The small Roman shrine of Hathor to the south of the courtyard is now used to store the mummies of sacred crocodiles from a nearby necropolis. The well north of the temple is complex and, because of the elevation of the temple, very deep. Like other wells in temple enclosures, it allowed pure water, in theory from the primeval waters themselves, to be drawn within the sacred area, avoiding pollution from the outside world.

Gebel el-Silsila

Some 65 km north of Aswan, at Gebel el-Silsila, steep sandstone cliffs narrow the stream and present a natural barrier to river traffic. The ancient Egyptian name of the place, *Kheny* (or *Khenu*), which has been translated as "The Place of Rowing," seems to reflect this fact. Local quarries, particularly those on the east bank, were exploited from the 18th Dynasty until the Greco-Roman Period.

On the west bank is the Great Speos (rock-cut chapel) of Haremhab. The seven deities to whom the chapel was dedicated were represented as seated statues in the niche at the back of the sanctuary, with the local crocodile god Sobek and King

area behind the enclosure is little explored, so that further early evidence may have been swept away or lie buried.

The earliest king named in the temple is Ptolemy VI Philometor; most of the decoration was completed by Ptolemy XII Auletes. In the early Roman Period the courtyard was decorated and the outer corridor added. The temple is dedicated to two triads of deities: Sobek, Hathor and Khons; and Haroeris (Horus the elder), Tasenetnofret (the good sister) and Panebtawy (the lord of the two lands). The last two have artificial names, which express the function of the goddess in such a group as a companion, and of the young god to be kingly. Sobek and his triad are the primary deities, as is shown by his occupying the southern part, because south is prior to north in Egyptian ordering schemes.

The birth house, nearest to the river, has lost its western half. It abuts closely on the pylon of the main temple, perhaps because space was short already in antiquity (the rear of the temple is similarly cramped against the enclosure wall). The pylon has a double gateway, which is the first sign of a complex plan, in which there is an axis for each main gateway and an unusually large number of intermediate rooms, culminating in two sanctuaries. From the first hypostyle hall runs a corridor which

Haremhab himself among them. Numerous rock-cut "shrines" (chambers), functioning as cenotaphs, were made south of the Speos by kings (Sethos I, Ramesses II, Merneptah) as well as high officials, particularly those of the 18th Dynasty.

The rock faces on both sides of the river abound in rock stelae and graffiti.

Edfu

The site of Edfu, near the river and raised above the broad valley around, is an ideal position for settlement, since it is safe from the inundation but not isolated near the desert. The Ptolemaic temple was part of a larger area extending to the east and south under the modern town, which must have balanced the extensive remains to the west. The western side has an inner and outer enclosure wall, which date to the Old Kingdom. A later wall runs outside the outer one, and may be of the 1st Intermediate Period. Within the walls and on top of them are remains of the Old Kingdom and Greco-Roman town site. The later wall overlaps an area of late Old Kingdom and 1st Intermediate Period tombs, which extends further to the west. These include quite large mastabas, and there are also scattered finds of stelae, statues and offering tables from the 2nd Intermediate Period and New Kingdom.

Only the base of the pylon of a temple of Ramesses III is preserved. It is oriented, conventionally, towards the Nile, and must have been part of a much smaller structure than its successor. The later temple alludes to this forerunner by aligning a gateway in its first court with that between the two massifs of the earlier pylon. It forms a complex with a small gateway to the south and, just south of the gate, the birth house, at right angles to the main temple. The temple is the most completely preserved in Egypt, and its form is archetypal. The building inscriptions, written in horizontal bands in the outer areas, give numerous details of construction. Building began in 237 (Ptolemy III Euergetes I). The inner part was finished in 212 (Ptolemy IV Philopator) and decorated by 142 (Ptolemy VIII Euergetes II). The outer hypostyle was built separately, being completed in 124 (Ptolemy VIII Euergetes II). Decoration of this and of the other outer parts was finished in 57. Mostly work continued regardless of the political situation, but it was suspended for more than 20 years during disturbances in Upper Egypt under Ptolemy IV and Ptolemy V Epiphanes.

The unusual orientation of the temple towards the south may be due to the nature of the site. Behind the pylon the courtyard, the only large one preserved, has columns with paired capitals of distinctive forms, as in other buildings of the

period, which give variety to otherwise uniform shapes. Gates lead behind the temple into an area bounded by the stone enclosure wall, which is a continuation of the outer wall of the courtyard. The scenes and inscriptions here and on the outer face of the enclosure wall include a list of donations of land to the temple, probably transferred from a demotic original, a narrative of its mythical foundation, and a grandiose set of reliefs with a "dramatic" text of a ritual in which Horus defeated his enemy Seth.

A striking feature of the inner part of the temple is the subtle exploitation of light – or of darkness. Some rooms are completely dark, while elsewhere the light comes from the openings between the columns of the hypostyle hall and from apertures in the roof or at the angle between the roof and a wall. The general progress is from light to dark, with the sanctuary receiving illumination only from the axis. The effect of all this must have been incomparably richer when the reliefs retained their original colors.

The monolithic naos of highly polished syenite in the sanctuary will have contained a wooden shrine with the cult image of the god – probably about 60

Top Aerial view from the north, taken in 1932. Both the temple's domination of the site and much of the town mound can be clearly seen. The monumental reliefs on the outside walls convey their message even at this distance.

Above Set of column capitals in the forecourt. Two are composite forms, one with multiple papyrus umbels (?) and the other the shape of a single umbel with stem decoration. The palm frond capital is an ancient type with solar associations, but is also aquatic, since date palms often grow by pools. The architraves contain solar scenes.

Right View east across the hypostyle hall at Edfu. The height and close spacing of the columns restrict the feeling of space; the result reflects the room's marsh or thicket symbolism. The columns have plant forms at the bottom, and several bands of emblematic motifs above and below central offering scenes.

cm high and made of wood, overlaid with gold and semiprecious stones – inside it. It is the oldest object in the temple, dating to Nectanebo II.

The outer areas of the birth house are much ruined, but the sanctuary and ambulatory are well preserved. In the south ambulatory the reliefs are sheltered from the prevailing north wind. Some of them preserve their color, giving an idea of the effect over large areas of the tones used in this period.

Like the other late temples, Edfu was emptied of its furniture and equipment when it fell out of use. We are fortunate, therefore, to have the pair of colossal statues of hawks flanking the entrance and a single one by the door into the hypostyle hall. A group of over-lifesize statues of naked boys – probably the young god Ihy or Harsomtus – that is now lying in the courtyard must also have formed part of the monumental decoration of the temple, relieving its present austere appearance.

Kom el-Ahmar

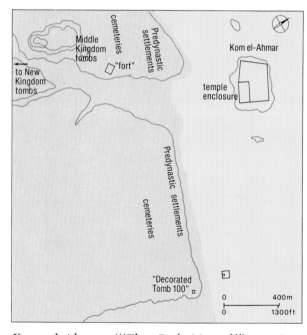

Kom el-Ahmar ("The Red Mound"), ancient *Nekhen*, lies a little over 1 km southwest of the village of el-Muissat, on the west bank of the Nile. *Nekhen* played an important part in Egyptian mythology: together with *Nekheb* (el-Kab) on the opposite bank, it represented the Upper Egyptian counterpart of the twin towns *Pe* and *Dep* (modern Tell el-Fara'in) in the delta. The jackal-headed figures known as "The Souls of *Nekhen*" might be personifications of the early rulers of *Nekhen*. The chief god of the town was a falcon with two tall plumes on its head (*Nekheny*, "The Nekhenite"), assimilated very early with Horus ("Horus the Nekhenite"), and the town's Greek name,

Hierakonpolis, acknowledged this fact. *Nekhen* was the early center of the 3rd Upper Egyptian nome. During the New Kingdom it was replaced in this role by el-Kab, and belonged to the territory administered by the viceroy of Kush.

Extensive remains of Predynastic settlements and cemeteries are discernible for some 3 km along the edge of the desert to the south and southwest of el-Muissat, and are particularly dense east of the wadi opposite which Kom el-Ahmar is situated. A brick-built structure of uncertain purpose ("The Fort"), probably Early Dynastic, stands some 500 m into the wadi. The famous "Decorated Tomb 100" was found in the easternmost part of the settlement/cemetery area at the end of the last century, but is now lost. This brick-built underground tomb of a modest size (4·5 by 2 by 1·5 m) had its west wall decorated with a remarkable painting showing boats, animals and men. It probably belonged to one of the local chiefs of the late Predynastic Period, and is important as an indicator of the growing social stratification of Egyptian society, as well as a document showing the conventions and motifs of Egyptian art in process of formation.

At the beginning of the 1st Dynasty the irregularly shaped town enclosure known as Kom el-Ahmar replaced the earlier settlement on the edge of the desert. In its south corner, occupying about

Above Small ivory and faience votive statuettes of the Early Dynastic Period, from the "Main Deposit" of the temple at Kom el-Ahmar. Oxford, Ashmolean Museum.

Left Seated lion, pottery with a shiny red slip, probably of the 3rd Dynasty. Several features of this sculpture are unusual, in particular the schematic treatment of the ears and the mane falling down on the chest of the animal like a bib in imitation of a headcloth. Height: 42·5 cm. Found in the temple. Oxford, Ashmolean Museum.

Limestone ceremonial mace head of king "Scorpion" (from the sign of a scorpion near the face of the king), perhaps identical with Naʿrmer. The main scene of the relief decoration shows a temple-founding ceremony with the king digging the first trench. Height: 25 cm. From the "Main Deposit." Oxford, Ashmolean Museum.

one sixth of the total area, was the temple complex. This was partially uncovered during the principal excavations at Hierakonpolis carried out in 1897–99. The excavators, J. E. Quibell and F. W. Green, faced great technical difficulties, for which Egyptian archaeology was not yet properly equipped. In its earliest form the brick-built temple apparently contained a mound of sand revetted with stones, perhaps the prototype of the hieroglyphic sign ⓞ with which the name of *Nekhen* was written. King Naʿrmer was the main benefactor, together with Khaʿsekhem/Khaʿsekhemwy. At some later point, many of the votive objects which had been presented to the temple were brought together and deposited in a cache (the so-called "Main Deposit"). It is not clear when and why this took place: it could have been caused by a rebuilding of the temple or by the uncertainty of the times. Many

of the objects in the "Main Deposit" (palettes, mace heads, stone vessels, carved ivory figures, etc.) date to the two Early Dynastic kings already mentioned, though a later date has been proposed for some uninscribed pieces. Monuments of practically all later periods have been found in the temple, but they are not very numerous or spectacular. Only those of the 6th Dynasty form an exception (two large copper statues representing Pepy I and Merenreʿ, a granite stela showing a king Pepy in the company of Horus and Hathor, a statue base of Pepy II, possibly also the head of a gold falcon image); there may have been alterations to the structure at that time.

Decorated and inscribed rock-cut tombs ranging from the 6th to the 18th Dynasties have been found in the wadi of the "Fort" and its subsidiary branches.

el-Kab

The earliest traces of man's activities in the area of el-Kab go back to about 6000 BC: the so-called Kabian is a microlithic industry which predates the known Neolithic cultures of Upper Egypt. Ancient *Nekheb*, on the east bank of the Nile, and *Nekhen* (Kom el-Ahmar), on the opposite side of the river, were very important settlements in the Predynastic and Early Dynastic Periods. This was reflected in the elevation of Nekhbet, the vulture goddess of *Nekheb*, to the status of the tutelary goddess of Egyptian kings (together with the cobra goddess Wadjit of Lower Egypt). Nekhbet was regarded as the Upper Egyptian goddess *par excellence*. Also known as "The White One of Nekhen," she was one of the deities who assisted at royal and divine births, and so was equated with the Greek Eileithyia

in the Greco-Roman Period, when the town was called Eileithyiaspolis. At least from the beginning of the 18th Dynasty *Nekheb* served as the capital of the 3rd Upper Egyptian nome, though it later relinquished this role in favor of Esna.

The view of el-Kab's town enclosure, measuring about 550 by 550 m and surrounded by massive brick-built walls, is most impressive. The enclosure contains the main temple of Nekhbet with several subsidiary structures, including a birth house, as well as smaller temples, a sacred lake and some early cemeteries.

It is likely that modest temple structures were erected at el-Kab as early as the Early Dynastic Period. This is suggested by the presence of a granite block bearing the name of Kha'sekhemwy. During the Middle Kingdom Nebhepetre' Mentuhotpe, Sebekhotpe III (*sed*-festival chapel) and Neferhotep III (Sekhemre'-s'ankhtawy) paid attention to the site. Major building activities in the temple of Nekhbet started in the 18th Dynasty. Almost all the kings of the period contributed in smaller or larger measure, but Tuthmosis III and Amenophis II seem to have been the most prominent among them. After the interlude of the 'Amarna Period the Ramessids continued to honor Nekhbet by adding to her temple. Taharqa of the 25th Dynasty, Psammetichus I of the 26th Dynasty and Darius I of the 27th Dynasty are also attested, but the shape in which the now much-dilapidated temple presented itself to archaeologists was mainly due to the kings of the 29th and 30th Dynasties (Hakoris and Nectanebo I and II).

Left One of the desert temples at el-Kab, the Ptolemaic rock-cut sanctuary of the goddess Shesmetet, seen from the south.

"At a Place called *Caab* . . . we discover'd something that look'd like a Piece of Antiquity . . . we came to the Remains of an antient Temple, consisting of Six Pillars in Two Rows, with their Roofs intire. A little to the North of these are the fragments of many other broken Pillars, and considerable other Ruins, and curiously wrought with Hieroglyphics, &c." (C. Perry, *A View of the Levant*, 1743, p. 361, describing the columns of the hypostyle hall of Hakoris in the temple of Nekhbet).

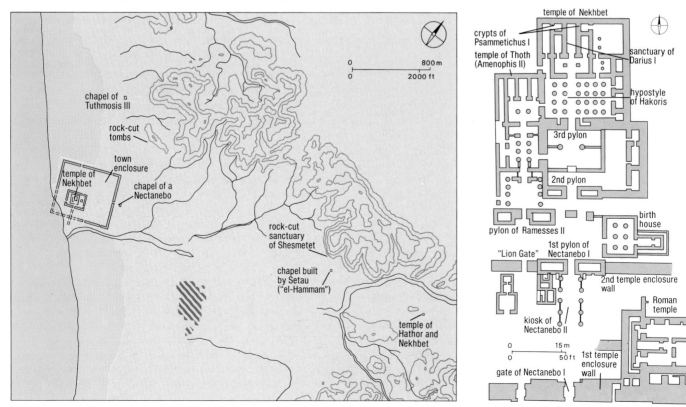

Temple of Khnum at Kom el-Deir,
northwest of Esna, now
destroyed; engraving made by
Napoleon's expedition of
1798–1800.

Facade of the temple of Khnum at
Esna; 1st century AD. The side
doorways into the hypostyle hall
have important mythological
texts, and were the normal
entrances for priests.

There are rock-cut tombs, mainly of the first half of the 18th Dynasty, but also of the Middle Kingdom and the Ramessid Period, some 400 m north of the town enclosure. Two of them, those of ʿAhmose Pennekhbet (No. 2) and of ʿAhmose, son of Ebana (No. 5), are renowned for their biographical texts. The capture of the Hyksos capital Avaris, the siege of Sharuhen in Palestine by King ʿAhmose, and Syrian and Nubian campaigns of the kings of the early 18th Dynasty are among the historical events mentioned in them. Another tomb, of the mayor of *Nekheb*, Pahery, is remarkable for its reliefs. There is a decorated tomb which probably dates to Ptolemy III Euergetes I northwest of the others, nearer the river.

Esna

Esna, ancient Egyptian *Iunyt* or *(Ta)senet*, was called in Greek Latopolis, after the *Lates* fish, which was held sacred there and buried in a cemetery west of the town. In the same area there are human burials of the Middle Kingdom to Late Period.

The temple of Esna is about 200 m from the river, in the middle of the modern town. Because of the accumulation of occupation debris and silt, it is now about 9 m below street level. The ceremonial way, which probably linked the quay with the temple, has disappeared. The quay has cartouches of Marcus Aurelius, and is still in use. Texts in the temple relate it to four others in the area, three to the north and one on the east bank, all of which have now disappeared completely, although parts of them were still visible in the 19th century. Recently another temple of the same period has been excavated at Kom Mer, 12 km to the south.

The temple is dedicated to Khnum with several other deities, of whom the most prominent are Neith and Heka, whose name means "magical power," and who is here a child deity. As it stands, it consists only of a completely preserved hypostyle hall, whose west wall formed the beginning of the inner temple. This wall is earlier than the rest, with reliefs of Ptolemy VI Philometor and VIII Euergetes II. The rest of the hypostyle is the latest major temple preserved, and is decorated inside and out with reliefs from the 1st to 3rd centuries AD. Some scenes, notably that of gods and the king netting birds, are most imposing.

The most significant feature of the decoration is the series of texts written on the columns. These give a full and rich picture of some of the festivals of the sacred year at Esna, which is set out in schematic form in a calendar, also inscribed on a column. There is in addition a remarkable pair of crypto-graphic hymns to Khnum, one written almost entirely with hieroglyphs of rams, and one written with crocodiles.

Two chapels, now destroyed, used to stand outside the enclosure. The first, about 750 m northwest of it, was built by Tuthmosis III; the other, outside the northeast enclosure wall, was the work of one of the Nectanebos. Some 2·2 km northeast of the enclosure, at the entrance to Wadi Hellal, there is the first of the so-called "desert temples," the partly free-standing and partly rock-cut sanctuary of the goddess Shesmetet (Smithis). It was built chiefly by Ptolemy VIII Euergetes II and Ptolemy IX Soter II. About 70 m southeast of it is the well-preserved chapel (known as "el-Hammam") built by the viceroy of Kush Setau during the reign of Ramesses II, and restored under the Ptolemies. It was probably dedicated to Reʿ-Harakhty, Hathor, Amun, Nekhbet and Ramesses II himself. Further away, about 3·4 km from the town enclosure, Tuthmosis IV and Amenophis III built a temple for Hathor "Mistress of the Entrance to the Valley" and Nekhbet.

el-Mo'alla

Two rock-cut decorated tombs of the beginning of the 1st Intermediate Period, belonging to 'Ankhtifi and Sebekhotpe, are the most important monuments at el-Mo'alla (probably to be equated with ancient Egyptian *Hefat*). Apart from its unconventional paintings, the tomb of 'Ankhtifi contains interesting biographical texts which describe the situation in the southern nomes following the end of the Old Kingdom.

Gebelein

The name of the locality means the same in Arabic as in ancient Egyptian: "The Two Hills." It derives from the most conspicuous landmark visible on the west bank of the Nile at the point where the 3rd and 4th Upper Egyptian nomes meet.

Tombs, mainly of the 1st Intermediate Period, were found on the west hill, while a temple of Hathor (hence the Greek name of the locality, Pathyris, from *Per-Hathor*, "The Domain of Hathor," or Aphroditopolis) stood on the east hill. The temple seems to have existed as early as the 3rd Dynasty, and reliefs, stelae or inscriptions dating to 'Nebhepetre' Mentuhotpe, several kings of the 13th (Djedneferre' Dedumose II, Djed'ankhre' Mentuemzaf and Sekhemre'-s'ankhtawy Neferhotep III) and 15th (Khian and 'Awoserre' Apophis) Dynasties

Far left top Tomb of 'Ankhtifi at el-Mo'alla: the deceased spearing fish from a papyrus boat. The figures of his wife and daughters standing behind him were destroyed by tomb robbers in recent years. Painting. 1st Intermediate Period.

Above and far left below Tomb of Iti at Gebelein. Three kneeling nude youths, perhaps engaged in gymnastics, and a scene of transport and storing grain in granaries. Painting. 1st Intermediate Period. Turin, Museo Egizio.

Left The Ptolemaic temple at Tod.

Black granite statue of the herald Sebekemsauf, the brother-in-law of one of the kings of the 2nd Intermediate Period. The sculpture, seen by John Gardner Wilkinson at Armant in the first half of the last century, is now in the Kunsthistorisches Museum in Vienna, but its base with the feet (on this photograph a cast) is in the National Museum of Ireland in Dublin. Height: 1·50 m.

have also been discovered. The temple still functioned in the Greco-Roman Period, and a number of demotic and Greek papyri have been found in the area. The town was situated in the plain below the east hill.

Tod

Apparently already in the reign of Userkaf of the 5th Dynasty there stood a brick-built chapel at ancient Egyptian *Djerty* (Tuphium of the Greco-Roman Period), on the east bank of the Nile. Major building activities connected with the local cult of the god Montu started in the Middle Kingdom, during the reigns of Nebhepetre' Mentuhotpe, S'ankhkare' Mentuhotpe and Senwosret I, but their temples are now destroyed. In the New Kingdom, Tuthmosis III erected a shrine, still partly preserved, for the bark of Montu, and Amenophis II, Sethos I, Amenmesse and Ramesses III and IV carried out some restoration work in it. Ptolemy VIII Euergetes II added his temple with a sacred lake in front of the temple of Senwosret I, and a Roman Period kiosk was located nearby.

Armant

Ancient *Iuny*, on the west bank of the Nile in the 4th Upper Egyptian nome, was one of the most important places of worship of the war god Montu, and until the beginning of the 18th Dynasty the capital of the whole nome, including Thebes. The modern name Armant derives from *Iunu-Montu*, Coptic *Ermont*, Greek Hermonthis.

A temple dedicated to Montu existed at Armant as early as the 11th Dynasty, the rulers of which perhaps originated there, and Nebhepetre' Mentuhotpe is the earliest builder known with certainty. Important additions were made during the 12th Dynasty and the New Kingdom, of which the remains of the pylon of Tuthmosis III are the only part still visible. The temple was destroyed some time during the Late Period, and its history can be traced only through reused or isolated blocks. In the reign of Nectanebo II a new temple was probably started, and the work was continued by the Ptolemies. The most important contribution to the appearance of the site was made by Cleopatra VII Philopator and Ptolemy XV Caesarion, who built a birth house with a lake. The building still existed in the first half of the last century, but is now completely destroyed. Two gates, one of them erected by Antoninus Pius, have also been found. The Bucheum (from ancient Egyptian *bekh*), the burial place of the sacred Buchis bulls of Armant, is located on the desert edge north of Armant. The earliest burial dates to Nectanebo II, and the Bucheum was in use for some 650 years, until the reign of Diocletian. The burial place of the "Mother of Buchis" cows has also been located. There are extensive cemeteries of all dates in the neighborhood of Armant.

THEBES

Ancient Egyptian *Waset* was called Thebai by the Greeks, but we are at a loss when searching for a reason for this. It has been suggested that the pronunciation of the Egyptian names *Ta-ipet* (*Ipet-resyt* was the Luxor temple) or *Djeme* (Medinet Habu) sounded similar to that of their Boeotian city, but the argument lacks conviction.

Waset was in the 4th Upper Egyptian nome, deep in the south. Its geographical position contributed greatly to the town's importance in history: it was close to Nubia and the eastern desert with their valuable mineral resources and trade routes, and distant from the restricting power centers in the north. Theban local rulers of the earlier part of Egyptian history pursued active expansionist policies, particularly during the 1st and 2nd Intermediate Periods; in the latter this was disguised as an Egyptian reaction against foreign invaders (the Hyksos). Monuments earlier than the end of the Old Kingdom are scarce, and *Waset* was little more than a provincial town. Its rise to prominence occurred during the 11th Dynasty; although the capital was moved to Itjtawy at the beginning of the 12th Dynasty, Thebes with its god Amun was established as the administrative center

of southern Upper Egypt. The peak came during the 18th Dynasty when the town acted as the capital of the country. Its temples were the most important and the wealthiest in the land, and the tombs prepared for the elite among its inhabitants on the west bank were the most luxurious Egypt ever saw. Even when in the later 18th Dynasty and during the Ramessid Period the residence and the center of royal activities moved to the north (el-ʿAmarna, Memphis and Pi-Riʿamsese), Theban temples continued to flourish, monarchs were still buried in the Valley of the Kings and the town retained some importance in the administrative life of the country. During the 3rd Intermediate Period Thebes, with the High Priest of Amun at its head, formed a counterbalance to the realm of the 21st- and 22nd-Dynasty kings, who ruled from Tanis in the delta. Theban influence ended only in the Late Period.

The main, and probably the earliest, part of the town and the principal temples were on the east bank. Across the river, on the west bank, was the necropolis with tombs and mortuary temples, but also the west part of the town; Amenophis III had his palace at el-Malqata, and in the Ramessid Period Thebes itself centered north of it, at Medinet Habu.

"The Pyramids, the Catacombs, and some other Things to be seen in Lower Egypt, are look'd upon as great Wonders; and are justly held in Preference to whatever the rest of the World can boast of. But if these challenge the Pre-eminence to all the extra Egyptian World, on the one hand, they must yield the Glory of Superiority to the many ancient Temples, &c. of Saaide [Upper Egypt] on the other" (C. Perry, *A View of the Levant*, 1743, Preface).

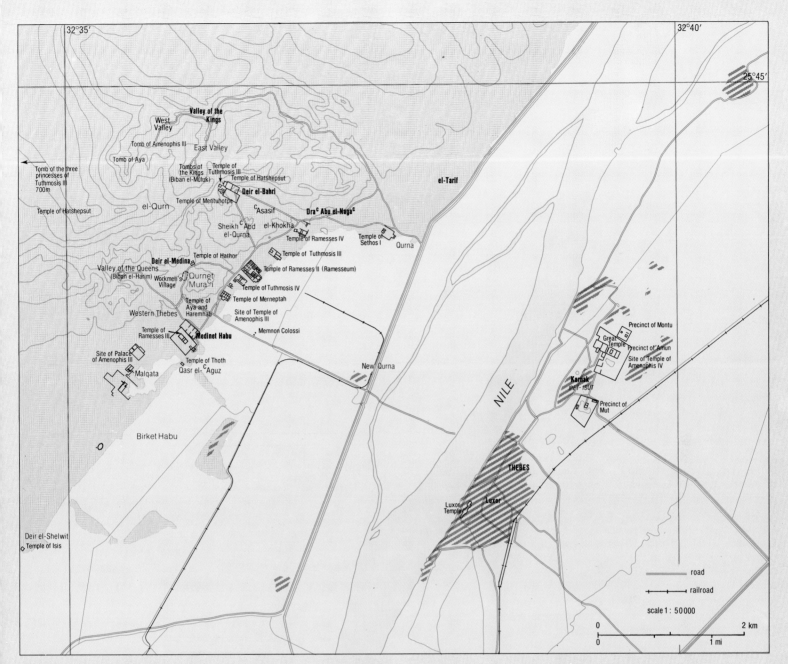

West Valley

Valley of the Kings

Tomb of Amenophis III

East Valley

Tomb of Aya

Tomb of the three princesses of Tuthmosis III 700m

el-Qurn

Temple of Hatshepsut

Tombs of the Kings (Biban el-Muluk)

Temple of Tuthmosis III

Temple of Hatshepsut

Deir el-Bahri

Temple of Mentuhotpe

ᶜAsasif

Draᶜ Abu el-Nagaᶜ

el-Tarif

Sheikh ᶜAbd el-Qurna

el-Khokha

Temple of Ramesses IV

Temple of Sethos I

Qurna

Temple of Hathor

Temple of Tuthmosis III

Deir el-Medina

Valley of the Queens (Biban el-Harim)

Workmen's Village

Qurnet Muraᶜi

Temple of Ramesses II (Ramesseum)

Temple of Tuthmosis IV

Temple of Aya and Haremhab

Temple of Merneptah

Western Thebes

Site of Temple of Amenophis III

Memnon Colossi

Temple of Ramesses III

Medinet Habu

New Qurna

Site of Palace of Amenophis III

Malqata

Temple of Thoth

Qasr el-ᶜAguz

Precinct of Montu

Great Temple

Precinct of Amun

Site of Temple of Amenophis IV

Karnak
IPET-ISUT

Precinct of Mut

NILE

Birket Habu

THEBES

Deir el-Shelwit

Temple of Isis

Luxor Temple

Luxor

road

railroad

scale 1 : 50 000

0   2 km

0   1 mi

32°35′   32°40′   25°45′

Luxor
Temple of Amun, chiefly of Amenophis III, Ramesses II and Alexander the Great.
Karnak
Precincts of Amun, Montu and Mut, with temple of Khons and numerous smaller temples and chapels, 12th Dynasty to Greco-Roman Period.
The West Bank: Temples
Deir el-Bahri: mortuary temples of Nebhepetreʿ Mentuhotpe and Hatshepsut, and temple of Amun by Tuthmosis III.
Ramesseum: mortuary temple of Ramesses II.
Medinet Habu: temple of Amun of the 18th Dynasty and later, and mortuary temple of Ramesses III.
Other mortuary temples, particularly those of Sethos I at Qurna and Amenophis III with "Memnon Colossi."

Royal Tombs
el-Tarif: 11th Dynasty.
Draʿ Abu el-Nagaʿ: 17th Dynasty.
Valley of the Kings: 18th to 20th Dynasties, including tomb of Tutʿankhamun.
Deir el-Medina: workmen's village.
Private Tombs
Tombs dating from the 6th Dynasty to Greco-Roman Period.

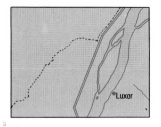

Luxor

Textual and archaeological evidence indicates that a sanctuary stood on the site of the Luxor temple or in its vicinity at the beginning of the 18th Dynasty, or even earlier, but the temple we see today was built essentially by two kings, Amenophis III (the inner part) and Ramesses II (the outer part). Several other rulers contributed to its relief decoration and inscriptions, added minor structures or made alterations, chiefly Tut'ankhamun, Haremhab and Alexander the Great. An earlier shrine of the Theban triad was incorporated into the court of Ramesses II. The overall length of the temple between the pylon and the rear wall is nearly 260 m.

The temple was dedicated to Amun (Amenemope) who at Luxor took the form of the ithyphallic Min. It was closely connected with the Great Temple of Amun at Karnak, and once a year, during the second and third months of the inundation season, a long religious festival was held at Luxor during which the image of Amun of Karnak visited his *Ipet-resyt*, ''Southern *Ipet*,'' as the temple was called.

At the end of the reign of the Roman Emperor Diocletian, just after 300 AD, the first of the antechambers in the inner part of the temple was converted into a sanctuary of the imperial cult serving the local military garrison and town. The standards and insignia of the legion were kept there. It was decorated with exquisite paintings which were still visible in the 19th century but are now almost completely lost. A small mosque of Abu el-Haggag was built in the court of Ramesses II in the Ayyubid Period (13th century AD), and still stands there.

An *alley of human-headed sphinxes of Nectanebo I* linked Karnak, some 3 km to the north, with Luxor, and brought the visitor to a *brick-built enclosure wall*. Several later structures stood in the forecourt which preceded the temple itself, including a colonnade of Shabaka (later dismantled) and chapels of Hathor, built by Taharqa, and of Sarapis, built by Hadrian. The burned brick walls visible to the east and west of the temple are remains of the late Roman town, contemporary with the imperial sanctuary.

The temple is fronted by a *pylon of Ramesses II*, with reliefs and texts on its outside relating the

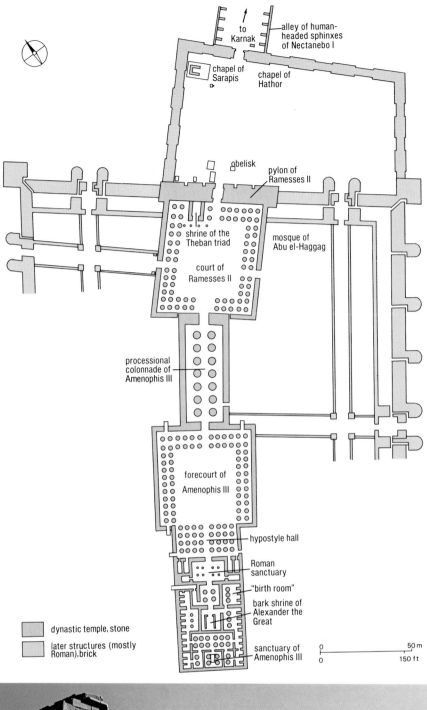

dynastic temple, stone

later structures (mostly Roman), brick

story of the famous battle against the Hittites at Qadesh in Syria in 1285 BC. Two red granite obelisks originally stood in front of the pylon but only one, approximately 25 m high, remains now: the other was removed to the Place de la Concorde in Paris in 1835–36. Several colossal statues of Ramesses II, two of them seated, flank the entrance. The central gateway of the pylon was partly decorated by Shabaka.

The *peristyle court of Ramesses II* which opens behind the pylon has 74 papyrus columns with scenes of the king before various deities. The columns are arranged in a double row around its sides, and are interrupted by a shrine consisting of three chapels (or bark stations) of Amun (center), Mut (left) and Khons (right), built by Hatshepsut and Tuthmosis III and redecorated by Ramesses II. It was the existence of this shrine which probably caused the considerable deviation of the axis of the buildings of Ramesses II from that of the earlier temple of Amenophis III. Colossal standing statues of the king are placed in the gaps between the front row of columns at the south end of the court.

The entrance to the *processional colonnade of Amenophis III*, with seven columns on either side, has two seated colossi of Ramesses II with Queen Nefertari by his right leg on the north side, while two seated double statues of Amun and Mut are on the south side. The walls behind the columns were decorated by Tut'ankhamun and Haremhab with reliefs depicting the Festival of Opet: those on the west wall show a procession of barks from Karnak to Luxor, while the eastern wall shows their homeward journey.

A *peristyle forecourt of Amenophis III* is fused with the *hypostyle hall*, which is the first room in the inner, originally roofed, part of the temple. This leads to a series of *four antechambers* with subsidiary rooms. The so-called "Birth Room," east of the second antechamber, is decorated with reliefs showing the symbolic "divine birth" of Amenophis III resulting from the union of his mother Mutemwia and the god Amun. Alexander the Great built a bark shrine in the third of the antechambers. The *sanctuary of Amenophis III* is the last room on the central axis of the temple.

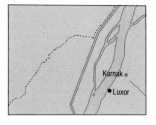

Karnak

The name Karnak, from that of a modern village nearby (el-Karnak), is used to describe a vast conglomeration of ruined temples, chapels and other buildings of various dates, measuring some 1·5 by at least 0·8 km. This was ancient Egyptian *Ipet-isut*, "The Most Select of Places," the main place of worship of the Theban triad with the god Amun at its head, and also the home of various "guest" deities. No site in Egypt makes a more over-whelming and lasting impression than this apparent chaos of walls, obelisks, columns, statues, stelae and decorated blocks. After the Theban kings and the god Amun came to prominence at the beginning of the Middle Kingdom, and particularly from the beginning of the 18th Dynasty, when the capital of Egypt was firmly established in Thebes, the temples of Karnak were built, enlarged, pulled down, added to and restored for more than 2,000 years. The temple of Amun was ideologically and economically the most important temple establishment in the whole of Egypt.

The site can conveniently be divided into three groups, which are defined geographically by the remains of brick-built walls enclosing the temple precincts. The largest and most important is the central enclosure, the temple of Amun proper. It is also the best preserved. The northern enclosure belongs to Montu, the original local god of the Theban area, while the enclosure of Mut lies to the south and is connected with Amun's precinct by an alley of ram-headed sphinxes. An avenue bordered by sphinxes linked Karnak with the Luxor temple, and canals connected the temples of Amun and Montu with the Nile.

The precinct of Amun

The trapezoidal central enclosure contains the Great Temple of Amun, built along two axes (east–west and north–south), a number of smaller temples and chapels and a sacred lake. East of the enclosure stood a now completely destroyed temple of Amenophis IV (Akhenaten), built on a huge scale, as well as two minor Ptolemaic structures, now also destroyed. Remains of some of the earliest buildings at Karnak, dating to Senwosret I, were discovered still *in situ* in the east part of the Great Temple, in the so-called Central Court behind Pylon VI.

The layout of the Great Temple can be described as consisting of a series of pylons of various dates, with courts or halls between them, leading to the main sanctuary. The earliest are Pylons IV and V, built by Tuthmosis I; from then on the temple was enlarged by building in a westerly and in a southerly direction.

Pylon I is preceded by a quay (probably reconstructed in its present form during the 25th Dynasty), and an avenue of ram-headed sphinxes

protecting the king, most of which bear the name of the high priest of Amun, Pinudjem I of the 21st Dynasty. South of the avenue there are several smaller structures, including a bark shrine of Psammuthis and Hakoris, and parapets of the 25th–26th Dynasties with texts connected with the ceremony of refilling the jars of the Theban triad. The date of the pylon itself is not quite certain: it is probably of the 30th Dynasty. The forecourt which opens behind it contains a triple bark shrine of Sethos I consisting of three contiguous chapels dedicated to Amun, Mut and Khons. In the center of the forecourt there are remains of a kiosk of unusual construction of Taharqa, with one of its columns standing. A small temple (bark station) of Ramesses III faces into the forecourt from the south.

Pylon II, probably a work of Haremhab, who reused a large number of earlier blocks to build it, is preceded by colossal statues of Ramesses II,

Top Ram-headed sphinxes ("crio-sphinxes") outside Pylon I. The ram was the sacred animal of Amun; the motif of an animal, bird or serpent "protecting" a king or even a private individual was common in Egyptian two- and three-dimensional sculpture.

Above left Headless statue of Sethos II kneeling with an offering table, now restored and set up north of the 4th column on the north side of the central aisle of the hypostyle hall.

Above The rear part of the Great Temple of Amun from the east.

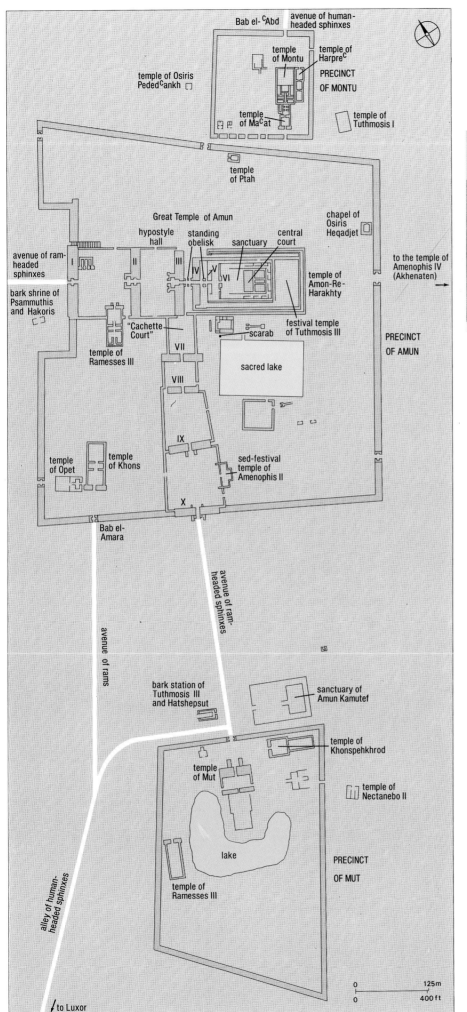

The small temple of Ramesses III between Pylons I and II: Osirid pillars on the west side of the court seen from the temple entrance. Reliefs on the sides of the pillars show the king before various gods.

including one (on the north) showing him with Princess Bent'anta. Behind the pylon, the now lost roof of the hypostyle hall, the most impressive part of the whole temple complex, was borne by 134 papyrus columns, of which the 12 in the central aisle are larger and have capitals of a different type. The relief decoration of the hypostyle hall is the work of Sethos I and Ramesses II. The exterior walls depict military campaigns of these kings in Palestine and Syria, including Ramesses II's battle at Qadesh.

Pylon III was built by Amenophis III, but the porch in front of it was decorated by Sethos I and Ramesses II. Numerous blocks from earlier buildings were found reused in the pylon: a *sed*-festival shrine of Senwosret I (the "White Chapel," now reerected to the north of the hypostyle hall), shrines of Amenophis I and II, Hatshepsut (the "Red Chapel," so called for its material, red quartzite) and Tuthmosis IV, and a pillared portico of the same king. The four obelisks which stood behind the pylon were erected by Tuthmosis I and III to mark the entrance to the original temple; only one obelisk of Tuthmosis I is still standing.

Between *Pylons IV and V*, both of Tuthmosis I, there is the earliest part of the temple still preserved, with 14 papyrus columns, originally gilded, and two obelisks of Hatshepsut (one standing, one fallen).

Pylon VI and the court which precedes it were built by Tuthmosis III. Behind them is a vestibule with two magnificent granite pillars with the emblems of Upper and Lower Egypt, both still standing. The bark shrine (sanctuary) dates to Philip Arrhidaeus and stands on the site of an earlier shrine built by Tuthmosis III.

Behind the Central Court is the Festival Temple of Tuthmosis III. One room in the temple is known as the "Botanical Garden," because of its representations of exotic plants, birds and animals.

Another four pylons were added along a new axis which extended the Great Temple of Amun in a southerly direction. The court north of Pylon VII is known as the "Cachette Court": it was here that a deposit of thousands of statues which originally stood in the temple was found at the beginning of this century. Remains of earlier buildings were also

found in this court, including pillars of Senwosret I and several chapels of Amenophis I. *Pylons VII and VIII* were built by Tuthmosis III, and the court between them contains his bark station.

Pylons IX and X are due to Haremhab. Many "talatat," blocks from buildings of Amenophis IV (Akhenaten), mostly dating before his move to el-ʿAmarna, were found reused in these pylons. A *sed*-festival temple of Amenophis II stands in the court between them.

Near the northwest corner of the temple's sacred lake there is a colossal statue of the sacred scarab beetle, dating to Amenophis III.

The temple of Khons stands in the southwest corner of the enclosure. Its propylon (a gate in the enclosure wall), built by Ptolemy III Euergetes I and known as the Bab el-ʿAmara, is approached from the south by an avenue of rams protecting Amenophis III. The pylon was decorated by Pinudjem I, the forecourt by Herihor, and the inner part by various Ramessids (at least part of the temple was built by Ramesses III); there is also some Ptolemaic relief work.

The temple of the hippopotamus goddess Opet, close to the last, was chiefly built by Ptolemy VIII Euergetes II. The decoration was completed by several later rulers, including Augustus. There is a symbolic "Crypt of Osiris" below the sanctuary at the back of the temple.

Nearly 20 other small chapels and temples are within the precinct of Amun, including a temple of Ptah built by Tuthmosis III, Shabaka, the Ptolemies and Tiberius (north of the Great Temple, close to the enclosure wall), and a chapel of Osiris Heqadjet "Ruler of Time" of Osorkon IV and Shebitku (northeast of the Great Temple, close to the enclosure wall).

The precinct of Montu

The square-shaped northern enclosure is the smallest of the three precincts. It contains the main temple of Montu, several smaller structures (particularly the temples of Harpreʿ and Maʿat) and a sacred lake. In 1970 an early temple of Montu, built by Tuthmosis I, was found outside the east enclosure wall.

The temple of Montu is fronted by a quay and an avenue of human-headed sphinxes which approaches the temple from the north. The propylon, known as Bab el-ʿAbd, was built by Ptolemy III Euergetes I and IV Philopator, and the temple by Amenophis III, but later kings, particularly Taharqa, carried out some modifications of the original plan.

The precinct of Mut

The southern enclosure contains the temple of Mut, surrounded by a crescent-shaped lake, and subsidiary structures, particularly the temple of Khonspekhrod, originally of the 18th Dynasty, and a temple of Ramesses III.

The temple of Mut was built by Amenophis III, but here too the propylon in the enclosure wall is Ptolemaic (Ptolemy II Philadelphus and III Euergetes I), and there are later additions to the temple by Taharqa and Nectanebo I among others. Amenophis III dedicated hundreds of black granite statues of the lioness goddess Sakhmet to the temple. Some of these can still be seen at Karnak.

Far left Ramesses II returning home from an expedition to Palestine, driving before him the captured "chiefs of Retjenu": bottom register on the south outside wall of the hypostyle hall, close to Pylon II.

Right A princess, perhaps Bentʿanta, standing between the feet of a colossal statue of her father Ramesses II (with added cartouches of Ramesses VI and the High Priest of Amun Pinudjem I of the 21st Dynasty). Restored and reerected before Pylon II of the Great Temple of Amun, on the north side of the entrance.

Below Countless private individuals had statues of themselves set up in the temples of Karnak. The main function of these sculptures was similar to that of votive stelae: to perpetuate the donor's presence in the temple in order for him to benefit from being by the side of the god.

Left The Chief Steward Senenmut, a contemporary of Hatshepsut, in his role of the tutor of the princess Nefrureʿ. Black granite. Height: 53 cm. Chicago, Field Museum of Natural History.

Below The Third Prophet of Montu, Pakhelkhons, kneels with a naos containing a statuette of Osiris. Black granite. Height: 42 cm. 3rd Intermediate Period. Baltimore (Md.), Walters Art Gallery.

"The Northernmost, said to be the statue of *Memnon*, is cover'd with a great Number of *Greek* and *Latin* Inscriptions; being so many testimonies of Persons who pretend to have heard it utter a Sound at Sun-rise" (C. Perry, *A View of the Levant*, 1743, p. 348).

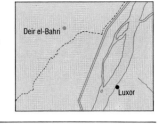

The West Bank

The temples

Across the Nile from the temples of Karnak and Luxor, the remains of temples occupy a stretch of some $7\frac{1}{2}$ km. Most of these were royal mortuary temples of the New Kingdom, and their main function was to maintain the cult of the deceased kings buried in their tombs cut in the cliffs further to the west, though gods also were worshiped there, particularly Amun and Re'-Harakhty. The most important of these temples are those of Deir el-Bahri, the Ramesseum and Medinet Habu. The mortuary temple of Sethos I stands at Qurna, while only huge seated statues, the "Memnon Colossi," and other fragmentary sculptures now mark the site of the temple of Amenophis III. Several of the temples on the west bank were not mortuary, such as the temples of Hathor (Deir el-Medina), Thoth (Qasr el-'Aguz) and Isis (Deir el-Shelwit), all of the Greco-Roman Period.

Deir el-Bahri
Deir el-Bahri, the place traditionally connected with the local cult of the cow goddess Hathor, almost directly opposite Karnak, was chosen by Nebhepetre' Mentuhotpe of the 11th Dynasty and Queen Hatshepsut of the 18th Dynasty for the site of their mortuary temples (in the case of Mentuhotpe the temple was directly connected with the burial, while Hatshepsut had two tombs prepared for her, one in a remote valley behind, the Wadi Sikket Taqet Zaid, the other in the Valley of the Kings). Shortly after the completion of Hatshepsut's temple, Tuthmosis III built a temple complex for the god Amun (*Djeser-akhet*) and a chapel for Hathor between the two earlier structures, and a kiosk (*Djeser-menu*) in the court of Mentuhotpe's temple.
The mortuary temple of Nebhepetre' Mentuhotpe (Akh-isut). Although the basic idea must have already been present in the minds of the

95

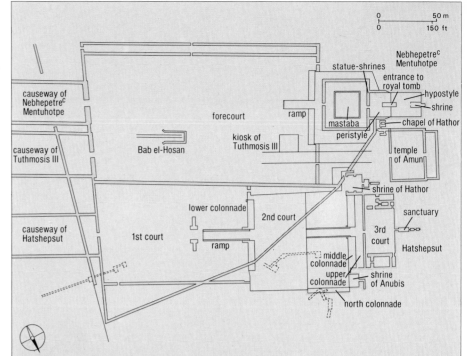

architects of the pyramid complexes of the Old Kingdom, a design which consciously placed different parts of a temple on terraces of varying height was not attempted in Egypt until Nebhepetreʿ Mentuhotpe built his temple at Deir el-Bahri. Another new element introduced there, the colonnade (portico) at the back of the terrace, may have derived from the appearance of the *saff*-tombs of the earlier kings of the 11th Dynasty.

The front, free-standing, part of the temple is approached by a 46-m-wide causeway from the now lost valley temple, and consists of a forecourt, enclosed by walls on its three sides, and a terrace with a now much-ruined mastaba-shaped structure, probably associated with the cult of the sun god. In the east part of the forecourt is the opening known as "Bab el-Hosan," which is connected by a long underground passage with a probably symbolic royal tomb, left unfinished. The west part of the forecourt originally contained a grove of tamarisk and sycamore trees on either side of an ascending ramp leading on to the terrace. Behind the colonnade at the west end of the forecourt and another on the terrace, were reliefs showing boat processions, foreign campaigns, hunting scenes etc.; of these a large number of small fragments are preserved in various museums. The mastaba, which was the dominant feature of the temple, is surrounded by a pillared ambulatory on all sides. In its west wall there are six statue-shrines (and, further west, tombs) of royal ladies of the reign of Nebhepetreʿ (from the north: Myt, ʿAshayt, Zadeh, Kawit, Kemsyt and Henhenet).

The inner part of the temple, cut into the cliff, consists of peristyle and hypostyle courts east and west of the entrance to an underground passage which after some 150 m leads to the tomb proper. Little of the royal burial and funerary equipment was found. The rock-cut shrine at the back of the inner part of the building was the main cult place of the deceased king in the temple.

The mortuary temple of Hatshepsut (*Djeser-djeseru*). The temple is a partly rock-cut and partly free-standing terraced structure. Its builders took up and developed the remarkable architectural ideas of its 550-year-old predecessor to the north of

which it stands. Even now, in its incompletely preserved state, the temple conveys a unique harmony between man's creation and the natural environment. The effect of its original appearance, with trees, flowerbeds and numerous sphinxes and statues, must have been even more overwhelming. The temple was built between years 7 and 22 of the reign of Hatshepsut and Tuthmosis III, and a number of high officials of the state were involved in its construction, including the influential "Chief Steward of Amun" Senenmut.

The valley temple of the complex is attested by its foundation deposits, but the building itself has disappeared, at least partly as a result of the proximity of the later temple of Ramesses IV. The monumental causeway, some 37 m wide, lined by sphinxes and provided with a bark chapel, led on to a series of three courts at different levels, approached by ramps and separated by colonnades (porticoes) protecting the now famous reliefs. These show huge barges specially constructed to bring obelisks from Aswan for the temple of Amun at Karnak (the lower colonnade), scenes of the divine birth and coronation of Hatshepsut (the north half

Top left Soldiers taking part in a boat procession: relief on the north wall of the hypostyle hall of the shrine of Hathor, in the south part of Hatshepsut's temple.

Above The temples at Deir el-Bahri from the cliff to the north.

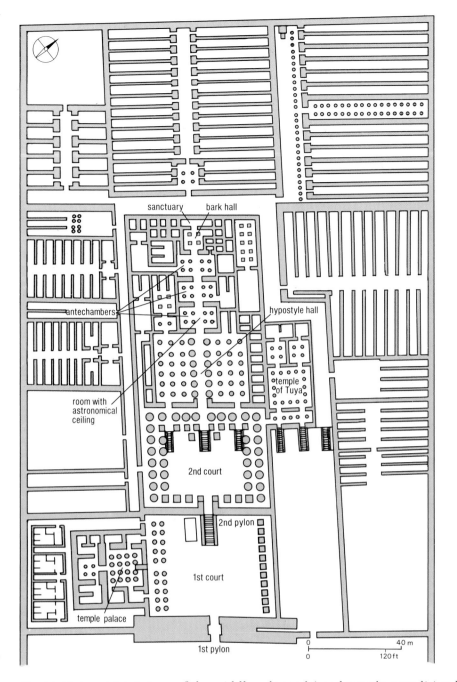

sanctuary   bark hall

antechambers

room with
astronomical
ceiling

hypostyle hall

temple
of Tuya

2nd court

2nd pylon

1st court

temple palace

1st pylon

0   40 m
0   120 ft

Top right The hypostyle hall of the Ramesseum from the southwest.

Above right The east wall of the hypostyle hall of the Ramesseum, south of the entrance, bottom register: detail of relief showing the assault on the fort of Dapur, ''the town which His Majesty sacked in the land of Amor,'' in year 8 of the reign of Ramesses II. The exact location of this northern Syrian town, perhaps in the region of Aleppo, is not known.

of the middle colonnade) and a trade expedition by sea to the exotic African land of Punt (the south half of the middle colonnade). The upper colonnade, formed by Osirid pillars flanked by colossal statues of the queen, preceded the upper court. Vaulted rooms on the north and south sides of this court were dedicated to Hatshepsut and her father Tuthmosis I, and the gods Reʿ-Harakhty and Amun. Theirs were the main cults maintained in the temple. A series of niches at the back (the west side) of the hall contained statues of the queen, and an entrance in the same wall led to the sanctuary proper. The innermost room of the present sanctuary was cut by Ptolemy VIII Euergetes II; otherwise, the temple's architecture is remarkably free from later interference. Special shrines of Anubis and Hathor were approached from the second court.

The mortuary temple of Ramesses II (*Khnemt-waset*) or Ramesseum

The mortuary complex of Ramesses II, somewhat misleadingly described by Diodorus as ''the tomb of Osymandyas'' (from Usermaʿatreʿ, part of the praenomen of Ramesses II), nowadays known as the Ramesseum, consists of the temple proper and the surrounding brick-built magazines and other buildings (the tomb of Ramesses II is in the Valley of the Kings).

The interior disposition of the stone-built temple is fairly orthodox, though somewhat more elaborate than usual: two courts, a hypostyle hall, a series of antechambers and subsidiary rooms, the bark hall and the sanctuary. The temple's overall plan is, unusually, a parallelogram rather than a rectangle. This was probably caused by retaining the orientation of an earlier small temple, dedicated to Tuya, the mother of Ramesses II, while making the pylons face the temple of Luxor on the east bank. Tuya's temple is north of the hypostyle hall of the Ramesseum.

The 1st and 2nd pylons of the Ramesseum are decorated with reliefs depicting, among other things, the battle of Qadesh (also known from Karnak, Luxor, Abydos and Abu Simbel). Two granite colossi of Ramesses II originally stood before a platform preceding the hypostyle hall: the upper part of the southern statue is now in the British Museum, but the head of the companion piece can still be seen in the Ramesseum. The first room behind the hypostyle hall has an astronomical ceiling and might have served as the temple's library. The usual temple palace stood south of the first court.

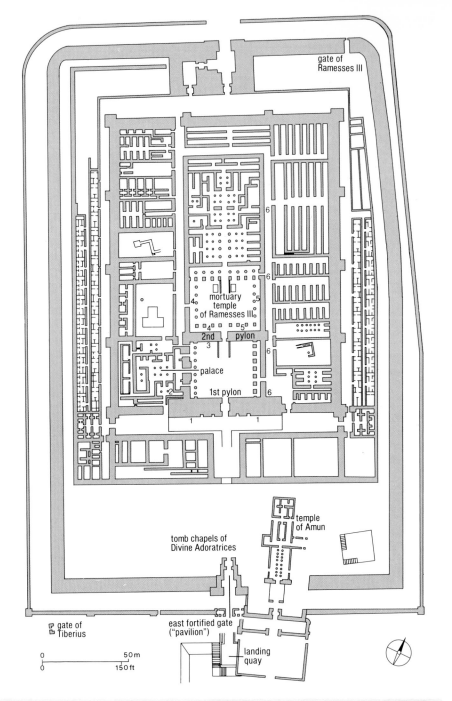

1 Ramesses III
smiting captives

2 Ramesses III
hunting

3 Ramesses III
presents captives
to Amun and Mut

4 festival of Sokar
and Libyan war

5 festivals of
Min and Amun

6 campaigns against
the Libyans, Asiatics
and the "sea peoples"

Medinet Habu

Situated opposite Luxor, ancient Egyptian *Tjamet* (or *Djamet*), Coptic *Djeme* (or *Djemi*), was one of the earliest places in the Theban area to be associated closely with Amun. Hatshepsut and Tuthmosis III built a temple for him there. Next to it, Ramesses III erected his mortuary temple, and enclosed both structures within massive brick-built walls. There were magazines, workshops, administrative buildings and dwellings of priests and officials within its enclosure walls. Medinet Habu became the focus of the administrative and economic life of the whole of Thebes, and performed this role for the next several hundred years. Even tombs and tomb chapels started being built there, in particular those of the Divine Adoratrices of the 25th and 26th Dynasties. The site continued to be inhabited well into the Middle Ages (9th century AD).

The temple of Amun (*Djeser-iset*). The original temple, built by Hatshepsut and Tuthmosis III, underwent many alterations and enlargements in the course of the following 1,500 years, mainly during Dynasties 20 (Ramesses III), 25 (Shabaka and Taharqa), 26, 29 (Hakoris), 30 (Nectanebo I) and the Greco-Roman Period (Ptolemy VIII Euergetes II, X Alexander I and Antoninus Pius). These considerably extended its plan by adding a columned hall, two pylons, and a court at the front.

The mortuary temple of Ramesses III (*Khnemt-neheh*). The temple used to be connected with the Nile by a canal, a feature of some importance since boat processions played an important part in religious festivals, and a landing quay was built outside the enclosure. The entrance to the temple enclosure was through one of the two fortified gates in the east and west; only the former, sometimes called the "Pavilion," now remains.

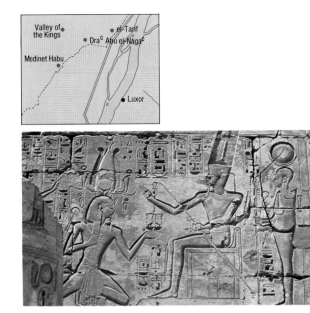

The temple itself is of orthodox design, and resembles closely the mortuary temple of Ramesses II (the Ramesseum), which it probably consciously imitates. South of the 1st court stood the brick-built palace, now badly damaged, which was used by the king during religious festivals held at Medinet Habu. Two building phases of the structure have been recognized. The palace's interior walls were originally decorated with exquisite faience tiles, similar to those known from contemporary palaces in the delta (Tell el-Yahudiya and Qantir). The "window of appearances" connected the palace with the temple.

Some of the reliefs at Medinet Habu are not only artistically but also historically important, because they record historical events of the reign of Ramesses III:

1st pylon: On the outside, the king is shown smiting foreign captives in front of Amun and Re'-Harakhty in symbolic scenes of triumph. The subjugated foreign lands and towns are represented by their names inscribed in rings that have human heads. Hunting scenes are on the short outside west face of the south massif.

2nd pylon: On the outside (east face) of the south massif, the king presents captives to Amun and Mut. On the inside, and also on the south and north walls of the 2nd court, are representations of the festivals of Sokar and Min.

The exterior of the temple: Campaigns against the Libyans, Asiatics and the "sea peoples" are shown on the north wall.

There are more strictly religious scenes on the walls of the rooms of the inner part of the temple.

Royal tombs

el-Tarif
The ambitious rulers of the early Theban 11th Dynasty, vying with the northern Herakleopolitan (9th/10th) Dynasty for supremacy over Egypt, built their tombs at el-Tarif, in river terms the northernmost part of the Theban necropolis. Although the tombs are comparable in type to contemporary provincial tombs elsewhere, their majestic size and truly monumental architecture connect them with the mortuary temple and tomb of the king who finally gained control over the whole of Egypt, Nebhepetre' Mentuhotpe, at Deir el-Bahri.

The tombs consist of an open excavation running into the rock which forms a huge court (as much as 300 m long and 60 m wide). At the back of the court a series of door-like openings creates the impression of a pillared facade. This gave the tombs the name *saff*-tombs (from *saff*, "row" in Arabic). The fairly modest burial chamber and other rooms are cut in the rock behind the facade, and a brick-built valley temple completes the complex. Little of the decoration of the tombs is preserved.

Three *saff*-tombs are known:
Inyotef I (Horus Sehertawy): Saff el-Dawaba
Inyotef II (Horus Wah'ankh): Saff el-Kisasiya
Inyotef III (Horus Nakhtnebtepnufer): Saff el-Baqar.

Dra' Abu el-Naga'
Theban rulers of the 17th Dynasty and their families were buried in modest tombs at Dra' Abu el-Naga', between el-Tarif and Deir el-Bahri. The relative position of these tombs and their ownership are known from a papyrus recording an inspection of them in about 1080 BC (the Abbott Papyrus). A number of inscribed objects, including the so-called *rishi*-coffins, decorated weapons and jewelry, were found during excavations conducted by Mariette before 1860. The architecture of the tombs, which may have had small brick-built pyramids, is little known.

The Valley of the Kings ("Biban el-Muluk")
After the defeat of the Hyksos the Theban rulers of the 18th Dynasty began to build themselves tombs in a style befitting kings of all Egypt. The tomb of Amenophis I was probably at Dra' Abu el-Naga'. Its position is not known for certain, but the esteem in which the king was held by the community of specialized workmen engaged in making royal tombs suggests that his was the earliest tomb of the new type. Tuthmosis I was the first to have his tomb cut in the cliffs of a desolate valley behind Deir el-Bahri, now known as the Valley of the Kings. The area is dominated by the peak of el-Qurn ("the horn"), and the valley consists of two main branches, the East Valley, with most of the tombs, and the West Valley, with the tombs of Amenophis

III and Aya. The total number of tombs is 62 (tomb No. 62 is that of Tutʿankhamun, discovered last), but some of them are not royal tombs, while the ownership of others is still disputed. The tombs were separated from the corresponding mortuary temples, which were built at the edge of cultivation. The motivation for separating temple and tomb was not just security: there were also religious and architectural reasons.

The plan of the royal tombs of the 18th to 20th Dynasties (the last is the tomb of Ramesses XI) in the Valley of the Kings consists of a long inclined rock-cut corridor with one or more halls (sometimes pillared), terminating in the burial chamber. In the earlier tombs the corridor turns right or left, usually at a right angle, after some distance, but from the end of the 18th Dynasty it was straight. Its length could be considerable: Haremhab's is 105 m long, Siptah's 88 m and Ramesses VI's 83 m. The decoration of the tombs is almost exclusively religious. There are numerous scenes of the king in the presence of gods, but the most striking elements are the texts and accompanying illustrations of various religious compositions ("books"), such as the Book of *Amduat* ("that which is in the netherworld"), of Gates, of Caverns, the Litany of Reʿ, and others. Early examples of these texts were made in such a way as to create the impression of huge funerary papyri unrolled on the tomb walls. From the end of the 18th Dynasty the decoration was carved in relief.

It is not easy to imagine the original wealth and beauty of the contents of these royal sepulchers. The only one which has been found largely intact and which provides a tantalizing glimpse of what is lost, that of Tutʿankhamun, may well not be typical.

The workmen's village at Deir el-Medina

The everyday life of the community of workmen ("Servants in the Place of Truth") employed in the

construction of royal tombs in the Valley of the Kings can be reconstructed in considerable detail from ostraca, papyri and other evidence. The ruins of the walled settlement (some 70 houses), in which workmen and their families lived from the reign of Tuthmosis I, can be seen in a small valley behind the hill of Qurnet Muraʿi, at Deir el-Medina. The workmen's own tombs and the chapels of their local gods are nearby.

The "gang" of workmen, numbering some 60 men or more, was divided into two "sides," each with a foreman, his deputy, and one or more scribes. Their superior was the vizier, who occasionally came, or sent one of the royal "butlers," to visit the site and inspect the progress of work. The workmen's wages were paid in goods, mainly grain, received at the end of each month. Other commodities, such as fish and vegetables, and occasionally meat, wine, salt etc., were also supplied. It was symptomatic of the period that during the 20th Dynasty there were times when the rations were overdue, and on several occasions the workmen resorted to demonstrations. The earliest recorded "industrial action" took place in the 29th year of Ramesses III. The workmen normally stayed at the site of the tomb in the Valley of the Kings during the working "week" of 10 days, returning to the village for rest days or for religious festivals which were also holidays.

Valley of the Kings.
Above left Tomb of Haremhab (No. 57): the king offers jars of wine to the hawk-headed Harsiese, "great god, king of the gods, lord of heaven," and stands in adoration before Hathor, "the chieftainess of Thebes, lady of all gods, mistress of heaven" (painted relief on east wall of the room preceding the sarcophagus chamber).

Above Tomb of Tuthmosis III (No. 34): scenes and texts of the 3rd "hour" (division) of the Book of *Amduat* (wall painting in the oval-shaped sarcophagus chamber).

Left Workmen's village at Deir el-Medina.

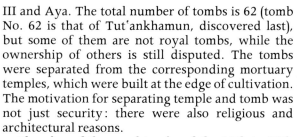

Tut'ankhamun: The Real Untold Story

"At last have made wonderful discovery in Valley; a magnificent tomb with seals intact; re-covered same for your arrival; congratulations" (Cable sent by Carter to Lord Carnarvon on the morning of 6 November 1922).

The tomb of Tut'ankhamun (No. 62 in the Valley of the Kings) was discovered in 1922 by the English Egyptologist Howard Carter, whose work was financed by the Earl of Carnarvon. It is the only royal tomb of the New Kingdom found largely intact, and will probably stay unique in this respect for ever. Although it is the most widely publicized discovery made in Egypt in this century, and despite all the public interest generated by the traveling exhibitions all over the world, the majority of Tut'ankhamun's treasures have not yet been properly evaluated by Egyptologists, so that this exceptional find has not yet made its full contribution to our knowledge of ancient Egypt. Tut'ankhamun's objects are kept in the Egyptian Museum in Cairo; the detailed notes taken by Carter and his collaborators during the years of painstaking clearing of the tomb are in the Griffith Institute in Oxford.

Some of the objects found in the tomb:
Connected with the mummy
four wooden shrines
quartzite sarcophagus
outer and middle wooden coffins
inner gold coffin
gold mask and trappings
gold diadem
gold dagger
canopic canopy
canopic chest
Funerary equipment
statuettes of the king
dismantled chariots
couches and beds
headrests
throne of gilded wood (*right*)
chairs and stools
boxes
vases and lamps
bows, bow cases and shields
sticks, whips and scepters
garments
writing palettes
gaming boards
jewelry
fans
musical instruments
model boats
shrines of wood and gold
statuettes of gods
shawabtis

Far left Tomb of the Vizier Ra'mose at Sheikh 'Abd el-Qurna (No. 55), of the early part of the reign of Amenophis IV. Relief.

Left Coffin base-board of Soter, early 2nd century AD, with a representation of the goddess Nut surrounded by signs of the zodiac. From a communal tomb at Sheikh 'Abd el-Qurna. London, British Museum.

Below Tomb of the God's Father Amenemone at Qurnet Mura'i (No. 277), of the early 19th Dynasty: episode from the funeral of the deceased. Painting.

Private tombs

The larger and more important Theban tombs are concentrated in several areas on the west bank. Starting from the river north, these are: Dra' Abu el-Naga', Deir el-Bahri, el-Khokha, 'Asasif, Sheikh 'Abd el-Qurna, Deir el-Medina and Qurnet Mura'i. Altogether 409 tombs received official numbers of the Egyptian Antiquities Service, but another five have been added recently. The tombs' dates range from the 6th Dynasty to the Greco-Roman Period, but the majority are of the New Kingdom. There are many further tombs, some large and decorated, others little more than simple graves. Perhaps the most important of these are in the Valley of the Queens, south of Deir el-Medina, and in smaller valleys nearby, including the "Tomb of Three Princesses" of the reign of Tuthmosis III in Wadi Qubbanet el-Qirud ("Valley of the Tombs of the Monkeys") with a treasure of gold and silver vessels, now in the Metropolitan Museum in New York.

As one would expect, many of the lesser tombs and burials at el-Tarif and Dra' Abu el-Naga', not included in the official series of Theban tombs, are contemporary with the royal tombs of the 11th and 17th Dynasties, but the latter area in particular continued to be used well into the Late Period. The same applies to the cemeteries of 'Asasif and el-Khokha around the causeways leading to the temples of the 11th and 18th Dynasties at Deir el-Bahri, and to Deir el-Bahri itself.

A number of important caches with group burials have been found. In 1891 E. Grébaut and G. Daressy found a large cache of coffins of "Priests of Amun" of the 3rd Intermediate Period at Deir el-Bahri. It was the second find of this type; already in 1858 Mariette had found a cache of coffins of "Priests of Montu." The most spectacular of these secret hideaways was that found in tomb No. 320, in the first of the valleys south of Deir el-Bahri, in 1881. It contained coffins and mummies of the most renowned Egyptian kings of the 17th to 20th Dynasties, assembled there for security during the 21st Dynasty.

Some of the tombs at Sheikh 'Abd el-Qurna, south of Deir el-Bahri, belonged to the family of the

Below Tomb of Amenemone at Qurnet Mura'i (No. 277), of the early 19th Dynasty: two anthropoid coffins of the deceased set up outside the tomb entrance during the funeral. Painting.

Right Tomb of the Servant in the Place of Truth Pashed at Deir el-Medina (No. 3), of the reign of Sethos I: the painted burial chamber.

celebrated commoner Senenmut of the reign of Hatshepsut. A tomb of the 3rd Intermediate Period (known as the "Prince of Wales Tomb"), with some 30 coffins (though this cache was probably at least partly set up in modern times, and the coffins brought from elsewhere), and another with 14 coffins, dating to the reign of Hadrian, were also found.

As the name suggests, the Valley of the Queens ("Biban el-Harim") contains tombs of queens and other members of the royal family, particularly those of Ramessid princes.

Most of the larger Theban tombs were rock-cut, and few of them had any free-standing super-structure. Their plans vary greatly; the following are only very general characteristics.

Late Old Kingdom. One or two rooms of an irregular shape, sometimes with pillars. Sloping shafts lead to one or more burial chambers.

Middle Kingdom. The rear wall of an open forecourt forms the facade of the tomb. A long corridor is followed by a chapel connected with the burial chamber by a sloping passage.

New Kingdom. An open forecourt, often with stelae, precedes the facade with a row of pottery "funerary cones" above the doorway. A transverse ("broad") hall, sometimes with stelae on the narrow walls, is followed by a "long" hall on the central axis of the tomb. The sanctuary has a statue niche or a false door. All inner rooms can have pillars. The shaft of the burial chamber is usually cut in the forecourt.

Ramessid tombs at Deir el-Medina combine a completely, or partly, free-standing superstructure (pylon, open court, portico and vaulted chapel with statue niche and brick-built pyramid above) with rock-cut chambers approached by a shaft.

Late Period. Some of these tombs are enormous and their plans very complex. Brick-built pylons and open courts precede a series of underground rooms, usually with pillars, leading to the burial chamber.

Painting is the usual method of decoration of Theban tombs, but relief is not uncommon. The subject matter includes both scenes of everyday life and religious themes, which predominate from the Ramessid Period on.

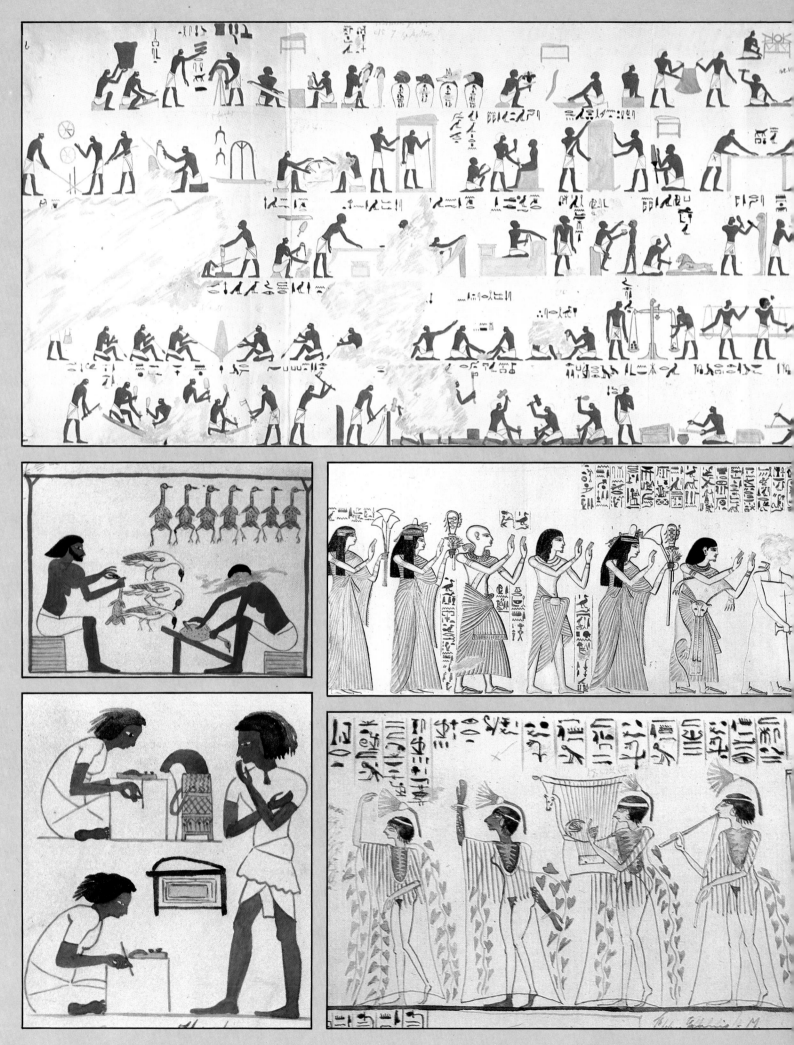

J.G.Wilkinson at Thebes

Modern Egyptologists stand on the shoulders of the scholars who, often under incredibly hard conditions, pioneered the discipline in the first half of the last century. It was a period during which Egyptology was assembling its basic corpus of material for study, a time of intensive recording and copying of Egyptian inscriptions, reliefs and paintings. Some of the works published at that time remain indispensable for a good Egyptological library even now, 150 years later.

John Gardner Wilkinson came to Egypt as a young man of 24 in 1821, a year before Champollion rediscovered the principles of the Egyptian script. For the next 12 years he stayed there continuously, and there was hardly an ancient Egyptian site which the skillful and compulsive copyist did not visit and record in his notebooks. His interest was almost an obsession: no inscription, however small or incomplete, was too insignificant for him. He was one of the first who mastered the conventions of Egyptian representation to such an extent that he was able to produce completely faithful copies. Thanks to this, his papers, now kept in the Griffith Institute in Oxford, contain a wealth of information on the most varied aspects of ancient Egypt. Wilkinson published the theoretical results of his work in a number of books, but not all of his copies; those which appeared in books were often badly disfigured by inadequate reproduction. His most important work was entitled *Manners and Customs of the Ancient Egyptians, including their private life, government, laws, arts, manufactures, religion, agriculture, and early history, derived from a comparison of the paintings, sculptures, and monuments still existing, with the accounts of ancient authors.* It was published in three volumes in 1837, and remained the best general treatment of ancient Egypt for almost 50 years. It brought to its author a

knighthood in 1839, and made him the first British Egyptologist of distinction.

Many a difficult problem has been solved by consulting Wilkinson's copies, because they show monuments as they were between 1821 and 1856 (the date of his last visit to Egypt). His work in Theban private tombs is a case in point: many of the scenes copied by Wilkinson have since been damaged or even completely destroyed, while others, including entire tombs, still await publication or are now inaccessible.

Top Craftsmen at work: relief from Theban Tomb 36 of the Chief Steward of the Divine Adoratrice, Ibi, of the reign of Psammetichus I (the scene partly imitates a relief of the 6th Dynasty at Deir el-Gabrawi). The following crafts are represented (from left): 1st register from top, leather workers making sandals, makers of stone vessels, shawabtis and canopic jars, metal workers; 2nd register, chariot makers, sculptors, joiners and makers of stone vessels; 3rd register, joiners, sculptors, jewelers; 4th register, metal workers, men carrying a wooden plank, boat builders; 5th register, boat builders and scribes. Now badly damaged.

Center left Two bearded men plucking geese: painting in Theban Tomb 88 of the Standard-Bearer of the Lord of the Two Lands, Pehsukher Tjenenu, dated to Tuthmosis III or Amenophis II. The scene takes place in a hut, and the birds

already dealt with are hung from its rafters. There are three other dead geese on the ground. Now damaged, the figure of the man on the left completely lost.

Bottom left Two scribes and an overseer, from a scene of the counting of cattle: painting in Theban Tomb 76 of the Fan-Bearer on the Right of the King Tjenuna, of the reign of Tuthmosis IV. The men are squatting in the typical posture of Egyptian scribes, with their feet tucked under their thighs, holding an unrolled papyrus (writing tables were not used in ancient Egypt). Containers for papyri are placed nearby. Now badly damaged.

Center right The Vizier Paser and his wife, followed by relatives, assist at the purification of offerings by censing and libation: relief in Theban Tomb 106 of Paser, Vizier of Sethos I and Ramesses II. The tomb has not yet been fully published, and

the scene is now almost completely destroyed.

Bottom right A Nubian dancing-girl accompanied by female and male musicians playing the lyre, double flute and harp: painting from Theban Tomb 113 of the Priest, Keeper of Secrets of the Domain of Amun, Keynebu, dated to the reign of Ramesses VIII. This Nubian dance, perhaps called *keskes*, is shown on several other monuments. Apart from the Nubian girl, the participants are Keynebu's sons and daughters; this may indicate the popularity of the dance in the Ramessid Period. Now completely destroyed.

NORTHERN UPPER EGYPT

Northern Upper Egypt extends between Thebes and Asyut. It was the heart of ancient Egypt, the cradle and forge of her earliest dynasties, the hinterland which remained Egyptian in times of crisis and from which, with Thebes at the head, attempts for new political unity were launched. Economically, control of access to the gold and minerals of the eastern desert was always of paramount importance, while politically Thebes in the south dictated the course of events from the 11th Dynasty.

Naqada, Qift and Abydos dominated the scene in the Predynastic and Early Dynastic Periods, with Dendara gaining in importance during the Old Kingdom. Abydos became something of a religious center for the whole country in the Middle Kingdom. The rise of Thebes stifled its northerly neighbors in the New Kingdom, though Abydos held its position, and Qift continued to be favored by royal building activities. The temple of Dendara is easily the most impressive structure of late antiquity in the area.

Left The name of this basalt statuette in the Ashmolean Museum in Oxford, the "MacGregor man," derives from the Revd. William MacGregor, from whom it was acquired at Sotheby's in 1922. The well-known collector had bought it, together with a group of ivory figurines, from a dealer. All the objects were claimed to have been found at Naqada, a site which produced large numbers of Predynastic and Early Dynastic artefacts. Most books on Egyptian art start with this magnificent piece, although recently its authenticity has been questioned on stylistic grounds. Height: 39 cm. Predynastic Period.

Far left Typical landscape of limestone cliffs west of the Nile near Nag' Hammadi, with a very narrow flat strip by the river. A geologist can read the history of the ice ages off the layering and terracing of the cliffs.

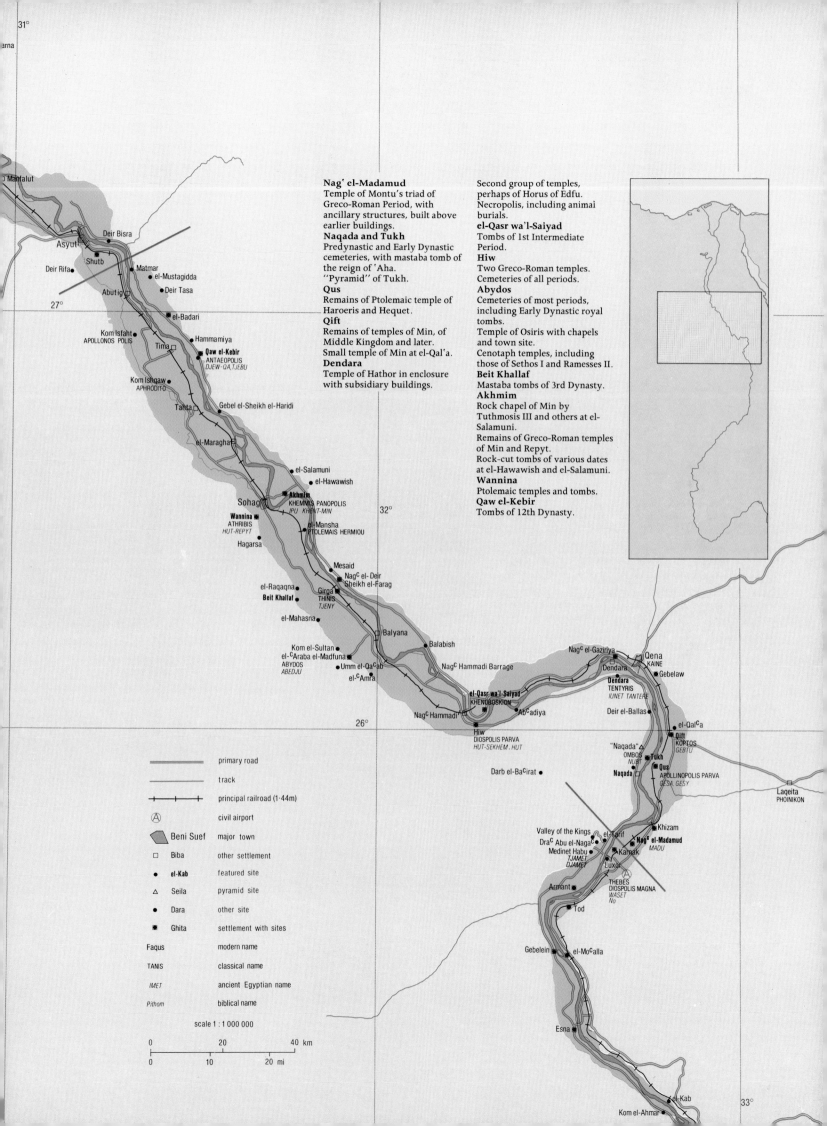

Nag' el-Madamud
Temple of Montu's triad of Greco-Roman Period, with ancillary structures, built above earlier buildings.

Naqada and Tukh
Predynastic and Early Dynastic cemeteries, with mastaba tomb of the reign of 'Aha.
"Pyramid" of Tukh.

Qus
Remains of Ptolemaic temple of Haroeris and Hequet.

Qift
Remains of temples of Min, of Middle Kingdom and later.
Small temple of Min at el-Qal'a.

Dendara
Temple of Hathor in enclosure with subsidiary buildings.

Second group of temples, perhaps of Horus of Edfu.
Necropolis, including animal burials.

el-Qasr wa'l-Saiyad
Tombs of 1st Intermediate Period.

Hiw
Two Greco-Roman temples.
Cemeteries of all periods.

Abydos
Cemeteries of most periods, including Early Dynastic royal tombs.
Temple of Osiris with chapels and town site.
Cenotaph temples, including those of Sethos I and Ramesses II.

Beit Khallaf
Mastaba tombs of 3rd Dynasty.

Akhmim
Rock chapel of Min by Tuthmosis III and others at el-Salamuni.
Remains of Greco-Roman temples of Min and Repyt.
Rock-cut tombs of various dates at el-Hawawish and el-Salamuni.

Wannina
Ptolemaic temples and tombs.

Qaw el-Kebir
Tombs of 12th Dynasty.

primary road
track
principal railroad (1·44m)
civil airport
Beni Suef major town
Biba other settlement
el-Kab featured site
Seila pyramid site
Dara other site
Ghita settlement with sites
Faqus modern name
TANIS classical name
IMET ancient Egyptian name
Pithom biblical name

scale 1 : 1 000 000

0   20   40 km
0   10   20 mi

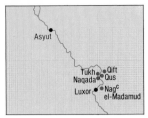

Below left Remains of the outer hypostyle hall of Ptolemy VIII Euergetes II in the temple of Montu at Nag' el-Madamud, seen from the northwest.

Below Lintel of Senwosret III from Nag' el-Madamud: double scene, with the king offering white bread (left) and cake (right) to Montu "Lord of Thebes." Paris, Musée du Louvre.

Nag' el-Madamud

In addition to Karnak, Tod and Armant, ancient Egyptian *Madu*, about 8 km northeast of Luxor, was an important place of worship of the falcon-headed god Montu in the Theban area.

The early temple at Madamud, now destroyed, dated to the Middle Kingdom (perhaps Nebhepetre' Mentuhotpe, mainly Senwosret III), but may have stood on the site of an earlier shrine. Kings of the late Middle Kingdom and the 2nd Intermediate Period continued to build there, particularly Amenemhet VII (Sedjefakare'), Sebekhotpe II (Sekhemre'-khutawy) and Sebekhotpe III (Sekhemre'-swadjtawy) of the 13th Dynasty, and Sebekemzaf I (Sekhemre'-wadjkha'u) of the 17th Dynasty, but none of their buildings has survived. There are also a few scattered monuments of the New Kingdom and the Late Period which indicate that the site was not forsaken at that time.

The temple of Montu, Ra'ttawy and Harpokrates, which is still partly standing, is of the Greco-Roman Period. It was built above the earlier structures, and a number of rulers contributed to its final appearance. A quay and remains of an avenue of sphinxes precede a gate in the brick-built enclosure wall of Tiberius. The facade of the temple itself is formed by three kiosks of Ptolemy XII Auletes, and from there one proceeds through the court of Antoninus Pius. From the outer hypostyle hall of Ptolemy VIII Euergetes II the temple is conventional in plan. Immediately behind is a second temple, dedicated to the sacred bull of Montu. Some of its rooms probably served to accommodate the animal itself. The exterior walls of the temples were decorated by Domitian and Trajan.

There was a sacred lake south of the temple of Montu, and a foundation deposit and blocks show that an early Ptolemaic temple (Ptolemy II Philadelphus, III Euergetes I, and IV Philopator) once stood in the southwest corner of the enclosure.

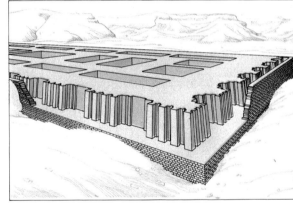

Naqada and Tukh

Archaeologists often use the names of important sites as descriptive terms for whole archaeological cultures. The last two Egyptian Predynastic cultures are usually called Naqada I and II, after the cemeteries excavated by W. M. Flinders Petrie in 1895. In this case the term is something of a misnomer: although Naqada is the largest modern settlement in the area, the cemeteries are in fact about 7 km north of it, between Tukh and el-Ballas.

About 3 km northwest of the village of Naqada, on the edge of the desert, an Early Dynastic mastaba tomb was found by J. de Morgan in 1897. It was a large (54 by 27 m) brick-built structure with a "palace facade" on all sides. Ivory tablets, vase fragments and clay sealings bearing the names of King 'Aha as well as Neithotpe, perhaps his wife and subsequently a queen regnant, were found. The tomb was most probably built for a local administrator of the beginning of the 1st Dynasty. The nearby cemeteries have also produced a number of stelae of the end of the Old Kingdom and the 1st Intermediate Period. The necropolis belonged to the town of Qus, on the east bank of the Nile.

The size of the cemeteries and settlement sites excavated by Petrie ("Naqada") shows that ancient

Above left Reconstruction of the Early Dynastic mastaba found by J. de Morgan at Naqada. The structure was surrounded by an enclosure wall some 1·1 m thick. In the center of the core of the mastaba were five rooms for the burial and equipment, surrounded by a further 16 compartments filled with gravel and sand.

Above Decorated pot of the Naqada I culture. Oxford, Ashmolean Museum.

Senwosret I, holding a *hep* (a ritual object of unknown origin) and an oar, performs a ceremonial *sed*-festival run before the god Min: limestone relief from the earlier structures below the Northern Temple at Qift. London, Petrie Collection (University College).

important town in the early part of Egyptian history. This was probably because at that time it served as the point of departure for expeditions to Wadi Hammamat quarries and the Red Sea. Nowadays only two pylons of the Ptolemaic temple of Haroeris and Heqet remain.

Qift

The town of *Gebtu* (Coptic *Kebto* or *Keft*, Greek Koptos [not connected with the word "Coptic"]), modern Qift, was the capital of the 5th Upper Egyptian nome. The town's prominence was due to its geographical position: it was here (or at Qus, a little to the south) that trading expeditions heading for the Red Sea coast and many mining expeditions into the eastern desert left the Nile valley. *Gebtu* soon became the most important religious center of the area, and its local god Min was also regarded as the god of the desert region to the east. Isis and Horus became prominent deities connected with Qift, particularly during the Greco-Roman Period; one of the reasons for this was a reinterpretation of the two falcons of the nome standard as Horus and Min. As one would expect, monuments discovered at Qift span the whole of Egyptian history, though only temple structures of the Late and Greco-Roman Periods were found *in situ*.

Remains of three temple groups surrounded by an enclosure wall were located during the excavations of W. M. Flinders Petrie (1893–94) and R. Weill and A. J. Reinach (1910–11).

The largely undecorated Northern Temple of Min and Isis, which still stands, was the work of an official called Sennuu on behalf of Ptolemy II Philadelphus, with some later additions of Ptolemy IV Philopator, Caligula and Nero (particularly the three pylons). The temple stands on the site of earlier structures of Amenemhet I, Senwosret I and Tuthmosis III, the last ruler being attested by a large number of foundation deposits. Remains of a chapel of Osiris erected by Amasis were found south of the 3rd pylon of the Northern Temple.

The site of the Middle Temple also had a long history: blocks of Senwosret I and a gate of Tuthmosis III with additions made by Osorkon (probably II) were found, and also a set of stelae ("Koptos Decrees"), dating to the 6th and 7th Dynasties, with copies of royal decrees concerning the temple and its personnel. The Middle Temple itself was built by Ptolemy II Philadelphus, with minor additions by Caligula, Claudius and Trajan.

Gates of Nectanebo II, Caligula and Claudius, and a chapel of Cleopatra VII Philopator and Ptolemy XV Caesarion were found at the site of the Southern Temple.

Claudius built a small temple (approximately 24 by 16 m) dedicated to Min, Isis and Horus northeast of Qift, at el-Qal'a.

Above Red granite colossal head of a Roman emperor, probably Caracalla, found at the 2nd pylon of the Northern Temple of Min and Isis at Qift. Height: 51 cm. Philadelphia (Pa.), Pennsylvania University Museum.

Below Qus at the time of Napoleon's expedition to Egypt: the west pylon of the temple of Haroeris and Heqet and the modern town.

Nubt (Greek Ombos), usually connected with modern Tukh, some 4 km to the southeast, must have been a very important town in the later Predynastic Period. The name probably derives from ancient Egyptian *nub*, "gold," on account of the proximity of gold mines in the eastern desert accessible from the Wadi Hammamat, and this could also explain the town's rise to prominence. The local god was Seth (*Nubty*, "The Ombite"), later regarded as the Upper Egyptian god *par excellence*. So far only a New Kingdom temple dedicated to him has been located. Various kings of the 18th Dynasty (Tuthmosis I and III, Amenophis II) and several Ramessids contributed to it.

A somewhat puzzling monument is the "pyramid" of Tukh. It is built of undressed stone, and its date and even its identification as a pyramid remain in doubt.

Qus

Judging by its cemeteries, Qus, northwest of Naqada, ancient Egyptian *Gesa* or *Gesy* (Apollinopolis Parva of the Greco-Roman Period), on the opposite bank of the Nile, must have been an

Below Dendara: central area of the main temple enclosure.

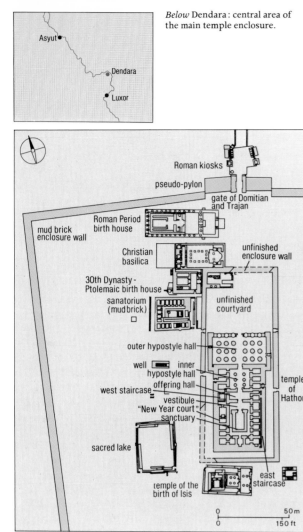

Above Temple of Hathor from the southwest, with reliefs of Ptolemy XV Caesarion and Cleopatra VII Philopator. The mutilated colossal sistrum originally had a wooden canopy. The characteristic lion gargoyles remove rain water from the roof.

Left Gateway of the Roman Period east of the main enclosure. This and a few remaining wall bases formed part of a complex perhaps dedicated to Horus of Edfu.

Dendara

Dendara, ancient Egyptian *Iunet* or *Tantere*, Greek Tentyris, was the capital of the 6th nome of Upper Egypt, and a town of some importance, but since antiquity the center of population in the area has moved to Qena on the east bank. The temple complex now stands isolated on the desert edge.

The necropolis of Dendara included tombs of the Early Dynastic Period, but its most important phase was the end of the Old Kingdom and the 1st Intermediate Period. The provinces were virtually autonomous at that time and, although Dendara was not the most important of the factions of Upper Egypt, its notables built a number of mastabas of some size, only one of which has any decoration apart from stelae and false doors. On the western side of the site are brick-vaulted catacombs of animal burials, primarily of birds and dogs, while cow burials have been found at various points in the necropolis – one of Hathor's forms being as a cow.

A small chapel of Nebhepetre' Mentuhotpe has been recovered from the site and is now reerected in the Cairo Museum. The building, which also has inscriptions of Merneptah, was more for the cult of the king than for the goddess, and was probably ancillary to the main temple of the time.

The temple complex is oriented, as usual, towards the Nile, which here flows east–west, so that the temple faces north, although this was symbolically "east" for the Egyptians. In this description the points of the compass are used.

The monumental gateway of Domitian and Trajan is set in the massive mud-brick enclosure wall, and leads to an open area with the Roman Period birth house on the west. This is the latest preserved temple of its type; it was the ritual location where Hathor gave birth to the young Ihy, who stands for the youthful phase of creator gods in general. The temple was built when the earlier structure, begun by Nectanebo I and decorated early in the Ptolemaic Period, was cut through by the foundations of the first court of the main temple of Hathor (which was never completed). Both birth houses are now accessible; they differ considerably in plan and in decoration.

Immediately south of the earlier birth house is a mud-brick "sanatorium," where visitors could bathe in the sacred waters or "incubate" – spend the night in the hope of having a healing dream of the goddess.

The main temple is the grandest and most elaborately decorated of its period; the massive foundations probably contain many of the blocks of the earlier structure it replaced. Fragments of earlier periods have been found on the site, but no buildings; Pepy I and Tuthmosis III in particular were remembered in the temple inscriptions.

The rear part of the temple was built first, probably at the end of the 2nd century BC. The earliest king named is Ptolemy XII Auletes, but mostly the cartouches are blank, probably because of the struggles in the royal family in the 1st century BC. The outer hypostyle hall was decorated between

Left The Roman hypostyle hall. The pale north light effectively brings out the relief surfaces, on some of which the white background is preserved.

Below Birth house, reign of Trajan: elaborately detailed relief of the king offering to Hathor, who is suckling the young Ihy, with a second Ihy behind.

the reigns of Augustus and Nero, and has a dedicatory inscription in Greek of 35 AD.

The temple follows the classic plan. The columns of the two hypostyle halls and the "new year court" have capitals in the form of a sistrum, a musical instrument sacred to Hathor. Their use evokes the image of Hathor as a cow appearing between the plants in the marsh of creation. There was also a relief of a sistrum at the center of the south outside wall, which was gilded, both to show its importance and to evoke Hathor, the "gold of the gods." All sistrum figures were severely mutilated in the early Christian Period.

Within the temple the most unusual parts are the decorated "crypts." These are suites of rooms on three stories, set in the thickness of the outside wall. Their main use was for storing cult equipment, archives and magical emblems for the temple's protection. Their decoration conforms to the temple's axis, and the most important reliefs, among which sistra are again prominent, were on the axis itself. Also within the thickness of the wall are the staircases, which lead up to and return from the roof. On the roof is a kiosk, in which the ritual of the goddess's union with the sun disk was performed. There is also a pair of shrines of Osiris, from one of which came the famous Dendara zodiac, now in the Louvre in Paris. Dendara was one of Osiris' many tombs, and the shrines, which have no direct link with Hathor, were used to celebrate his resurrection. His death may have been reenacted in the sacred lake to the west of the temple.

Immediately south of the Hathor temple is the temple of the birth of Isis, decorated under Augustus, and using foundation blocks from a destroyed Ptolemaic building. The east gateway of the enclosure, also Roman in date, leads to this temple, which is unique in having a dual orientation, in which the outer rooms face east and the inner ones north towards the temple of Hathor. The central scene of Isis' birth has been mutilated.

East of the temple lay part of the town, with a temple of Horus of Edfu in its midst. This may be the same as some temple remains of the Roman Period about 500 m from the main enclosure.

The triads of deities worshiped at Edfu and at Dendara were very similar, consisting of Horus, Hathor (or Isis) and Ihy or Harsomtus. Hathor of Dendara and Horus of Edfu met at a sacred marriage ceremony, when she made a progress to the south.

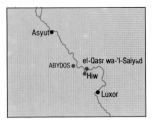

el-Qasr wa-'l-Saiyad

The rock-cut tombs near the modern village el-Qasr wa-'l-Saiyad, northeast of Hiw, on the right bank of the Nile in the 7th Upper Egyptian nome, date to the beginning of the 1st Intermediate Period. Only two of them, of the "Great Overlords of the Nome" Idu Seneni and Tjauti, deserve special attention because of their preserved relief decoration.

Hiw

During the reign of Senwosret I, a royal estate named "Kheperkare' [Senwosret I] the Justified is Mighty" was founded on the west bank of the Nile in the 7th Upper Egyptian nome. The locality soon became more important than the original nome capital, and its long-winded name started being abbreviated to *Hut-sekhem* or *Hut. Hut-sekhem* was reinterpreted as "The Mansion of the Sistrum," an allusion to the local goddess Bat worshiped in the form of a sistrum-shaped object with human head and bovine ears and horns. However, already during the New Kingdom the goddess Bat was completely assimilated to Hathor of the neighboring Dendara. In the Greco-Roman Period Hiw was known as Diospolis Mikra or Diospolis Parva. The Coptic version of the name, *Ho* (or *Hou*), led to the name by which the place is known nowadays.

Despite the fact that they are mentioned in Egyptian texts (e.g. Papyrus Harris I, recording a temple donation in the reign of Ramesses III), no pharaonic temples have yet been discovered at Hiw. The only two existing structures date to the Greco-Roman Period: one was probably built by Ptolemy VI Philometor, the other by Nerva and Hadrian.

About 1·5 km south of the temples, there used to be a Ptolemaic tomb of a certain Harsiese Dionysius. It is now destroyed but, fortunately, some of the early Egyptologists (Wilkinson, Nestor l'Hôte,

Burton, Hay and others) recorded its texts and relief decoration in the first half of the last century.

East of the town, there are extensive cemeteries of all periods, and burials of sacred animals (dogs, ibises and falcons) of the Greco-Roman Period.

Abydos

Ancient Egyptian *Abedju* (Coptic *Ebot* or *Abot*) was the most important burial ground in the land at the beginning of the Early Dynastic Period, and has produced traces of settlement going back to the Predynastic Naqada I Period. The political importance of the town of Abydos and its relationship with the nome capital *Tjeny* (perhaps modern Girga) is less clear.

The temple of the local necropolis god Khentamentiu ("Foremost of the Westerners," i.e. ruler of the dead) was an important religious center in the first dynasties. During the 5th and 6th Dynasties the god became identified with the originally Lower Egyptian Osiris, and in the Middle Kingdom Abydos was the chief popular religious center of Egypt. The "mysteries of Osiris," during which there was a ritual enactment of the death and resurrection of the god, attracted pilgrims from all over Egypt. Many people wished to share in the ceremonies in the afterlife, as a token of sharing in Osiris' resurrection, and they built small brick cenotaphs and set up stelae in the area between the temple of Osiris and the cemeteries. The cemeteries themselves, which extend for about 1·5 km southwest of Kom el-Sultan as far as the temple of Sethos I, are far more extensive than other local burial grounds. In the Middle Kingdom kings began to build cenotaphs at Abydos, and in the 19th Dynasty this culminated in the temples of Sethos I and Ramesses II. Later Period private tombs at Abydos commonly had brick-built pyramids with a stone pyramidion (capstone).

Burials of dogs or jackals, ibises and falcons, dating to the Late and Greco-Roman Periods, have also been found.

Left Fragments of furniture from the Early Dynastic royal tombs at Abydos. Left: piece of schist of unknown use, carved with extraordinary accuracy and skill. Right: leg of a bed, in the form of a bull's hind leg, with tenon for insertion in the frame and holes for leather lashings; ivory. Oxford, Ashmolean Museum.

Bottom left Baying hippopotamus made of pottery, from an early Naqada II grave at Hiw. Animal sculpture of the Predynastic and Early Dynastic Periods is often superior in quality to human figures of the time. Oxford, Ashmolean Museum.

Below Clapper in the form of a forearm (a common musical instrument), made of bone and inscribed for the Female Servant of the Goddess Heqet, Sithathor. 2nd Intermediate Period. From Hiw. London, British Museum.

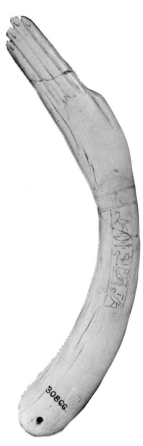

Temple of Sethos I, relief in the king's chapel showing the Iunmutef priest or deity before the mummified king, who is seated on a throne on top of the hieroglyph for "festival." The text is an elaborate version of a censing formula.

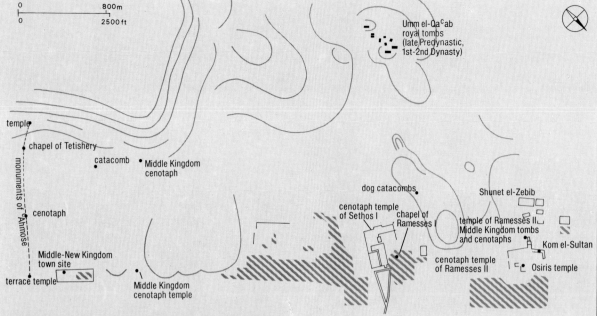

Left Map of the area with ancient remains, stretching along the edge of the cultivation for 5 km. The ancient city, which probably extended on to the floodplain, was concentrated at the northern end, with royal and private funerary monuments towards the south.

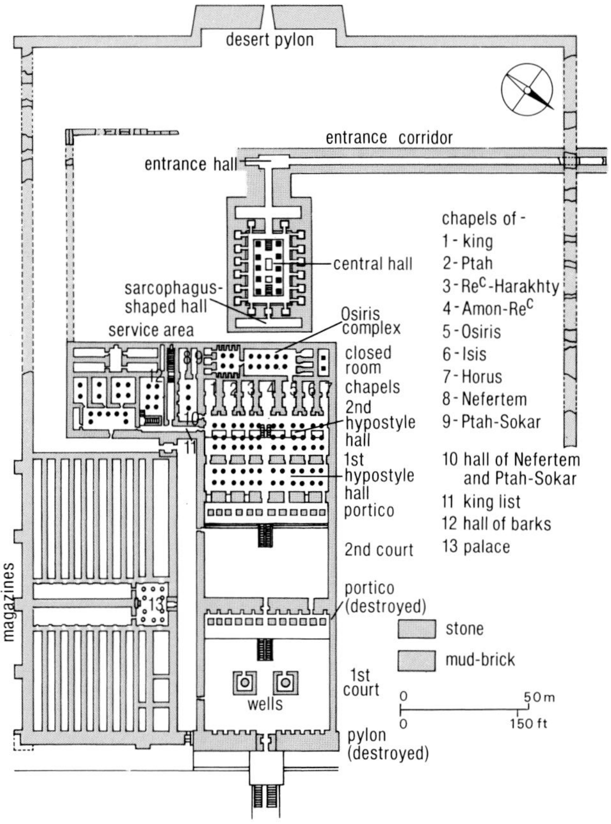

The early royal tombs

In 1895–96 É. Amélineau excavated a series of tombs containing objects with the names of Early Dynastic kings at Umm el-Qaʿab ("Mother of Pots" – so called for the large amount of pottery found in the area). After Amélineau's somewhat unsatisfactory campaigns, W. M. Flinders Petrie reworked the site in 1900–01. Monuments of all the kings of the 1st Dynasty and two of the 2nd Dynasty (Peribsen and Khaʿsekhemwy) were discovered. The superstructures of the tombs had been lost, and only brick-lined pits with rows of subsidiary burials remained. The finds included magnificent stone name stelae of the kings, and small objects such as clay sealings, ivory and ebony labels, parts of stone vessels and fragmentary furniture. The tomb of Djer was later regarded as the tomb of Osiris himself, and was surrounded by votive pottery of the 18th Dynasty and later.

The cemetery went back beyond the beginning of the 1st Dynasty, and may also have been the burial place of the latest Predynastic kings.

There are further Early Dynastic remains near the cultivation, in the area of the temple of Osiris. These consist of cemeteries surrounding bare areas which may have had temporary buildings erected on them for the mortuary ceremonies of particular kings. The Shunet el-Zebib, a massive mud-brick enclosure a little way into the desert, is thought to be a monumental version of one of these areas, possibly the ancestor of the step pyramid enclosure at

Saqqara. A Coptic monastery to the north also seems to be built on foundations of huge Early Dynastic walls.

The town and temple of Osiris

The center of the ancient walled town is the mound called Kom el-Sultan. The most important feature of the town must have been the temple, at first of Khentamentiu and from the 12th Dynasty of Osiris. The temple was built in brick, with only a few elements, such as door jambs and lintels, in stone. This accounts in part for its almost complete destruction. The earliest objects found are of the beginning of the 1st Dynasty: a vase fragment of

Far left Temple of Ramesses II from northwest. Most of the structure is preserved up to about 2 meters. In the foreground is the inner suite of rooms with mortuary scenes; beyond are the two hypostyle halls, with square pillars instead of columns, and the portico. Outside the modern entrance was a further court with a side chapel, and a pylon.

Structural supports are in sandstone, which can span considerable widths, but the relief surfaces are in limestone; the two gateways are of gray granite. Similar composite techniques are found in the temple of Sethos I.

Temple plan labels:

desert pylon

entrance corridor

entrance hall

central hall

sarcophagus-shaped hall

service area

Osiris complex

closed room chapels

2nd hypostyle hall

1st hypostyle hall

portico

2nd court

portico (destroyed)

1st court

wells

pylon (destroyed)

magazines

chapels of –
1 - king
2 - Ptah
3 - Reʿ-Harakhty
4 - Amon-Reʿ
5 - Osiris
6 - Isis
7 - Horus
8 - Nefertem
9 - Ptah-Sokar
10 - hall of Nefertem and Ptah-Sokar
11 - king list
12 - hall of barks
13 - palace

stone

mud-brick

0   50m
0   150 ft

Above Temple of Ramesses II, courtyard; fattened ox with drover, from a procession of festival offerings. The ox is identified as being from the estate of this temple. On the right is another drover and the head of an oryx.

Above right Temple of Ramesses II, 1st hypostyle hall, north wall. Personification of Dendara, from a series carrying food offerings and libations. The figure's fatness symbolizes abundance, and its blue flesh and green wig are part of a patterning scheme, also symbolic. The text identifies him with the king: "Ramesses has come, bringing food offerings" (the right band relates to the next figure). Above is part of a scene with priests carrying a divine bark in procession.

King ʿAha, and a number of small stone and faience figures of men, animals and reptiles. Starting with Khufu of the 4th Dynasty (an ivory statuette, the only preserved likeness of him), almost all kings of the Old Kingdom down to Pepy II are attested among the finds. In the Middle Kingdom Nebhepetreʿ Mentuhotpe probably added a small shrine to the existing temple, and from then on many kings are attested down to the 17th Dynasty. In the 18th Dynasty Amenophis I, Tuthmosis III and Amenophis III did rebuilding work, and all the major Ramessids are represented, Ramesses II by a complete temple nearby, while in the Late Period Apries, Amasis and Nectanebo I feature prominently. The temple probably continued to function well into the Greco-Roman Period. The site of Kom el-Sultan is enclosed by massive mud-brick walls of the 30th Dynasty.

Royal cenotaph temples

The cenotaph temples are secondary mortuary temples of their builders, serving regular deities and the cult of the deceased king as Osiris. Senwosret III is the first king who is known to have built one, some 3 km south of Kom el-Sultan. All the other identifiable buildings in the same area seem to be connected with ʿAhmose, including one he built for his grandmother Tetisheri. Several temples of the 18th Dynasty are known from texts but have not been located.

The temple of Sethos I (the "Memnonium" of Strabo) has a highly unusual L-shaped plan, but its internal arrangements are a variation of the norm. It has two pylons (the outer one almost completely lost) with two courts and pillared porticoes, followed by two hypostyle halls and seven chapels side by side. Moving from the south, the chapels were dedicated to Sethos I, Ptah, Reʿ-Harakhty, Amon-Reʿ, Osiris, Isis and Horus. The Osiris chapel leads into an area devoted to the Osiris cult, running the whole width of the temple, and including two halls and two sets of three chapels for Osiris, Isis and Horus. Its strangest feature is a room with two pillars that was designed to be completely inaccessible. The southern extension of the temple contains rooms for the cult of the Memphite gods Nefertem and Ptah-Sokar and a gallery in which is a magnificent relief of Sethos I and Ramesses II lassoing a bull and, on the other side, one of Egypt's few king lists, here serving the cult of the royal ancestors. The gallery leads to a set of storerooms. In front of this extension is a brick-built palace with storerooms that was probably used when the king visited during festivals.

The reliefs in the inner parts of the temple, which were completed by Sethos I, are exceptionally fine. The outer areas, including the first hypostyle hall, were completed by Ramesses II, in some instances overlaying the work of his father.

Behind the temple of Sethos I and on the same axis is the cenotaph proper. Both in its plan and in its decoration (mainly executed by Merneptah) it resembles a royal tomb. It is approached from the north through a long, sloping corridor. The main rooms are a hall imitating an island and another resembling a sarcophagus, with an astronomical ceiling. The massive granite architraves roofed only part of the island hall, the center remaining open. It was meant as a recreation of the primeval waters – the island being surrounded by the ground water – with in their midst the solid primeval mound on which barley was probably germinated to symbolize the resurrection of Osiris.

Ramesses II built himself a smaller temple northwest of his father's. This is noteworthy for the excellent color preservation on its reliefs, which may be seen in full sunlight. The plan is very similar to that of the temple of Medinet Habu.

Beit Khallaf

Five large brick-built mastabas (the dimensions of K.1 are 85 by 45 m) with clay sealings bearing the names of Zanakht and Netjerykhet (Djoser) were found near the village of Beit Khallaf, some 20 km northwest of Abydos. The tombs were probably made for administrators of the Thinite area of the early 3rd Dynasty.

Akhmim

Akhmim (ancient Egyptian *Ipu* or *Khent-min*, Coptic *Khmin* or *Shmin*, hence Greek Khemmis and the modern name), on the east bank of the Nile, was once the flourishing center of the important 9th Upper Egyptian nome. Very little of its past glory remains nowadays: nothing is left of the town, the temples were almost completely dismantled and their material reused in nearby villages in the Middle Ages, and the extensive cemeteries of ancient Akhmim have never been systematically explored.

Northeast of Akhmim, at el-Salamuni, there is a rock chapel dedicated to the local god Min. Min was equated with Pan by the Greeks, so that another name given to the town in Classical antiquity was Panopolis. The chapel was probably cut by Tuthmosis III. During the reign of Aya it was decorated by the "First Prophet of Min," Nakhtmin. The reliefs show Aya and his wife Teye before local gods, and some 1,000 years later representations of Ptolemy II Philadelphus, depicted in a similar fashion, were added by his contemporary, the "Chief Priest of Min" Harma'kheru.

Far left Offering table of Harsiese from Akhmim, with fecundity figures bearing trays with gifts, and the owner and his *ba* (represented as a human-headed bird) receiving libation from a tree goddess. Granite. About 56 by 53 cm. Ptolemaic Period. London, British Museum.

Left Lid of the outer anthropoid coffin of Espamai, a priest at Akhmim in the 26th or 27th Dynasty. The Pyramid Texts on the lid were compiled some 2,000 years earlier. Wood. Height: 2·10 m. West Berlin Museum.

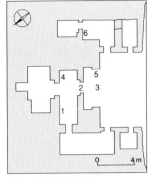

1 two registers: *Ptolemy II
Philadelphus before Min
and other deities*

2 above doorway: *Aya
and Queen Teye before Min
and other deities*

3 above doorway: *Aya and
Queen Teye before Min and Hathor,
and before Horus and Mehyt*

4 *Tuthmosis III before Min*

5 *Tuthmosis III before Amon-Re*

6 *Tuthmosis III
before deities*

Above Rock-cut chapel of Min
near Akhmim.

Right Limestone sarcophagus lid
of the Prophet Shepen-min, the
son of Heprenpu and Tashent-
min, probably of the Ptolemaic
Period. Theophoric names (those
containing names of deities) are
good evidence of the probable
provenance of the monument: in
this case the names of the owner
and his mother relate them to the
local god Min. Height: 1·80 m.
Copenhagen, Ny Carlsberg
Glyptotek.

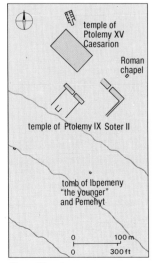

Above Wannina.

Far right Head of a statue of Ibu,
probably a contemporary of
Senwosret III, from his tomb at
Qaw el-Kebir. Painted limestone.
Height: 25 cm. Turin, Museo
Egizio.

Wannina

Wannina, some 10 km southwest of Akhmim, is the
site of a temple (ancient *Hut-Repyt*, hence Greek
Athribis) built for the goddess Triphis (Repyt) in the
reign of Ptolemy XV Caesarion. South of it, there
was an earlier temple of Ptolemy IX Soter II. One of
the tombs nearby, belonging to the brothers
Ibpemeny "the younger" and Pemehyt of the late
2nd century AD, has two zodiacs on its ceiling.

Qaw el-Kebir

Several large terraced funerary complexes built by
officials of the 10th Upper Egyptian nome in the
area of the modern village Qaw el-Kebir (ancient
Tjebu, later *Djew-qa*, Antaiopolis of the Greco-
Roman Period) during the 12th Dynasty represent
the peak of private funerary architecture of the
Middle Kingdom. A causeway approached a series
of courts and halls, partly cut in the rock, from the
valley. The innermost room of the chapel was
connected by a shaft with the burial chamber.

Cemeteries of other dates have been found in the
vicinity. A Ptolemaic temple (probably of Ptolemy
IV Philopator, enlarged and restored under Ptolemy
VI Philometor and Marcus Aurelius) which stood
near the river was destroyed in the first half of the
last century.

The two temples which once stood west of the
modern town of Akhmim were built for Min (Pan)
and the goddess Repyt (Triphis), regarded as his
companion. Both apparently dated from the Greco-
Roman Period; although some earlier blocks were
also found, it is not clear whether they belonged
to these temples or whether they were reused.

Several groups of rock-cut tombs of various dates
are known in the area, at el-Hawawish, northeast of
Akhmim, and at el-Salamuni, some 3 km further
north. The ceilings of the tombs of the Greco-Roman
Period at el-Salamuni are decorated with painted
circular zodiacs. Some of the tombs at el-Hawawish
were made for officials of the Panopolite nome
during the late Old Kingdom and the early Middle
Kingdom.

A large number of monuments, in particular
stelae and coffins, which are known from various
museum collections, can be ascribed to Akhmim,
although it is not possible to establish the exact
circumstances of their discovery.

MIDDLE EGYPT

Wooden models of boats are common finds from rock-cut tombs of Middle Egypt: sailing boat from Beni Hasan, 12th Dynasty. Length: 71·5 cm. Oxford, Ashmolean Museum.

The term Middle Egypt describes the area between Asyut and Memphis, therefore, somewhat confusingly, the northern part of Upper Egypt of the traditional terminology; both limits are geographically well defined and historically significant. Asyut became the southernmost area of the Herakleopolitan kingdom during the 1st Intermediate Period. The boundary between the southern and northern administrative regions remained in its vicinity until the end of the New Kingdom.

The area is characterized by the provincial tombs of the late Old Kingdom and the 1st Intermediate Period cut in the cliffs on the edge of the desert plateau. Ihnasya el-Medina was the residence of the Herakleopolitans, while in the 12th Dynasty the capital was further north, at Itjtawy, somewhere near el-Lisht. During the Middle Kingdom the Faiyum gained in importance, never to lose it. el-'Amarna became the royal residence for a few years in the 18th Dynasty. During the 3rd Intermediate and Late Periods Middle Egypt was the meeting ground of the delta and the south. In late antiquity it prospered and traded extensively with the oases: although smaller and less spectacular than their southern contemporaries, many temples testify to the renewed vitality of Middle Egyptian towns.

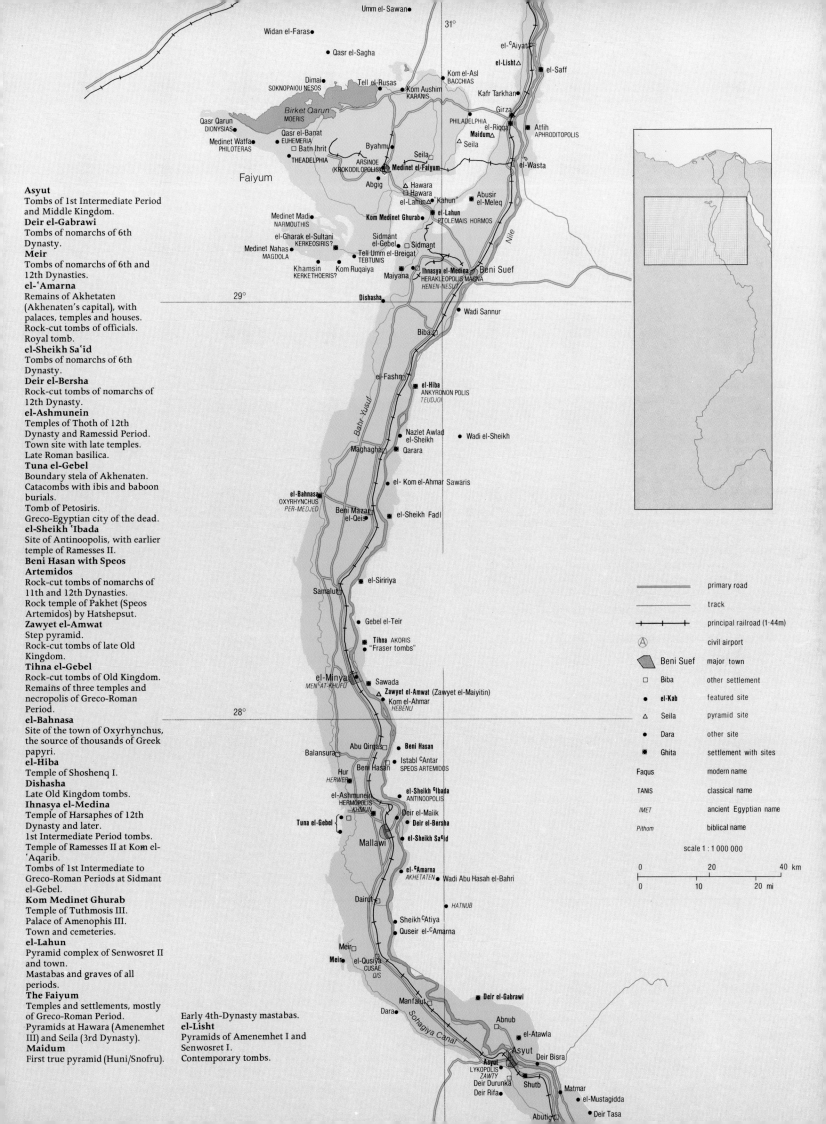

Asyut
Tombs of 1st Intermediate Period and Middle Kingdom.
Deir el-Gabrawi
Tombs of nomarchs of 6th Dynasty.
Meir
Tombs of nomarchs of 6th and 12th Dynasties.
el-ʿAmarna
Remains of Akhetaten (Akhenaten's capital), with palaces, temples and houses.
Rock-cut tombs of officials.
Royal tomb.
el-Sheikh Saʿid
Tombs of nomarchs of 6th Dynasty.
Deir el-Bersha
Rock-cut tombs of nomarchs of 12th Dynasty.
el-Ashmunein
Temples of Thoth of 12th Dynasty and Ramessid Period.
Town site with late temples.
Late Roman basilica.
Tuna el-Gebel
Boundary stela of Akhenaten.
Catacombs with ibis and baboon burials.
Tomb of Petosiris.
Greco-Egyptian city of the dead.
el-Sheikh ʿIbada
Site of Antinoopolis, with earlier temple of Ramesses II.
Beni Hasan with Speos Artemidos
Rock-cut tombs of nomarchs of 11th and 12th Dynasties.
Rock temple of Pakhet (Speos Artemidos) by Hatshepsut.
Zawyet el-Amwat
Step pyramid.
Rock-cut tombs of late Old Kingdom.
Tihna el-Gebel
Rock-cut tombs of Old Kingdom.
Remains of three temples and necropolis of Greco-Roman Period.
el-Bahnasa
Site of the town of Oxyrhynchus, the source of thousands of Greek papyri.
el-Hiba
Temple of Shoshenq I.
Dishasha
Late Old Kingdom tombs.
Ihnasya el-Medina
Temple of Harsaphes of 12th Dynasty and later.
1st Intermediate Period tombs.
Temple of Ramesses II at Kom el-ʿAqarib.
Tombs of 1st Intermediate to Greco-Roman Periods at Sidmant el-Gebel.
Kom Medinet Ghurab
Temple of Tuthmosis III.
Palace of Amenophis III.
Town and cemeteries.
el-Lahun
Pyramid complex of Senwosret II and town.
Mastabas and graves of all periods.
The Faiyum
Temples and settlements, mostly of Greco-Roman Period.
Pyramids at Hawara (Amenemhet III) and Seila (3rd Dynasty).
Maidum
First true pyramid (Huni/Snofru).

Early 4th-Dynasty mastabas.
el-Lisht
Pyramids of Amenemhet I and Senwosret I.
Contemporary tombs.

primary road
track
principal railroad (1·44m)
(A) civil airport
Beni Suef major town
□ Biba other settlement
• el-Kab featured site
△ Seila pyramid site
• Dara other site
■ Ghita settlement with sites

Faqus modern name
TANIS classical name
IMET ancient Egyptian name
Pithom biblical name

scale 1 : 1 000 000

0   20   40 km
0   10   20 mi

Asyut

Asyut (ancient Egyptian *Zawty*) was the capital of the 13th nome of Upper Egypt. Its place in Egyptian history was ensured by its strategic position at a point where the Libyan desert encroaches on the cultivated land and narrows the Nile valley, and where the Darb el-Arba'in caravan route departs for el-Kharga oasis and further south.

Although the town of Asyut and its shrines (particularly the temple of the local wolf god Wepwawet) are often mentioned in Egyptian texts, the actual remains so far discovered are almost exclusively connected with Asyut necropolis, west of the modern town. The most important tombs date to Dynasties 9/10 and 12, but two Ramessid tombs have also been found (those of Siese and Amenhotpe).

During the 1st Intermediate Period, the "Great Overlords of the Lycopolite Nome," Khety I, Itefibi and Khety II, were staunch supporters of the Herakleopolitan kings, and the nome formed the southernmost limit of the Herakleopolitan dominion. Biographical texts from Asyut provide valuable information on the history of the conflict with "the southern nomes" (i.e. the 11th Dynasty). The ultimate victory of Thebes adversely affected the status of Djefaiha'py I–III, the nome officials of the 12th Dynasty, but their tombs retained the high artistic standards of the earlier period.

Deir el-Gabrawi

During the 6th Dynasty, the powerful nomarchs of the 12th Upper Egyptian nome were buried in two groups of rock-cut tombs near the modern village of Deir el-Gabrawi. Some of these local rulers also held the title of the "Great Overlord of the Abydene Nome," and so controlled a large area extending from the 8th nome (Abydos) in the south as far north as the 12th (or 13th) nome.

It is remarkable that some of the scenes in the tomb of one of them, Ibi, were copied about 1,600 years later, during the reign of Psammetichus I, in the Theban tomb (No. 36) of a man of the same name.

Meir

There is nothing at el-Qusiya, on the west bank of the Nile, to suggest that this is the site of ancient *Qis* (Cusae), once the center of the 14th Upper Egyptian nome. Some 7 km west of el-Qusiya is the village of

Meir, which gave its name to several groups of tombs further west, in a low slope leading on to the desert plateau.

The most important of these rock-cut tombs belong to the men who were in charge of the nome during the 6th and 12th Dynasties. It is of the greatest interest that for both these periods the sequence of tombs is unbroken as the hereditary office passed from one man to his son or younger brother.

The decoration was, as a rule, executed in relief. Some astonishingly lively scenes were created by

"William," the blue faience hippopotamus decorated with aquatic plants, in the Metropolitan Museum of Art in New York. It was found at Meir in tomb B.3 of Senbi, dating to Senwosret I – Amenemhet II. Height: 11·5 cm.

the craftsmen of the 12th Dynasty, e.g. the desert-hunt scene in tomb B.1 of Senbi, dating to Amenemhet I. In the latest of the tombs, that of Wekh-hotpe (C.1), the walls were only painted.

In the past, Meir suffered much from illicit digging. The most prominent among the archaeologists who worked there in the first half of this century was Aylward M. Blackman.

el-ʿAmarna

el-ʿAmarna (also Tell el-ʿAmarna), ancient Egyptian Akhetaten ("The Horizon of the Sun Disk"), was the short-lived capital of Egypt, the royal residence during much of the reign of King Akhenaten, and the center of the new state religion introduced at that time. It is one of the very few Egyptian towns which it has been possible to excavate to any significant extent. Its layout and architecture are fairly well known because the site was abandoned some 15 years after it had been founded, and the town thus escaped the destruction which would have resulted from continuous habitation. King Akhenaten built it on virgin soil, not tarnished by an earlier presence of people and their gods, but the exact reasons for his choice of the large bay on the east bank of the Nile, north of the massif of Gebel

Abu Feda, are not known. Recently it has been suggested that the appearance of the landscape, resembling a large "horizon" hieroglyph ☐ might have been one of them.

The boundaries of Akhetaten were marked by a chain of stelae surrounding the area on both banks of the river. On the west bank, the northernmost of these (Stela A) is at Tuna el-Gebel, while on the east bank Akhetaten extended close to the tombs of el-Sheikh Saʿid (Stela X).

Although it has produced a number of famous works of art, for the visitor el-ʿAmarna is disappointing because there are hardly any buildings standing. The spoliation started soon after the town was abandoned, with the removal of stone to building sites nearby, notably to el-Ashmunein.

Except for the side facing the river, the plain of

Left Wekh-hotpe (the owner of tomb C.1 at Meir) with his two wives Khnemhotpe and Nebkau, and a small daughter. Granite. Height: 37 cm. Reign of Senwosret II or III. Boston (Mass.), Museum of Fine Arts.

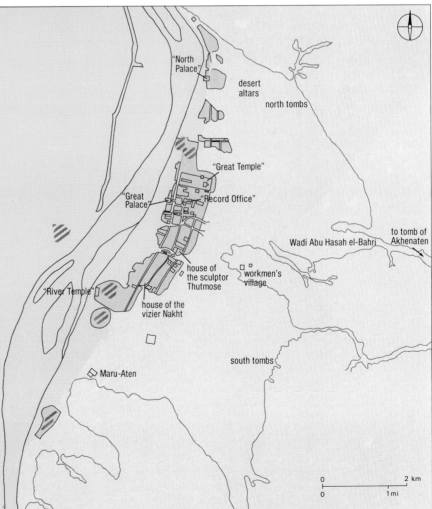

Below left Blind singers, one of the smaller groups below a large scene of Akhenaten and family offering to the Aten. Tomb of Meryreʿ I (No. 4) at el-ʿAmarna, south wall of the pillared hall, east side.

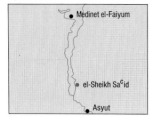

el-'Amarna is entirely enclosed by rock cliffs, occasionally broken by wadis. The bay is some 10 km long and about 5 km deep, but the town itself occupies only the area closest to the river. Its most important central part contained the *Per-Aten-em-Akhetaten* ("The Temple of the Aten in Akhetaten"), known as "The Great Temple," and the official state building, "The Great Palace." The main features of the latter were (1) the "State Apartments," formed by a series of courts and columned halls and built of stone, (2) the "Harim," with adjacent servants' quarters, and (3) the so-called "Coronation Hall." Akhenaten's private residence was across the road from "The Great Palace" and was connected with it by a bridge. Close to it was the "Record Office," which in 1887 produced the cuneiform diplomatic correspondence ('Amarna Letters) exchanged between Amenophis III, Akhenaten and Tut'ankhamun, and rulers and vassals of Palestine, Syria, Mesopotamia and Asia Minor. This conglomeration of official buildings

was surrounded by private houses, workshops, sculptors' studios etc., on the north and south sides. The names of the owners of many of the houses are known from inscribed architectural elements found during their excavation (the sculptor Thutmose, the vizier Nakht and others).

Near the southern extremity of the 'Amarna bay there was the *Maru-Aten*, a group of buildings which also included a lake, a kiosk on an island and flower beds, and was adorned with painted pavements. At the north end of the bay there stood the "North Palace" and perhaps yet another royal residence. However, the exact purpose of some of el-'Amarna's buildings is still a matter of conjecture.

'Amarna officials had their tombs cut in the cliffs encircling the plain. Thebes and Saqqara apart, el-'Amarna is the only site which can be described as a New Kingdom necropolis of importance. The tombs form two large groups, and their plan is similar to that of the Theban tombs of the 18th Dynasty: (1) an outer court, (2) and (3) a long hall and a broad hall,

Left Painted limestone bust of Nefertiti wearing her characteristic crown with the uraeus. It was found with many other pieces in the studio of the sculptor Thutmose during the German excavations at el-'Amarna in 1912. Height: 48 cm. West Berlin Museum.

Above Painting from the king's private residence, showing two small daughters of Akhenaten, Neferneferuaten-tasherit and Neferneferure'. This is part of a much larger composition which included the whole royal family (the heel of a foot of the seated Nefertiti is next to the head of the princess on the right). Oxford, Ashmolean Museum.

Left Fragment of a red quartzite female statue, probably of Nefertiti. This is one of the most sensitive studies of the female body from the 'Amarna Period, belonging to the same class as the similarly incomplete sculptures of princesses in the Petrie Collection at University College in London and the Ashmolean Museum in Oxford. Height: 29 cm. Paris, Musée du Louvre.

Below "Talatat," the typical building blocks of Akhenaten: the king's hand holding an olive branch, and attendants kissing the ground in obeisance. New York, Schimmel collection.

both sometimes with columns, (4) a statue niche. The decoration was in sunk relief. The date is betrayed by the novel subject-matter and the unusual artistic conventions of 'Amarna art. How many of these tombs were actually put to use is not clear; some of their owners had other tombs made elsewhere, either before the move to el-'Amarna or afterwards. Tomb No. 25 of the south group was prepared for Aya, who later became the penultimate king of the 18th Dynasty and was buried in a tomb in the Valley of the Kings at Thebes (No. 23).

For his own family tomb Akhenaten chose a ravine about 6 km from the mouth of the large Wadi Abu Hasah el-Bahri, which it joins.

el-Sheikh Sa'id

The tombs of the men governing the Hare nome (15th Upper Egyptian nome) during the 6th Dynasty were cut in the steep cliffs named after a Muslim saint buried in the area. Their importance is greatly enhanced by the absence of contemporary evidence from el-Ashmunein, the capital of the nome.

Deir el-Bersha

Almost opposite the town of Mallawi, on the east bank of the Nile, a valley called the Wadi el-Nakhla breaks through the cliffs and runs in a southeasterly direction. Apart from limestone quarries of various periods it contains a number of rock-cut tombs. Some of them belong to the nomarchs of the 15th Upper Egyptian nome and date to the 12th Dynasty, though several are probably a little earlier. The name Deir el-Bersha, by which the site is known, is from that of the village west of the wadi.

The most spectacular of the tombs was made for the "Great Overlord of the Hare nome" called Djehutihotpe, who lived during the reigns of Amenemhet II, Senwosret II and Senwosret III. The chapel consists of a deep portico of two columns with palm capitals, and the inner room with a niche at the back. The decoration is executed in very low relief, at places only in paint. The west wall of the inner room bears the famous scene of the transport of a colossal statue from the alabaster quarries at Hatnub.

The tombs were excavated by expeditions of the Egypt Exploration Fund (P. E. Newberry and others) between 1891 and 1893, and the combined mission of the Harvard University and the Boston Museum of Fine Arts in 1915 (G. A. Reisner and others).

el-Ashmunein

el-Ashmunein, ancient Egyptian *Khmun* ("8-town"), named for the group of eight deities (ogdoad) who represented the world before creation, was called in Greek Hermopolis after Hermes (= Egyptian Thoth). It was the capital of the 15th Upper Egyptian nome and the main cult center of Thoth, the god of healing and of wisdom, and the patron of scribes. No early remains have been found there, but this is probably the result of chance destruction.

The site is in a broad and rich area of the Nile valley. It is now very badly ruined, with small parts of temples standing above the general rubble. Only the Roman Period *agora* with its early Christian basilica is at all well preserved, giving evidence of the great prosperity of the town in late antiquity.

A native Egyptian monument that was still

Above Wadi el-Nakhla.

Below Scene in the tomb of Djehutihotpe at Deir el-Bersha (copied by John Gardner Wilkinson before 1856).

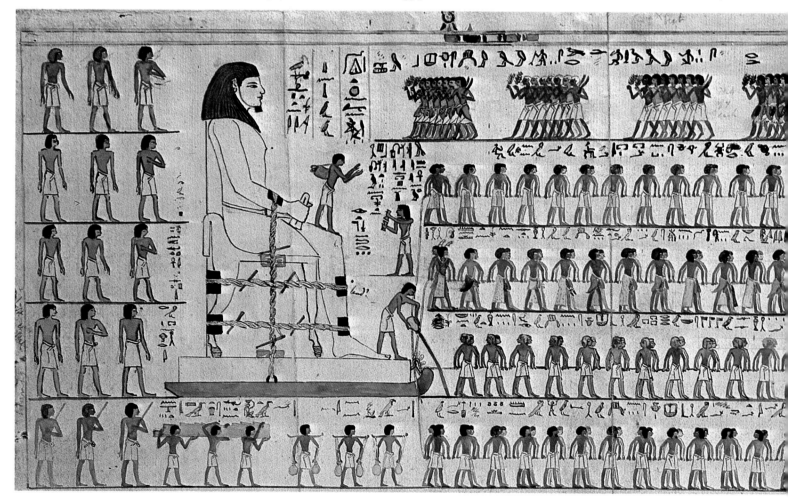

Below Granite columns of the late Roman basilica at el-Ashmunein, the only surviving large building of its kind in Egypt.

Above Ramessid calcite statuette of a priest with leopard-skin garment and a baboon squatting around his neck. The man probably dedicated a baboon in the temple of Thoth at el-Ashmunein. Oxford, Ashmolean Museum.

standing in 1820 consisted of two rows of columns from the hypostyle hall of the temple of Thoth, dating to Alexander the Great and Philip Arrhidaeus. About 200 m south of this temple was an earlier pylon of Ramesses II, in whose foundations more than 1,500 blocks from dismantled temples of Akhenaten at el-ʿAmarna were found by a German expedition under Günther Roeder between 1929 and 1939. Other monuments of the Dynastic Period that can now be seen are the entrance to a temple of Amenemhet II and the first pylon of a 19th-Dynasty temple of Amun with reliefs of Sethos II. All these buildings were in a central sacred area of the town, surrounded by a massive mud-brick enclosure of the 30th Dynasty.

The prosperity of the Greco-Roman Period was due to agriculture and to the prestige of Thoth, who was worshiped as Hermes Trismegistos ("thrice-great Hermes") by Greek and Egyptian alike, and had the Hermetic Corpus of mystical writings ascribed to him. Hermopolis and Tuna el-Gebel became centers of pilgrimage for Greeks and Egyptians.

Tuna el-Gebel

The site of Tuna el-Gebel is scattered for about 3 km along the desert 7 km west of el-Ashmunein. A boundary stela of Akhenaten, the earliest monument, is one of the most accessible of a series of such stelae. A group of six, of which this is the northwestern (stela A), is named in the text as marking the limits of el-ʿAmarna with its agricultural hinterland. The monument consists of a rock-cut "shrine" a little way up the escarpment, with the stela, with its much-eroded text, to one side. The top of the stela has a relief of the royal couple adoring the solar disk. Beside it are two pair statues of the king and queen, also rock-cut, whose arms are in different gestures, probably of adoration and of offering; the pairs are accompanied by much smaller figures of princesses.

To the south is the late necropolis of el-Ashmunein. The earliest objects found here are Aramaic papyri of the 5th century BC. These administrative documents of the Persian occupation were in a jar in the catacombs of ibis and baboon burials that are the largest feature of the site, and included a baboon sarcophagus dated to the Persian King Darius I. Most of the material in the catacombs was Greco-Roman in date, and a selection of pottery, bronze statuettes and mummies is now shown in the museum in the nearby town of Mallawi. Ibis and baboon are the two chief sacred animals of Thoth, the god of el-Ashmunein.

The site also contains the almost unique tomb of the family of Petosiris, which dates to the reign of Philip Arrhidaeus. It is in the form of a temple, with

an entrance portico and a cult chapel behind (the burials are in underground chambers). In the portico there are scenes of daily life and of offering bearers in a mixed Egyptian-Greek style. The chapel contains traditional religious scenes and important texts, including an extensive description of works in the temples of Hermopolis.

South of the tomb of Petosiris is a large Greek city of the dead of the first centuries AD, with tombs and mortuary houses decorated in a complex mixture of Greek and Egyptian styles. Both the galleries and the city of the dead were excavated by the Egyptian Egyptologist Sami Gabra between the two world wars.

el-Sheikh ʿIbada

This is the site of the ancient Antinoopolis, founded by Emperor Hadrian in 130 AD to commemorate his favorite Antinous who had drowned here. Among the earlier monuments the largest is the temple of Ramesses II, dedicated to the gods of el-Ashmunein and Heliopolis.

Beni Hasan with Speos Artemidos

Beni Hasan, some 23 km south of el-Minya, on the east bank of the Nile, is the most important and informative Middle Kingdom provincial necropolis between Asyut and Memphis. It contains 39 large rock-cut tombs, at least eight of them belonging to the "Great Overlords of the Oryx nome" (the 16th nome of Upper Egypt) of the end of the 11th and the early 12th Dynasties.

The biographical text in the tomb (No. 2) of the last of the holders of the title, Amenemhet, is dated "Year 43, month 2 of the inundation season, day 15" of the reign of Senwosret I. Although the tombs of his two successors, Khnumhotpe II (No. 13) and Khnumhotpe III (No. 3), do not show an appreciable diminution of material resources, the centralization that was gradually achieved by the early kings of the 12th Dynasty ultimately broke the string of the families of nomarchs in the whole of Middle Egypt, and large rock-cut tombs ceased to be built. The plan of the latest among the tombs consists of (1) an outer court with a portico formed by two pillars, (2) a rectangular main room with four polygonal pillars and (3) a statue niche. The decoration, now rapidly deteriorating, is painted throughout, and military activities, such as siege scenes, figure very prominently. Below these tombs there are others, more modest, some of which go back to the 6th Dynasty.

South of Beni Hasan is Speos Artemidos (locally known as Istabl ʿAntar), a rock temple dedicated to the local lioness goddess Pakhet, built by Queen Hatshepsut. The architrave bears a long dedicatory text with the famous denunciation of the Hyksos.

Zawyet el-Amwat

The most important features at this site are a step pyramid, perhaps of the 3rd Dynasty, and a necropolis of rock-cut tombs, mainly of the end of the Old Kingdom, which belonged to ancient *Hebenu* (modern Kom el-Ahmar), the early capital of the 16th Upper Egyptian nome.

Tihna el-Gebel

The rock-cut tombs ("Fraser Tombs") at Tihna date to the Old Kingdom. About 2 km north of them, close to the modern village, there are remains of the ancient town Akoris and three small temples and a necropolis of the Greco-Roman Period.

Left Greco-Egyptian painting in mortuary "house" 21 at Tuna el-Gebel, c. 2nd century AD. Apart from the decorative panel at the bottom, the motifs are Egyptian, and the hieroglyphs are intelligible. Above: Horus and Thoth pour libations over the deceased, shown in Greek style; to the right is her "shadow," shown as a symbolically black, emaciated corpse. Below: adoring figures of the "Mistress of the West," Atum and two further deities face into an opening.

Right Gold statuette of the god Harsaphes, with an inscription on the lower side of its base naming Neferkareʿ Peftjauʿawybast, the local king at Herakleopolis contemporary with Piye of the 25th Dynasty. Height: about 6 cm. From the hypostyle hall of the temple at Ihnasya el-Medina. Boston (Mass.), Museum of Fine Arts.

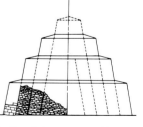

Section of the step pyramid at Zawyet el-Amwat.

The detective side of Egyptology: a keen eye, retentive memory and sense of detail can often help to identify errant monuments. The tomb relief on the right, now in the collection of the Museo Arqueológico Nacional in Madrid, was found during the excavation of a 1st Intermediate Period cemetery south of the temple of Harsaphes at Ihnasya el-Medina in 1968. The fragment on the left was, in disguise, on the New York art market already in 1964, incorrectly dated and with a misleading indication of its provenance.

Above Wooden statue of the Lector-Priest Meryre'-haishtef as a naked youth. This type of wooden statue is characteristic of the end of the Old Kingdom, and similar pieces are known from Memphite as well as provincial cemeteries. Height: 51 cm. 6th Dynasty. From Sidmant el-Gebel. London, British Museum.

el-Bahnasa

Little is known about *Per-medjed* (Coptic *Pemdje*), the capital of the 19th Upper Egyptian nome, from the Dynastic Period. Although it played an interesting part in Egyptian mythology, its pharaonic remains are unknown.

The town came to prominence during the Greco-Roman Period when it was called Oxyrhynchus, after the local cult of the *Mormyrus* fish. Its rubbish heaps have produced many thousands of Greek papyri (Grenfell and Hunt, 1896–1907), equaled in numbers only by those found in the towns of the Faiyum.

el-Hiba

This is a town site (ancient Egyptian *Teudjoi*) with a much-destroyed temple built by Shoshenq I. It was the northern limit of the Thebaid during the 21st–25th Dynasties.

Dishasha

Dishasha is known for its late Old Kingdom tombs, including some belonging to the chief officials of the 20th Upper Egyptian nome. The rock-cut tomb of Inti contains a rare scene of the siege of a fortified town.

Ihnasya el-Medina

About 15 km west of Beni Suef, on the right bank of the Bahr Yusuf, is the modern village of Ihnasya el-Medina. The village derives its name from ancient Egyptian *Henen-nesut* (Coptic *Hnes*), the capital of the 20th Upper Egyptian nome, which was situated nearby, probably mainly west of it. As the chief god of the ancient town was the ram-headed Harsaphes (Egyptian Herishef, literally "He who is on his Lake"), later identified with Greek Herakles, it acquired the Classical name Herakleopolis Magna.

The remains of the temple of Harsaphes lie southwest of the village, and have been excavated by E. Naville (1891–92), W. M. Flinders Petrie (1904) and in recent years by a Spanish expedition (J. López). The earliest monuments date to the 12th Dynasty. During the 18th Dynasty the temple was enlarged, but the major rebuilding program was due to Ramesses II. The temple continued to be used during the 3rd Intermediate and Late Periods.

The most prominent part Herakleopolis ever played in Egyptian history was during the 1st Intermediate Period when it was the seat of the rulers of the 9th/10th (Herakleopolitan) Dynasty. No temples of this or earlier periods have yet been located, but tombs of contemporary officials have been found some 300 m south of the temple.

Southeast of the temple of Harsaphes, at Kom el-ʿAqarib, there was another temple built by Ramesses II. Sidmant el-Gebel, about 7 km to the west, was probably the main necropolis serving the town, with graves and rock-cut tombs ranging from the 1st Intermediate to the Greco-Roman Periods.

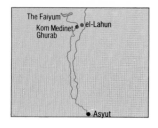

Kom Medinet Ghurab

At the south side of the entrance to the Faiyum, on the edge of the desert some 3 km southwest of el-Lahun, there are scanty remains of two temples and adjacent town quarters and cemeteries. The larger of the temples was built by Tuthmosis III, and the settlement thrived during the second half of the 18th and in the 19th Dynasty. A number of objects found there represent or are connected with Amenophis III and Queen Teye, and one of the buildings is often described as a palace of his reign.

el-Lahun

The pyramid of el-Lahun, some 3 km north of the modern town of this name, was built by Senwosret II. It is on the right side of the opening through which the Bahr Yusuf enters the Faiyum, opposite Kom Medinet Ghurab, and overlooks the area to which the kings of the 12th Dynasty devoted much attention. Its builders used a natural knoll of rock for siting the pyramid, and employed the well-established Middle Kingdom method of core construction. This was based on stone retaining walls radiating from the center, and the filling of chambers formed between them with mud bricks.

The stone outer casing produced an effect comparable to that of pyramids completely built of stone, but nowadays, with the revetment gone, the structure is little more than a large mound of earth. The entrance to the interior of the pyramid was through two shafts near the south face; this is very unusual (normally the entrance is in the north face) and presented W. M. Flinders Petrie, the excavator, with considerable problems.

Beautiful Middle Kingdom jewelry, comparable to that discovered at Dahshur, was found south of the pyramid, in the shaft tomb of Princess Sithathoriunet.

There are mastabas and graves dating to practically all periods of Egyptian history in the neighborhood of the pyramid.

The valley temple lies about 1 km to the east, near the line of cultivation. Close to it is the walled settlement of el-Lahun (also known as Kahun), excavated by Petrie. Most of the town was planned and laid out at the same time, with streets and houses arranged in neat geometrical rows. At least three town quarters, separated by walls, can be distinguished: (1) the "acropolis," perhaps intended for the king himself, (2) the eastern quarter, with large mansions (about 40 by 60 m) centered around a court and consisting of as many as 70 or 80 rooms, (3) the western quarter of smaller uniform dwellings (about 10 by 10 m) with 4 to 12 rooms. The town housed priests and officials connected with the pyramid; although it is unique to date, it must have been one of many built near pyramid complexes. The town is famous because of the hundreds of hieratic papyri ("Kahun Papyri") found there. These contained texts of varying nature, such as literary, mathematical, medical and veterinary works, and also legal and temple documents, accounts, letters etc.

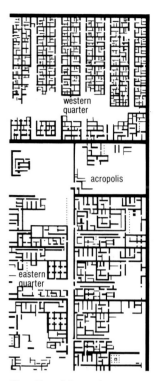

Above Plan of the northern part of the town of el-Lahun.

Left Head of a queen, probably Teye, the wife of Amenophis III, from Kom Medinet Ghurab. The shrewd and world-weary expression of the queen makes this head perhaps the most individually conceived female portrait known from ancient Egypt. Yewwood, glass, gesso, cloth etc. Height: 9·5 cm. West Berlin Museum.

Below The pyramid of Senwosret II at el-Lahun.

Top right The temple at Qasr el-Sagha.

Far right Black granite colossal statue of a king (almost certainly Amenemhet III) dressed as a priest, wearing an unusual heavy wig, and carrying two hawk-headed standards (long staves sacred to the local god). Height: 1 m. 12th Dynasty. From Mit Faris in the Faiyum. Cairo, Egyptian Museum.

The following are the most important places of interest in the Faiyum:

Kom Aushim (Karanis)
A temple of the Greco-Roman Period dedicated to the local gods Petesuchos and Pnepheros.

Dimai (Soknopaiou Nesos)
A Ptolemaic temple of Soknopaios (a form of the crocodile god Sobek).

Qasr el-Sagha
An unfinished Middle Kingdom temple.

Qasr Qarun (Dionysias)
A late Ptolemaic temple.

Batn Ihrit (Theadelphia)
A Ptolemaic temple of Pnepheros.

Byahmu
The masonry-built bases of a pair of colossal seated statues of Amenemhet III.

Medinet el-Faiyum, also el-Medina (Krokodilopolis or Arsinoe)
A 12th-Dynasty temple of Sobek, rebuilt or enlarged in later times.

Abgig
A large freestanding stela (previously called "obelisk") of Senwosret I, now removed to Medinet el-Faiyum.

Hawara
The pyramid of Amenemhet III (another pyramid of the same king stands at Dahshur). A large mortuary temple (known as "The Labyrinth" to Classical authors), formerly to be seen south of the pyramid.
Cemeteries of rock-cut tombs and graves (Middle Kingdom and Late and Greco-Roman Periods).

Seila
A small step pyramid, dated with some hesitation to the 3rd Dynasty.

Medinet Madi (Narmouthis)
A temple complex of the serpent goddess Renenutet (Termuthis), initially built by Amenemhet III and IV, with Ptolemaic additions.

Tell Umm el-Breigat (Tebtunis)
Ptolemaic temple and town.

Kom Ruqaiya
Rock-cut tombs, probably of the 12th Dynasty.

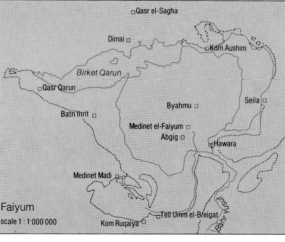

Faiyum
scale 1 : 1'000 000

The Faiyum

Although usually described as an oasis, the Faiyum is connected with the Nile by a river arm known as the Bahr Yusuf (Arabic: "The River of Joseph"). The Faiyum (ancient Egyptian *She-resy*, "The Southern Lake," later divided into *She-resy* and *Mer-wer*, "The Great Lake," Greek Moeris) is a large, extremely fertile depression some 65 km from east to west, with a lake (modern Birket Qarun, Lake Moeris of Classical writers) in its northwestern part. Nowadays the lake only occupies about one fifth of the Faiyum and is some 44 m below sea level, but in the past it was much larger, teeming with wild life, and with abundant vegetation on its shores. Crocodiles must have been very common in the region, hence the role of the species as the chief deity of the area (Sobek, Greek Suchos). The name

Faiyum derives from that of the lake, Coptic *Peiom*.

Two periods in Egyptian history were of great significance for the area. When during the 12th Dynasty the capital of Egypt was moved to el-Lisht, measures were taken to enhance the economic importance of the nearby Faiyum, probably by reducing the inflow of water into the lake and reclaiming land. The majority of temples and settlements uncovered so far date to the Greco-Roman Period, when the area once again became the focus of royal attention. The lake was artificially reduced to win further arable land, and new settlers, particularly Greco-Macedonian veterans, were introduced there by Ptolemy II Philadelphus. Thousands of Egyptian (demotic) and Greek papyri have been found in Faiyum town sites of this period.

131

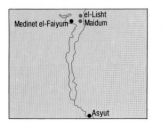

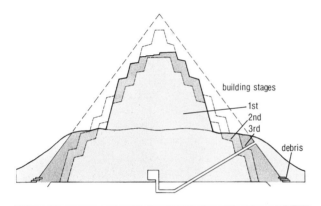

building stages
1st
2nd
3rd
debris

Maidum

The unmistakable view of Maidum is one showing a huge tower-shaped structure appearing above a hill formed by stone debris. These are the remains of the first true pyramid ever attempted in Egypt, and the earliest-known developed pyramid complex (together with the "Bent Pyramid" at Dahshur).

Experiments with the design of the pyramid are the cause of its present appearance. The monument started as a seven-stepped pyramid, but was subsequently altered into an eight-stepped structure; finally the steps were filled and an outer casing was applied to complete its conversion into a proper pyramidal form. The king for whom the pyramid was begun was probably Huni, the last ruler of the 3rd Dynasty, but since New Kingdom graffiti tell us that the Egyptians themselves later connected it with Huni's successor Snofru, the latter may have been responsible for its completion. However, the smooth dressing of the walls which were originally intended to be exposed as outer faces of the step pyramid (some can still be seen on the pyramid) did not provide sufficient bonding for later fill leaning against them. Furthermore, the outer casing did not rest on sound

Top left External masonry of the buttress walls and the less carefully built interior.

Above Aerial view of the pyramid from the east, showing the causeway, the mortuary temple, and the vast amount of material now surrounding the remains of the pyramid core following the partial collapse of the structure.

Above left Section of the pyramid looking west.

Left Statues of the Greatest of the Seers (i.e. High Priest) of Heliopolis and King's Son of his Body (of Snofru) Re'hotpe and his wife Nofret. Limestone with remarkably well-preserved original coloring. Height: 1·20 and 1·18 m. Cairo, Egyptian Museum.

foundations, and the method employed in laying its blocks was not well chosen. As a result of these constructional deficiencies the bases of the four outer buttress walls gave way and the walls slid down and collapsed, creating the tower that we see today. The date at which this happened is still hotly disputed; attempts have been made to connect this "building disaster" with the change of the angle of the "Bent Pyramid" at Dahshur, but the presence of an extensive contemporary necropolis speaks against such an early date. Bar the discovery of some unexpected textual or pictorial evidence elsewhere, only further excavations in the immediate vicinity of the pyramid can provide a satisfactory solution to this problem.

Cemeteries of large brick-built mastabas of the beginning of the 4th Dynasty lie to the north and east of the pyramid. The best-known among them are the twin mastabas of Re'hotpe and his wife Nofret, and of Neferma'at and his wife Itet.

Although the site has not been by any means systematically explored, a number of excavators have worked at it. The most distinguished of them were A. Mariette, W. M. Flinders Petrie and Alan Rowe.

Below Limestone relief of archers: one of the many Memphite blocks of the Old Kingdom reused at el-Lisht by Amenemhet I. Most of these reliefs come from royal monuments and are of superb quality. New York, Metropolitan Museum of Art.

Below right The goddess Seshat records foreign captives and booty: limestone relief of the 12th Dynasty which continues an Old Kingdom tradition of similar scenes in royal temples. From the mortuary temple of Senwosret I at el-Lisht. New York, Metropolitan Museum of Art.

el-Lisht

Early in his reign, King Amenemhet I of the 12th Dynasty moved the administrative capital of Egypt and the royal residence from Thebes to Itjtawy, a newly founded walled town somewhere between the Faiyum and Memphis. Paradoxical though it may seem, nothing has yet been found of the town itself, and its exact location is still unknown. It is, however, certain that the pyramid field of el-Lisht was its main necropolis, and so Itjtawy probably spread in the cultivated area to the east of it. The town retained its importance for at least 300 years, only to relinquish it to the Hyksos center Avaris in the northeastern delta and to Thebes during the 2nd Intermediate Period.

The main features of el-Lisht are the two dilapidated pyramids of Amenemhet I and his son Senwosret I, some 1·5 km apart, surrounded by smaller pyramids and mastabas of members of the royal family and officials and cemeteries of ordinary graves. The proximity of the Memphite necropolis provided Amenemhet I with a source of conveniently prepared building material, and as a result a large number of decorated blocks originating in earlier royal temples have been recovered from the core of the pyramid by archaeologists.

The most interesting among the 12th-Dynasty mastabas near the north pyramid of Amenemhet I belong to the Vizier Inyotefoqer, the Chief Steward Nakht, the Overseer of Sealers Rehuerdjersen and the Mistress of the House Senebtisy, while close to the south pyramid of Senwosret I there are the tombs of the High Priest of Heliopolis Imhotep, the Steward Sehetepibre'-'ankh, the High Priest of Memphis Senwosret-'ankh and others. The monuments of el-Lisht have been explored by the expeditions of the Institut Français d'Archéologie Orientale (1894–95) and the Metropolitan Museum of Art in New York (1906–34).

MEMPHIS

The city of Memphis, which has now disappeared almost completely, was the administrative and religious center of the 1st Lower Egyptian nome. It was the royal residence and capital of Egypt during the Early Dynastic Period and the Old Kingdom, and many later kings maintained a palace there. The city's temples were among the most important in the land. Memphis always remained one of the most populous and renowned places of Egypt and, indeed, of the whole ancient world, inhabited by a truly cosmopolitan community. Its harbor and local workshops played an important part in Egypt's foreign trade.

A reflection of the size and importance of Memphis is the stretch, more than 30 km long, covered by its cemeteries, on the edge of the desert on the west bank of the Nile. These together form the Memphite necropolis: (1) Dahshur, (2) Saqqara, (3) Abusir, (4) Zawyet el-'Aryan, (5) Giza, (6) Abu Rawash. Administratively, Giza and Abu Rawash were already in the 2nd nome of Lower Egypt.

The names by which the various parts of the Memphite necropolis are now known derive from the names of modern villages nearby. Egyptians themselves had no special term for the whole necropolis, but a number of ancient Egyptian place names which used to be applied to its various parts are known, such as *Rasetau* (probably southern Giza). The most conspicuous features of the necropolis, the royal pyramids, sometimes lent their names to the adjacent quarters of the city which had grown out of the original "pyramid towns" of priests and pyramid officials. One of these terms, the name of the pyramid of Pepy I at Saqqara, *Mennufer*, Coptic *Menfe*, and Memphis in its Grecized form, was adopted as early as the 18th Dynasty to describe the whole city.

The town itself, or whatever may remain of its palaces, temples and houses, is to be sought in the cultivated area to the east of the necropolis, buried under the deposits of silt left behind by Nile inundations, and covered by modern settlements, fields and vegetation. So far only small parts have been revealed at Mit Rahina and at Saqqara (east of the pyramid of Teti). The position of the city, or at least of its center, probably did not remain stable throughout Egyptian history, new thriving areas gaining in importance to the detriment of others whose popularity had waned. This must have been one reason for the very long expanse covered by the city's cemeteries, though undoubtedly there were others, such as the search for suitable sites for the large-scale projects of building pyramids. Our modern concept of the city of Memphis and of its shadowy counterpart, the Memphite necropolis, is therefore very artificial, because neither of them ever existed completely at any one time.

Classical sources as well as archaeological discoveries show that Memphis became one of the most important administrative centers of the country at the very beginning of Egyptian history, after 2920

BC. Herodotus says that it was Menes, the traditional first king of Egypt, who raised a dike to protect the city from the inundations of the Nile. According to Manetho the successor of Menes, called Athothis, was the builder of the earliest of the palaces of Memphis. The oldest name of the district was *Ineb-hedj*, "The White Wall," possibly reflecting the appearance of its fortified residence to which it could also be applied. Perhaps the most apt was the term which appeared in the Middle Kingdom, '*Ankh-tawy*, "That which Binds the Two Lands," stressing the strategic position of the town at the tip of the economically important delta, between Lower and Upper Egypt of the traditional terminology. This, indeed, was probably the reason why the rulers of the 1st Dynasty chose the area for the site of the capital.

One of the most familiar faces of Memphis: the calcite sphinx at Mit Rahina.

Only Thebes in the south was comparable in religious, political and economic importance to Memphis, yet our knowledge of the remains of this truly national shrine of Egypt is infinitely smaller. For foreigners Memphis represented Egypt. According to some scholars, the name of one of its New Kingdom temples and of the neighboring quarters of the city, *Hikuptah* ("The Temple of the *ka* of Ptah"), gave rise to the name of the whole country, Greek Aigyptos, and our Egypt. This is also the etymology of the word "Coptic."

The city of Memphis did not survive the gradual eclipse of ancient Egyptian civilization in the early centuries of our era. Economically, it suffered even earlier from the growth of Alexandria. Its religious importance was lost when Theodosius I (379–95 AD) decreed that Christianity should be the religion of the whole of the Roman Empire. The final *coup de grâce* was delivered in 641 AD, when the Muslim conqueror 'Amr ibn el-'Asi founded a new capital of Egypt, el-Fustat, on the east bank of the Nile at the south end of modern Cairo.

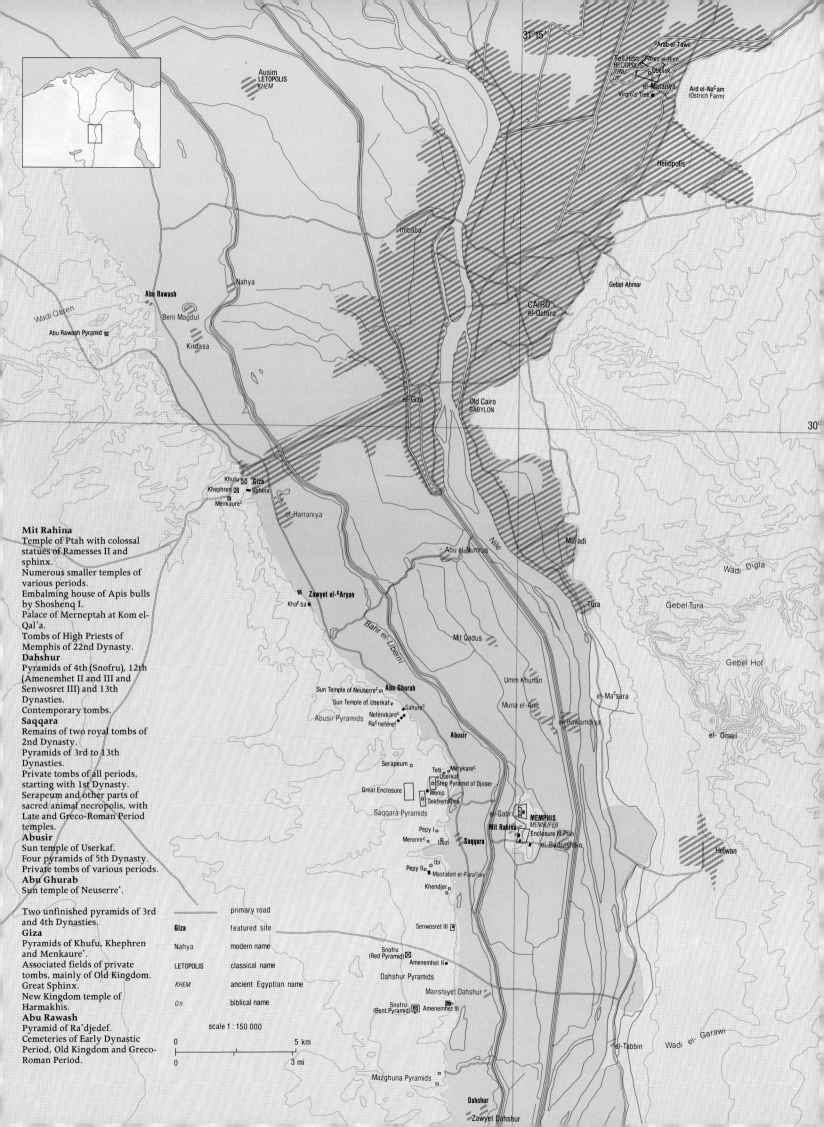

Ausim
LETOPOLIS
KHEM

°Arab el-Tawil
Tell Hisn
HELIOPOLIS
IUNU
On
Obelisk
el-Matariya
Virgin's Tree
Ard el-Naᶜam
(Ostrich Farm)

Heliopolis

31°15′

Imbaba

Gebel Ahmar

CAIRO
el-Qahira

Abu Rawash

Wadi Qaren

Beni Magdul

Nahya

Kirdasa

el-Giza

Old Cairo
BABYLON

30°

Khufu ⊠ **Giza**
Khephren ⊠ ▪ Sphinx
Menkaureᶜ ▪

el-Harraniya

Nile

Maᶜadi

Mit Rahina
Temple of Ptah with colossal
statues of Ramesses II and
sphinx.
Numerous smaller temples of
various periods.
Embalming house of Apis bulls
by Shoshenq I.
Palace of Merneptah at Kom el-
Qalʿa.
Tombs of High Priests of
Memphis of 22nd Dynasty.
Dahshur
Pyramids of 4th (Snofru), 12th
(Amenemhet II and III and
Senwosret III) and 13th
Dynasties.
Contemporary tombs.
Saqqara
Remains of two royal tombs of
2nd Dynasty.
Pyramids of 3rd to 13th
Dynasties.
Private tombs of all periods,
starting with 1st Dynasty.
Serapeum and other parts of
sacred animal necropolis, with
Late and Greco-Roman Period
temples.
Abusir
Sun temple of Userkaf.
Four pyramids of 5th Dynasty.
Private tombs of various periods.
Abu Ghurab
Sun temple of Neuserreʿ.

Two unfinished pyramids of 3rd
and 4th Dynasties.
Giza
Pyramids of Khufu, Khephren
and Menkaureʿ.
Associated fields of private
tombs, mainly of Old Kingdom.
Great Sphinx.
New Kingdom temple of
Harmakhis.
Abu Rawash
Pyramid of Raʿdjedef.
Cemeteries of Early Dynastic
Period, Old Kingdom and Greco-
Roman Period.

Abu el-Nummus

Wadi Digla

Gebel Tura

Tura

Zawyet el-ᶜAryan
Khaᶜba ▪

Bahr el-Libeini

Mit Qadus

Gebel Hof

Sun Temple of Neuserreᶜ
Sun Temple of Userkaf
Abu Ghurab
Sahureᶜ
Umm Khunan

Abusir Pyramids
Neferirkareᶜ
Raᶜneferef

el-Maᶜsara

Muna el-Amir

Abusir

el-Hawamdiya

el- Omari

Serapeum

Teti
Merykareᶜ
Userkaf
Step Pyramid of Djoser

Great Enclosure
Wenis
Sekhemkhet

Saqqara Pyramids

el-Gabri
MEMPHIS
MENNUFER

el-Gabri
Mit Rahina
Enclosure of Ptah
el-Badrashein

Pepy I
Merenreᶜ
Izezi
Saqqara

Helwan

Pepy II
Ibi
Mastabet el-Faraᶜun

Khendjer

Senwosret III ▪

Giza   featured site

Nahya   modern name

LETOPOLIS   classical name

KHEM   ancient Egyptian name

On   biblical name

scale 1 : 150 000

Snofru
(Red Pyramid) ⊠
Amenemhet II ▪

Dahshur Pyramids

Manshiyet Dahshur

0   5 km

0   3 mi

Snofru
(Bent Pyramid) ⊠ Amenemhet III

el-Tabbin   Wadi el-Garawi

Mazghuna Pyramids

Dahshur

Zawyet Dahshur

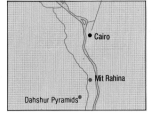

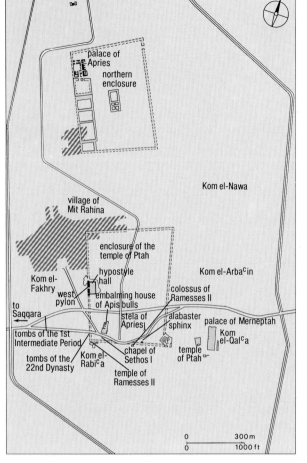

Map of Mit Rahina showing: palace of Apries, northern enclosure, Kom el-Nawa, village of Mit Rahina, enclosure of the temple of Ptah, hypostyle hall, Kom el-Arbaᶜin, Kom el-Fakhry, west pylon, embalming house of Apis bulls, colossus of Ramesses II, to Saqqara, stela of Apries, alabaster sphinx, palace of Merneptah, tombs of the 1st Intermediate Period, Kom el-Qalᶜa, tombs of the 22nd Dynasty, Kom el-Rabiᶜa, chapel of Sethos I, temple of Ptah, temple of Ramesses II. Scale: 300 m / 1000 ft

Mit Rahina

Extensive remains of ancient Memphis can be seen in a picturesque setting of palm groves close to the modern village of Mit Rahina.

The most important of the still discernible structures is the enclosure of the temple of Ptah, with colossal statues of Ramesses II and a large alabaster sphinx of approximately the same date. Ptah was the chief Memphite god, and in Classical antiquity was identified with Hephaistos and Vulcan. Only a small west section of the temple complex, once one of the largest in Egypt, has been systematically excavated (mainly by W. M. Flinders Petrie between 1908 and 1913), due to technical difficulties and the proximity of the village. The west pylon, leading into the columned hypostyle hall, was built by Ramesses II, but elsewhere in the enclosure isolated earlier elements were found (a lintel of Amenemhet III, blocks of Amenophis III etc.), suggesting the presence of older structures in the vicinity. Apart from the west pylon with the hypostyle hall, Ramesses II also built the gates on the north and south sides of the enclosure and had, in characteristic fashion, colossal statues of himself placed outside the gates. Yet another, smaller,

temple was built just outside the southwest corner of the enclosure during his reign. Later kings continued constructing within the enclosure. Thus Shoshenq I added an embalming house of Apis bulls, and Shabaka and Amasis erected smaller chapels there.

Foundation deposits discovered west of the Ptah enclosure indicate the position of an earlier temple, built by Tuthmosis IV and enlarged by other rulers of the 18th Dynasty.

An enclosure of the Late Period is visible north of the precinct of Ptah. The names of Psammetichus II and Apries of the 26th Dynasty, and of Teos of the 30th Dynasty, have been found there.

A number of mounds formed by continuous habitation are situated to the south and east of the Ptah enclosure. The most important among them are Kom el-Rabiʿa, with the temple of Hathor built by Ramesses II, and Kom el-Qalʿa, with a smaller temple dedicated to Ptah and a palace of Merneptah. The last was excavated by C. S. Fisher and the expedition of the University Museum in Philadelphia (Pa.) some 50 years ago, but still awaits publication.

There are few tombs at Mit Rahina. The most important among them date to the 1st Intermediate Period or early Middle Kingdom, at Kom el-Fakhry, and to the 22nd Dynasty (tombs of the High Priests of Memphis called Shoshenq, Tjekerti, Peteese and Harsiese), close to the southwest corner of the Ptah enclosure.

Fallen granite colossus of Ramesses II wearing the white crown, found near the south gate of the enclosure of the temple of Ptah, some 30 m from the famous huge statue of the same king made of limestone. The original colors of the colossus are still partly preserved. Fragments of a companion piece were also discovered, as well as lower parts of smaller seated colossi.

Dahshur

The pyramid field of Dahshur forms the southernmost extension of the Memphite necropolis. The site is some 3·5 km long, and the pyramid variously called "Bent," "Blunted," "Rhomboidal" or "False," the only one of its shape in Egypt, is the most conspicuous landmark on the horizon of Dahshur.

For royal tombs, the change from the 3rd to the 4th Dynasty is signaled by the transition from step pyramid to true pyramid. This radical move was initiated and completed during the reigns of the last king of the 3rd Dynasty, Huni, and the first king of the new dynasty, Snofru. The pyramids in which the process can be observed are at Maidum and Dahshur. The southern pyramid at Dahshur was the earliest to be planned as a true pyramid from its inception. However, when the structure reached more than half of its intended height, the slope of its outer faces was sharply reduced (from 54°27'44" to 43°22'), thus creating the characteristic "bent" silhouette, and the method of laying the casing and packing blocks was improved. This change of design was probably caused by constructional flaws which had appeared either in the structure itself or in its contemporary at Maidum. The Bent Pyramid is unique in having two separate entrances, one in its northern face and another in the western face. Large areas of the pyramid have retained their original smooth exterior casing. South of the pyramid there is the usual subsidiary ritual pyramid. The valley temple is situated about 700 m northeast of the pyramid, and has provided a series of remarkable reliefs, some of them showing processions of female figures personifying Snofru's estates in Upper and Lower Egypt.

Snofru, apparently, was not content with one pyramid at Dahshur but had another, the so-called "Red" or "Pink Pyramid" (from the color of the reddish limestone used to build it) erected some 2 km to the north. The reason for this has not been established, but the fact that the incline of the faces of the later pyramid was from the very beginning that of the upper part of the Bent Pyramid may be significant. The dimensions of the base of this pyramid (220 by 220 m) are surpassed only by those of the Great Pyramid of Khufu at Giza.

The remaining pyramids at Dahshur, at some distance from each other and not forming any group, are smaller structures of the 12th Dynasty, of Amenemhet II (the so-called "White Pyramid"), Senwosret III and Amenemhet III (the so-called "Black Pyramid"). The last two are brick built. A remarkable discovery of at least six wooden boats was made near the pyramid of Senwosret III, comparable to the find of a dismantled boat of Khufu at Giza. Near the pyramid of Amenemhet III there is the tomb of an ephemeral king Awibre' Hor, and a small pyramidal structure of Amenyqemau, both of the 13th Dynasty.

Following the usual pattern, the pyramids are accompanied by tombs of members of the royal family, officials and priests. Near the pyramids of Amenemhet II and Senwosret III, but still within the pyramid enclosure walls, there are the mastabas of princesses (Iti, Khnemt, Itiwert and Sitmerhut, all daughters of Amenemhet II, and Ment and Sentsenebtisi, daughters of Senwosret III) and queens. These tombs contained some superb examples of Middle Kingdom jewelry (bracelets, pectorals, collars, necklaces etc.), now in the Cairo Museum.

Among the archaeologists who have excavated at Dahshur, two names are prominent: J. de Morgan, to whom we owe our knowledge of the Middle Kingdom pyramids and tombs (1894–95), and Ahmed Fakhry, who explored the Bent Pyramid (1951–55). In recent years, excavations at Dahshur have been resumed by the German Archaeological Institute.

The "Bent Pyramid" and the "Red Pyramid" of Dahshur seen behind the landmarks of south Saqqara, the "Mastabet el-Fara'un" and the pyramid of Pepy II, and showing how artificial the dividing line between Saqqara and Dahshur is.

Right Ka-statue, with the uplifted arms of the hieroglyphic sign *ka* on its head, from the tomb of King Awibre' Hor. Wood, remains of paint and gilt. Height: 1·75 m. Cairo, Egyptian Museum.

Left Granite pyramidion (capstone) of Amenemhet III from Dahshur. Height: 1·40 m. Cairo, Egyptian Museum.

The Pyramids: Types and Construction

Between 2630 and 1640 BC, Egyptian kings built for themselves tombs in the form of pyramids. Architectural as well as religious considerations played a part in the pyramid's introduction and development; although united by their purpose, pyramids differ in their form, size, interior design and other details. There are two basic types: the step pyramid and the true pyramid.

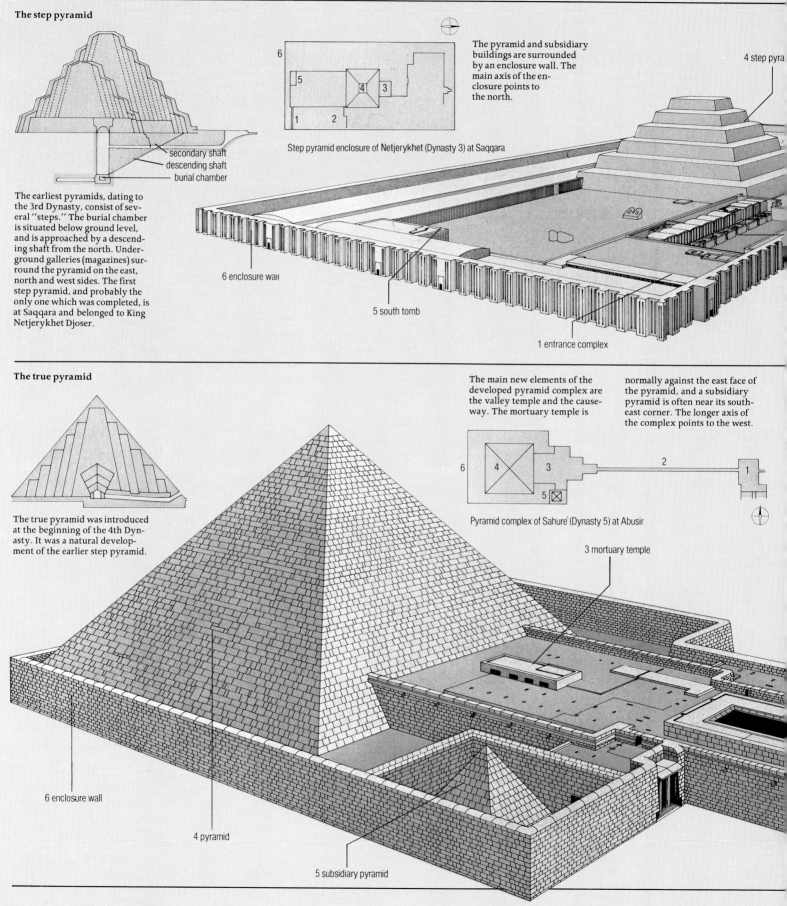

The step pyramid

secondary shaft
descending shaft
burial chamber

The earliest pyramids, dating to the 3rd Dynasty, consist of several "steps." The burial chamber is situated below ground level, and is approached by a descending shaft from the north. Underground galleries (magazines) surround the pyramid on the east, north and west sides. The first step pyramid, and probably the only one which was completed, is at Saqqara and belonged to King Netjerykhet Djoser.

The pyramid and subsidiary buildings are surrounded by an enclosure wall. The main axis of the enclosure points to the north.

Step pyramid enclosure of Netjerykhet (Dynasty 3) at Saqqara

4 step pyra

6 enclosure wall

5 south tomb

1 entrance complex

The true pyramid

The true pyramid was introduced at the beginning of the 4th Dynasty. It was a natural development of the earlier step pyramid.

The main new elements of the developed pyramid complex are the valley temple and the causeway. The mortuary temple is normally against the east face of the pyramid, and a subsidiary pyramid is often near its southeast corner. The longer axis of the complex points to the west.

Pyramid complex of Sahure (Dynasty 5) at Abusir

3 mortuary temple

6 enclosure wall

4 pyramid

5 subsidiary pyramid

138

Internal construction

In most true pyramids, the structure consists of a series of buttress walls (coatings of masonry) surrounding the central core. The

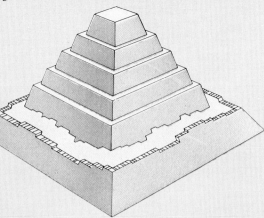

buttress walls decrease in height from the center outwards; in other words, there is a step pyramid within most true pyramids. This clever internal arrangement

added stability to the structure but evolved historically, together with the pyramid itself. Packing blocks were used to fill the "steps" formed by the faces of the outermost buttress walls, and casing blocks (often of better-quality Tura limestone) completed the transformation into a true pyramid.

A different method of construction was employed in the pyramids of the 12th and 13th Dynasties. The main reason for its introduction was economy: it was suitable for relatively modest structures in inferior materials. Solid stone walls ran from the center of the pyramid, while shorter cross walls created a series of internal chambers filled with stone blocks, rubble or mud bricks. The whole structure then received the usual outer casing. Although quite effective in the

short term, this could not compare with the earlier constructional methods, and all pyramids built in this way are now very dilapidated.

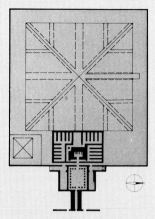

3 mortuary temple

2 Sed-festival complex

The subsidiary buildings, in particular the south tomb and the mortuary temple, ensured the deceased king's well-being in his new existence, and served to maintain his cult. Djoser's *sed*-festival complex is a special feature not attested elsewhere.

The funerary monument of Sahure' at Abusir is a good example of the pyramid complex. The landing stages of the valley temple show that it could be approached by boat. The ascending causeway connects it with the mortuary temple. This consists of the outer part, with an entrance passage and a columned court, and the inner part, with five niches for statues, magazines to the north and south, and a sanctuary. In most pyramids the interior is reached by a descending passage starting in the north face. The roof of the burial chamber is formed by the largest and heaviest blocks in the whole structure.

Building ramps

A major problem facing the pyramid builders was how to lift the heavy stone blocks to the required height. The only method proved to have been used by the ancient Egyptians is based on ramps. These were inclined planes, built of mud brick and rubble, along which the blocks were dragged on sledges (wheeled transport was not used in the

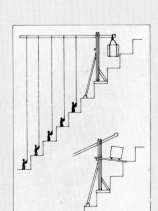

pyramid age). As the pyramid grew in height, the length of the ramp and the width of its base were increased in order to maintain a constant gradient (about 1 to 10) and to prevent the ramp from collapsing. Several ramps approaching the pyramid from different sides were probably used.

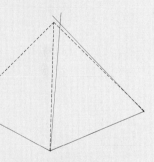

There are many theories concerning the actual arrangement of building ramps. Assuming that the "step pyramid within the pyramid" was built first, the ramps could have run from one step to another rather than approaching the pyramid face at right angles.

Other methods of lifting

The size of the ramps and the volume of material required to build them have prompted alternative suggestions as to how the problem of raising the building blocks was solved. One, proposed by L. Croon, uses the principle of the *shaduf*. The Egyptians knew the *shaduf* for raising water, but there is no evidence that they used a similar device for lifting weights.

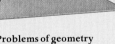

This is the main objection to this and similar ideas.

Models of "rockers," wooden cradle-like appliances, are known, and it has been thought that these were used to lift stone blocks. The rocker, with the stone placed on it, would have been raised by positioning wedges below its sides and rocking it up onto them. Stones might have been handled this way at some stage, but as a main lifting method this does not seem adequate.

Problems of geometry

A very slight error in the angle of incline of a pyramid would have resulted in a substantial misalignment of the edges at the apex. The principles of pyramid construction are familiar, but the exact procedure and practices remain unknown.

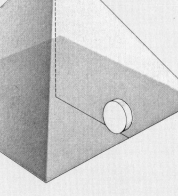

Some of the pyramid measurements show an accurate use of π (e.g. height of Khufu's

$$\text{pyramid} = \frac{\text{perimeter of the base}}{2\pi}.$$

The mathematical knowledge of

the Egyptians was not sufficient to arrive at this by calculation, but it could have been produced "accidentally," for example through measuring distances by counting revolutions of a drum.

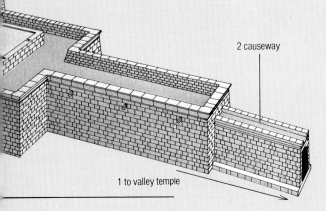

2 causeway

1 to valley temple

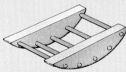

The Pyramids: Checklist

This list contains all the royal pyramids known from Egypt to date. The pyramids tend to form pyramid fields which are referred to by the names of the modern villages situated nearby. There are various reasons for these groupings but, broadly speaking, the Old Kingdom pyramids were concentrated near Memphis while those of the Middle Kingdom were built close to Itjtawy (near modern el-Lisht), the capital of the land at that time. At the beginning of the 4th Dynasty the pyramids, together with the buildings associated with them, started being named. During the 12th Dynasty each part of the pyramid complex probably had a name of its own.

△ true pyramid

▱ step pyramid

△ bent pyramid

▭ sarcophagus-shaped pyramid

Each entry in the table lists the following information (if available): king's name and dynasty; ancient name of pyramid in hieroglyphs and English; modern name; dimensions (α = angle of incline); associated pyramids (△).

Abu Rawash

△ Ra'djedef/Dyn 4
"The Pyramid which is the *Sehedu*-star"
104·5m sq; α = 60°
Subsidiary △
Unfinished; remains of granite casing

Giza

△ Khufu/Dyn 4
"The Pyramid which is the Place of Sunrise and Sunset"
Modern name: "The Great Pyramid" or "The First Pyramid of Giza"
230m sq; α = 51°50'35''; original ht 146m
Subsidiary △; queens △ △ △
5 boat pits, one containing a dismantled wooden boat, one as yet unopened

△ Khephren/Dyn 4
"The Great Pyramid"
Modern name: "The Second Pyramid of Giza"
214·5m sq; α = 53°7'48''; ht 143·5m
Subsidiary △
Lowest course of casing in granite; remains of original limestone casing near summit; 5 boat pits

△ Menkaure'/Dyn 4
"The Divine Pyramid"
Modern name: "The Third Pyramid of Giza"
105m sq; α = 51°20'25''; original ht 65·5m
queens △ △ △
Pyramid refurnished during Dyn 26; bottom 16 courses of casing in granite

Zawyet el-'Aryan

△ Owner unknown (probably the successor of Khephren)
Name unknown
Modern name: "The Unfinished Pyramid"
209m sq
Only the underground part begun; sarcophagus of unusual form found embedded in floor of burial chamber

▱ Probably Kha'ba/Dyn 3
Modern name: "The Layer Pyramid" or "el-Medowwara"
78·5m sq
Ownership inferred from inscribed alabaster vessels found nearby; unfinished

Abusir

△ Sahure'/Dyn 5
"The Pyramid where the *Ba*-spirit rises"
78·5m sq; α = 50°11'40''; original ht 47m
Subsidiary △

△ Neuserre'/Dyn 5
"The Pyramid which is Established of Places"
81m sq; α = 51°50'35''; original ht 51·5m
Subsidiary △
Valley Temple and part of causeway originally built for Neferirkare' and usurped

△ Neferirkare'/Dyn 5
"The Pyramid of the *Ba*-spirit"
105m sq; α = 53°7'48''; original ht 70m
Valley Temple and causeway unfinished at time of king's death and later usurped by Neuserre'

△ Probably Ra'neferef/Dyn 5
"The Pyramid which is Divine of the *Ba*-spirits"
65m sq
Hardly begun; name of Pyramid known from titles of priests connected with it but identification, though logical, is not supported by any evidence

Saqqara

△ Teti/Dyn 6
"The Pyramid which is Enduring of Places"
78·5m sq; α = 53°7'48''; original ht 52·5m
Subsidiary △; queens △ (Iput I), △ (Khuit)
Pyramid Texts

△ Probably Merykare'/Dyn 9 or 10
"The Pyramid which is Flourishing of Places"
Estimated 50m sq

△ Pepy I/Dyn 6
"The Established and

No evidence for ownership except for titles of priests buried nearby; not yet excavated

△ Userkaf/Dyn 5
"The Pyramid which is Pure of Places"
Modern name: "el-Haram el-Makharbish"
73·5m sq; α = 53°7'48''; original ht 49m
Subsidiary △
Mortuary Temple placed, unusually, south of Pyramid

▱ Netjerykhet (Djoser)/Dyn 3
Modern name: "The Step Pyramid" or "el-Haram el-Mudarrag"
140 × 118m; ht 60m
Begun as a mastaba tomb; plan modified 6 times; final form of superstructure a pyramid in 6 steps, the earliest pyramid built in Egypt

△ Wenis/Dyn 5
"The Pyramid which is Beautiful of Places"
57·5m sq; α = 56° 18' 35''; original ht 43m
Subsidiary △
Pyramid Texts
Causeway decorated by series of remarkable reliefs; 2 boat pits

▱ Sekhemkhet/Dyn 3
Modern name: "The Buried Pyramid"
120m sq
Unfinished; raised to ht of only c.7m; sealed but empty sarcophagus found in burial chamber

▱ (probably) Owner unknown, perhaps a king of Dyn 3
Modern name: "The Great Enclosure"
Outlines of enclosure walls only; not yet excavated; perhaps only begun, but on a grandiose scale; possibly not a pyramid at all or not of Dyn 3

△ Pepy I/Dyn 6
"The Established and

Beautiful Pyramid"
78·5m sq; α = 53°7'48''; original ht 52·5m
Pyramid Texts
Pyramid lent its name to city of Memphis

△ Izezi/Dyn 5
"The Beautiful Pyramid"
Modern name: "el-Shawwaf"
78·5m sq; α = 53°7'48''; original ht 52·5m
queen △

△ Merenre'/Dyn 6
"The Shining and Beautiful Pyramid"
78·5m sq; α = 53°7'48''; original ht 52·5m
Pyramid Texts

△ Ibi/Dyn 8
Name unknown
31·5m sq; α = ?; original ht ?
Pyramid too damaged to provide accurate measurements; Mortuary Temple only brick-built; apparently no Valley Temple or causeway; Pyramid Texts

△ Pepy II/Dyn 6
"The Established and Living Pyramid"
78·5m sq; α = 53°7'48''; original ht 52·5m
Subsidiary △; queens △ (Neit), △ (Iput II), △ (Wedjebten);
Pyramid Texts

▭ Shepseskaf/Dyn 4
"The Purified Pyramid"
100 × 72m
Not really a pyramid but a sarcophagus-shaped structure though even the Egyptians sometimes used to write its name with the sign showing a pyramid

△ Khendjer/Dyn 13
Name unknown
52·5m sq; α = 55°; original ht 37m
queen (?) △
Mainly brick-built

△ Owner unknown/Dyn 13
Name unknown
80m sq; α = ?; original ht ?
Too damaged to provide accurate measurements; mainly brick-built; at present only c. 3m high

Dahshur

△ Senwosret III/Dyn 12
Name not certain
105m sq; α = 56°18'35''; original ht 78·5m
Brick-built; 6 wooden boats buried near Pyramid

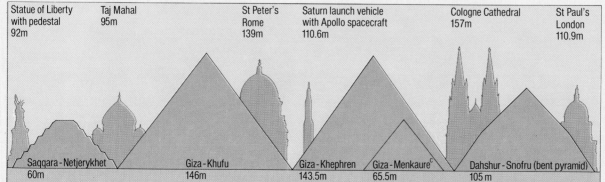

| Statue of Liberty with pedestal 92m | Taj Mahal 95m | St Peter's Rome 139m | Saturn launch vehicle with Apollo spacecraft 110.6m | Cologne Cathedral 157m | St Paul's London 110.9m |

| Saqqara - Netjerykhet 60m | Giza - Khufu 146m | Giza - Khephren 143.5m | Giza - Menkaure' 65.5m | Dahshur - Snofru (bent pyramid) 105 m |

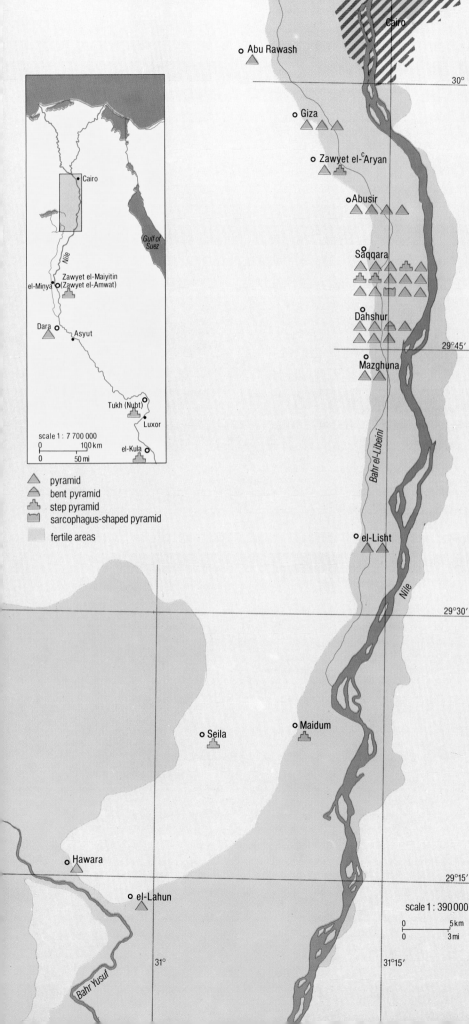

Map labels: Cairo, Abu Rawash, Giza, Zawyet el-ᶜAryan, Abusir, Saqqara, Dahshur, Mazghuna, el-Lisht, Maidum, Seila, Hawara, el-Lahun, Bahr el-Libeini, Nile

Inset map labels: Cairo, Gulf of Suez, Nile, Zawyet el-Maiyitin (Zawyet el-Amwat), el-Minya, Dara, Asyut, Tukh (Nubt), Luxor, el-Kula

scale 1 : 7 700 000
0 100 km
0 50 mi

Legend:
- pyramid
- bent pyramid
- step pyramid
- sarcophagus-shaped pyramid
- fertile areas

scale 1 : 390 000
0 5 km
0 3 mi

Snofru/Dyn 4

"The Shining Pyramid"
Modern names: "The Red Pyramid," etc
220m sq; α = 43°22'; original ht 104m

Snofru (another pyramid)/Dyn 4

"The Southern Shining Pyramid"
Modern names: "The Bent Pyramid," etc
183·5m sq; α1 = 54° 27' 44"; α2 = 43° 22'; intended ht 128·5m; original ht 105m
Subsidiary △
The only Egyptian pyramid of this form

Amenemhet II/Dyn 12

"The Mighty Pyramid"
Modern name: "The White Pyramid"
More than 50m sq; α = ?; original ht ? Too damaged to provide accurate measurements

Owner unknown, date unknown
No data available

Amenemhet III/Dyn 12
Name not certain
Modern name: "The Black Pyramid"
105m sq; α = 57°15'50"; original ht 81·5m; brick-built

Amenyqemau/Dyn 13
Name unknown
45m sq; unfinished

Mazghuna

Owner unknown, perhaps Amenemhet IV or Nefrusobk of Dyn 12, or more likely a king of Dyn 13
Name unknown
Superstructure, probably stone-built, now completely lost

Owner unknown, perhaps Amenemhet IV or Nefrusobk of Dyn 12, or more likely a king of Dyn 13
Name unknown
52·5m sq; α = ?; original ht ?
Brick-built

el-Lisht

Amenemhet I/Dyn 12

"The High and Beautiful Pyramid" or

"The Pyramid of the Places of Arising," and possibly others
78·5m sq; α = 54°27'44"; original ht 55m
Many decorated Old Kingdom blocks reused as building material in the core

Senwosret I/Dyn 12

"The Pyramid

which is Favored of Places" or

"The Pyramid which overlooks the Two Lands"
105m sq; α = 49°23'55"; original ht 61m
Subsidiary △; queens and princesses △△△△△△△△

Maidum

altered to △ Probably Huni/Dyn 3
147m sq; α = 51°50'35"; original ht 93·5m
Subsidiary △
Perhaps completed by Snofru

Seila

Owner unknown (most probably not a royal pyramid), thought to be of Dyn 3
26m sq
Never properly investigated

Hawara

Amenemhet III/Dyn 12
100m sq; α = 48°45'; original ht 58m
Name not certain
Brick-built

el-Lahun

Senwosret II/Dyn 12

"The Shining Pyramid," and probably others
106m sq; α = 42° 35'; original ht 48m
queen △

Zawyet el-Maiyitin (or Zawyet el-Amwat)

Owner unknown (most probably not a royal pyramid), thought to be of Dyn 3
18m sq

Dara

Probably Khui/Dyns 7–10
Name unknown
130m sq
Brick-built; present ht only 4m

Tukh (Nubt)

Owner unknown (most probably not a royal pyramid), thought to be of Dyn 3
18m sq

el-Kula

Owner unknown (most probably not a royal pyramid), thought to be of Dyn 3
18m sq

Location unknown

Menkauhor/Dyn 5
Undoubtedly at Saqqara

"The Pyramid which is Divine of Places"

Neferkareᶜ/Dyns 7 or 8
Almost certainly at Saqqara

"The Enduring and Living Pyramid"

Ity/Dyns 7/10

"The Pyramid of the Ba-spirits"

141

Below left Limestone gaming disk with calcite-inlaid black paste border and two owls with outstretched wings. Found with 44 others in the tomb of Hemaka, an official of King Den. Diameter: 9·7 cm. Cairo, Egyptian Museum.

Right "The Scribe 'Ahmose, son of Yeptah, came to see the Temple of Djoser. He found it as though heaven were within it, Re' rising in it." (Hieratic graffito of the 18th Dynasty.)

Saqqara

Saqqara is the most attractive and the most interesting site in Lower Egypt, though it must be stressed that the infinitely lesser chances of preservation of monuments in the delta distort any attempt at a fair comparison. It is the most important link in the chain of cemeteries belonging to the ancient city of Memphis, and covers an area over 6 km long, measuring more than 1·5 km at its widest.

Before the pyramids (Dynasties 1 and 2)

The earliest royal name which the archaeologists have so far met at Saqqara is that of Na'rmer, whom some Egyptologists equate with Menes, the legendary founder of Memphis. It is engraved on a porphyry bowl which, together with thousands of other complete and fragmentary vessels of magnificent craftsmanship, was discovered in one of the subterranean magazines under the Step Pyramid of Djoser. The earliest mastaba tomb at Saqqara is only a little later, dating to the reign of King 'Aha (Menes according to another school of thought, probably Na'rmer's successor).

Mastaba tombs of the 1st Dynasty form an almost continuous line along the eastern edge of the large plateau north of the Step Pyramid of Djoser, above the modern village of Abusir. Their superstructures, built of sun-dried bricks and provided with a paneled "palace facade," were of considerable size: tomb S 3504, for example, of the reign of King Wadj, measured 56·45 by 25·45 m. Chambers for funerary equipment were situated in the core of the mastaba, while the substructure contained a centrally placed burial chamber and subsidiary rooms. The most important of these mastabas were excavated by W. B. Emery between 1936 and 1956. It was believed that at least some of them were royal tombs, mainly because of their size, but now most

scholars consider them to be the tombs of high officials resident at Memphis.

At the end of the 1st Dynasty the "palace-facade" paneling on the outside of the mastaba was reduced to two niches in the east face, of which that near the southeast corner was the more important and became the focus of the mortuary cult of the deceased. The generally smaller private mastabas of the 2nd Dynasty continued to be built in an apparently haphazard way in the area west of the large tombs of the 1st Dynasty. A large complex of underground rock-cut chambers has also been located under the east side of the pyramid of Wenis, and another about 140 m east of it. Nothing has been preserved of their brick-built superstructures, but the names on some clay sealings, originally used to seal jars and other articles of burial equipment, suggest that these galleries were made during the reigns of two early kings of the 2nd Dynasty, Re'neb and Ninetjer. When this fact is connected with the finding of a stela of Re'neb, probably reused in a modern village nearby (though the exact circumstances of the discovery are not clear), it seems likely that the galleries were once royal tombs, and that Egyptian kings were first buried at Saqqara as early as the beginning of the 2nd Dynasty.

The pyramid builders (Dynasties 3–13)

The pyramids. Altogether 15 royal pyramids, treated here in chronological order, are known from Saqqara. Most of them have now lost their original, strictly geometrical, forms and are reduced to artificial hills. Incredible though it may seem, it is almost certain that other pyramids are still to be discovered (for example that of Menkauhor).

(1) The Step Pyramid of Netjerykhet Djoser was built some time after 2630 BC. It was the first pyramid in Egyptian history, and the earliest stone structure of its size in the world. The pioneering character of the project is shown by the hesitation about its form, probably largely influenced by the new building material. Altogether six different plans were adopted in the course of the construction: the monument was started as a large mastaba tomb, thus following the well-established Saqqara tradition, but ended up as a pyramid of six steps. The design of the Step Pyramid was traditionally credited to Imuthes (in Egyptian: Imhotep), described by Manetho some 2,400 years later as "the inventor of the art of building with hewn stone." During the excavation of the entrance complex of the Step Pyramid in 1925–26 the name of Imhotep was, indeed, found inscribed on the pedestal of a statue of Netjerykhet, and so provided fascinating contemporary evidence for the correctness of Manetho's statement.

The complex of buildings near the southeast corner of the pyramid represents a stone replica of the chapels and pavilions built for the celebration of the *sed* festival. The festival was held to mark the

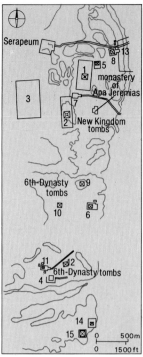

1	Netjerykhet Djoser	6	Izezi	11	Pepy II
2	Sekhemkhet	7	Wenis	12	Ibi
3	"Great Enclosure"	8	Teti	13	Merykare[c](?)
4	Shepseskaf	9	Pepy I	14	Khendjer
5	Userkaf	10	Merenre[c]	15	unknown king of 13th Dynasty

beginning of a new phase in the reign of the king, and the presence of these buildings in lasting stone guaranteed that Djoser would not be unprepared for the many celebrations of the *sed* festival he hoped to enjoy in his life after death. A closed room (*serdab*) near the northeast corner of the pyramid contained his seated statue, the earliest large stone royal statue known from Egypt.

For more than 50 years the Step Pyramid has been connected with the name of the French Egyptologist Jean-Philippe Lauer. At present his remarkable work is concentrated on the chapels in the *sed*-festival court; no visitor to Saqqara should miss a

chance to see these unique examples of the earliest Egyptian stone architecture restored to their original beauty.

(2) King Sekhemkhet intended to build an even larger step structure southwest of that of his predecessor, but the pyramid remained unfinished and gradually disappeared under the sand. It was only in 1950 that it was discovered by the Egyptian Egyptologist M. Zakaria Goneim, who aptly called it "The Buried Pyramid."

(3) Aerial photographs show the outlines of a huge enclosed area (known as the "Great Enclosure" to Egyptologists), as yet unexcavated, west of the

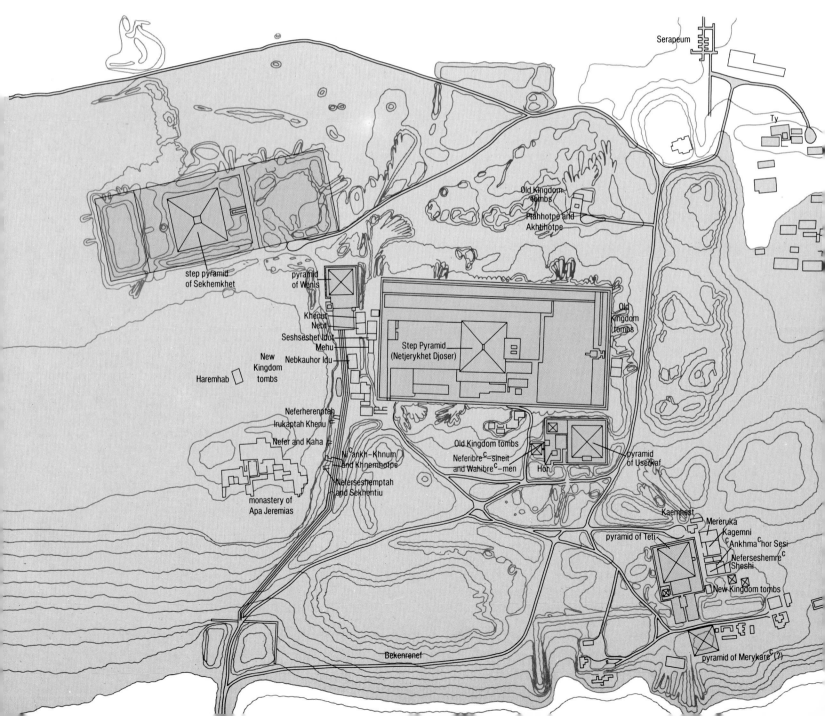

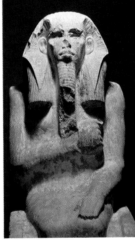

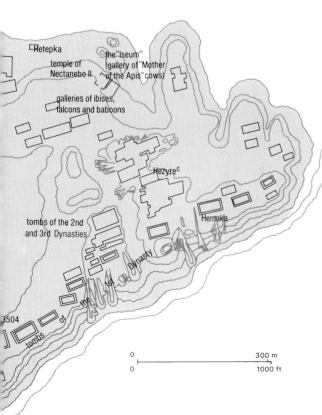

Hetepka

the "Iseum"
(gallery of "Mother
of the Apis" cows)

temple of
Nectanebo II

galleries of ibises,
falcons and baboons

Hezyre^c

Hemaka

tombs of the 2nd
and 3rd Dynasties

tombs of the 1st Dynasty

3504

0   300 m
0   1000 ft

Top left Step Pyramid of Netjerykhet Djoser: entrance near the southeast corner of the recessed enclosure wall; *top right* colonnade with engaged ribbed columns (partly attached to the wall behind), linking the entrance with the court south of the pyramid; *above left* "South Building" in the *sed*-festival complex. All much restored.

Above Upper part of the limestone seated statue of Djoser found in the *serdab*. The king is clad in a ceremonial robe, and wears an unusual headdress. The pose, with the right arm bent and the hand clenched against the chest, is typically archaic. Most of the paint, yellow for the skin and black for the hair and beard, has been lost; the mutilation of the face is the result of the gouging out of the inlaid eyes. Height: 1·40 m. Cairo, Egyptian Museum.

Above right Pyramid complex of Wenis: two boat pits, some 39 m long, by the south side of the causeway, about 180 m east of the pyramd.

enclosure of Sekhemkhet. There may be another building of the same type immediately west of the Step Pyramid of Djoser. These could be monuments of the 3rd Dynasty, but only future excavations can settle the problems of their dating and ownership.

(4) The burial complex of Shepseskaf, one of the last kings of the 4th Dynasty, is not a pyramid but a structure resembling a huge sarcophagus. It is known as "Mastabet el-Fara'un." The only parallel is the Giza tomb of Khentkaus, the mother of the early kings of the 5th Dynasty.

(5) Userkaf, the first king of the 5th Dynasty, built his pyramid near the northeast corner of Djoser's enclosure, but his successors abandoned Saqqara for Abusir, further north. It is likely that the return to Saqqara was initiated by Menkauhor, but his pyramid has not yet been located.

(6) The pyramid of Menkauhor's successor, Izezi, was built in the southern part of Saqqara.

(7) The pyramid of Wenis, the last king of the 5th Dynasty, stands near the southwest corner of the step pyramid enclosure of Djoser. The walls of the interior of this pyramid are inscribed with the Pyramid Texts, a collection of spells designed to help the deceased king in the netherworld, which may have been used during the burial ceremony. The pyramid of Wenis was the first to contain the Pyramid Texts, which subsequently became a standard feature of Old Kingdom pyramids.

On the south face of the pyramid there is a hieroglyphic inscription of Kha'emwese, one of the sons of Ramesses II. It records restoration work carried out by the prince, who was known for his interest in ancient monuments. Kha'emwese was connected with the Memphite region in his function

Below Wooden panel showing the Chief of Dentists and Physicians Hezyre' of the 3rd Dynasty. Originally in a niche in his tomb. Cairo, Egyptian Museum.

as the High Priest of Ptah.

The causeway, linking the mortuary temple against the east face of the pyramid with the valley temple, was decorated with reliefs. These depict, among other scenes, boats transporting granite columns and architraves from the granite quarries near Aswan to the building site of Wenis' pyramid. The journey, we are told, took seven days.

(8) The pyramid of Teti, the founder of the 6th Dynasty, is the northernmost royal pyramid of Saqqara. The other rulers of the dynasty, Pepy I (9), Merenre' (10) and Pepy II (11), followed Izezi's example and moved to the southern part of Saqqara. Since 1965, the interior passages and rooms of the pyramids of the 6th Dynasty have been systematically cleared, and the Pyramid Texts inscribed on their walls copied and studied by Jean Leclant and Jean-Philippe Lauer.

(12) The small brick-built pyramid of the little-known King Ibi of the 8th Dynasty is in the same area.

(13) The as yet unexcavated remains of the pyramid discernible to the east of the pyramid of Teti, at north Saqqara, might belong to King Merykare', one of the two reasonably well-known kings of the Herakleopolitan Period (9th/10th Dynasty). This assumption is based on the fact that the part of Memphis adjacent to the pyramid complex of Teti was very popular at that time: the area is densely covered by contemporary tombs, some of them belonging to priests of Merykare', and the city quarter is mentioned (as *Djed-isut*, from the name of Teti's pyramid) in the ancient Egyptian literary composition known as the "Instruction for Merykare'."

(14) and (15) The two southernmost Saqqara pyramids belong to kings of the 13th Dynasty and, characteristically for the period, are built of

sun-dried bricks. The owner of one of these pyramids was Khendjer, while the other remains anonymous.

Private tombs. The largest conglomeration of private tombs, contemporary with the pyramids, occupies the area north of the Step Pyramid of Djoser, and is a natural outgrowth of the earlier cemeteries of Dynasties 1 and 2. Many of these tombs, mainly of Dynasties 3–5, were partly excavated more than a century ago under the direction of the French archaeologist Auguste Mariette. Archaeological techniques and practices used during the excavation were those of the period. Before long the tombs were sanded up again and are now inaccessible.

All Old Kingdom pyramids are surrounded by cemeteries of private tombs. Those which were situated south of the Step Pyramid were in the way when the pyramid of Wenis was begun, with the result that some of them were literally covered by Wenis' causeway, and so avoided the destruction and plundering of later times (the much later tomb of King Tut'ankhamun in the Valley of the Kings at Thebes escaped looting for similar reasons). Some of these were partly rock-cut, a less usual occurrence at Saqqara where the rock is not very suitable for this form of tomb. Tombs of the late Old Kingdom and of the 1st Intermediate Period, which have been found north and east of the pyramid of Teti and around the pyramid of Pepy II, are also of exceptional interest, mainly on account of their relief decoration or their unusual architectural features.

The series of private tombs at Saqqara is uninterrupted for at least the first ten Egyptian dynasties (2920–2040 BC), and possibly even longer. The cult niche in the east face of the mastaba of the 1st and 2nd Dynasties was withdrawn into the body

Right Sheikh el-Beled, "the headman of the village," was the name given to this statue by the local workmen who discovered it in 1860. It is made of wood (the arms were carved as separate pieces and joined to the body) and was originally covered with plaster coating and painted, with the eyes inlaid. The feet and lower parts of the legs and the stick are modern. The statue is uninscribed, but the tomb in which it was found belonged to the Chief Lector-Priest Ka'aper of the early 5th Dynasty. It is an apparently realistic portrait of a corpulent aging man, and one of the finest of its type. Height: 1·10 m. Cairo, Egyptian Museum.

Far right Reliefs from Old Kingdom tombs. From the top: fowl-yard, with men force-feeding geese and cranes (from an unknown tomb of the 5th Dynasty, in East Berlin Museum); group of butchers felling an ox (Mereruka, reign of Teti); members of the household approaching the deceased with offerings for his tomb, partly unfinished (Akhtihotpe, end of the 5th Dynasty); cattle crossing a canal, with a hippopotamus and fish (Kagemni, reign of Teti); shrine with a statue of the deceased dragged on a sled to the tomb (Hetepka, late 5th or early 6th Dynasty).

of the mastaba during the 3rd or early 4th Dynasty, probably in order to protect its decorated parts more effectively against the elements. It was connected with the outside by means of a passage, thus creating the classical Saqqara cruciform chapel. This, the simplest tomb chapel, developed further during the 5th and 6th Dynasties through the addition of more rooms. These finally filled practically the whole body of the mastaba, originally a solid mass of mud brick or stone, and provided large areas suitable for relief decoration. The most famous Saqqara mastabas of the Old Kingdom are of this type, for example the mastaba of Ty with a portico, a pillared court and another four rooms, and the family tomb of Mereruka.

The New Kingdom

Private tombs. Only one important burial of the period immediately preceding the rise of the 18th Dynasty has so far been found at Saqqara. In view of the politically and socially unsettled situation in the country at that time, this is not altogether surprising. Much more puzzling, however, is the absence of tombs which could be dated to the early and middle 18th Dynasty, i.e. before the reign of Amenophis III. Several texts record hunting and other activities of Egyptian princes in the Giza area, the inference being that Memphis was at least a temporary abode for some members of the royal family, probably including the king himself, and therefore required an establishment to accommodate them and staff to maintain it. Furthermore, it is hard to conceive that there would not be a substantial number of administrative personnel in the Memphite area, and Memphite temples must have been served by a permanent priesthood. Unless the tombs of these people were not at Saqqara – a somewhat unlikely proposition – we must assume that they have not yet been discovered. The most promising area in which to look for them is the escarpment on the east edge of the necropolis, particularly between the pyramid of Teti and the northern tip of the plateau north of it. The tombs were probably rock-cut; this would conform to what we know about provincial tombs of the 18th Dynasty elsewhere (e.g. el-Kab), and would explain the almost total absence of isolated relief fragments. So far only a few rock-cut tombs of the New Kingdom, among them one belonging to a vizier called 'Aperia, have been found at Saqqara.

The large stone-built (as opposed to rock-cut) tomb of the New Kingdom appeared at Saqqara in the reign of Amenophis III, but the majority of those known so far are somewhat later. When Tut'ankhamun abandoned el-'Amarna, the royal residence was moved to Memphis rather than to Thebes. Memphis, and Saqqara as its most important cemetery, retained this position until the reign of Ramesses II, when the center of activities shifted to the northeastern delta. The finest Saqqara tombs

of the New Kingdom therefore date between the reigns of Tut'ankhamun and Ramesses II; they cover some 100 years, and present a fairly uniform group. The best craftsmen and artists in the land accompanied the court and took part in their preparation. The high artistic standard of relief work at Saqqara during this period was not achieved again in private monuments of the New Kingdom. Unfortunately, very few of these Saqqara tombs have been excavated under controlled conditions. They were fairly close to the surface, sometimes overlaying tombs of the Old Kingdom, and so they became an easy prey for collectors of antiquities of the last century, for whom the situation was made even easier by the proximity of Saqqara to Cairo. It was quite simple to dismantle the tombs, which were lined with stone blocks, and remove the decorated reliefs. New Kingdom tombs, as known at present, are concentrated in two areas of Saqqara: (1) in the vicinity of the pyramid complex of Teti; (2) in the area south of the causeway of Wenis, defined by the ruins of the Coptic monastery of Apa Jeremias to the east and the pyramid enclosure of Sekhemkhet to the west.

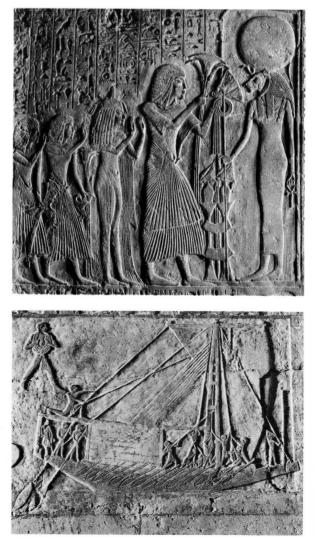

Opposite above The Overseer of Craftsmen Amenemone, followed by his wife Tahesyt and sons, offers papyrus and lotus flowers to Sakhmet, the lioness-headed Memphite goddess. End of the 18th Dynasty. Cairo, Egyptian Museum.

Opposite below Hoisting the mast of a sailing boat on the Nile, on the east wall, and (*above*) part of the west wall, with a series of false doors of various members of the family, in the tomb chapel of the Director of Singers, Nufer. Mid- to late 5th Dynasty.

Center left The Inspector of Hairdressers, Hetepka, represented on the jambs and the rear wall of the niche of his false door. Late 5th or early 6th Dynasty.

Left Painted limestone statue of a scribe reading from a papyrus, his eyes fixed on his listener. A roll of papyrus is placed on the flat surface formed by his kilt stretched over his knees, and while his left hand presses the beginning of the papyrus roll against it, his right hand is ready to unroll it as required. The papyrus still bears traces of a text in ink, but the statue itself is uninscribed and the exact circumstances of its discovery are not known, so that the owner remains anonymous. This type of sculpture was introduced in the 4th Dynasty and remained popular. Height: 49 cm. 5th Dynasty. Cairo, Egyptian Museum.

The Memphite tomb of Haremhab, east wall of the 2nd columned court. A group of courtiers dressed in long pleated costumes billowing at the front, fashionable at the end of the 18th Dynasty, and sporting long walking sticks with ornamental knobs, take part in a social occasion. Their individual tastes are shown by the different types of wig they wear. The event is a review of African and Asiatic captives brought from military campaigns abroad by the "General of the Generals" Haremhab. The captives are dragged into his presence unwillingly and subjected to various indignities by Egyptian soldiers escorting them. The scene is surprisingly unconventional, and the harsh treatment meted out to the foreigners contrasts markedly with the effeminate finery of the courtiers. The relief is very fine, with beautifully modeled details such as the hands of the men, and is in many respects a continuation of the best 'Amarna tradition. Some of the relief fragments which have been known for a long time could now be directly fitted on to this wall (a block with black captives in the Museo Civico in Bologna, and another which used to be in the Zizinia collection in Alexandria).

A spectacular discovery, and one which settled an Egyptological dispute of long standing, was made a few years ago by the Anglo-Dutch expedition of the Egypt Exploration Society and the National Museum of Antiquities, Leiden, led by G. T. Martin. Since the first half of the last century, many national museums, in particular those of Berlin, Bologna, Leiden, Leningrad, London and Vienna, have proudly displayed reliefs and stelae from the tomb of the Great Commander of the Army, Haremhab. Haremhab was the military power behind the throne in the post-'Amarna period,

during the reigns of Tut'ankhamun and Aya, and himself became king at the close of the 18th Dynasty. His royal tomb is in the Valley of the Kings at Thebes (No. 57), but the monuments in museums must have come from an earlier tomb which he had built for himself before ascending the throne. The position of the tomb from which the monuments came was nowhere precisely recorded, and even the area of Egypt in which it was situated was not certain. Both Thebes and Memphis were initially considered until the Belgian Egyptologist Jean Capart advanced strong arguments in favor of a

Those allowed to enter the underground parts of the animal necropolis during an animal funeral used to leave behind small votive stelae as tokens of their piety. Nowadays only their emplacements are sometimes left.

Memphite location in 1921. However, it was not until 54 years later, in January 1975, that he was proved right, and the position of the tomb was established with certainty.

The main features of the plan of the typical Saqqara tomb chapel of the New Kingdom were an open court, sometimes with columns on one or more of its sides, and the cult room situated at the back of the mastaba. The main element of the cult room was a stela, usually placed on the central east–west axis of the tomb, while there were often further stelae and statues in other parts of the mastaba. A small pyramid was usually built above the cult room. The mouth of the shaft leading to the underground burial chamber opened into the court.

The tombs of Apis bulls. The cult of the Apis bull was closely connected with that of the chief Memphite god Ptah. From the reign of Amenophis III onwards the tombs of the mummified Apis bulls are known from the Serapeum at Saqqara.

The Late and Greco-Roman Periods

Private tombs. During the 26th Dynasty the designers of Egyptian tombs apparently achieved what they had vainly attempted for the previous two millennia: they designed an almost completely safe tomb. In many Saqqara tombs of this period a vaulted burial chamber was built at the bottom of a very large and deep shaft which was subsequently filled with sand. Somewhat paradoxically, removing the enormous mass of this unstable material from the shaft presented the tomb robbers with much greater technical difficulties than cutting through or around the stone blocking of the shafts of the earlier periods. The other type of tomb known from this period is the more conventional rock-cut tomb.

The majority of the tombs of the Late and Greco-Roman Periods are near the Step Pyramid enclosure:
(1) to the north, approximately along the avenue of sphinxes leading to the Serapeum: mainly 30th Dynasty and Greco-Roman;
(2) to the east, particularly shaft tombs in the area of the pyramid of Userkaf, with rock-cut tombs further east, in the face of the cliff: mainly 26th Dynasty;
(3) to the west: mainly Greco-Roman;
(4) to the south, and close to the pyramid of Wenis: mainly 26th and 27th Dynasties, but also a large Ptolemaic tomb.

The Serapeum and other parts of the sacred animal necropolis. The Apis bulls were by far the most important cult animals buried at Saqqara. Already during the New Kingdom Ramesses II abandoned the earlier isolated tombs and started an underground gallery (the so-called Lesser Vaults) in which the mummified bodies of Apis bulls were deposited in large niches on either side. As there was only one of these animals at a time, an Apis bull burial occurred about once every 14 years. The gallery of Ramesses II ultimately reached a length of 68 m. A second gallery (the so-called Greater Vaults), cut at right angles to the earlier one, was inaugurated during the 26th Dynasty, and the first Apis bull laid to rest there died in year 52 of Psammetichus I. This gallery, of a total length of 198 m, remained in use until the Greco-Roman Period.

A complex of chapels and smaller temples grew up in the neighborhood of the catacombs of Apis bulls, together forming the Serapeum (from *Usir-Hapy*, i.e. the deceased Apis bull, Greek Osorapis, later identified with the artificially introduced god Sarapis of the Ptolemies). Nectanebo I and II of the 30th Dynasty were the two most distinguished contributors, the former probably also setting up the alley of human-headed sphinxes that approached the Serapeum from the city of Memphis, in the east, below the Saqqara plateau. It is said that in 1850 one of these sphinxes, which was visible above the sand, gave Auguste Mariette the idea that the Serapeum mentioned by Classical authors should be sought at Saqqara. New unpublished evidence indicates that the English antiquarian A. C. Harris came to the same conclusion several years earlier.

At the eastern end of the alley of sphinxes, immediately adjoining the city of Memphis, there were temples, among them the famous Anubieion and the Asklepieion, most of which were built by the Ptolemies. In the vicinity were cemeteries of mummified jackals and cats.

The excavations conducted since 1964 by the Egypt Exploration Society near the northwestern edge of the Saqqara necropolis have revealed galleries of the mummified "Mother of the Apis" cows, falcons, ibises and baboons.

Below Abusir from the northeast: the pyramid of Sahure' in the foreground, followed by those of Neuserre' and Neferirkare', with the remains of Ra'neferef's structure at the back. This aerial view was taken before the excavations of the Czechoslovak Institute of Egyptology (still in progress).

Right Cultivation extends close to the valley temples, though there are still the long ascending causeways to climb before one reaches the pyramids. That of Sahure' measures about 230 m, but the unfinished causeway of Neferirkare' was planned to be almost twice as long.

Abusir

The sun temple

The northernmost monument at Abusir, halfway between Abu Ghurab and the Abusir pyramids and isolated from all other buildings, is the sun temple built by King Userkaf. This is the earliest preserved sun temple in Egypt, so its simplicity and lack of relief decoration come as no surprise; but Userkaf's reign of only seven years did not allow him to complete the temple. Some Egyptian texts write its name with a hieroglyphic sign showing only an obelisk base surrounded by an enclosure wall. This seems to indicate that the obelisk itself was a later feature, and the excavation and architectural study of the temple undertaken by H. Ricke and G. Haeny between 1954 and 1957 indeed show this to be the case. Altogether four building phases of the upper part of the temple can be discerned, the first three of them dating to the 5th Dynasty.

Some uncertainty remains attached to the lower part of the monument, the so-called valley temple. A suggestion has been made (by S. Schott and H. Ricke) that this structure was connected with the cult of the goddess Neith, who originated in the delta but became very popular in the Memphite area during the Old Kingdom. Her common Memphite epithets were "North-of-the-Wall" (presumably indicating that her sanctuary in this region was situated north of the town wall of the capital Memphis) and "Opener-of-the-Ways" (a reference to her bellicose character, a "path-finder"). Her temple has not yet been positively located. Absence of any inscriptional evidence from Abusir referring to Neith, however, demands that the problem be approached with caution.

The pyramids

The founder of the 5th Dynasty, Userkaf, built his pyramid at Saqqara, but four of the next five kings moved to Abusir (the pyramid of Shepseskare' has not yet been located).

The pyramid complex of Sahure' was a magnificent structure both in size and in its decoration. Its plan can serve as a typical example of Egyptian royal funerary architecture of the 5th Dynasty. The basic building material throughout its temples was local limestone, with finer limestone from the quarries at Tura (ferried across the river from the east bank) employed for reliefs, red granite from Aswan used for columns, door jambs and lintels, and black basalt for pavements. The pyramid also was built of local limestone, with Tura limestone reserved for its outer casing and the lining of passages, and granite used for some of its interior elements. The quality of the core masonry was very poor; it was originally concealed behind the outer casing, and this saved labor. As a result, however, the structure is now little more than a huge pile of rubble.

Although most of the limestone relief decoration and inscriptions from the temples were turned into lime by industrious entrepreneurs of later times (only a little more than one hundredth of the original 10,000 square m of decoration has been preserved), the fragmentary scenes are spectacular in their subject matter as well as their technical accomplishment. It is true that the decoration of none of the earlier pyramid temples has been preserved to any significant degree, so that comparative material is lacking, but all the same it is certain that the architects and artists employed in building the pyramid complex of Sahure' were faced with entirely new problems. Their solutions set the standard for many generations to come.

The theme of the reliefs is the king himself, his

King Userkaf or the goddess Neith? An almost perfectly preserved head of a graywacke statue wearing the Egyptian red crown, found near the sun temple. This type of headdress was worn by the king, but also by the goddess Neith; the former seems a more likely identification. Cairo, Egyptian Museum.

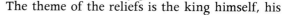

worldly activities and achievements as well as scenes characterizing his position in relation to the gods. Perhaps the most remarkable are the large wall compositions showing Sahure' shooting desert animals with a bow and arrows and Egyptian seagoing boats returning from an Asiatic expedition. The technique of the scenes is the best "low" raised relief (painted, as was always the practice) in which figures and texts project only a few millimeters above the surface of the stone.

The pyramid complexes of Neferirkare' and Neuserre' have suffered even more than that of their predecessor. Neferirkare' designed his funerary complex on a larger scale than Sahure', but did not succeed in completing it; indeed, its unfinished lower part was later appropriated by Neuserre', who diverted the causeway to his own pyramid temple. There is no tangible evidence which would identify the remains of the fourth pyramid, which is generally regarded as belonging to Ra'neferef. Nevertheless, the name of Ra'neferef's pyramid is mentioned in Egyptian texts and the identification, though not certain, is very probably correct.

The exploration of the pyramids at Abusir was carried out by L. Borchardt at the beginning of this century.

The mastaba tombs

Among the private tombs at Abusir by far the most important is the family mastaba of Ptahshepses, the vizier (the highest state official) and son-in-law of Neuserre'. It is one of the largest private tombs of the Old Kingdom, so much so that in the first half of the 19th century C. R. Lepsius numbered it as his nineteenth Egyptian pyramid. The mastaba has recently been excavated by the Czechoslovak Institute of Egyptology.

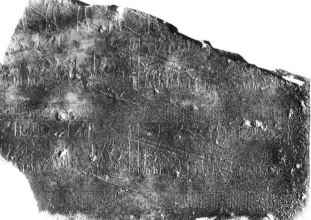

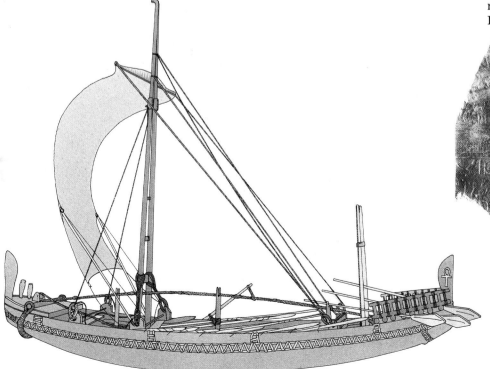

Although the mortuary temple of Sahure' produced the earliest pictorial record of Egyptian seagoing boats, their sophisticated features point to a long period of maritime activities before that (their appearance is shown here in a reconstruction). In particular, in the absence of a keel, Egyptian boats had to rely on a hogging truss (a cable connecting the prow and the stern of the vessel) for longitudinal rigidity. Old Kingdom representations of seagoing boats are rare: in addition to these only reliefs from the causeway of Wenis and another reused at el-Lisht are known. East Berlin Museum.

Abu Ghurab

The rulers of the 5th Dynasty, with the exception of the last two, expressed their preference for the Heliopolitan sun god Re᾿ by building special temples designed for his worship. The names of altogether six of these temples are known from Egyptian texts but the remains of only two have so far been located by archaeologists.

The sun temple built by King Neuserre᾿ at Abu Ghurab is a splendid example of this type of building, and one unlikely to be surpassed even if the four as yet unaccounted for are found in the future. In its general features it owes much to the typical pyramid complex of the same period. Its main axis is east–west and it consists of:
(1) the valley temple (close to a canal, so that it could be approached by boat)

(2) the causeway (linking the valley temple with the upper part of the complex)
(3) the upper temple.

The dominant feature of the upper temple was a large open court with an altar and a masonry-built (not monolithic) obelisk, the symbol of the sun god. A corridor around the temple and the chapel south of the obelisk were decorated with scenes showing the king taking part in the ceremonies of the *sed* festival. Much more unusual were, however, scenes in the "Room of the Seasons." The creative influence the sun god exerted on nature was expressed there by scenes characteristic of the Egyptian countryside in the *akhet* season (the inundation) and in the *shemu* season (the harvest). Reliefs of this type are very unusual in the royal monuments of the Old Kingdom, and are only partly paralleled by much less extensive representations in the pyramid complexes of the same king at Abusir and of Wenis at Saqqara.

Left Open court of the upper temple at Abu Ghurab from the east, with the obelisk base and the altar, and (*right*) the latter seen from the west. The unusually shaped alabaster altar consists of four *hetep* signs, each representing a simple offering mat with a loaf of bread placed on it; its diameter is some 6 m. The large calcite basins in the southeastern corner of the court belong to the slaughterhouse in the north, and may have served to catch the blood of sacrificed animals.

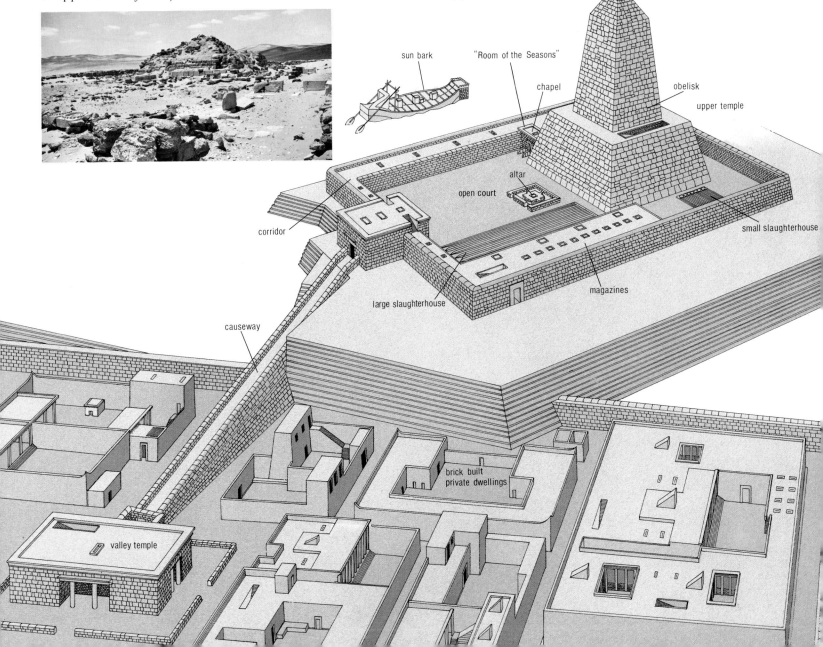

South of the upper temple was a brick-built imitation of the bark of the sun god (about 30 m long).

The temple, known to early travelers as the "Pyramid of Reegah," was uncovered by the German archaeologists Ludwig Borchardt, Heinrich Schäfer and F. W. von Bissing in 1898–1901, and its relief fragments were scattered among many museums and collections, mainly in Germany. Many of them perished during World War II. Drawings of those from the "Room of the Seasons" were published only recently, but their evaluation, nearly 80 years after their discovery, has not yet been completed.

Zawyet el-'Aryan

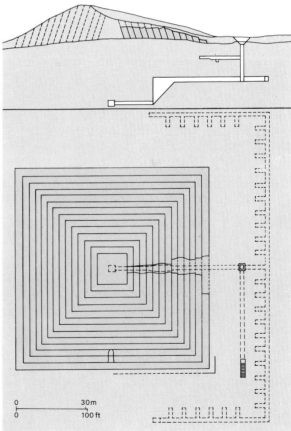

Plan and section of the "Layer Pyramid."

Neither of the two pyramids at Zawyet el-'Aryan was completed. The earlier one, the "Layer Pyramid," which was started as a step pyramid, is attributed to King Kha'ba of the 3rd Dynasty, while the other, the "Unfinished Pyramid," is dated to the 4th Dynasty by its more advanced architectural features.

One of the tombs near the pyramid of Kha'ba contained clay sealings and a pottery fragment with the name of the late Predynastic ruler Na'rmer.

Below Egyptian countryside in summer (*shemu*), on a relief from the west wall of the "Room of the Seasons" at Abu Ghurab: mullet in water, and two registers of animals, some of them giving birth, including addax (upper register, 5th from left), oryx (upper register, 4th from left, also below), gazelle, with an ostrich (upper register); the hounds on the left of the lower register belong with the figure of a hunter, of which only a basket for carrying young captured animals which was slung over the shoulder remains. East Berlin Museum.

Giza

The three Giza pyramids of the 4th Dynasty start looming on the horizon as soon as one has passed through the Cairo suburb which lent them its name and proceeds in a southwesterly direction along Shari'a al-Ahram (Avenue of the Pyramids). The history of the site, however, goes back much further, at least to the reign of King Ninetjer of the 2nd Dynasty, whose name occurs on some jar sealings found in a tomb in the southern part of the site. An even earlier tomb of the reign of King Wadj of the 1st Dynasty was located to the south of the area usually described as the Giza necropolis.

The present appearance of the site is the result of the natural configuration of the terrain combined with man's activities, in particular the quarrying of the local, fossil-rich limestone which was used as a building material for the pyramids and mastabas, and the leveling of the site by dumping builders' refuse. The most pronounced effects of the quarrying activities can be seen to the southeast of the pyramids of Khephren and Menkaure'.

The site falls naturally into two well-defined groups situated on higher ground and separated by a broad wadi. The first and much the larger and more important unit consists of the pyramids and the surrounding fields of private mastabas. The valley temples belonging to the pyramids, and the Great Sphinx with the adjacent temples, are situated below this elevated plateau. The smaller and less important group, containing only private tombs, is on a ridge to the southeast.

The systematic study of the site started in the first half of the 19th century. Among the early explorers the most prominent were Giovanni Battista Caviglia, Giovanni Battista Belzoni, R. W. Howard Vyse and J. S. Perring. C. R. Lepsius and the Prussian Expedition worked there in the early 1840s. Auguste Mariette and W. M. Flinders Petrie were active at the site in the second half of the last and at the beginning of this century. George Andrew Reisner, Hermann Junker and Selim Hassan, however, contributed more than anybody else to our knowledge of Giza. Although probably more systematically excavated than any other Egyptian site, its exploration cannot even now be regarded as completed.

The pyramid complex of Khufu

Khufu's pyramid, usually called the "Great Pyramid," must be one of the most famous monuments in the world. Its majestic size and perfection of construction have made it the focus of attention of visitors to the Memphite area since time immemorial. The pyramid was almost certainly robbed of its original contents during the period of political instability and social unrest which followed the collapse of the central royal power after

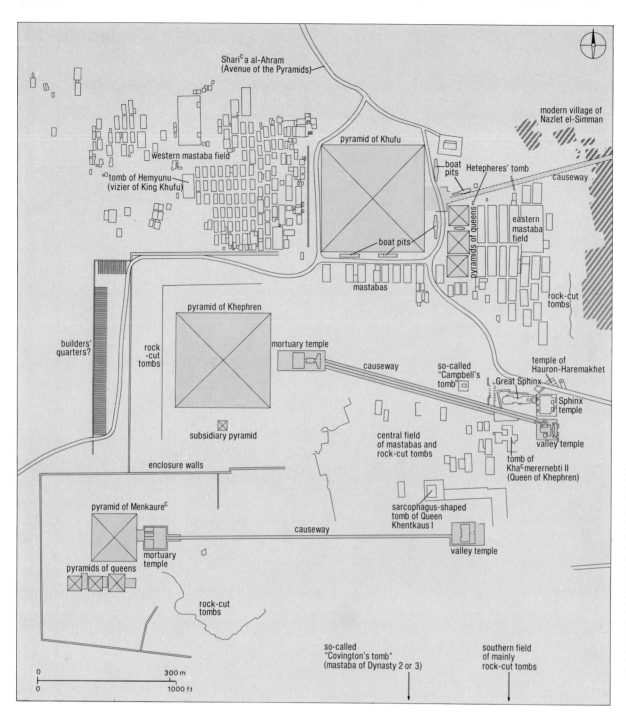

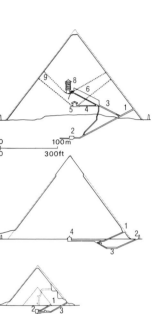

Above Sections of the pyramids looking west:
Khufu: 1 descending passage, 2 burial chamber of the 1st plan, 3 ascending passage, 4 level passage, 5 burial chamber of the 2nd plan ("Queen's Chamber"), 6 great gallery, 7 burial chamber of the 3rd plan ("King's Chamber"), 8 weight-relieving rooms, 9 "air shafts" (perhaps of religious significance).
Khephren: 1 upper entrance, 2 lower entrance, 3 burial chamber of the 1st plan, 4 burial chamber of the 2nd plan.
Menkaure': I abandoned descending passage of the 1st plan, 2 burial chamber of the 1st plan, 3 descending passage, 4 burial chamber of the 3rd plan.

the end of the Old Kingdom but definite evidence is lacking. Reuse of Khufu's decorated blocks started at el-Lisht during the reign of Amenemhet I. Modern explorers found the Great Pyramid empty, with only the massive granite sarcophagus in the burial chamber of the 3rd construction plan indicating its original purpose.

During the Middle Ages the outer limestone casing of the pyramid was completely stripped off, with the result that many buildings of old Giza and Cairo probably owe their stone material to the Great Pyramid. Today it is, apart from the small pyramids of Khufu's queens, the only element of the original pyramid complex which remains spectacularly obvious and, despite all spoliation, seems little affected. The valley temple is buried somewhere under the houses of the modern village of Nazlet el-Simman, and there is little chance of recovering it in the foreseeable future. The causeway, discernible on old maps of the site and still visible in the last century, also disappeared when the modern village

started growing. Only a patch of a basalt pavement against the east face of the pyramid shows the position of the pyramid temple. Khufu may not have succeeded in his plan to provide a safe place where his body might rest eternally, but he seems to have been completely successful in building an almost indestructible monument.

The interior of the Great Pyramid (see section) shows that the initial plan underwent at least two alterations in the process of the construction. The modern visitor enters the pyramid by an opening forced by Caliph Ma'amun's men in the 9th century AD, which is situated below and somewhat west of the original entrance. The descending passage leads to the burial chamber of the 1st plan below ground level. Before this could have been completed, the design was enlarged and altered in favor of the burial chamber of the 2nd plan, which is placed in the mass of the pyramid and approached by the ascending and level passages. Yet another change of the plan caused even this to be abandoned, and the

Right "There is no way to ruin it, but by beginning at the top. It rests upon a basis too firm to be attacked on that part; and whoever would undertake it, would find as much difficulty, as there was to raise it" (F. L. Norden, *Travels in Egypt and Nubia*, i, 1757, p. 72).

ascending passage was extended by the great gallery to reach the burial chamber of the 3rd plan. The great gallery, with its high corbeled ceiling, is easily the most impressive part of the whole interior. One of its purposes was probably to provide space for storing the granite blocks which were slid down the ascending passage after the funeral to seal it permanently. The frequent changes of plan are not so difficult to understand when one realizes that the architects were faced with the impossible task of being expected to have the complex ready to receive the burial when the king's death occurred, yet not being able to predict this "completion date" with any certainty.

Even nowadays building the Great Pyramid would present considerable technological and managerial problems. The project must have been more or less completed by the end of Khufu's 23-year reign, and that meant that every year 100,000 large blocks (i.e. about 285 a day), each weighing on average $2\frac{1}{2}$ tons, must have been quarried, dressed, brought to the building site and set in place. As the building progressed, the height to which it was necessary to lift the blocks increased, while at the same time the working platform at the top of the pyramid was rapidly decreasing in size. Once the project was "off the ground," transport of material was almost certainly exclusively effected by human force, because restricted space prevented the use of draft animals. Even such simple devices as the pulley or wheeled carriages were yet to be invented, and the problems connected with moving and lifting of heavy stone blocks must have been enormous. At least as many people as those actually dealing with the stone blocks must have been engaged in auxiliary works such as construction of inclined ramps along which the blocks were dragged, maintenance of tools, provision of food and water etc. Because of the uncertainty about the methods the Egyptians actually used, any estimate of the size of the labor force must remain a mere guess.

The sheer size of the task, the accuracy with which the structure was designed and built, the fact that no burial is on record as having ever been found in the Great Pyramid, and the seemingly absurd idea that the object of all this exercise would have been to provide a tomb for one individual, have worried scholars as well as amateurs for a long time. The interest does not seem to be abating even now but, unfortunately, not all "students" of the Great Pyramid adhere to strict scholarly methods; the esoteric approach to the pyramid is normally called "pyramidology." It would, however, be futile to maintain that Egyptologists have solved all problems connected with this or other pyramids.

A remarkable discovery was made in the early 1950s. A rectangular pit close to the south face of the pyramid of Khufu was found to contain parts of a dismantled wooden boat. In the airtight surroundings they remained almost perfectly preserved, and

Left The great gallery of Khufu's pyramid, as seen by the artists accompanying Napoleon's expedition. "You advance on with crouching. For though it is twenty-two feet in height, and has a raised way on each side, it is, however, so steep and slippery, that if you happen to fail of the holes, made for facilitating the ascent, you slide backwards, and return, in spite of yourself, quite to the resting place" (F. L. Norden, *Travels in Egypt and Nubia*, i, 1757, p. 79). Nowadays the "advance" is much easier.

Right One enters the valley temple of Khephren through one of the two doorways in its eastern facade: short passages lead into a transverse antechamber connected by another short passage with main T-shaped pillared hall.

Below When C. R. Lepsius and his team visited Giza in 1842–43, Khufu's causeway was still clearly visible. According to Herodotus the causeway was "all of stone polished and carven with figures"; although some decorated blocks have been found, his statement has not yet been fully confirmed.

the vessel, which is over 40 m long and has a displacement of about 40 tons, has now been reassembled, though it is not yet accessible to visitors. The location of another pit, almost certainly containing another boat, is known, but the pit is still to be opened. The boats were perhaps used to convey the body of the deceased king to the place of purification and embalmment and finally to the valley temple.

The pyramid complex of Khephren

Khufu's son and successor Ra'djedef started constructing his own pyramid at Abu Rawash, north of Giza, but the next king, Khephren, another son of Khufu, built his funerary complex beside his father's. Although it was designed on a more modest scale, a slight increase in the incline of the faces of the pyramid produced the effect of a structure comparable in size to the Great Pyramid. The pyramid (usually known as the "Second Pyramid") retains some of its original smooth outer casing near its summit, perhaps due to a change in the method of positioning the blocks.

The valley temple of Khephren's complex, next to the Great Sphinx, is a soberly designed building which, in the absence of almost any decoration, relies on the effect produced by the polished granite casing of the walls of its rooms and its calcite floors. A pit in one of the rooms contained a set of diorite-gneiss and graywacke sculptures of Khephren,

Left Khephren and Horus, the majesty of the pharaoh and his proximity to gods: an abstract concept expressed in stone. This type of sculpture was probably already introduced in the reign of Khufu, and certainly more than one piece was made for Khephren's temples. Epigones exist, but they all fade into nothingness in comparison. Diorite-gneiss. Height: 1·68 m. Cairo, Egyptian Museum.

Top right Menkaure' with Hathor "Lady of the Sycamore in all her Places (of worship)" and a personification of the 7th Upper Egyptian nome. Graywacke. Height: 96 cm. From the valley temple of Menkaure'. Cairo, Egyptian Museum.

Center right Restored columned portico of the family tomb of Seshemnefer, near the southeast corner of the pyramid of Khufu. Two seated statues and six small obelisks originally flanked the approach. End of the 5th or early 6th Dynasty.

Bottom right The dwarf Seneb with his wife Sentyotes and a small son and daughter. Painted limestone. Height: 33 cm. Mid-6th Dynasty or a little later. From Seneb's tomb west of the pyramid of Khufu. Cairo, Egyptian Museum.

Below "Reserve head" of an unknown lady. Limestone. Height: 25 cm. Reign of Khufu. From the tomb of Kanefer, west of the pyramid of Khufu. Berkeley (Ca.), Robert H. Lowie Museum of Anthropology.

deposited there in a later period, among them probably the most famous Egyptian statue, which shows the king seated with a hawk perched on the back of the throne.

The pyramid complex of Menkaure'

The pyramid complex of Menkaure', another king of the 4th Dynasty, is somewhat dwarfed by its two Giza companions. Although hastily finished in mud brick, its valley temple produced a superb collection of royal statues. Some of these were triads (groups of three figures) and showed the king accompanied by the Memphite goddess Hathor and personifications of nomes (provinces) of Egypt. There was also a standing double statue of the king and one of his wives, the earliest of this type in Egyptian sculpture.

The pyramid (known as the "Third Pyramid") was refurnished, probably during the 26th Dynasty when the cult of the kings buried at Giza was revived. The basalt sarcophagus found in the burial chamber was, unfortunately, lost at sea while being shipped to England so that its date cannot be verified, but remains of a wooden coffin, purporting to be that of Menkaure', were certainly put in the pyramid some 1,800 years later. An inscription discovered in 1968 on the remains of the casing near the entrance of the pyramid probably refers to this remarkable ancient effort of restoration.

Private tombs

Close to each pyramid complex there are fields of tombs of officials and priests. This proximity is explained by the fact that many of these tombs were presented by the king himself, built by royal craftsmen, and benefited from the redistribution of offerings brought to the nearby pyramid complexes. A large number of people buried in these tombs were connected with the Giza necropolis by priestly functions in their lifetime.

The most extensive mastaba fields are to the west, south and east of the pyramid of Khufu. The nuclei of the west and east fields, contemporary with the Great Pyramid, consist of stone-built mastabas of a uniform size and arranged in regular rows. These fields continued to be used through the rest of the Old Kingdom, with smaller tombs often being added in between the larger mastabas. The quarries to the southeast of the pyramids of Khephren and Menkaure', with their artificially created rock faces, provided ideal conditions for rock-cut tombs, the earliest of this type in Egypt.

A typical mastaba, such as was built at Giza in the reign of Khufu, had a stone-built superstructure with a rectangular plan and slightly sloping faces. A shaft sunk through this superstructure and cut in the rock substratum terminated in a simple burial chamber. This shaft was permanently sealed after the burial had been deposited in the chamber. The original cult chapel consisted of one or two brick-built rooms against the east face of the

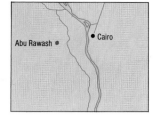

mastaba. The main element of this primitive chapel was an inscribed slab stela with a representation of the deceased seated at a table and with a list of offerings. Offerings were brought for the *ka* (spirit) of the deceased before this stela on prescribed days. There were no other decorated elements in the tomb.

The mastabas at Giza were the earliest private stone-built tombs in Egypt, and so it is not surprising that the original simple design underwent a rapid development. The greatest changes occurred in the chapel. In some of the mastabas an interior chapel was introduced, i.e. the offering room and subsidiary rooms were contained in the core of the mastaba itself, while others continued to be built with an exterior chapel. The slab stela was replaced by a false door, and the walls of the chapel began to be lined with fine limestone and decorated with reliefs.

The chief royal wives were the only persons apart from the king himself who were granted the privilege of being buried in small pyramids, situated close to the main pyramidal structure. However, the tomb of Queen Hetepheres, the wife of Snofru and the mother of Khufu, which was found to the east of the Great Pyramid in 1925, lacked a superstructure of any kind and, indeed, the most important object in the tomb, the queen's mummy, was missing. The whole tomb gave the impression of being a rather hasty reburial, and one can only speculate as to whether the original tomb, perhaps near one of Snofru's pyramids at Dahshur, could have been plundered and the mummy of the queen destroyed.

The Great Sphinx

The concept of the sphinx, a creature with a human head and a lion's body, is not known from Egypt before the reign of Ra'djedef, Khephren's immediate predecessor. The perfection with which these two incongruous elements were blended on a huge scale in the Great Sphinx is admirable, but the idea behind this creation is still rather obscure. The temple in front of it bears some resemblance to the later sun temples built by the kings of the 5th Dynasty at Abu Ghurab and Abusir, but there is no evidence for the religious significance of the Great Sphinx during the Old Kingdom. It was only some 1,000 years later that the colossal statue started being identified with the god Harmakhis ("Horus on the Horizon").

The sand which tends to cover the Sphinx has had to be cleared several times. Probably the earliest clearance was undertaken by King Tuthmosis IV, who left a record of it on the so-called "Dream Stela" erected between its forepaws.

Giza after the end of the Old Kingdom

With the end of the Old Kingdom the heyday of Giza's glory was over, and for the next 600 years nothing of significance took place there. It was only

The Great Sphinx before the removal of the sand covering its body: a photograph taken before 1875.

Left Sethos I embraced by a goddess, perhaps Isis, on the doorway to the outer hall of the temple of Harmakhis.

Below Lid of the basalt anthropoid sarcophagus of Ptahhotpe, a contemporary of Darius I. From "Campbell's Tomb," close to Khephren's causeway. Oxford, Ashmolean Museum.

in the New Kingdom that the site profited from the renewed importance of Memphis (Mit Rahina). King Amenophis II of the 18th Dynasty built a small brick temple for Harmakhis northeast of the Great Sphinx, and Sethos I later enlarged it. The site became a place of pilgrimage, and several kings and many private individuals dedicated their votive stelae there.

During the 21st Dynasty the chapel of the southern of the queens' pyramids in the Khufu complex was reconstructed into a temple of Isis "Mistress-of-the-Pyramid." The temple was enlarged during the 26th Dynasty, and the refurnishing of the burial in the Third Pyramid might have been due to the priests of this temple. Several large isolated tombs of this period are scattered along the causeway of Khephren, and doorways leading to the plundered remains of others can be seen in the rock face west of the Great Sphinx.

Abu Rawash

The site, which took its name from the village of Abu Rawash situated to the east, served as the necropolis for an important administrative center as early as the very beginning of Egyptian history. Excavations have revealed objects inscribed with the names of two kings of the 1st Dynasty, 'Aha and Den.

King Ra'djedef, who chose the commanding plateau of Abu Rawash for the site of his pyramid complex, did not therefore move on to virgin ground. The pyramid is the northernmost in the Memphite necropolis, and remains of building material visible at the site indicate that it was planned to be at least partly cased with red granite. The causeway, about 1,500 m long, approaches the pyramid and its temple from the northeast instead of from the customary east, but this was determined by the character of the terrain rather than any religious considerations. Because Ra'djedef reigned for only eight years, his funerary monument hardly got beyond the initial stages of its construction. Its most important parts have been excavated, but the burial chamber has not been reached in modern times.

Despite its incompleteness the pyramid complex gave us some excellent examples of royal sculpture of the first half of the 4th Dynasty, though even these are sadly fragmentary. The statues are made of the hard red quartzite of Gebel Ahmar (east of modern Cairo). Apart from providing us with the probably somewhat idealized features of the king, one of them is an attractive seated statue with a small figure of Ra'djedef's queen Khentetka shown kneeling holding the leg of her husband. Although eagerly taken up by makers of private statues, this type was not repeated in royal sculpture.

The site of Abu Rawash never regained its short-lived importance under Ra'djedef. However, one of the several late structures at Wadi Qaren, north of the pyramid, yielded the upper part of a beautiful statuette of Queen Arsinoe II, the sister and wife of Ptolemy II Philadelphus.

Above When discovered during the excavations of the Institut Français d'Archéologie Orientale by F. Bisson de la Roque in 1922–23, this alabaster head of Arsinoe II still possessed an equally attractive torso, now lost. Present height: 12·2 cm. New York, Metropolitan Museum of Art.

Right Quartzite head of King Ra'djedef wearing the royal *nemes* headcloth with the uraeus: the best-preserved of many fragments of at least 20 statues, originally painted. Found by E. Chassinat in 1900–01. Height: 28 cm. Paris, Musée du Louvre.

LOWER EGYPT–THE DELTA

MEDITERRANEAN SEA

Top Silver coffin of Psusennes I, from San el-Hagar. Cairo, Egyptian Museum.

Center Granite naos of Amasis at Tell el-Rub'a.

Bottom Remains of the temples at San el-Hagar.

The delta's most ancient history is still buried deep under the silt and little known, but no one doubts the antiquity of its towns or its economic importance from the very earliest times.

The eastern delta was the sensitive shoulder which Egypt rubbed with Asia. At the end of the Middle Kingdom it was overrun by Asiatics; later it became the Egyptian base for campaigns to Asia.

When the royal residence was moved to Pi-Ri'amsese in the 19th Dynasty, the delta took over the leadership from the rest of Egypt. Several of its towns saw their rulers at the helm of Egypt during the 3rd Intermediate and Late Periods. Its proximity to the political and economic centers of the ancient world favored the delta's development under the Ptolemies and the Romans.

Ausim
Scattered Late Period monuments.
Kom Abu Billo
Early Ptolemaic temple of Hathor. Necropolis with burials from 6th Dynasty to early centuries AD.
Kom el-Hisn
Temple of Sakhmet-Hathor of Middle Kingdom and later. Cemeteries of Middle and New Kingdoms.
Naukratis
Greek trading town, with temples of Greek gods, as well as Amun and Thoth.
Alexandria
Ptolemaic and Roman temple of Sarapis (Serapeum). Catacombs with sculpture and relief decoration, including Kom el-Shuqafa. Many fragmentary Classical remains.
Abusir (Taposiris Magna)
Unfinished Ptolemaic temple. Animal necropolis.
Sa el-Hagar
Few visible remains of temple of Neith, but many objects in museums.
Tell el-Fara'in
Three mounds, two with town remains, one with temple enclosure.
Behbeit el-Hagar
Temple of Isis of Late and Ptolemaic Periods.
Tell Atrib
Temple of Amasis. Town, temples and necropolis of Greco-Roman Period. Tomb of Queen Takhut.
Tell el-Muqdam
Remains of temple of Mihos. Tomb of Queen Kamama.
Samannud
Remains of temple of Onuris-Shu, of Late and Greco-Roman Periods.
el-Baqliya
Town and temple of Thoth at Tell el-Naqus. Necropolis with cemetery of ibises at Tell el-Zereiki. Other remains at Tell el-Rub'a.
Tell el-Rub'a and Tell el-Timai
Late Old Kingdom mastabas, temple of Amasis and cemetery of rams at Tell el-Rub'a. Greco-Roman Period structures at Tell el-Timai.

Heliopolis
Temple of Re' and ancillary structures of all periods at Tell Hisn, with obelisk of Senwosret I. Tombs of High Priests of Heliopolis of 6th Dynasty and others of Late Period. Ramessid tombs of Mnevis bulls at 'Arab el-Tawil.
Tell el-Yahudiya
Earthwork enclosure of late Middle Kingdom or 2nd Intermediate Period, containing temple and palace of Ramesses II. Remains of temple and town of Onias. Cemeteries of Middle Kingdom and later.
Tell Basta
Temple of Bastet by Osorkon II and others. Smaller temples of 6th, 12th, 18th and 22nd Dynasties and Greco-Roman Period. Cemeteries of animals, especially cats.
Saft el-Hinna
Temple enclosure of Sopd.
el-Khata'na and Qantir
Mounds indicating settlements of Middle Kingdom, 2nd Intermediate and Ramessid Periods. Remains of 12th-Dynasty chapel at Tell el-Qirqafa. Temple of Seth at Tell el-Dab'a (Avaris?). Middle Kingdom town and temple at Ezbet Rushdi el-Saghira. Palace of 19th and 20th Dynasties at Qantir (Pi-Ri'amsese?). Remains of colossus of Ramesses II at Tell Abu el-Shafi'a.
Tell Nabasha
Enclosure with Ramessid temple of Wadjit and temple by Amasis. Remains of Greco-Roman town. Cemetery of Late Period.
San el-Hagar
Enclosure with temple of Amun by Psusennes I and others, with ancillary buildings. Precinct of Mut, built by Siamun, Apries and Ptolemy IV Philopator. Six royal tombs of 21st and 22nd Dynasties.
Tell el-Maskhuta
Temple enclosure.

ALEXANDRIA
el-Iskandariya

CANOPUS · Abuqir
Abuqir
PHAROS
ALEXANDRIA
RAKOTE
Rose
Ras
Lake Idku
Lake Mariut
Kom el-Kanater
Abusir
TAPOSIRIS MAGNA
el-Gharbaniyat
Karm Abu Girg
Wadi el-Natrun
Qaret el-Da

	primary road
	track
—+—+—	principal railroad (1·44m)
Ⓐ	civil airport
Beni Suef	major town
▢ Biba	other settlement
• el-Kab	featured site
△ Seila	pyramid site
▽ Kubri	stela site
• Dara	other site
▪ Ghita	settlement with sites
Faqus	modern name
TANIS	classical name
IMET	ancient Egyptian name
Pithom	biblical name

scale 1 : 1 000 000

0 .... 20 .... 40 km

0 ...... 10 ...... 20 mi

Qasr Qaru

31°

30°

31°　　　　　　　　　　　　　　　　　　　　　32°

Baltim

Lake Burullus

Damietta
Dumyat

Lake Manzala

Port Said

el - Balamun

Tell el-Faraᶜin
BUTO
PE and DEP. PER-WADJIT

Shirbin

Kom Tennis

el-Matariya

Tell el-Farama
PELUSIUM

Disuq

Kafr el-Sheikh

el-Manzala

31°

OLIS PARVA

Sakha
XOIS

Dikirnis

Behbeit el-Hagar
*ISEUM
HEBYT*

el-Mansura

Tell el-Heir
Migdol

Sa el-Hagar
*SAIS
ZAU*

el-Mahalla el-Kubra

el-Baqliya
HERMOPOLIS PARVA
BAḤ

Tell el-Rubᶜa
MENDES
PER-BANEBDJEDET

San el-Hagar
TANIS
DJAⁿNET

el-Beda

ra

el-Niqrash

el-Giᶜeit

NAUKRATIS

Abusir
BUSIRIS

Samannud
SEBENNYTOS
TJEBNUTJER

Tell el-Timai
THMUIS
ᶜANPET DJEDET

Tell el-Samarra

Tell el-Ginn

Manshiyet Abu ᶜOmar

el-Qantara

Tell Dafana
DAPHNAE

Tell Abu Sefa
SILE

Kom el-Hisn
IMU

el-Simbellawein

Gezira Sangaha

Tell Nabasha
Tell Farᶜun, Tell Bedawi
IMET

Kom Hamada

el-Balamun

el-Rubᶜaiyin

Qantir

el-Khataᶜna

Tell el-Dabᶜa
AVARIS
PI-RI-AMSESE
Raamses

Tanta

Kufur Nigm

Hurbeit
PHARBAITHOS

el-Khataᶜna

Zifta

Mit Ghamr

Tell el-Muqdam
LEONTOPOLIS

Abu Kebir

Faqus
PHAKUSSA

Farasha

Shibin el-Kom

Mit Yaᶜish

Beni Anir
Zagazig

Wadi Tumilat

Tell el-Maskhuta
TJEKU Pithom

Ismailia
Lake Timsah

Kom Abu Billo
TERENUTHIS

Minuf

Benna

Tell Basta
BUBASTIS
BAST

Ismailia Canal

Tell el-Rataba

Tell el-Sahaba

Tell Atrib
ATHRIBIS
HUT-HERYIB.HUT-TAHERY-IBT

Minya el-Qamh

Saft el-Hinna
PER-SOPDU

Merimda Beni Salama

Bilbeis

Ghita

*Great
Bitter Lake*

Kabret

Little Bitter Lake

el-Qatta

Shibin el-Qanatir

Tell el-Yahudiya
LEONTOPOLIS
NAY-TA-HUT

Sweet Water Canal

Gebel Abu Hassa

Gebel Murr

Suez Canal

Tell Hisn
HELIOPOLIS
IUNU

Arab el-Tawil

Ausim
LETOPOLIS
KHEM

el-Matariya

Abu Naᶜam

Kubri

Abu Rawash

Gebel Ahmar

30°

CAIRO
el-Qahira

Suez
Quizum
KLYSMA

Giza

Old Cairo
BABYLON
Maᶜadi

el-Suweis

Zawyet el-ᶜAryan

Wadi Digla

Tura

Abu Ghurab
Abusir

Mit Rahina
MEMPHIS

Helwan

Saqqara

Dahshur

Manshiyet Dahshur

Mazghuna

Wadi el-Garawi

Dahshur

Umm el-Sawan

Widan el-Faras

Qasr el-Sagha

el-ᶜAiyat

Dimai

el-Lisht

Kom Aushim

Birket Qarun

DERIS

FAIYUM

Maidum

Atfih

Byahmu

Seila

Medinet el-Faiyum

Hawara

el-Wasta

el-Lahun

el-Lahun

Kom Medinet Ghurab

nef Madi

harak el-Sultani

Ihnasya el-Medina

Beni Suef

29°

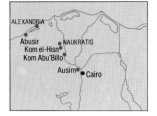

Ausim

Ancient Egyptian *Khem* (Greek Letopolis), some 13 km northwest of modern Cairo, was the capital of the 2nd Lower Egyptian nome. The nome and its falcon god Khenty-irty (a form of Horus, also referred to as Khenty-Khem, "The Foremost One of *Khem*") are mentioned in Egyptian texts as early as the 4th Dynasty, but so far only a few late monuments, bearing the names of Necho II, Psammetichus II, Hakoris and Nectanebo I, have been found at the site.

Kom Abu Billo

At the point where the route leading from Wadi Natrun approaches the Rosetta branch of the Nile, there lies the town of Tarrana (from Coptic *Terenouti* and classical Terenuthis). The name derives from that of the serpent goddess Renenutet (Termuthis) who was probably worshiped in the area. The remains of the temple and the necropolis have been found nearby, at the mound of Kom Abu Billo.

The temple of Kom Abu Billo, dedicated to Hathor "Mistress of Mefket" (ancient Tarrana, but *mefket* also means turquoise), was located by F. Ll. Griffith in 1887–88. It was not possible to establish its complete plan, but blocks decorated with exquisite low raised relief showed it to be one of the few surviving works of Ptolemy I Soter, completed by Ptolemy II Philadelphus. Burials of cattle in the vicinity are probably connected with the cult of Hathor.

The large necropolis of Kom Abu Billo contains burials ranging from the 6th Dynasty to the 4th century AD. A number of New Kingdom pottery sarcophagi (called "slipper coffins"), with their lids modeled to imitate often very grotesque faces, have been found. The site is particularly well known for a special type of tomb stela dating to the first four centuries AD (called "Terenuthis stelae"). The deceased, represented in un-Egyptian style, is usually standing with upraised arms or reclining on a couch, with a short text in demotic or Greek below.

Kom el-Hisn

A large mound, measuring some 500 m across, called Kom el-Hisn, covers the remains of the ancient town of *Imu*. From the New Kingdom onwards this was the capital of the 3rd Lower Egyptian nome,

replacing the earlier *Hut-ihyt*, which has not yet been located.

The most important feature at Kom el-Hisn is the rectangular outline of a temple enclosure (about 115 by 64 m). Statues of Amenemhet III and Ramesses II found there identify the temple as belonging to Sakhmet-Hathor. Hathor was the traditional goddess of the area.

The tomb of the "Overseer of Prophets" Khesuwer of the Middle Kingdom was found southwest of the temple enclosure.

Extensive cemeteries (at least 700 graves) of the Middle and New Kingdoms have been excavated in the vicinity. Many of the Middle Kingdom burials of men contained weapons (battle-axes, spears and daggers).

Naukratis

A mound near the villages el-Gi'eif, el-Nibeira and el-Niqrash (the last perhaps preserving the ancient name), in the 5th (Saite) nome of Lower Egypt, is the site of the Greek trading post Naukratis. The Greeks (initially Milesians) settled in the area some time during the 26th Dynasty, and under Amasis the town was granted a monopoly of Greek trade.

Naukratis contained several temples of Greek

Above Early Ptolemaic reliefs from Kom Abu Billo: Hathor, in Bolton Museum and Art Gallery, and Ptolemy I Soter, in Oxford, Ashmolean Museum.

Below Basalt royal head, probably of Amenemhet III, found in the tomb of Khesuwer at Kom el-Hisn, though originally from the temple nearby. The identification rests on the discovery of another sculpture of Amenemhet III in the temple. Height: 35 cm. Cairo, Egyptian Museum.

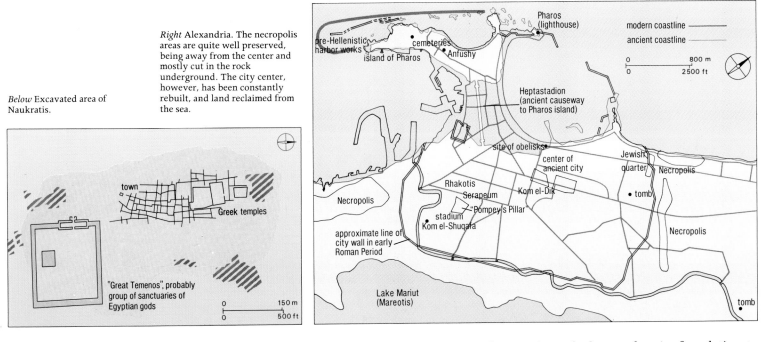

Right Alexandria. The necropolis areas are quite well preserved, being away from the center and mostly cut in the rock underground. The city center, however, has been constantly rebuilt, and land reclaimed from the sea.

Below Excavated area of Naukratis.

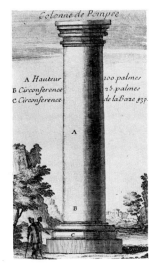

Above Engraving of "Pompey's pillar" in the Serapeum at Alexandria (reign of Diocletian), from Gemelli Careri, *Voyage du tour du monde*, i, Paris, 1729, p. 36. All the picture – evidently the engraver's free invention – records is dimensions; form and proportions are different from those of the original, and the scene is a landscape of European inspiration, not part of a Near Eastern city.

gods but also an Egyptian temple, dedicated probably to Amun and Thoth, in its southern part. Hardly anything of these monuments can be seen nowadays.

Alexandria

In the Egyptian language Alexandria was called Raqote, a name that was used by Ptolemy I Soter in a text inscribed before he was proclaimed king in 305, and was taken over from an Egyptian settlement on the site. Apart from Raqote, pre-Ptolemaic sea walls that have been found under water north and west of the island of Pharos are of quite uncertain date. A quarter of the city continued to be called Rhakotis by the Greek population. It was one of those where native Egyptians lived, and contained monuments in an Egyptian style. A second native quarter was a walled settlement on Pharos, near which are Egyptianizing tombs of the late Ptolemaic Period. Among the lower classes there was widespread intermarriage between Greeks and Egyptians, but otherwise Alexandria was a Greek city of very mixed population, whose most important non-Greek element was the Jewish community. As the chief city and port of the Hellenistic world it did, however, play a vital part in the dissemination of Egyptian lore in Classical antiquity.

The Serapeum, the most important temple of the Greco-Egyptian god Sarapis, was in the quarter of

Rhakotis. Bilingual plaques date its foundation to the reign of Ptolemy III Euergetes I. The present remains, including the famous "Pompey's pillar" of the reign of Diocletian, date mainly to the first centuries AD, but incorporate a considerable amount of pharaonic Egyptian material, most notably sphinxes and other large sculpture, whose function will have been to set the scene. Objects like these, and numerous smaller pieces, were also exported, no doubt through Alexandria, to be used in Roman temples of Sarapis and Isis, or in the grounds of Hadrian's villa at Tivoli and Diocletian's palace at Split. The monuments in which they were placed were not in an Egyptian style.

Near the Serapeum is the catacomb of Kom el-Shuqafa. It dates to the 1st–2nd century AD, and contains a remarkable complex of burial areas with Egyptianizing scenes and motifs. Chambers near ground level have retained some painted decoration, while only sculpture and relief remain in the deeper parts. Unlike the tomb of Petosiris at Tuna el-Gebel, which has Grecizing scenes by Egyptian artists, the catacomb has Egyptian motifs in a simplified Classical style. For the Isis cult such work was influential in the Roman world at large, starting by running parallel with the use of genuine Egyptian objects and ending by assuming greater importance. The style was probably Alexandrian in origin.

Right Painted tomb near Kom el-Shuqafa in Alexandria, c. 2nd century AD. The ornamentation is Classical, but the main scene is Egyptian-inspired, showing a winged disk above the mummy on a bier, with two mourning figures and two kites; both these pairs derive from Isis and Nephthys.

Abusir

About 45 km west of Alexandria is Abusir, ancient Taposiris Magna, an important town in the Ptolemaic Period, which has an unfinished temple in native Egyptian style. The enclosure is in limestone instead of the traditional mud brick, but uses mud-brick building techniques. The east side of the enclosure wall is in the form of an entrance pylon. The temple is uninscribed, and so cannot be dated precisely. Nearby was a large animal necropolis, which is a further indication of the town's significance as a native center.

The Chief of Physicians
Psammetik-seneb kneeling with
a naos of Neith: basalt statue
originally set up in the temple of
the goddess at Sa el-Hagar.
Heavily restored, probably in the
18th century. Height: 63 cm.
26th Dynasty. Vatican, Museo
Gregoriano Egizio.

Sa el-Hagar

Sais (ancient Egyptian *Zau*) and its goddess Neith are known from the very beginning of Egyptian history. The town was the capital of the 5th Lower Egyptian nome, which until the 12th Dynasty also incorporated the area south of it, later the 4th nome. Politically, Sais came to prominence only towards the end of the 8th century BC when its ambitious local princes Tefnakhte and Bocchoris (24th Dynasty) clashed with the rulers of the 25th (Nubian) Dynasty. During the 26th Dynasty it was the capital of the country, with temples, royal palaces and tombs of the kings of the Saite Dynasty. Some idea about its topography can be gleaned from the remarks of Herodotus, who wrote in the middle of the 5th century BC.

Despite the city's famous past, no monuments except some isolated stone blocks are visible in the area nowadays. Even at the end of the last century it was still possible to trace remains of a huge rectangular enclosure (some 800 by 700 m, according to the plan published by G. Foucart in 1898) north of the village of Sa el-Hagar, on the right bank of the Rosetta branch of the Nile. Fifty years earlier, in the middle of the last century, the artists of Lepsius's expedition recorded a view of the sizable remains of the walls. The relatively recent but very quick disappearance of the enclosure was due to the activities of the *sabbakhin* who look for old mud-brick structures as a source of cheap fertilizer. Stone blocks had already been removed to be used as building material in the Middle Ages. It has been possible to locate some of them in various towns and villages along the Rosetta branch.

There is a substantial number of monuments, such as statues, stelae, sarcophagi etc., in museums whose texts show them to come from Sais. The great majority of them date to the 26th Dynasty, and none so far is earlier than the 3rd Intermediate Period.

Sa el-Hagar has been little explored by archaeologists, and the few small excavations have not been very successful.

Tell el-Fara'in

Tell el-Fara'in ("The Mound of the Pharaohs"), in the 6th Lower Egyptian nome, is the site of Buto (from ancient Egyptian *Per-Wadjit*, "The Domain of Wadjit," Coptic *Pouto*). The town was held to have consisted of two parts, called *Pe* and *Dep*, and was the home of the cobra goddess Wadjit, the tutelary goddess of Lower Egypt. In this it was paralleled by Upper Egyptian *Nekheb* (el-Kab) and *Nekhen* (Kom el-Ahmar) and the vulture goddess Nekhbet. "The

Souls of Pe," falcon-headed figures connected with Buto, may have represented the early local rulers ("Lower Egyptian kings") of the area.

The site of Tell el-Fara'in consists of three mounds, two with town remains and one with a temple enclosure. This corresponds to the expected layout of Buto, but the results of excavations carried out so far do not suggest that the town's size was commensurate with its ideological importance throughout Egyptian history. Apart from one Early Dynastic cylinder seal there are a few objects of the ubiquitous Ramesses II and a donation stela of year 38 of Shoshenq V; the rest are Late Period pieces of little significance.

Above Offering-bearers from the tomb of Harhotpe at Tell el-Fara'in, probably of the 30th Dynasty. Cairo, Egyptian Museum.

Below The ruins of Sa el-Hagar as seen by the artists of Lepsius's expedition in 1842.

Below A typical temple statue: Djeho, son of Neb'ankh and Hetepher, kneeling with a naos containing a statuette of Osiris. Hard black stone. Height: 54 cm. Ptolemaic. No recorded provenance, but according to its inscriptions certainly from Tell Atrib. Lisbon, Fundação Calouste Gulbenkian.

Early Ptolemaic granite relief from the temple of Isis at Behbeit el-Hagar, showing the king censing before a god with hawk's head and lunar disk, perhaps Khons, with parts of further scenes on either side. Richmond (Va.), Museum of Fine Arts.

classical image of Egypt. When temples to Isis were built, especially in Rome in the early empire, they were often adorned with them. Monuments of the Nectanebos and of Isis appear to have been particularly favored, and a block from this temple was found in the chief Isis temple in Rome.

Behbeit el-Hagar

Behbeit el-Hagar is the site of one of the most important temples of Isis in Egypt. It is near Samannud (ancient Sebennytos), the home town of the kings of the 30th Dynasty, who were reputed to have a special devotion to Isis. It is likely that the foundation dates to that period, or that a large temple was built on the site of an unimportant predecessor.

The temple is like many Late Period monuments in being built in hard stone, in this case granite, but it is the only remaining example of a structure of this size that uses only hard stone. The ruins occupy an area 80 by 55 m, and are set in an enclosure of which two sides can still be distinguished. The temple itself, however, has collapsed completely, either through quarrying activities or after an earthquake, and its plan has not been recovered; all that is visible is a disorderly mass of relief blocks and some architectural elements. The reliefs are very fine work of Nectanebo I–II and of Ptolemy II Philadelphus and III Euergetes I, much more delicate than that of the Greco-Roman temples of Upper Egypt. Reliefs in this style and material played an important part in formulating the

Tell Atrib

Tell Atrib, north of the town of Benha on the right bank of the Damietta branch of the Nile, derives its name from ancient Egyptian *Hut-hery-ib* (or *Hut-ta-hery-ibt*), Coptic *Athrebi* and Greek Athribis. It was the capital of the 10th Lower Egyptian nome, and the name *Kem-wer* ("The Great Black One," i.e. bull) could equally be applied to the local god, the nome and its capital. In the Dynastic Period the crocodile (or falcon) god Khentekhtai became the most prominent local deity.

Egyptian texts show that the history of Tell Atrib goes back at least to the beginning of the 4th Dynasty, but the remains of the earliest temple found there are dated by foundation deposits to the reign of Amasis. A town, temples and necropolis of the Greco-Roman Period have also been located. The topography of the little-excavated Tell Atrib still presents difficulties. Isolated monuments of various dates are known from, or have been ascribed to, Tell Atrib on the basis of their inscriptions, though none of them is earlier than the 12th Dynasty. As with all delta sites, caution is required when dealing with objects which might have been brought from elsewhere and reused. Many monuments have been found by the *sabbakhin* whose activities have seriously affected the site: in 1924 a large cache (some 50 kg) of silver treasure consisting of ingots, amulets, rings, earrings etc., dating to the 25th–30th Dynasties, was discovered by them. Other monuments have been uncovered accidentally by peasants or workmen, e.g. the tombs of Queen Takhut (wife of Psammetichus II), of a woman called Tadubaste, and Pefteu'awyamun Tjaiemhorimu of the Late Period, all in the north part of the tell.

Uninscribed statue of the 12th Dynasty from Tell Atrib. Granite. Height: 63.5 cm. London, British Museum.

Tell el-Muqdam

Some of the most extensive man-made mounds of earth in the Egyptian delta are on the right bank of the Damietta branch of the Nile, about 10 km southeast of Mit Ghamr, at Tell el-Muqdam. This is the site of ancient Leontopolis, an important town in the 11th Lower Egyptian nome and its capital during the Ptolemaic Period. There are indications that Tell el-Muqdam was the seat of a line of kings of

the 23rd Dynasty and perhaps their burial place, but so far only the tomb of Queen Kamama, the mother of Osorkon IV, has been found.

The temple of the local lion god Mihos (Greek Miysis), situated in the east part of the ruins, suffered the fate of many similar buildings in the delta: most of its stone blocks have been removed and reused, leaving even the date of the structure uncertain. Another tell in the neighborhood, Mit Ya'ish, has produced material of the 22nd Dynasty (a stela of Osorkon III) and of the Ptolemaic Period.

Some monuments (particularly statues) of earlier dates have been found usurped by later rulers and probably removed from their original places. At Tell el-Muqdam this certainly applies to the statue of a 14th- (or 13th-) Dynasty king Nehesy, usurped by Merneptah, and possibly to others, particularly some of Senwosret III. The number of monuments found in controlled excavations is small, but the original provenance of others (from the reign of Ramesses II or earlier) can be established from their inscriptions and other indications. Many objects, particularly statuettes of lions in bronze and other materials, which used to be in D. M. Fouquet's private collection, dispersed in 1922, derived from Tell el-Muqdam.

Samannud

Ancient *Tjebnutjer* (Coptic *Djebenoute* or *Djemnouti*, Greek Sebennytos), now on the left bank of the Damietta branch of the Nile, was the capital of the 12th Lower Egyptian nome and a town of some importance towards the end of the pharaonic period: according to Manetho, himself a native of Sebennytos, the kings of the 30th Dynasty came from there.

A large mound west of the modern town marks

the remains of the temple of the local god Onuris-Shu. The granite blocks bear the names of Nectanebo II, Alexander IV, Philip Arrhidaeus and Ptolemy II Philadelphus. Some earlier monuments are said to have come from Samannud or its neighborhood, including an Old Kingdom false door of a certain Sesni, an altar of Amenemhet I, a statue dated to Psammetichus I, a fragment of a shrine of Nepherites (probably I) and sculpture of the reign of Nectanebo I. No blocks or other architectural elements of buildings earlier than the 30th Dynasty have been reported.

el-Baqliya

South of the modern village el-Baqliya, three low mounds, rising only a few meters above the cultivated land, mark the site of the ancient *Ba'h* (Hermopolis Parva of the Greco-Roman Period), the capital of the 15th Lower Egyptian nome.

Tell el-Naqus probably covers the town and the temple of the local god Thoth. Outlines of an enclosure measuring some 350 by 384 m are visible,

Above Bronze inlay of the animal sacred to the god Mihos, originally probably part of a piece of temple furniture; early Ptolemaic, from Tell el-Muqdam. Height: 14·7 cm. Formerly in the Fouquet collection, now in the Brooklyn Museum (N.Y.).

Below left Procession of personifications bringing symbolic offerings to the god Onuris-Shu on behalf of Nectanebo II. Granite relief from the temple at Samannud. Baltimore (Md.), Walters Art Gallery.

Below Nekht-harhebi, whose "good name" was Nekht-harmenkhib, a contemporary of Psammetichus II, is known from his six statues from various delta sites, and his sarcophagus found at Sa el-Hagar. This sandstone kneeling statue, 1·48 m high, probably comes from el-Baqliya. Paris, Musée du Louvre.

Mastaba tombs and houses uncovered by the expedition of the Institute of Fine Arts of New York University at Tell el-Rubʻa in 1977.

The Manager of the Estate Tetu, son of Nekhti: the *hotep-di-nesu* formula running down the front of his long kilt invokes Atum "Lord of Heliopolis" and so indicates the provenance of the statuette. Granite. Height: 27 cm. West Berlin Museum.

but few remains can be seen inside. There are some granite blocks lying outside the enclosure, including a large bell-shaped capital of a papyrus column which probably gave the tell its name ("The Mound of the Bell").

The necropolis belonging to the town, including a cemetery of ibises, was probably situated at Tell el-Zereiki.

Tell el-Rubʻa covers further, as yet unidentified, remains: a quartzite monolithic naos (shrine) dedicated to Thoth by Apries was found there, as well as the torso of a granite statue of Nectanebo I.

Blocks of Psammetichus I and Nectanebo I and a fragment of a basalt sarcophagus of a certain ʻAhmose of the 26th Dynasty have been found in the area of el-Baqliya. In recent years another statue of Nectanebo I was discovered, and in 1970 a granite block statue of a scribe called Nehesy, a contemporary of Ramesses II. The latter is so far the earliest monument known from the little-excavated el-Baqliya.

Tell el-Rubʻa and Tell el-Timai

Two mounds several hundred meters apart, northwest of the modern town of el-Simbellawein, in the central delta, were in turn the site of the capital of the 16th Lower Egyptian nome: the northern Tell el-Rubʻa (ancient Egyptian *Per-banebdjedet*, "The Domain of the Ram Lord of *Djedet*," Greek Mendes) was in the Greco-Roman Period replaced in this role by the southern Tell el-Timai (Greek Thmuis). The earlier names of Tell el-Rubʻa were *ʻAnpet* and *Djedet*. Originally, the fish goddess Hatmehyt was the local deity, but in the Dynastic Period the most prominent local cult was that of the Ram (*Ba*) of Mendes (*Djedet*). A cemetery of sacred rams with large sarcophagi, in which the animals were buried, can be seen in the northwest corner of the enclosure of Tell el-Rubʻa.

The nome is mentioned in Egyptian texts as early as the 4th Dynasty, and the earliest monuments found at Tell el-Rubʻa are mastaba tombs of the late Old Kingdom. A number of isolated monuments of the Ramessid kings, in particular Ramesses II, Merneptah and Ramesses III, suggest that there is a temple structure of that date, but none has yet been found. The earliest known temple, attested by its foundation deposits, was built by Amasis. A red granite monolithic naos, nearly 8 m high, dedicated by the same king, dominates the scene, but apart from the incompletely preserved enclosure walls nothing is left of the temple itself, and no fragments of temple reliefs have been found in the area. In the Late Period Tell el-Rubʻa reached the peak of its glory, and, as the kings of the 29th Dynasty are said to have originated from there, it might even have functioned as the royal residence and capital.

Tell el-Timai, much spoiled by the *sabbakhin*, contains remains of brick-built structures of the Greco-Roman Period.

Heliopolis

Ancient Egyptian *Iunu* (Coptic and biblical *On*), the capital of the 13th Lower Egyptian nome, is at and around Tell Hisn, northwest of the modern el-Matariya (effectively a Cairo suburb, north of Misr el-Gedida). The temples of the sun god Reʻ, Reʻ-Atum or Reʻ-Harakhty, at Heliopolis were among the most important and influential religious institutions in the land, economically and, still more, ideologically. The Heliopolitan doctrine with the god creator Atum and the sun god Reʻ (hence the Greek name of the town, from *helios* = sun) at its center played a very prominent part in the shaping of Egyptian religious and political history. The *benu* bird (phoenix) and the Mnevis bull were worshiped as manifestations of the god, and Hathor "Mistress of Hetpet" and Iusʻas were the female deities connected with Heliopolis.

Despite the town's importance, no spectacular monuments can be seen in the area nowadays, except a still-standing obelisk of Senwosret I. Because Cairo is so near, most of the stone was removed from the temples and reused a long time ago, while the fact that the area is cultivated or built over hinders archaeological work. The main temple and probably also the town at Tell Hisn were surrounded by massive brick-built double walls. The enclosed area has been estimated to measure some 1,100 by 475 m, but the architectural history of the site and its precise topography are not clear. Isolated monuments (statues, reliefs, obelisks, offering tables etc.) dating between the 3rd Dynasty (Djoser) and the Ptolemaic Period have been found in abundance, and excavations, particularly those carried out in recent years and still in progress,

Below Small polychrome faience tiles representing lotus flowers, probably from the temple palace of Ramesses III at Tell el-Yahudiya. Brooklyn Museum (N.Y.).

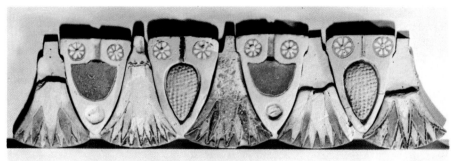

have revealed a number of buildings described as temples built by various New Kingdom kings: Amenophis III (restored by Ramesses II), Sethos I, Ramesses II and IX, Merneptah. It remains to be seen whether these buildings are temples in their own right attached to the great temple of Re' (at least ten of which are known to have existed at Heliopolis during the New Kingdom), or whether they are parts of the temple of Re' itself.

Tombs of the high priests of Heliopolis during the 6th Dynasty have been located some 550 m southeast of the obelisk of Senwosret I, near the southeast corner of the enclosure. Proceeding in the same general direction, at el-Matariya, about 950 m from the obelisk, there were tombs of the Late Period, while at a distance of some 3 km, at Ard el-Na'am ("The Ostrich Farm"), objects indicating the presence of further tombs of the Ramessid and Late Periods have been found.

Tombs of Mnevis bulls, mainly of the Ramessid Period, have been discovered about 1·3 km northeast of the obelisk, at 'Arab el-Tawil.

Tell el-Yahudiya

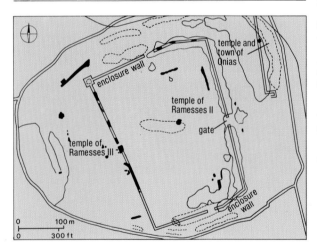

Tell el-Yahudiya ("The Mound of the Jews"), ancient Egyptian *Nay-ta-hut*, Greek Leontopolis, lies some 2 km southeast of the village of Shibin el-Qanatir, within the ancient 13th (Heliopolitan) nome of Lower Egypt.

The most conspicuous, as well as the most puzzling, feature of the site is the remains of a rectangular earthwork enclosure, the so-called "Hyksos Camp," measuring some 515 by 490 m. It is usually interpreted as fortifications and dated to the late Middle Kingdom or the 2nd Intermediate Period. No good Egyptian parallels for such massive defensive enclosure walls, plastered over and sloping ("glacis") on the outside and almost vertical inside, can be found, and so the builders of the enclosure have been sought outside Egypt, the immigrants from northwest Asia during the Hyksos

Period being the obvious choice. There is, however, a strong possibility that the structure is of a religious rather than military character.

Inside the enclosure, in its northeastern part, colossal statues of Ramesses II were found, which suggest that this was the site of a temple of that date. In its western part there stood a temple of Ramesses III, and faience tiles decorated with rosettes, *rekhyt* birds symbolic of the king's subjects, cartouches and foreign captives, probably originating in the temple palace and now in various museum collections, come from there.

Outside the enclosure, near its northeastern corner, are remains of a temple and town which the exiled Jewish priest Onias was given permission to build by Ptolemy VI Philometor. The settlement flourished for more than 200 years until the temple was closed by Vespasian in 71 AD.

Cemeteries of various dates, starting with the Middle Kingdom, extend to the east of the enclosure.

Above Obelisk of Senwosret I at Heliopolis. Granite. Height: about 20 m.

Tell Basta

Tell Basta, southeast of Zaqaziq, is the site of the ancient *Bast* (classical Bubastis, from *Per-Bastet*, "The Domain of Bastet"), the town of the lioness goddess Bastet (Bubastis), and the capital of the 18th Lower Egyptian nome during the Late Period. The town gained prominence very early in Egyptian history, at least partly because of its strategically important location controlling the routes from Memphis to Sinai (Wadi Tumilat) and to Asia.

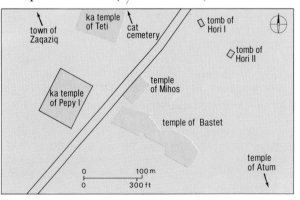

Right Bronze statuette of a cat, the sacred animal of Bastet of Bubastis (Tell Basta). Probably Late Period. Oxford, Ashmolean Museum.

Above Silver jug with a goat handle of gold, from a 19th-Dynasty hoard of gold and silver vessels and jewelry found at Tell Basta in 1906. Height: 16·8 cm; weight: 602 g. Cairo, Egyptian Museum.

Far right Bronze bust of a king, probably from Qantir. It is usually thought to show Ramesses II, but a much later date seems more likely. Height: 36 cm. Hildesheim, Roemer-Pelizaeus-Museum.

Below The form and finish brought to perfection, not diminished even by the present fragmentary state of the sculpture: Nectanebo I from Saft el-Hinna. Granite. Height: 67 cm. London, British Museum.

Politically, the peak of the town's influence was reached during the 22nd Dynasty, the kings of which came from Bubastis. The decline of Bubastis occurred in the first centuries AD.

The main temple, dedicated to Bastet, was excavated by E. Naville between 1887 and 1889. It was not possible to establish the plan of the edifice, some 200 or 300 m long, beyond its basic division into the entrance hall of Osorkon II, the *sed*-festival hall and the hypostyle hall of Osorkon III, and the hall of Nectanebo II. In the middle of the 5th century BC Herodotus described the temple as standing on an island, with two water channels running on its sides, and being on a much lower level than the city in the middle of which it was located. The excavation confirmed the correctness of both of these statements, though the channels would have been more appropriately described as the two arms of the sacred lake. Blocks of various dates, including some bearing the names of kings of the 4th Dynasty, were found reused in the temple.

Among the other buildings discovered at Tell Basta, there are the *ka* temples of Teti (a structure measuring some 108 by 50 m, about 250 m northwest of the temple of Bastet) and Pepy I, the *sed*-festival chapels of Amenemhet III and Amenophis III, a temple of Atum built by Osorkon II, a temple of Mihos (the lion god regarded as the son of Bastet) dedicated by Osorkon III, and a temple of the Roman Period.

Several burials of important officials have been found at Tell Basta, among them the vizier Iuti of the 19th Dynasty and two viceroys of Kush called Hori, who were father and son, of the end of the 19th and the 20th Dynasties. Some Old Kingdom monuments indicating the presence of tombs of this date were found recently. Extensive cemeteries of sacred animals, particularly cats (associated with Bastet from the 3rd Intermediate Period onwards) have also been located.

Saft el-Hinna

The village of Saft el-Hinna, east of Zaqaziq, stands on the site of ancient *Per-Sopdu* ("The Domain of Sopd"), the earlier capital of the 20th nome of Lower Egypt. In 1885 E. Naville partly uncovered the brick-built enclosure walls of the local temple, measuring some 75 (or more) by 40 m, as well as a number of uninscribed basalt blocks.

Few inscribed monuments have been found at Saft el-Hinna: statue fragments of Ramesses II are among the earliest, but the remains of a granite naos dedicated to Sopd by Nectanebo I are the most impressive.

The district of el-Khata'na and Qantir

el-Khata'na and Qantir are villages some 6 and 9 km respectively north of Faqus, in the northeastern delta. A number of sandy mounds in the area show signs of settlements of the Middle Kingdom and the 2nd Intermediate Period, and of the Ramessid Period. Avaris, the Hyksos center during the 2nd Intermediate Period, and Pi-Ri'amsese, the delta residence of the Ramessids and Raamses of the Exodus, are probably to be located somewhere here (Avaris perhaps in the south, at Tell el-Dab'a, and Pi-Ri'amsese probably in the north, near Qantir).

The southernmost site of importance, near el-Khata'na, is Tell el-Qirqafa, where remains of the

granite gate of a columned chapel of Amenemhet I and Senwosret III were found.

At Tell el-Dabʻa, east of the last, statues of Queen Nefrusobk and King Harnedjheriotef (Hetepibreʻ) were among the finds of the late 12th and 13th Dynasties. In the 2nd Intermediate Period Tell el-Dabʻa witnessed a large influx of foreign migrants from Asia, contemporary with the rise of the 15th (Hyksos) Dynasty. An apparent hiatus during the 18th Dynasty was followed by building activities under Haremhab and the Ramessids. These included a large temple structure (180 by 140 m), probably dedicated to Seth.

A Middle Kingdom town and a temple built by Amenemhet I were found at Ezbet Rushdi el-Saghira, north of Tell el-Dabʻa.

In the 1920s a number of decorated glazed tiles were reported to have been discovered in the vicinity of Qantir. Subsequent excavations confirmed that the tiles, bearing floral designs, fish, ducks, plants etc., had come from a palace of the 19th and 20th Dynasties. Some of them were inscribed with the names of Sethos I and Ramesses II. Importantly, contemporary stelae, statues, blocks from doorways and other monuments were also found.

At Tell Abu el-Shafiʻa, north of Qantir, there is the base of a seated colossus of Ramesses II, perhaps indicating the position of a temple.

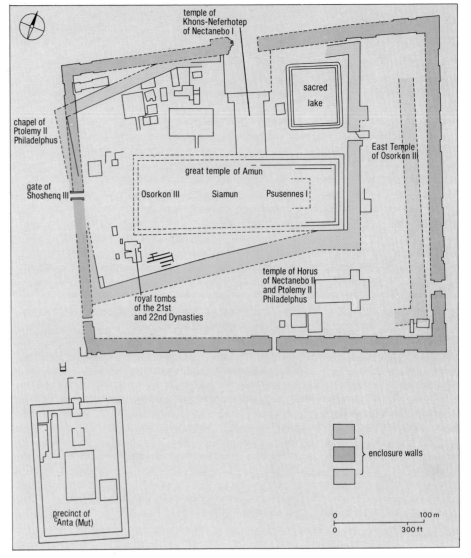

Tell Nabasha

A large mound, some 1·5 km across, in the northeastern delta, is the site of ancient Egyptian *Imet*. During the New Kingdom this was the capital of the district which was later divided into the 18th (capital: Bubastis) and 19th (capital: Tanis) Lower Egyptian nomes. The modern names of the locality are Tell Nabasha, Tell Farʻun or Tell Bedawi.

The outlines of the brick-built temple enclosure of the goddess Wadjit, measuring some 215 by 205 m, are still discernible. The enclosure originally contained at least two temples. The larger one (about 65 by 30 m), approached from the east, was probably built under the Ramessids (Ramesses II and others are attested). Although Middle Kingdom sphinxes usurped by later kings were found, it is likely that these had been brought from elsewhere. The smaller temple (about 30 by 15 m), near the northeast corner of the earlier temple and with its longer axis pointing to the north, is dated to Amasis by its foundation deposits. Reused Middle Kingdom monuments were also discovered here.

Remains of a town of the Greco-Roman Period were located southeast of the temple enclosure, and a cemetery, mostly of the Late Period, lies in the plain further to the east.

San el-Hagar

Situated in the northeastern part of the Nile delta, ancient *Djaʻnet* (Greek Tanis, modern San el-Hagar) was the residence and the burial place of the kings of the 21st and 22nd Dynasties. In the Late Period it became the capital of the 19th Lower Egyptian nome. In the present state of our archaeological knowledge of the delta it is easily the most impressive ancient site there, and one of the largest. The problems which one encounters when trying to interpret the monuments of Tanis in order to trace its history epitomize the difficulties connected with all the delta sites. The most prominent excavators at San el-Hagar have been A. Mariette in the second half of the last century, W. M. Flinders Petrie (1883–86) and P. Montet (1929–51).

The salient feature of San el-Hagar is a large brick-built rectangular enclosure measuring about 430 by 370 m. The enclosure walls were, amazingly, some 15 m thick and probably about 10 m high. Inside this precinct there is another, inner enclosure, with stamped bricks dating it to Psusennes I, which contains the great temple of Amun. Nowadays the temple is a mass of inscribed and decorated blocks, columns, obelisks and statues of various dates, some of them even bearing the names of rulers of the Old and Middle Kingdoms (Khufu, Khephren, Teti, Pepy I and II, Senwosret I).

Above San el-Hagar.

Below Seated colossus of Ramesses II, from Tell Nabasha. Granite. Height: 2·02 m. Boston (Mass.), Museum of Fine Arts.

Brutality personified? Not many Egyptian statues give a more powerful and awe-inspiring effect than this sphinx with its mane closely enveloping the face. Originally a work of the 12th Dynasty (probably of Amenemhet III), it was subsequently "usurped" by kings who added their names on it: Ramesses II, Merneptah and Psusennes I. The sphinx had been moved several times before it was set up at San el-Hagar by the last-named king. Granite. Length: 2·25 m. Cairo, Egyptian Museum.

blocks from several of these buildings, in particular a temple and a *sed*-festival chapel of Shoshenq V and a temple of Psammetichus I, were later reused by Nectanebo I when he built the sacred lake and a temple of Khons-Neferhotep nearby. Outside the enclosure, near the approach to the great temple, there stood a chapel of Ptolemy II Philadelphus.

The kings who built between the walls of the inner and outer enclosures were Osorkon III ("The East Temple") and Nectanebo II with Ptolemy II Philadelphus (temple of Horus). Outside the outer enclosure, near its southwest corner, there was a precinct of ʿAnta (Mut), built mainly by Siamun and Apries, and rebuilt by Ptolemy IV Philopator.

In 1939 P. Montet found a group of royal tombs of the 21st and 22nd Dynasties inside the inner enclosure, near the southwest corner of the great temple. The habit of building tombs within temple precincts was characteristic of the 3rd Intermediate Period, and was probably dictated by the unstable conditions of the country. In all six tombs were found at San el-Hagar, belonging to Psusennes I, Amenemope, Osorkon III and Shoshenq III, with the two remaining tombs being anonymous. There probably were no superstructures or, at least, none were found. The underground parts, in most cases consisting of several rooms, were built of limestone (many of the blocks were reused material of an earlier date), granite or mud brick, and were entered through a shaft. The walls of the tombs of Psusennes I, Osorkon III and Shoshenq III were decorated with reliefs and inscriptions. Some of the tombs contained several burials, with sarcophagi often made of granite and usurped. Two additional royal burials were found: the sarcophagus used by Takelot II was discovered in one of the rooms of the tomb of Osorkon III, while the silver falcon-headed coffin of Shoshenq II was placed in the tomb of Psusennes I. The sarcophagus and coffin of Amenemope were discovered in the tomb of Psusennes I. Silver coffins and gold mummy masks and jewelry, such as pectorals, bracelets and collars, are the most spectacular finds. Apart from the tomb of Tutʿankhamun of the 18th Dynasty, the royal tombs of San el-Hagar are the only ones that have been discovered essentially intact.

However, the majority of the inscribed monuments are connected with Ramesses II, and this led P. Montet, the greatest expert on Tanis monuments, to believe that this was the site of the ancient Pi-Riʿamsese, the delta capital of the Ramessids. Nevertheless, none of the buildings so far excavated can be shown convincingly to have been built before the reign of Psusennes I of the 21st Dynasty, and the inescapable conclusion, therefore, is that all the Ramessid and earlier monuments must have been brought from other places. Some were reused as building material (a near-universal Egyptian practice; in the delta stone monuments often traveled considerable distances), while others were used to adorn the newly built temples.

Psusennes I is attested with certainty by foundation deposits in the sanctuary in the easternmost part of the great temple. Later Siamun contributed by building in the same general area, possibly adding a pylon and a court (the second from the outside), while Osorkon III (again, known by his foundation deposits) of the 22nd Dynasty completed the plan of the temple by adding another pylon and a court (the first from the outside). Finally Shoshenq III built a gate in the enclosure wall through which one approaches the first pylon. The only later name certainly connected with the great temple at San el-Hagar is that of Nectanebo I, who probably carried out some restoration work there.

Apart from the great temple there were other, smaller structures within the inner enclosure. The

Tell el-Maskhuta

In 1883 E. Naville excavated a large brick-built enclosure (some 210 by 210 m) with a badly damaged temple at Tell el-Maskhuta, in Wadi Tumilat (in the Late Period a canal through this wadi enabled ships to sail from the Nile into the Red Sea). Most scholars, though not all, identify Tell el-Maskhuta with ancient Egyptian *Tjeku* and Pithom (probably from *Per-Atum*, "The Domain of Atum") of the Exodus, and the capital of the 8th Lower Egyptian nome.

NUBIA

Nubia, the area south of the 1st cataract, was from the earliest times regarded as belonging to Egypt by right. Apart from forming a buffer zone at the southern frontier, it was a region through which exotic African goods reached Egypt, and an important source of gold, minerals and wood, but also of valued recruits for the Egyptian army and police force.

The crude Old Kingdom methods of exploitation consisted of raids aiming at bringing back captives and cattle. In the Middle Kingdom the area under direct military control, exercised through a series of strategically placed fortresses, extended to the 2nd cataract. During the New Kingdom the Egyptians went beyond the 4th cataract; in Lower Nubia many rock-cut temples were built, dating chiefly to the reign of Ramesses II. In the Late Period Nubia produced a royal dynasty, the 25th of Egypt, but after an unsuccessful encounter with the Assyrians its Napatan rulers withdrew to the 4th cataract, ceased to take an active interest in Egyptian affairs, and developed their own, Meroïtic, culture. A number of temples were built in the northern part of Lower Nubia during the condominium of the two cultures in the Ptolemaic and early Roman Periods.

In the 1960s many Nubian temples were removed to new locations in an act of international cooperation unprecedented in the history of archaeology.

Above The Roman Period temple of Sarapis at el-Maharraqa, painted by the French architect Hector Horeau in 1838. The temple was removed to the vicinity of el-Sebu'a in 1965–66.

Left The temple of Ramesses II at el-Sebu'a, as it used to be before the creation of the Lake Nasser: (*above*) one of the sphinxes in the outer court.

Aksha
Dibeira West • Dibe
Ashk
Argin
Gezira
BUHEN • Wadi Hal
ᶜAbd el-Qadir
Gebel Sheikh Suleiman • Koi • Meinarti
Abusir • Dorginarti
Second Cataract
Mirgissa • Abka
Dabenarti
Gamai

31°

Murshid West

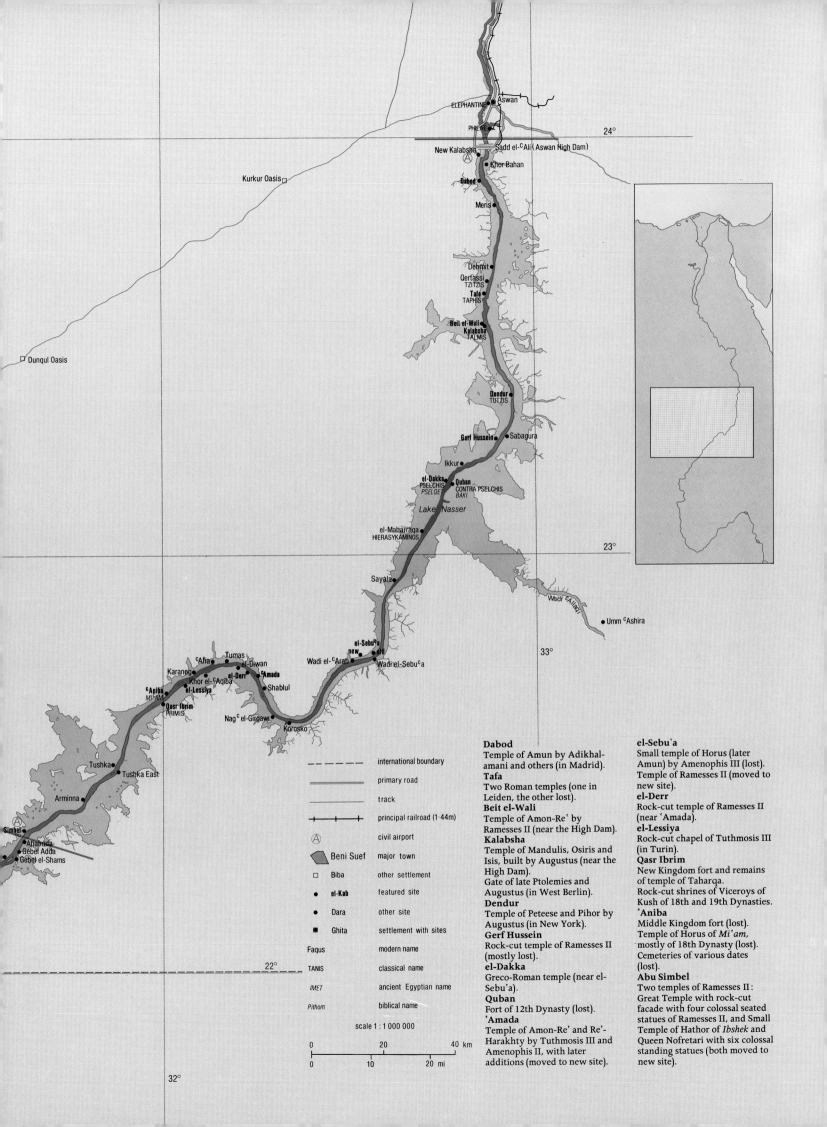

ELEPHANTINE · Aswan

PHILAE

24°

New Kalabsha · Sadd el-ʿAli (Aswan High Dam)
· Khor Bahan
Dabod
Meris

Kurkur Oasis □

Dehmit
Qertassi
TZITZIS
Tafa
TAPHIS
Beit el-Wali
Kalabsha
TALMIS

Dunqul Oasis □

Dendur
TUTZIS

Gerf Hussein · Sabagura

Ikkur ·
el-Dakka · **Quban**
PSELCHIS   CONTRA PSELCHIS
PSELQET   *BAKI*

Lake Nasser

el-Maharraqa
HIERASYKAMINOS

23°

Sayala

Wadi ʿAllaqi

· Umm ʿAshira

33°

el-Sebuʿa
new   old
Wadi el-ʿArab
Wadi el-Sebuʿa

ʿAfia · Tumas
Karanog · el-Diwan
· el-Derr   ʿAmada
Khor el-ʿAqiba
ʿAniba · el-Lessiya · Shablul
MIʿAM
Qasr Ibrim
PRIMIS

Nagʿ el-Girgawi
Korosko

Tushka
Tushka East

Arminna

Simbel
Abahuda
Gebel Adda
Gebel el-Shams

---

international boundary
primary road
track
principal railroad (1·44m)
Ⓐ civil airport
Beni Suef   major town
□ Biba   other settlement
· el-Kab   featured site
· Dara   other site
■ Ghita   settlement with sites

Faqus   modern name
TANIS   classical name
IMET   ancient Egyptian name
Pithom   biblical name

scale 1 : 1 000 000

0   20   40 km
0   10   20 mi

22°

32°

Dabod
Temple of Amun by Adikhal-
amani and others (in Madrid).
Tafa
Two Roman temples (one in
Leiden, the other lost).
Beit el-Wali
Temple of Amon-Reʿ by
Ramesses II (near the High Dam).
Kalabsha
Temple of Mandulis, Osiris and
Isis, built by Augustus (near the
High Dam).
Gate of late Ptolemies and
Augustus (in West Berlin).
Dendur
Temple of Peteese and Pihor by
Augustus (in New York).
Gerf Hussein
Rock-cut temple of Ramesses II
(mostly lost).
el-Dakka
Greco-Roman temple (near el-
Sebuʿa).
Quban
Fort of 12th Dynasty (lost).
ʿAmada
Temple of Amon-Reʿ and Reʿ-
Harakhty by Tuthmosis III and
Amenophis II, with later
additions (moved to new site).

el-Sebuʿa
Small temple of Horus (later
Amun) by Amenophis III (lost).
Temple of Ramesses II (moved to
new site).
el-Derr
Rock-cut temple of Ramesses II
(near ʿAmada).
el-Lessiya
Rock-cut chapel of Tuthmosis III
(in Turin).
Qasr Ibrim
New Kingdom fort and remains
of temple of Taharqa.
Rock-cut shrines of Viceroys of
Kush of 18th and 19th Dynasties.
ʿAniba
Middle Kingdom fort (lost).
Temple of Horus of *Miʿam*,
mostly of 18th Dynasty (lost).
Cemeteries of various dates
(lost).
Abu Simbel
Two temples of Ramesses II:
Great Temple with rock-cut
facade with four colossal seated
statues of Ramesses II, and Small
Temple of Hathor of *Ibshek* and
Queen Nofretari with six colossal
standing statues (both moved to
new site).

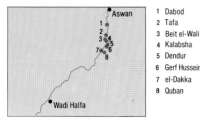

1	Dabod
2	Tafa
3	Beit el-Wali
4	Kalabsha
5	Dendur
6	Gerf Hussein
7	el-Dakka
8	Quban

Dabod

The early temple of Dabod was built and decorated by the Meroïtic ruler Adikhalamani, probably in the first half of the 3rd century BC, and was dedicated to Amun. In the Greco-Roman Period several Ptolemies (VI Philometor, VIII Euergetes II and XII Auletes) enlarged it and rededicated it to Isis. The decoration of the vestibule dates to the Emperors Augustus and Tiberius. Old views show a series of three pylons in front of the temple, but only two were to be seen in this century.

In the years 1960–61 the temple was dismantled and in 1968 presented to Spain; since 1970 it has adorned one of the parks of Madrid.

Tafa

Two temples of Roman date used to stand at Tafa. The so-called "North Temple," with no relief decoration, was dismantled in 1960 and given to the Rijksmuseum van Oudheden in Leiden. The "South Temple" was lost as early as the end of the last century.

There were two sanctuaries of Isis of the same date in the area, one of them overlooking the dangerous "minor" cataract of Bab el-Kalabsha.

Beit el-Wali

The small rock-cut temple of Beit el-Wali, on the west bank of the Nile, was built by Ramesses II and dedicated to Amon-Reʿ and other gods. Originally fronted by a brick-built pylon, its simple plan consists of an entrance hall (at one time roofed with a brick-built vault), a columned hall and the sanctuary. The temple has now been moved to a new site (New Kalabsha) close to the new Aswan dam.

Kalabsha

The largest free-standing temple of Egyptian Nubia, measuring some 74 m from the pylon to the rear wall and about 33 m wide, was built at Kalabsha (ancient Talmis) in the reign of Augustus, and was dedicated to the Nubian god Mandulis, accompanied by Osiris and Isis. In front of the pylon there is a quay and a terrace, and to reach the sanctuary one proceeds through a forecourt, a hypostyle hall and two vestibules. Only the three inner rooms are fully decorated with reliefs. The walls of the temple precinct also enclose a birth house (in the southwest corner), and a chapel built probably by Ptolemy IX Soter II (in the northeast corner).

Since the beginning of this century the temple was under water for most of the year. In 1962–63 it was dismantled and its 13,000 blocks transferred to the vicinity of the new Aswan dam (New Kalabsha), where it was rebuilt. During the dismantling operation reused blocks from a gate built by the late Ptolemies and Augustus were found. The gate, 7·35 m high, has now been reerected in the Ägyptisches Museum in West Berlin.

Dendur

In order to save it from the waters of Lake Nasser, the temple of Dendur was dismantled in 1963 and a few years later presented by the Egyptian government to the United States and shipped to New York. Its 642 blocks have now been reassembled at the Metropolitan Museum of Art where (since

The temple of Kalabsha in 1839; watercolor painting by Hector Horeau.

Far right Forecourt of the temple of Ramesses II at Gerf Hussein from the south. View taken before the creation of Lake Nasser.

Below right The temple of Kalabsha at its new site near the Aswan High Dam.

Bottom right The deities of the Kalabsha temple: Mandulis, wearing his characteristic headdress, followed by Isis. Relief on the intercolumnar wall at the back of the forecourt, north of the entrance to the hypostyle hall.

September 1978) the temple forms the Sackler wing of the museum.

Augustus built the small temple (the main building measures about 13·5 by 7 m) for two local "saints," Peteese and Pihor, sons of Quper. The exact reason for their deification at Dendur is not clear; perhaps they drowned at that spot. The original place of their worship was a rock chamber behind the temple, which may have dated back to the 26th Dynasty. The temple, fronted by a terrace, has a simple plan: a pylon and the main building some 10 m behind it. The latter consists of a columned pronaos, a vestibule and the sanctuary. The reliefs in the temple show Augustus before various deities, among them the two deified brothers and the Nubian gods Arensnuphis and Mandulis.

Gerf Hussein

"The Temple of Ri'amsese-meryamun [Ramesses II] in the Domain of Ptah" at Gerf Hussein was built by the viceroy of Kush, Setau, sometime between years

35 and 50 of Ramesses II. The gods to whom it was dedicated were represented by four seated statues in the niche at the back of the sanctuary: Ptah, the deified Ramesses II, Ptah-tanen with a hawk above his head, and Hathor.

The temple, on the west bank of the Nile, was partly free-standing and partly cut in the rock, and its plan was remarkably similar to that of the great temple of Abu Simbel. Unfortunately, most of it fell victim to the progress of modern civilization, and disappeared under the newly created Lake Nasser.

el-Dakka

Several rulers contributed to the building and decoration of the temple of el-Dakka (ancient Egyptian *Pselqet*, classical Pselchis), notably Ptolemy IV Philopator, Ptolemy VIII Euergetes II, the Meroïtic King Arqamani of the turn of the 3rd century BC, and the Roman emperors Augustus and Tiberius.

Between 1962 and 1968 the temple was dismantled and removed to a new site near el-Sebu'a. During the work a number of reused blocks were found. These come from an earlier temple built by Hatshepsut and Tuthmosis III for Horus of *Baki* (Quban), probably on the opposite side of the river.

Quban

The fort of Quban (ancient Egyptian *Baki*, classical Contra Pselchis) was built at the beginning of the 12th Dynasty, probably by Senwosret I, but may have had a precursor in the Old Kingdom. During the New Kingdom Quban was the most important settlement in Nubia north of 'Aniba, controlling access to the gold mines of Wadi 'Allaqi. Several ruined temple structures have been reported from the area.

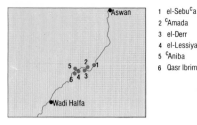

1 el-Sebuᶜa
2 ᶜAmada
3 el-Derr
4 el-Lessiya
5 ᶜAniba
6 Qasr Ibrim

ʿAmada

The temple of ʿAmada was originally built by Tuthmosis III and Amenophis II, and was dedicated to the gods Amon-Reʿ and Reʿ-Harakhty. A hypostyle hall was later added by Tuthmosis IV. Various kings of the 19th Dynasty, in particular Sethos I and Ramesses II, carried out minor restorations and added to the temple's decoration.

There are two important historical inscriptions in the ʿAmada temple. The earlier of them, dated to year 3 of Amenophis II, is on a round-topped stela on the rear (eastern) wall of the sanctuary. The text describes a victorious military campaign into Asia: "His Majesty returned in joy to his father Amun after he had slain with his own mace the seven chiefs in the district of *Takhesy*, who were then hung upside down from the prow of the boat of His Majesty." The other text, on a stela engraved on the left (northern) thickness of the entrance doorway, concerns the defeat of an invasion of Egypt from Libya in year 4 of Merneptah.

Between December 1964 and February 1975 the temple was moved to a new position, some 65 m higher and 2·5 km away from its original site. Part of the temple, weighing about 900 tons, was transported to its new setting in one piece.

el-Sebuʿa

el-Sebuʿa, on the west bank of the Nile, was the site of two temples of the New Kingdom.

The earlier temple was built by Amenophis III. In its first stage it consisted of a rock-cut sanctuary (about 3 by 2 m) fronted by a brick-built pylon, a court and a hall, partly decorated with wall paintings. Originally the temple seems to have been dedicated to one of the local Nubian forms of Horus, but his representations were altered to Amun at some later point. During the ʿAmarna persecution of images of Amun the decoration suffered, but Ramesses II restored it and also extended the temple by building in front of the pylon of the original plan.

The large temple of el-Sebuʿa, known as "The Temple of Riʿamsese-meryamun [Ramesses II] in the Domain of Amun," was built about 150 m northeast of the temple of Amenophis III; monuments and representations of the viceroy of Kush, Setau, indicate that this was between regnal years 35 and 50 of Ramesses II. The temple is partly free-standing and partly rock-cut.

Proceeding along its central axis, one passes through a series of three pylons and courts to reach the hypostyle hall (later converted into a Coptic church) where the rock-cut part of the temple starts.

The antechamber opens into two side rooms, two side chapels and the sanctuary itself. The statues in the niche of the sanctuary are destroyed, but there is little doubt that they represented Amon-Re', Re'-Harakhty and Ramesses II himself.

During the UNESCO campaign to save the monuments of Nubia the temple was removed to a new site, some 4 km to the west.

el-Derr

The only Nubian rock-cut temple built by Ramesses II on the right bank of the Nile used to stand at el-Derr. The position was probably due to the fact that the river on its approach to the Korosko bend flows in an "unnatural" southeasterly direction. In 1964 the temple was dismantled and removed to a new site near 'Amada.

"The Temple of Ri'amsese-meryamun [Ramesses II] in the Domain of Re''' was built in the second half of the king's reign, and in plan and decoration resembles the Great Temple of Abu Simbel (minus the colossal seated statues against the facade). After cleaning, the temple's relief decoration is unusually bright and vivid, contrasting strongly with the more subdued color tones to which we are used from elsewhere. The chief deities worshiped in the temple had seated statues in the sanctuary niche: Re'-Harakhty, Ramesses II himself, Amon-Re' and Ptah.

el-Lessiya

At el-Lessiya, on the right bank of the Nile, a small chapel was cut in the reign of Tuthmosis III. The plan consists of a single room (5·5 by 3 m) with a niche (2 by 3 m), and the relief decoration shows the king before various deities, including the Nubian god Dedwen and the deified Senwosret III. The niche originally contained statues of Tuthmosis III between Horus of *Mi'am* ('Aniba) and Satis, but these were damaged during the 'Amarna Period, and Ramesses II had them restored to represent himself between Amon-Re' and Horus of *Mi'am*.

The chapel was presented to Italy in 1966 and is now in the Museo Egizio in Turin.

Qasr Ibrim

The central of the three sandstone massifs which used to loom south of the village of Ibrim (the name probably derives from the classical Primis), on the

east bank of the Nile, was the most important one. On its top, the fort of Qasr Ibrim ("The Castle of Ibrim") no doubt stood on pharaonic foundations, as suggested by a number of reused or isolated monuments dating to the New Kingdom (the earliest is a stela of year 8 of Amenophis I) and a temple structure of Taharqa (with a painting showing the king offering to a god). Parts of the fortress were constructed during the short stay of the Roman garrison under the prefect Gaius Petronius in the reign of Augustus, and from then on Qasr Ibrim remained occupied until the beginning of the last century.

Rock-cut shrines (chapels) dedicated to the reigning king and various gods were made by viceroys of Kush of the 18th and 19th Dynasties at the bottom of the cliff. During the salvage operation carried out while the new Aswan dam was being built, their reliefs were cut away and removed to the vicinity of el-Sebu'a.

The large rock stela of Sethos I and the contemporary viceroy of Kush, Amenemope, which used to be south of the fort, has been transferred to the neighborhood of the reconstructed Kalabsha temple at Aswan.

'Aniba

'Aniba, ancient *Mi'am*, was prominent in the New Kingdom, when it served as the administrative center of *Wawat* (Lower Nubia, between the 1st and 2nd cataracts).

The town contained a fort, probably of Middle Kingdom origin, and the temple of Horus of *Mi'am*. The temple may go back to the beginning of the 12th Dynasty (Senwosret I), but most of the evidence dates to the 18th Dynasty (Tuthmosis III and later kings).

There were cemeteries of various dates in the vicinity, including tombs of the New Kingdom. One of these, the rock-cut tomb of Penniut, the deputy of *Wawat* under Ramesses VI, has now been removed to a new site near 'Amada.

Abu Simbel

Of the seven temples in Nubia built by Ramesses II (Beit el-Wali, Gerf Hussein, el-Sebuʻa, el-Derr, two at Abu Simbel, and Aksha), the rock temples at Abu Simbel (Ibsambul), on the west bank of the Nile, are the most impressive.

The Great Temple was first reported by J. L. Burckhardt in 1813 and opened by G. B. Belzoni in 1817. As a result of the widely publicized dismantling and removal operation it has become one of the best-known monuments of Egypt. Its ancient name was simply "The Temple of Riʻamsese-meryamun [Ramesses II]," and it was probably built early in the reign of the king.

A gateway leads into a forecourt and on to a terrace. There the visitor is confronted by the temple's rock-cut facade, some 30 m high and 35 m wide, with four colossal seated statues of Ramesses II (about 21 m high), accompanied by smaller standing statues of relatives by his legs. These are as follows:

1st southern colossus: Queen Nofretari by the king's left leg, the king's mother (and the wife of Sethos I) Muttuya by his right leg, and Prince Amenhirkhopshef in front.

2nd southern colossus (in the same order as for the previous statue): Princesses Bentʻanta, Nebettawy and one unnamed, probably Esenofre.

1st northern colossus: Queen Nofretari by the king's right leg, Princess Beketmut by his left leg and Prince Riʻamsese in front.

2nd northern colossus: Princess Merytamun, Queen Muttuya and Princess Nofretari.

A niche above the temple entrance contains a symbolic sculptural group representing a cryptographic writing of the praenomen of Ramesses II, Usermaʻatreʻ: the falcon-headed god Reʻ has by his right leg the hieroglyph showing the head and neck of an animal which is read as user while the goddess by his left leg stands for maʻat. At the top of the temple facade is a row of statues of baboons in adoring attitudes whose cries were held to welcome the rising sun.

The temple was built in such a way that twice a year, when the rising sun appeared above the horizon on the east bank of the Nile, its rays penetrated the temple entrance, shot through the great hall with eight pillars in the form of colossal statues of the king, the second pillared hall, the vestibule and the sanctuary, and rested on the four statues in the niche at the back, which they illuminated fully. The statues represented the three most important state gods of the Ramessid Period: the Memphite Ptah (first on the left), the Theban Amon-Reʻ (second) and the Heliopolitan Reʻ-Harakhty (fourth). The third figure from the left was the king himself.

The Great Temple of Abu Simbel bears witness to the deification of Ramesses II during his lifetime, including scenes showing the king performing rites before the sacred bark of his deified self (on the north wall of the second pillared hall, and on the north wall of the sanctuary). The reliefs in the great hall show scenes of historical or symbolic character: on the long north wall the battle of Qadesh in Syria, and on the south wall the Syrian, Libyan and Nubian wars.

The Small Temple of Abu Simbel, contemporary with the Great Temple, was dedicated to Hathor of Ibshek and Queen Nofretari. The facade is formed by six colossal standing statues (about 10 m high) cut in the rock. Four of them represent the king and two the queen, each being flanked by princes and princesses. In its plan the Small Temple is an abbreviated version of the Great Temple: a hall with Hathor pillars, a vestibule with side rooms, and the sanctuary. The niche at the back contains a statue of a Hathor cow protecting the king.

Between 1964 and 1968 both temples were removed to their new location, about 210 m further away from the river and 65 m higher, at the cost of some 40 million US dollars.

Left The gods of the Great Temple in the niche of the sanctuary.

Right The much more romantic Abu Simbel of the first half of the last century (David Roberts, November 1838).

Below right The "Abu Simbel Salvage Operation" was one of the results of the appeal of UNESCO to all its member states to help to rescue the monuments of Nubia threatened by the building of the new dam at Aswan. The protection of the temples at Abu Simbel, cut in the living rock, presented considerable technical and financial difficulties. Several projects were considered; that which was finally chosen consisted in dismantling the temple facades and the walls of their rooms by cutting them into large blocks, removing these, and rebuilding the temples inside concrete dome-shaped structures in a simulated environment. A cofferdam had to be built while the dismantling operation was in progress because of the already rising water of Lake Nasser. The whole huge Lego game was successfully completed, and the resited temples were reopened officially on 22 September 1968.

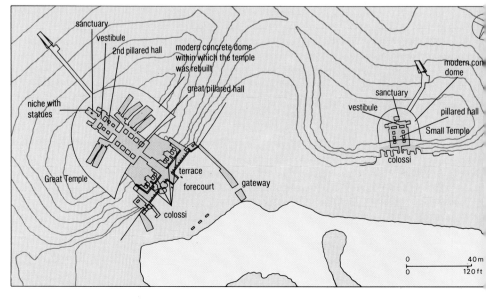

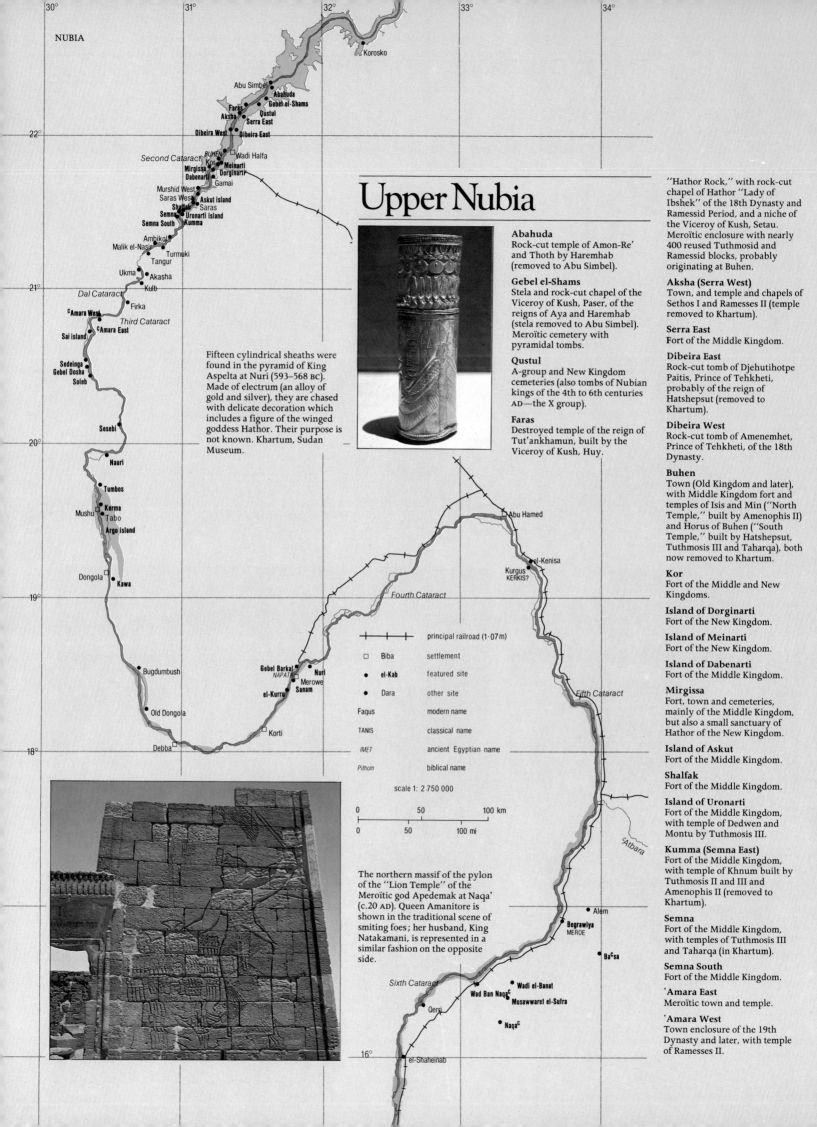

Upper Nubia

NUBIA

30° 31° 32° 33° 34°

Korosko

Abu Simbel
Abahuda
Faras   Gebel el-Shams
Aksha   Qustul
         Serra East
Dibeira West   Dibeira East

Second Cataract
BUHEN   Wadi Halfa
KOR   Meinarti
Mirgissa   Dorginarti
Dabenarti
Gamai
Murshid West
Saras West   Askut island
Shalfak   Saras
Semna   Uronarti island
Semna South   Kumma
Ambikol
Malik el-Nasir
Turmuki
Tangur
Ukma   Akasha
Dal Cataract   Kulb
Firka
ᶜAmara West   Third Cataract
Sai island   ᶜAmara East
Sedeinga
Gebel Dosha
Soleb
Sesebi
Nauri
Tumbos
Mushu   Kerma
    Tabo
Argo island
Dongola   Kawa
Old Dongola
Debba   Korti

Bugdumbush
Gebel Barkal   Nuri
NAPATA   Merowe
el-Kurru   Sanam

Abu Hamed
el-Kenisa
Kurgus
KERKIS?
Fourth Cataract

Fifth Cataract

ᶜAtbara

Alem
Begrawiya
MEROE
Baᶜsa

Sixth Cataract
Wadi el-Banat
Wad Ban Naqaᶜ   Musawwaret el-Sufra
Qersi
Naqaᶜ
el-Shaheinab

Key

| principal railroad (1·07 m) |
□ Biba	settlement
● el-Kab	featured site
● Dara	other site
Faqus	modern name
TANIS	classical name
IMET	ancient Egyptian name
Pithom	biblical name

scale 1: 2·750 000

0   50   100 km
0   50   100 mi

Fifteen cylindrical sheaths were found in the pyramid of King Aspelta at Nuri (593–568 BC). Made of electrum (an alloy of gold and silver), they are chased with delicate decoration which includes a figure of the winged goddess Hathor. Their purpose is not known. Khartum, Sudan Museum.

The northern massif of the pylon of the "Lion Temple" of the Meroïtic god Apedemak at Naqa' (c.20 AD). Queen Amanitore is shown in the traditional scene of smiting foes; her husband, King Natakamani, is represented in a similar fashion on the opposite side.

Abahuda
Rock-cut temple of Amon-Reʿ and Thoth by Haremhab (removed to Abu Simbel).

Gebel el-Shams
Stela and rock-cut chapel of the Viceroy of Kush, Paser, of the reigns of Aya and Haremhab (stela removed to Abu Simbel). Meroïtic cemetery with pyramidal tombs.

Qustul
A-group and New Kingdom cemeteries (also tombs of Nubian kings of the 4th to 6th centuries AD—the X group).

Faras
Destroyed temple of the reign of Tutʿankhamun, built by the Viceroy of Kush, Huy.

"Hathor Rock," with rock-cut chapel of Hathor "Lady of Ibshek" of the 18th Dynasty and Ramessid Period, and a niche of the Viceroy of Kush, Setau. Meroïtic enclosure with nearly 400 reused Tuthmosid and Ramessid blocks, probably originating at Buhen.

Aksha (Serra West)
Town, and temple and chapels of Sethos I and Ramesses II (temple removed to Khartum).

Serra East
Fort of the Middle Kingdom.

Dibeira East
Rock-cut tomb of Djehutihotpe Paitis, Prince of Tehkheti, probably of the reign of Hatshepsut (removed to Khartum).

Dibeira West
Rock-cut tomb of Amenemhet, Prince of Tehkheti, of the 18th Dynasty.

Buhen
Town (Old Kingdom and later), with Middle Kingdom fort and temples of Isis and Min ("North Temple," built by Amenophis II) and Horus of Buhen ("South Temple," built by Hatshepsut, Tuthmosis III and Taharqa), both now removed to Khartum.

Kor
Fort of the Middle and New Kingdoms.

Island of Dorginarti
Fort of the New Kingdom.

Island of Meinarti
Fort of the New Kingdom.

Island of Dabenarti
Fort of the Middle Kingdom.

Mirgissa
Fort, town and cemeteries, mainly of the Middle Kingdom, but also a small sanctuary of Hathor of the New Kingdom.

Island of Askut
Fort of the Middle Kingdom.

Shalfak
Fort of the Middle Kingdom.

Island of Uronarti
Fort of the Middle Kingdom, with temple of Dedwen and Montu by Tuthmosis III.

Kumma (Semna East)
Fort of the Middle Kingdom, with temple of Khnum built by Tuthmosis II and III and Amenophis II (removed to Khartum).

Semna
Fort of the Middle Kingdom, with temples of Tuthmosis III and Taharqa (in Khartum).

Semna South
Fort of the Middle Kingdom.

ᶜAmara East
Meroïtic town and temple.

ᶜAmara West
Town enclosure of the 19th Dynasty and later, with temple of Ramesses II.

Island of Sai
Town and fort with temple, 18th Dynasty and Meroïtic.

Sedeinga
Temple of Amenophis III. Meroïtic cemeteries.

Gebel Dosha
Rock-cut chapel of Tuthmosis III.

Soleb
Temple of Amenophis III. Cemetery of the New Kingdom.

Sesebi
New Kingdom town with temples of the Aten and the Theban triad, built by Akhenaten and Sethos I.

Nauri
Rock-cut stela of year 4 of Sethos I.

Tumbos
Stelae of Tuthmosis I and others, including the Viceroy of Kush, Setau, of the reign of Ramesses II.

Kerma
Settlement of the 2nd Intermediate Period, and cemetery with tumuli with reused Egyptian objects, including statues, stelae, and stone vessels. Colossal mudbrick tower (*deffufa*).

Island of Argo
Temple at Tabo, of the 25th Dynasty (Taharqa, reusing New Kingdom blocks) and Meroïtic.

Kawa
Temples of Amun, built mainly by Tut'ankhamun, Taharqa and Napatan and Meroïtic kings.

el-Kurru
Pyramid field, including burials of kings of the 25th Dynasty.

Sanam
Palace, storerooms and cemeteries of the 25th Dynasty, with temple of Amon-Reʿ built by Taharqa.

Gebel Barkal
Meroïtic pyramid field. A number of temples and chapels dedicated to Amon-Reʿ, built by kings of the New Kingdom, Piye and Taharqa, and Napatan and Meroïtic kings.

Nuri
Pyramid field, including burial of Taharqa and those of various Napatan and Meroïtic kings.

Meroë (Begrawiya)
Temples and pyramid fields of the Meroïtic Period.

Baʿsa
Meroïtic temple.

Wadi el-Banat
Destroyed Meroïtic temple.

Wadi Ban Naqaʿ
Destroyed Meroïtic temple.

Musawwarat el-Sufra
Meroïtic temples.

Naqaʿ
Meroïtic temples.

The Oases

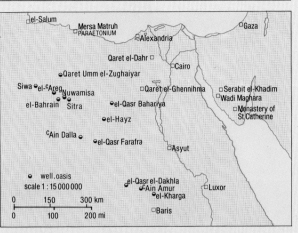

The western oases consist of a series of wind-eroded depressions in the Libyan desert, where there are natural springs, and wells are bored more than 100 meters below ground. There is enough water for agriculture, but wells are scattered and may fail. The population (75,000 in 1966) is spread over wide areas, with barren tracts between settlements.

The oases have been inhabited since Paleolithic times, and el-Kharga, the largest, has produced traces of very early agriculture, but their importance was due more to their location than to their produce. The local economy's fortunes fluctuated with those of Egypt proper, and for the Roman Period there is ample evidence for trade with the Nile valley.

Our knowledge of the area's early history is still rudimentary. For the Old–New Kingdoms the four southern oases are mentioned in Egyptian texts, and there have been some finds, chiefly in el-Dakhla. They were probably all administered by Egypt during these periods. From the 3rd Intermediate Period remains are more frequent, and prosperity increased until the Roman Period, when some Greeks settled. Siwa was colonized in the 26th Dynasty, and remained in Egyptian control; its population, now Berber-speaking, was probably always more Libyan than Egyptian.

In late Roman times there was widespread depopulation. The oasis economy has never recovered fully, so that the naturally good conditions for preserving sites are enhanced.

Below left el-Dakhla oasis, the village of el-Smant el-Kharab. In antiquity lakes were more prominent in the oases than they are now. Preservation is so good that it can be difficult to distinguish a Roman farmhouse from a recently abandoned one.

el-Kharga
ʿAin Amur Temple and settlement of the Roman Period.
Hibis Well-preserved temple of Amun, Darius, Nectanebo II and Ptolemaic.
Qasr el-Ghueida Temple of Amun, Mut and Khons, 25th Dynasty – Ptolemaic.
Gebel el-Teir Rock inscriptions, 26th Dynasty – Ptolemaic.
Nadura Temple of the Roman Period.
Qasr Zaiyan Ptolemaic and Roman temple.
Qasr Dush Temple of Sarapis and Isis, Roman.

el-Dakhla
Many Old Kingdom settlements and cemeteries.
Balat Town site; mastabas of the 6th Dynasty and 1st Intermediate Period; temple of Mut, New Kingdom; tombs of the 3rd Intermediate and Roman Periods.
Amhada Tombs of the 1st Intermediate Period.
Mut Destroyed temple; objects of the 3rd Intermediate Period.
el-Qasr Temple of Thoth, Greco-Roman; necropolis.
Deir el-Hagar Temple, 1st century AD.
Qaret el-Muzawwaqa Decorated tombs of the Roman Period.
el-Smant el-Kharab Roman town site with small temple (ruined).

Farafra
No native Egyptian remains, but evidence for Roman occupation.

Bahariya
Monuments near *el-Qasr* and *el-Bawiti*:
Tomb of Amenhotpe Huy (18th–19th Dynasty).
Chapels and tombs of the reigns of Apries and Amasis and of the Greco-Roman Period.
Temple of Alexander the Great. Destroyed Roman "triumphal arch."
el-Hayz Small center of the Roman Period.

Siwa
Aghurmi 26th Dynasty and Ptolemaic temple, assumed to be where Alexander the Great consulted the oracle of Ammon.
Umm el-ʿEbeida Temple of Nectanebo II.
Gebel el-Mawta Necropolis, 26th Dynasty and Greco-Roman, including some decorated tombs. Cemeteries and small, undecorated temples at a number of further sites.

Small oases with ancient remains: Qaret Umm el-Zughaiyar, el-ʿAreg, Nuwamisa, el-Bahrain, Sitra.

Sinai

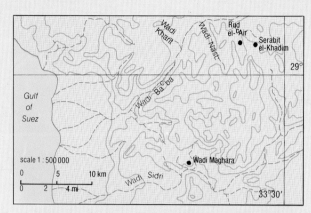

Right Head of a statuette of Teye, the chief consort of Amenophis III, identified by a cartouche bearing her name on the headdress. Green steatite. Height 6·5 cm. Found at Serabit el-Khadim. Cairo, Egyptian Museum.

Below left A relief of King Sekhemkhet, rediscovered at Wadi Maghara in 1973. It is almost identical with another, some 35 m to the south. The two reliefs are among the earliest Egyptian inscriptions at Sinai.

Below A recently taken view of the temple of Hathor at Serabit el-Khadim, showing some of the stelae that are still standing.

The Egyptians were attracted by the mineral deposits of the valleys of southwestern Sinai as early as the 3rd Dynasty. The objective of the expeditions regularly sent out to work the mines during the Old to New Kingdoms was to bring back turquoise and to acquire copper; the copper workings over much of Sinai are mostly not associated with Egyptian finds. Egyptian activities in Sinai ceased at the end of the New Kingdom.

There were several routes which these expeditions could follow, and the choice probably varied with the period: the long overland journey around the Gulf of Suez or the combined land/sea/land travel which in its first stage involved crossing the eastern desert, and perhaps also the Nile/sea/land route through the Wadi Tumilat canal.

The mines of the Wadi Maghara were the first to be exploited, with the earliest rock inscriptions and reliefs dating to Zanakht, Netjerykhet (Djoser) and Sekhemkhet. The last Old Kingdom expedition was that of Pepy II in the "year of the 2nd census" (around his 3rd year); although some Middle and New Kingdom rulers are attested (Amenemhet III and IV, Hatshepsut and Tuthmosis III, perhaps

Ramesses II), the site did not regain its former significance.

The most important site of Egyptian activities in Sinai is Serabit el-Khadim with its temple of Hathor. The temple's earliest part, the rock-cut "Cave of Hathor" preceded by a court and a portico, goes back to the beginning of the 12th Dynasty. In the New Kingdom, a shrine for Sopd, the god of the eastern desert, was built to the south, and the temple of Hathor was much enlarged (mainly by Hatshepsut and Tuthmosis III). Thoth was also worshiped locally, together with several deified kings of the past, notably Snofru. Ramesses VI is the last ruler whose name has been encountered. A new Middle Kingdom rock text has recently been found at Rud el-ʿAir, some 1·5 km west of the Serabit el-Khadim temple. Several others have been known from there for some time.

A rock text of Sahureʿ and a large stela of Senwosret I date the third important center of turquoise mining, which was located recently in the Wadi Kharit. Nearby, in the Wadi Nasb, were found a rock stela of year 20 of Amenemhet III and Middle Kingdom and Ramessid texts.

PART THREE
ASPECTS OF EGYPTIAN SOCIETY

EVERYDAY LIFE

Agricultural scenes in Theban tomb No. 1 at Deir el-Medina, belonging to Sennedjem, of the reign of Sethos I. The setting is the mythical Fields of Ialu, where Sennedjem, accompanied by his wife Iyneferti, is shown reaping grain, plowing with a pair of dappled cattle, and harvesting flax. Only the heads of grain were cut off with a short-handled wooden sickle, whose serrated blade was formed of sharp flakes of flint; the remaining much-valued straw was pulled up later. Many examples of sickles and whips of the types used by Sennedjem have been preserved.

There is no one method of studying the everyday life of the ancient Egyptians, but a mosaic of different approaches which draw on various sources. Tomb reliefs and paintings provide a wealth of material; although only members of the top stratum of society were buried in large decorated tombs, subsidiary scenes afford glimpses of the life of ordinary people. These are supplemented by tomb models and objects of daily use which often form part of funerary equipment; less common are those found in excavations of settlements. Literary and administrative texts on papyri and ostraca are invaluable because they provide details not available from elsewhere.

190

Farms and Vineyards

For sowing, the ground was prepared by plowing, usually done with oxen, or hoeing. The seed was then scattered and cattle, sheep or goats were used to tread it in.

The monotony of the reapers' work was relieved by a flute player. After cutting, the ears of grain were collected into baskets and either carried or transported on donkeys to threshing floors. The threshing was done by cattle, sheep or goats which were driven over the ears and trod the grain out. The chaff was separated laboriously by winnowing and sifting. The grain was then deposited in granaries.

Scenes of watering grapevines and picking and crushing grapes are often shown. The crushing was done by men treading grapes in a vat, often to the accompaniment of the rhythmical beating of resonant sticks, and the must was later strained by twisting in a sack. Hieratic labels on wine jars found in excavations give us names of many vineyards and vintners as well as the vintage of the wines they originally contained.

Plowing, Middle Kingdom.

Reaping grain, 5th Dynasty.

Granary, Middle Kingdom.

Winnowing and carrying ears of grain to granary, 18th Dynasty.

Threshing with cattle, 18th Dynasty.

Picking grapes, 18th Dynasty.

Herds and Herdsmen

Scenes from the life of herdsmen include cows being mounted by bulls, calving, suckling calves or being milked; bulls fighting, cattle being fed, and goats browsing on trees or bushes. Inspections of cattle, goats, donkeys, sheep and fowl by the owner of the estate, during which they were counted and their numbers were recorded, were a regular occurrence. Herdsmen may be shown cooking and eating, skinning a goat hung from a tree, or making mats, apparently their favorite pastime. The prestige of stock rearing was reflected in the number of officials bearing titles connected with it.

Inspection of cattle, 18th Dynasty.

Herdsman with goats, 19th Dynasty.

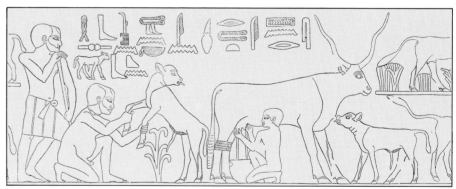

Milking, 5th Dynasty.

Hunter with dogs, 5th Dynasty.

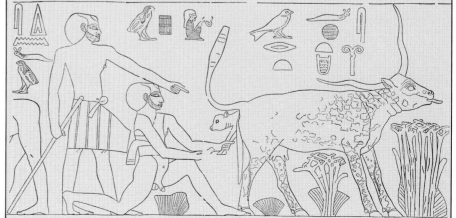

Cow calving, 5th Dynasty.

Hunting and Fishing

The contribution of the hunting of desert animals to the Egyptian economy was limited, and the activity soon became the sport of the rich.

Marsh scenes with people fishing, fowling, harvesting papyrus and making papyrus rafts are usually closely associated with cattle-breeding activities. The final stage of seining (or netting) fish by fishermen is often shown, as are several other methods, in particular catching fish in baskets and by means of small hand-held clap-nets. Spearing fish and angling, both usually done from a small papyrus raft, must have been regarded as enjoyable relaxations. Hippopotamus hunting was probably a necessary task rather than a sport.

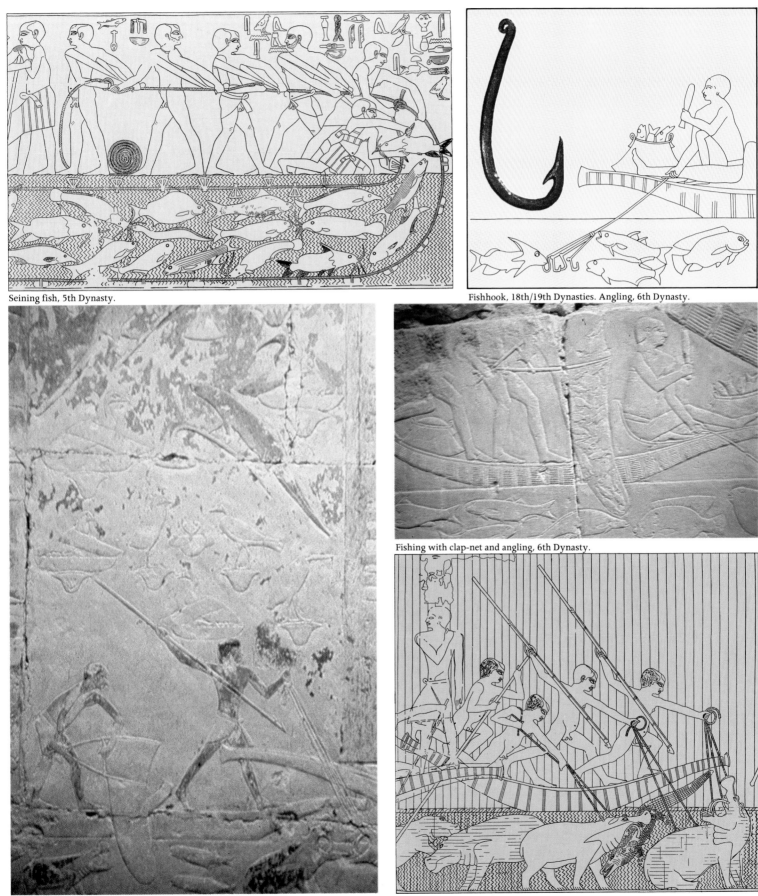

Seining fish, 5th Dynasty.

Fishhook, 18th/19th Dynasties. Angling, 6th Dynasty.

Fishing with clap-net and angling, 6th Dynasty.

Fishing with clap-net and hippopotamus hunt, 6th Dynasty.

Hippopotamus hunt, 5th Dynasty.

Trades and Crafts

Important stages in the manufacture of objects by craftsmen are shown with surprising technical knowledge in tomb reliefs and paintings: a goldworker is weighing gold; joiners are adding final touches to wooden *djed*-signs (symbolizing endurance) for a shrine; boat-builders have nearly completed the hull of a large wooden boat; men with blowpipes are busy smelting metal. Other craftsmen often represented include sculptors (the making of statues was as much a craft as an art), carpenters, leather-workers, potters, makers of stone vessels, rope-makers and brick-makers. Many models as well as real tools of craftsmen have been found.

Goldsmith, joiners, jewelers and engravers, 18th Dynasty.

Model tools, 18th Dynasty.

Boat-builders, 5th Dynasty.

Metalworkers, 5th Dynasty.

Because of their role in ensuring that the tomb was provided with meat offerings, scenes and models of butchers were among the commonest.

There were many different qualities and shapes of bread and cakes. The grinding of grain was common to all, but different methods of baking were employed. Sometimes the dough was poured into preheated earthenware pots and gently baked without direct fire.

Egyptian beer was brewed by fermenting part-baked bread; brewers standing in vats treading pieces of bread or leaning over a large vessel straining the mash are a common theme in statuettes, models and reliefs.

Butchers, 18th Dynasty.

Preheating pots for baking bread, 5th Dynasty.

Butchers, bakers and brewers, Middle Kingdom.

Granaries with grain, 5th Dynasty.

Brewer, cook and woman grinding grain, First Intermediate Period.

Brewing, Middle Kingdom.

Domestic Life

A number of musical instruments were known from the earliest times, and many of them have been found in excavations. The flute, double clarinet, double oboe and trumpet were the commonest wind instruments; stringed instruments included various types of harp, lute and lyre, and the tambourine and drum were the normal membranophones. On another level, sistra and clappers were used as percussion instruments in rituals.

Occasional finds of model houses usefully complement information gathered from excavations of settlements. Our knowledge of ancient Egyptian domestic architecture is still very incomplete, particularly for the Early Dynastic Period and Old Kingdom, in comparison with what we know about the architecture of temples and tombs.

Details of the day-to-day running of ancient Egyptian households remain obscure, and only exceptionally are we able to penetrate beyond the rather general and very selective information provided by tombs. An attempt to reconstruct an ordinary day, month or year in the life of an ancient Egyptian family would still involve much guessing, a telling indicator of the difficulties Egyptologists face.

Female musicians and dancers, 18th Dynasty.

Model house, Middle Kingdom.

Offering bearers, Middle Kingdom.

Reed brush, 18th Dynasty.

Basketwork and matting, Middle Kingdom.

Sandals, 18th Dynasty or Greco-Roman Period.

''Place myrrh upon your head, and clothe yourself in fine linen,'' exhorts the ''Song of the Harper.'' Rich Egyptians appreciated beautiful objects of daily use, in particular toilet articles, such as combs, ointment spoons (often in the form of a musician, a servant carrying a large jar on his shoulders, or a swimming girl), kohl-containers (for eye makeup), vases, and mirrors (made of polished copper or bronze, usually circular, with a decorative handle). They liked to surround themselves with elegant furniture (chairs, stools, beds, chests and boxes) and valued fine clothes, wigs and jewelry. They also enjoyed good food, drink, music, singing and dancing (they do not seem to have participated actively in dances, but rather watched dancing displays).

Representations of banquets are very common, particularly in Theban tombs of the New Kingdom. One of the features of these merry-making scenes is the cone of a scented greasy substance (the ''myrrh'' of the ''Song of the Harper'') placed on the wig of each reveler; as the party progressed, these slowly melted and gave off a pleasant aroma.

Ancient Egyptian children played much the same games and amused themselves in similar ways to Egyptian children of today. A number of simple toys have been found, though wooden horses on wheels are not known before the Greco-Roman Period.

Detail of banquet scene, 18th Dynasty.

Comb, 19th Dynasty.

Toilet spoon, 18th Dynasty.

Mirror, New Kingdom.

Toy horse, Greco-Roman Period.

Folding stool, 18th Dynasty.

SCRIBES AND WRITING

The invention of writing around 3000 BC defines the beginning of Egyptian history more than any other single change. Similarly, literacy set the chief cultures of the ancient Near East apart from their contemporaries, opening up new possibilities in social organization and in the transmission, and occasionally criticism, of growing bodies of received knowledge. But the script was complex, and literacy was confined to a small elite. Not until the spread of alphabetic scripts was anything like the full potential of writing for society exploited.

It seems that there was no separate, illiterate class of nobility, as a landed aristocracy might be. All high-ranking people had scribal careers in official-dom, army or priesthood; kings too were literate. Among administrative titles the highest do not allude to writing, but we know from representations that such people were scribes; they had surpassed the level of achievement at which writing was the main occupation, not bypassed it. In all spheres writing formed the basis of official organization.

A scribe was trained in his first job by another scribe, and the children of important people could enter office very young – perhaps about the age of 12. After his training, or in its later stages, the scribe would rise gradually through the administrative hierarchy. Basic literacy was probably acquired before he started a job. At Deir el-Medina, the only school for which we have evidence, the initial training seems to have been copying passages from a cursive hieroglyphic text called the "Book of Kemyt." From there the scribe progressed to classic works of literature and, after moving to a job, to contemporary miscellanies of model letters, satirical compositions, poems and panegyrics, which may have been set as daily exercises by pupil-masters. A surprising number of these have been preserved, which suggests that they may ultimately have been put in their owners' tombs.

There are two noteworthy features of this training. First, it was mainly in cursive writing, which was from the beginning the commonest form. Further instruction was probably needed for proficiency in the monumental hieroglyphic script, which was therefore comprehensible to rather fewer people; in the Late Period the two forms diverged sharply. Second, although the Egyptians dissolved their language into a syllabary and had an "alphabetical" order into which lists were some-times arranged, learning was by copying sentences or words, not by starting from individual signs. Writing was perceived in groups of signs, and there was little stimulus to minute analysis of the script.

Apart from administration, letters etc., the cursive script was used for non-essential purposes, the most interesting of which, from our point of view, was transmitting works of literature. Literary texts are preserved both from schools and from other sources. They include narrative fiction, instruction and "philosophical" texts, cult and

Top Granite scribe statue of the Chief Lector-Priest Petamenope, c. 650 BC. The figure is in the traditional cross-legged writing pose, with a papyrus spread between the knees. The statue form is a conscious revival of an Old Kingdom model by one of the richest men of the Late Period. Quartzite, height 75 cm. From Karnak. Cairo, Egyptian Museum.

Above Typical scribe's palette with a long slot for reed pens (the original ones are preserved) in addition to depressions with cakes of ink. Middle Kingdom. Wood. From Beni Hasan. Oxford, Ashmolean Museum.

The scribe's basic tools make up the hieroglyph on the left, which shows a palette with depressions for cakes of red and black pigment mixed with gum, a water pot or bag, and a reed pen or papyrus smoother, all tied together. Ink was made by adding water to the cake of pigment. The scribe painted rather than wrote, with his hand held above the surface. Because of the right-to-left direction of writing, originally in vertical columns, he would have smudged his text if he let his hand rest. In hieratic he could write about a dozen signs before recharging his pen.

religious hymns, love poetry, royal inscriptions and miscellaneous texts used secondarily as literature, and various genres we would not consider literary: medical and mathematical texts, rituals, and some mortuary books. The chief center of production was the "house of life," a scriptorium attached to temples, which evidently made copies of the entire range of traditional writings, not only of belles-lettres. The tradition continued almost without a break into the 3rd century AD, although few texts survived the transition from hieratic to demotic. Some literary works became generally familiar and were alluded to in later texts, playing on a lettered culture common to writer and reader.

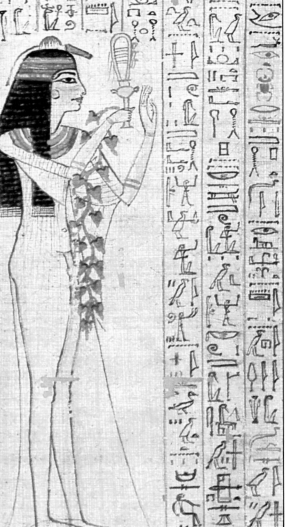

Above Specimen of literary hieratic of the 12th Dynasty with transcription into hieroglyphs. Translation: "The vizier Ptahhotpe says: Sovereign, my lord, decrepitude has come, old age has descended, feebleness has arrived, dotage has returned; one is lying in a second childhood all the time. Eyes are feeble, ears deaf, and the tired heart fails. The mouth is silent and cannot speak." Pap. Prisse 4.2–4. Paris, Bibliothèque Nationale.

Below Extract from a statement of the misfortunes of Peteese's family, perhaps submitted to a high financial official in the reign of Darius I. The text and transcription between the lines read from right to left, but the individual words of the transcription read from left to right. Translation: "The master of harbors dispatched a military officer, saying: 'Arrest anybody Peteese (an ancestor of the author)/tells you to arrest.' The officer came to Teudjoi (el-Hiba), and Peteese had the two priests arrested. He went north with them to the royal palace./In Pharaoh's presence Peteese recounted everything they had done. Pharaoh passed sentence on the two priests." From el-Hiba. Manchester, John Rylands Library, Pap. 9.

p3-dj-jst jw ntj nb rmt n jmhtj m-sm dd mr-ms' w' jw ''-n-mr p' dj

pr-'' pr'p'r jrmw hdjf 2 w'b p' n mhw p'-dj-jst dj t'jw-d'j r jw mr-ms' p' n-jmw mhw mj nk dd r

2 s(?) w'b p' n hp jrw pr-'' dj pr-'' m-b'h jjrw nb md p'-dj-jst dd

There are several forms of the script. Hieroglyphic was used for monumental and ornamental inscriptions, cursive hieroglyphs for religious texts and the "Book of Kemyt," and hieratic, the normal cursive, for everyday purposes. In the 3rd Intermediate Period some monumental inscriptions were written in hieratic, which was also the point of departure for abnormal hieratic, used in the Theban area in the 9th–7th centuries, and for demotic, the cursive of the north after 700 and of all Egypt by 600. Hieratic can always be transcribed into hieroglyphs, although the result is not the same as a text originally composed in hieroglyphic, but demotic is self-sufficient, referring at most to hieratic. Cursive hieroglyphs died out in the first millennium BC, while hieratic was used for religious texts until the end; demotic was used for business, literature and occasional inscriptions on stone.

The spoken language developed continuously, but written forms changed only fitfully, and were linked to the script form used to write them. Between the Old and Middle Kingdoms, the period of Old and Middle Egyptian, the change was more or less consistent with the script, but speech and writing had diverged greatly by the 18th Dynasty. Late Egyptian, the spoken language of the New Kingdom, was used for hieratic documents of the 19th–20th Dynasties, while hieroglyphic texts were still written in a loose form of Middle Egyptian; hieratic forms began to differ between Middle Egyptian religious texts and Late Egyptian business documents. Demotic, roughly the spoken language of the 7th–6th centuries BC, supplanted Late Egyptian, but Middle Egyptian remained the formal, monumental language until the end of Egyptian civilization. In the 2nd century AD Egyptian magical texts began to be written in Greek letters, and from the 4th century this developed into Coptic, the language of Christian Egypt, which gradually gave way to Arabic after 640 AD.

Egyptian is a member of the Afro-Asiatic language family, which includes Semitic and groups in Africa ranging from Berber in the northwest to Chadic (around Lake Chad) and Kushitic and Omotic in southern Sudan and Ethiopia. It resembles Semitic most closely, but nonetheless forms a branch of its own. In word formation and phonetics the two have much in common, including tricon-sonantal roots and the consonants '('ayin), q and ḥ, but Egyptian's structure is as far from Semitic's as modern English is from Latin.

Right Ink hieroglyphs and vignette from the Book of the Dead papyrus of the lady Anhai, 19th Dynasty. The red groups of signs (rubrics) mark the beginnings of sections. The text is corrupt and untranslatable, but derives from a formula for appearing in the form of Ptah and another for eating, drinking and taking up a throne in the next world. London, British Museum.

Left A pair of demotic questions to the oracle of Sobek and Isis at Soknopaiou Nesos (Dimai) in the Faiyum; 149 or 138 BC. The two tiny slips of papyrus (7·5 × 5·5 cm) were placed before the god, and in some way the relevant one was chosen and removed. The texts are almost identical; the first reads: "Plea of the servant Teshnufe (son of) Ma're', who says/before his master Sobek lord of Pay, great god,/and Isis, perfect of throne. If my/soundest course is to plow/the bank of the lake this year,/year 33,/and I should not sow, let this slip/be brought out to me." The second has the corresponding negative provision "if it is not my soundest course . . . ," and omits the reference to sowing, which is not applicable.

All the forms of the script use signs in two overlapping categories: phonograms (phonetic signs) and semograms (conveying meaning). The phonograms form a syllabary, but one in which the vowels are not specified. Because they write consonants + any vowel or no vowel, the information they convey is only consonants. Transcriptions are into consonantal skeletons. The examples of different types of sign are drawn from the text illustrated *right*. In theory there are vast numbers of possible writings of any word, but in practice words have standard writings, mostly of phonograms with semograms at the end. These are read as groups, not broken down into their components – as is true also of reading an alphabetic script. Standard writings make the script easily legible, and are particularly important in hieratic and demotic, with their simplified sign forms.

Inscription on a naos of Tuthmosis IV, recording the king's discovery of a stone. The lines of text and transcription give a step-by-step analysis of the Egyptian and its translation into English.
(a) Copy of the hieroglyphs, written from left to right for convenience. Signs enclosed by [ ] are restored.
(b) Sign-by-sign transcription, divided into words, with indication of taxograms and orthograms above the line. (+) marks a phonogram complement, which is not to be read separately. Logograms are written in CAPITALS; there is no sharp distinction between a single phonogram writing a whole world and a logogram. *nsjt* is a complex historical writing that has to be read as a group.
(c) Conventional Egyptologist's transcription, giving the linguistic structure of the text.
(d) Word-for-word indication of the meaning of the Egyptian.
(e) English translation.

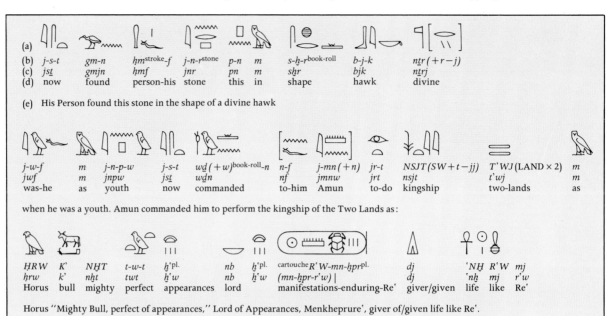

(a)
(b) j-s-t   gm-n   ḥm^stroke-f   j-n-r^stone   p-n   m   s-ḫ-r^book-roll   b-j-k   nṯr(+r-j)
(c) jst   gmjn   ḥmf   jnr   pn   m   sḫr   bjk   nṯrj
(d) now   found   person-his   stone   this   in   shape   hawk   divine

(e)   His Person found this stone in the shape of a divine hawk

j-w-f   m   j-n-p-w   j-s-t   wḏ(+w)^book-roll-n   n-f   j-mn(+n)   jr-t   NSJT(SW+t-jj)   T'WJ(LAND×2)   m
jwf   m   jnpw   jst   wḏn   nf   jmnw   jrt   nsjt   t'wj   m
was-he   as   youth   now   commanded   to-him   Amun   to-do   kingship   two-lands   as

when he was a youth. Amun commanded him to perform the kingship of the Two Lands as:

ḤRW   K'   NḪT   t-w-t   ḫ'^pl.   nb   ḫ'^pl.   cartouche R'W-mn-ḫpr^pl.   dj   'NḪ   R'W   mj
ḥrw   k'   nḫt   twt   ḫ'w   nb   ḫ'w   (mn-ḫpr-r'w)| dj   'nḫ   mj   r'w
Horus   bull   mighty   perfect   appearances   lord   appearances   manifestations-enduring-Re'   giver/given   life   like   Re'

Horus "Mighty Bull, perfect of appearances," Lord of Appearances, Menkheprure', giver of/given life like Re'.

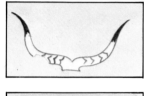

Representational aspects
Most hieroglyphs are pictures; they may evolve with the artistic styles of different periods. This group shows a pair of cattle horns and a clump of papyrus, both in versions of the Old and of the Middle Kingdom, and a reed mat.

Derivation of values

	s	from *sw* "length of cloth"
	t	from *tj* "loaf of bread"
	gm	from *gmt* "black ibis"
	r	from *r'* "mouth"
	p	from *pj* "mat"
	jr	from *jrt* "eye"
	ḫ'	from *ḫ'j* "appear (the sun over the horizon)"

A sign's consonantal reading is mostly determined by what it represents, but one sign may have several values, and may function both as a phonogram and as a semogram. , a seated man, may read *rmṯ* "human being," *zj* "man" or *rḫw* "companion," or may be a taxogram, as in *ḥm-nṯr* "priest."

	Uniconsonantal		Biconsonantal		Triconsonantal	
	j (y)		*gm*		*nṯr*	
	s		*wḏ*		*ḫpr*	
	t		*mn*		(Quadriconsonantal)	
	n		*jr*		*hsmn*	
	r		*sw*			
	p		*ḫ'*			
	m		*nb*			
	ḫ		*dj*			
	b		*mj*			
	k					
	w					
	f					

Above Signs can write one to four consonants. Uniconsonantal signs are common, but a set of them is not an alphabet, because in theory it writes vowels with the consonants, and it has no special position among phonograms as a whole.

Right There are two types of semogram: logograms, which write complete words, and signs that are placed after the phonograms in a word. The most important of these are taxograms, or determinatives, which indicate the class or area of meaning to which a word belongs. Strokes, or orthograms, show that a preceding sign is a logogram; sets of two or three strokes write the dual or the plural.

Logograms

	ḥm "person" (of the king)
	t' t'wj "land, two lands"
	k' "bull"
	nḫt "mighty"
	r'w "Re'"
	'nḫ "life"

Taxograms

	stone
	book-roll: abstraction, word
	cartouche; surrounds royal names

Orthograms

| | logogram indicator |
| | plural indicator |

The writing of the signs in a text fixes the direction of reading. Signs facing right – the normal direction – show that the text reads from right to left. Columns or lines may be used. Here an identical text has been written once from right to left and once from left to right. Offering formula on a false door in the mastaba of Kahayf. Late 6th Dynasty. Giza.

Ornamental caption to a hunting scene in the tomb of Amenemhet at Thebes (no. 82, reign of Tuthmosis III). Words containing the name of Amun have been erased, probably during the 'Amarna Period. The text reads: "Crossing the valleys, treading the hills, taking pleasure, shooting the game of the desert, by the one beloved of his lord, steward of the vizier, scribe accountant of the grain of [Amun, Amenemhet], justified."

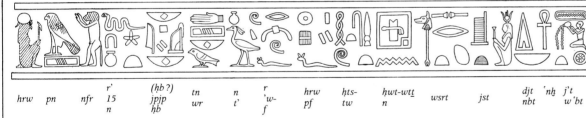

hrw	pn	nfr	r' 15 n	(ḥb ?) jpjp ḥb	tn wr	n	r t' f	'w- f	hrw pf	ḥts- tw	ḥwt-wtt n	wsrt	jst	djt nbt	'nḥ	j't w'bt

Above Outline hieroglyphs in a caption in the tomb of Pere' at Thebes (no. 139, reign of Tuthmosis IV). The text reads: "Going north to the district of Poqer [Abydos]; seeing Wennofre [Osiris] at the festival." The sign *m* has been replaced by ⟶, also *m*, in order to make a better grouping. Both versions are now visible. a sign is changed in form: (human mouth), *r*, becomes . The result of all this is that a single value may be written by many different signs: , all *m* (from a total of more than 25), and one sign can have many values: , *š s ḫ ḥ n m jnr*.

Cryptography

The use of the script's principles in a deliberately misleading way is called cryptography. This is found at all periods, chiefly as a challenge to persuade the reader to read a standard formula. During the Late and Greco-Roman Periods, however, the hieroglyphic script was elaborated from a repertory of a few hundred signs to one of several thousand, using every possible method for devising new signs and combinations, and not observing the former economy of means. At this stage hieroglyphs had lost their connection with the everyday script. They could be read only by a tiny elite, mainly of priests, who wished to cultivate complexity almost for its own sake.

Above Facsimile of an ornamental inscription of the reign of Tiberius in the birth house at Philae. Translation: "This good day, the 2nd of Epiphi [month name]: This festival, the great festival of the entire land; that day when the birth house was completed for the mighty one, Isis, giver of life, mistress of the Abaton [see page 73]." The transcription follows the grouping of the signs. The writing, especially of the first few words, uses numerous non-traditional sign-values. Examples of early and late values are:

p; early *bjk*

n; early *š*

t'; early *'ḫ*

t; early *d*

Some signs do not occur in early periods: *nfr*. In other cases

A letter of the 11th Dynasty (2002 BC) that never reached its destination. The papyrus is folded into a packet (8 × 4 cm) and sealed, with the addressee's name above the seal. The text reads: "The overseer of Lower Egypt, Re'nofre." From Deir el-Bahri. New York, Metropolitan Museum of Art.

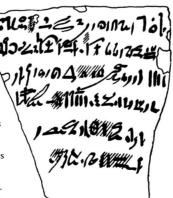

Ostraca were used for writing drafts of texts or as cheap substitutes for papyrus. In this example an illiterate man asks another to write a pledge for him in respect of a debt; the ostracon was probably kept by the creditor until the matter was settled. At this date – between Ramesses III and IX – the tunic was equivalent in value to 1–3 sacks of grain.

Translation: "Year 5, month 3 of *peret* (approx. winter), day 22. What the guardian of the estate Penrenenutet said: 'By Amun and the ruler, if I enter a(nother) week without having given this tunic to Harmin, it (my debt) will be doubled to my debit.' Done (i.e. written) by the foreman of the gang Nekhemmut." From Deir el-Medina. London, Petrie Collection (University College).

THE ARMY

The earliest battle in the history of mankind whose course can be reconstructed in detail took place near the city of Qadesh on the river Orontes in 1285 BC. The combatants were Ramesses II and the Hittite king Muwatallis, and at stake was the control of Syria. In the end, both armies suffered heavily, but neither was annihilated. Ramesses II gained a moral victory, but the encounter was indecisive.

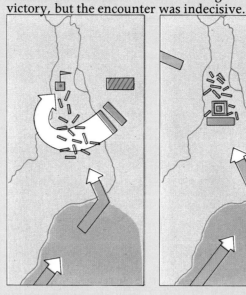

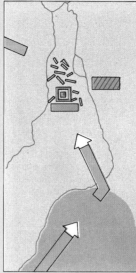

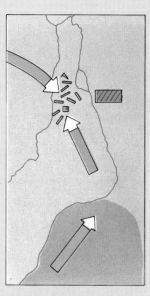

	Egyptian infantry and chariotry, total 20,000 men		Hittite chariotry, 3,500 chariots with 10,500 men
●	Ramesses II		
🚩	Egyptian camp		Hittite infantry, 8,000 men

1. The Egyptian army consisted of four divisions, with a smaller unit operating independently. Through false information planted on them, the Egyptians were misled into believing that the Hittite host had retreated. The Egyptian divisions advanced northwards along the Orontes, unaware that the Hittites lay concealed beyond Qadesh.

2. The Egyptian van, the division of Amun led by the king himself, reached the rendezvous point northwest of the city and set up camp. When the division of Preˤ, suspecting no danger, approached, its right flank was subjected to a devastating charge of Hittite chariotry.

3. The division of Preˤ, caught by surprise, was broken and scattered. Survivors of the Hittite ambush were fleeing northwards in the direction of the Egyptian camp, with Hittite chariots in pursuit. The division of Ptah was still emerging from the Robaui forest south of the town of Shabtuna and crossing on to the west bank of the river, and was too far away to render any assistance to the attacked unit.

4. The camp was overrun and the division of Amun suffered heavy losses. The king and his guard desperately tried to fight their way to meet the approaching division of Ptah. Muwatallis committed his chariot reserve in order to bring the battle to a quick conclusion.

5. By his gallant, though forced, action the Egyptian king gained enough time: the special task force appeared at last, and with the division of Ptah now reaching the scene, crushed the Hittite chariotry. Muwatallis' infantry remained inactive beyond the river.

One of the advantages Egypt derived from her unique geographical position was relative safety. Nomadic tribes in the deserts on either side of the Nile valley soon ceased to pose a serious threat to the highly organized and much more powerful Egyptian civilization; only during periods of instability were they a force to be reckoned with. Colonial expansion in the 12th Dynasty led to intensive campaigning and building of fortresses in Nubia, but it was not until the 18th Dynasty that the Egyptians encountered real opposition, when they entered the military arena of the Near East by contending for Syria and Palestine.

The word *mesha'*, "army," originally described both military forces and peaceful expeditions sent to quarry minerals: "task force" would be the most fitting translation. During the Old Kingdom, when an emergency arose, a body of men was mustered to back the small specialized permanent units. The situation changed in the 1st Intermediate Period: instability brought about the creation of private armies of nomarchs and the use of non-Egyptian mercenary troops. The Middle Kingdom already knew well-organized standing military units, supplemented when needed by local militia. The force consisted mainly of infantry, with boat personnel integrated into it. The 2nd Intermediate Period and the 18th Dynasty saw an unprecedented advance in the development of weapons, military organization (the appearance of chariotry, organization of infantry into companies of some 250 men led by a standard-bearer), strategy and tactics. The standing army and professional army officers began to play an important part in internal politics. In the Late Period, foreign mercenaries formed the core.

Ancient Egyptian weapons of various types are known from contemporary representations and models as well as archaeological finds.

The bow, the most important long-range weapon, was used at all times, either the archaic compound horn-bow consisting of two antelope horns joined by a wooden central piece, or the wooden, slightly double-convex, "self" bow. During the 2nd Intermediate Period the composite bow was introduced from Asia. It was made of laminated strips of various materials, and had a much-improved range and power. When strung, the bow acquired a characteristic triangular shape. *The quiver* was in use from the Old Kingdom onwards.

The spear was employed throughout Egyptian history.

The mace with a stone mace-head of varying form, the most powerful weapon of close combat in the Predynastic Period, was in historic times replaced by *the battle-ax* with a copper ax-head. Some of the early semicircular ax-heads differed little from contemporary tools of craftsmen, but already during the Old Kingdom a specialized shallow type appeared. This, and the scalloped ax-head, were characteristic of the weapons of the Middle Kingdom. In the 2nd Intermediate Period a new type with a narrow ax-blade and therefore much-improved power of penetration appeared, probably an indigenous development. *The scimitar* (sickle sword), an Asiatic weapon used in the same way as the Egyptian battle-ax (as a cutting or piercing rather than thrusting weapon), is also met in the New Kingdom.

Cudgels, clubs and *throwing-sticks* of various types remained in use as side arms at all times. *The dagger* was used in the same way.

Personal protection was afforded by *the shield*, already attested during the late Predynastic Period. Light *body armor* was known from the New Kingdom but its use remained limited.

The two-wheeled horse-drawn *chariot*, introduced to Egypt in the 2nd Intermediate Period, was a light vehicle, made of wood with some leather and metal elements. It was manned by two soldiers: the charioteer, and the chariot-warrior armed with a bow and spear and carrying a shield. The chariot's main contribution to the art of warfare was mobility and the element of surprise connected with it: in the attack, the chariots approached at full speed and the chariot-warriors delivered their arrows while passing the massed enemy ranks. The chariot was not armored in any way and therefore was not suitable for a direct attack. Once the enemy lines were broken, the chariotry was ideally suited for pursuing and harassing the scattered foot soldiers. Judging from the appearance of special titles, the chariotry formed a separate arm of the Egyptian army from the reign of Amenophis III.

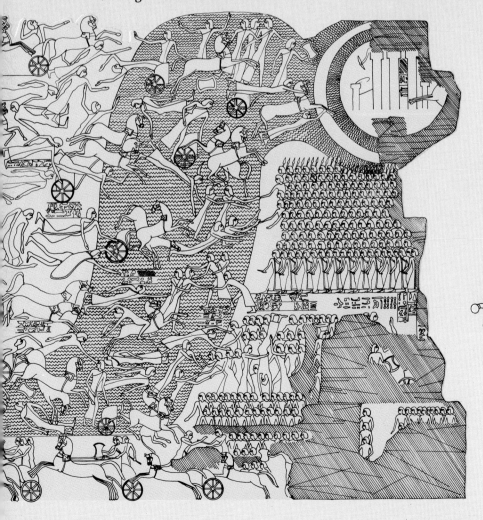

WOMEN IN SOCIETY

The position of women in Egypt is neatly summarized in their roles in early tomb decoration. At the top of the hierarchy is the wife, or sometimes the mother, of the tomb owner, who is simply but elegantly dressed, and sits at leisure with her husband at a table of offerings, in a statue group or on a false door. She sometimes accompanies her husband when he watches scenes of work, but is more often shown when offerings are presented to the couple; this distinction may show that she is normally expected to stay at home. At the other extreme are scenes or statuettes of servant girls and of women engaged in menial tasks, making bread and beer, spinning and weaving. These too are sedentary activities, probably conducted in the domestic quarters of a house or estate. The female flesh color, yellow, indicates among other things less exposure to the sun than the male red, and therefore a more enclosed existence – as it does on successful male bureaucrats.

It may have been unsafe for women to venture out. Ramesses III is made to say in a posthumous text, "I enabled the woman of Egypt to go her way, her journeys being extended where she wanted, without any other person assaulting her on the road" – which implies that this was not always the case.

In early tombs women are absent from the most important work shown and from the most pleasurable diversions, but do not have to engage in the roughest tasks. Men, for example, make wine, which is more strenuous than brewing. Apart from scenes of musicians and of very athletic girls' dances, the role of women in early periods seems very decorous, although this may be because we cannot interpret our sources fully. In the New Kingdom women become much more prominent, their clothing more elaborate, and the erotic content of scenes in which they appear more definite – if still heavily coded. The Late Period mostly returns to earlier decorum.

Women did not hold any important titles, except some priestly ones, and apart from a few members of

Women in different roles and artistic media
Far left bottom The corpulent Ka'aper embraces his slender wife. His body depicts wise and prosperous age, hers the blander feminine ideal. Embraces are very rarely shown. The small musical scenes and the monkey have erotic overtones. In his mastaba at Saqqara. Early 5th Dynasty.

Left Wooden statue of a servant carrying offerings, unusual for its large size (c.110 cm) and for the coloring of the garments. The type derives from Old Kingdom reliefs of bearers bringing the produce of estates. c.2020 BC. From Theban Tomb 280 of Meketre'. New York, Metropolitan Museum of Art.

Below left Sketch of a woman performing an acrobatic dance on a 19th-Dynasty limestone ostracon from Deir el-Medina. Width 16·8 cm. Turin, Museo Egizio.

the royal family and queens regnant they had little political power. Their commonest title, "mistress of the house," is a term of respect, and may mean little more than "Mrs." Almost all were illiterate, and therefore barred from the bureaucracy – to which they are in any case unlikely to have aspired – and from the major intellectual areas of culture. Symptomatic of this is the fact that age and wisdom were qualities respected in men, who were represented as corpulent elder statesmen, but not in women. Even a man's mother is indistinguishable from his wife in tomb depictions; both are youthful figures. The way women are shown is, of course, part of men's definition of them, and displays a public, ideal state of affairs. In reality women's influence may not have been so circumscribed, and they may have been far more varied in their roles than our evidence would suggest.

Family structures, for example, appear severely simplified. The norms of tomb and stela decoration leave no room for the widow or widower, the divorcee, homosexuals, or deviations from monogamy – yet all of these are known to have occurred. A story recounts an affair between a king and a military officer, and there are homosexual episodes in the myth of Horus and Seth. There was a limited amount of polygyny in the Old and Middle Kingdoms, and the king could have many wives, although only one – in addition to his mother, if she was still alive – bore the title "great royal wife."

Marriage

Egyptians were mostly monogamous. Inheritance passed from father to children, but followed no very rigid pattern, and family property was defined by a marriage settlement – documentation of which is not known before the 3rd Intermediate Period – and by deeds of transfer made either between the living or as wills. In all of this the woman's role was important, though not equal to that of her husband. She brought a proportion of the property into the marriage, which was in theory a new household, not an extension of parental home, and had some rights over it in a divorce. She could also make a will and leave her property as she wished, although the extent of this freedom is not known. It is most striking that we have no evidence either for marriage ceremonies of any sort or for judicial processes in divorce. Even so, the legal status of a couple living together was different from that of a married pair. There is even a case where a man is accused for having intercourse with a woman who is living with another man but not married to him, something which might seem unlikely to constitute an offence. Despite these relatively free institutions, a woman's adultery was, at least in theory, a serious offence. Apart from gradations of this sort, mortality and the frequency of divorce led to complicated situations with regard to property and inheritance. Life expectancy was probably around 20, so that it was not unusual for a man or a woman

Above Black granite statue group of Tuthmosis IV and his mother Ti'a. Kings shown with their mothers may not yet have had a chief wife, but this is unlikely here, because Tuthmosis had three in ten years. Height 110 cm. From Karnak. Cairo, Egyptian Museum.

Right Mereruka's wife plays the harp to him on a bed. Beneath are pots and chests containing "the best of the treasures of gold, all sorts of oil, and clothing." These are probably all for the adornment of the couple in their amorous encounters. In his tomb at Saqqara. Reign of Teti.

Left Miy, a lady of the court of Amenophis III, ebony statuette from a tomb near the royal harem complex at Kom Medinet Ghurab; one of a group of similar works. Height 15·6 cm. Brooklyn Museum.

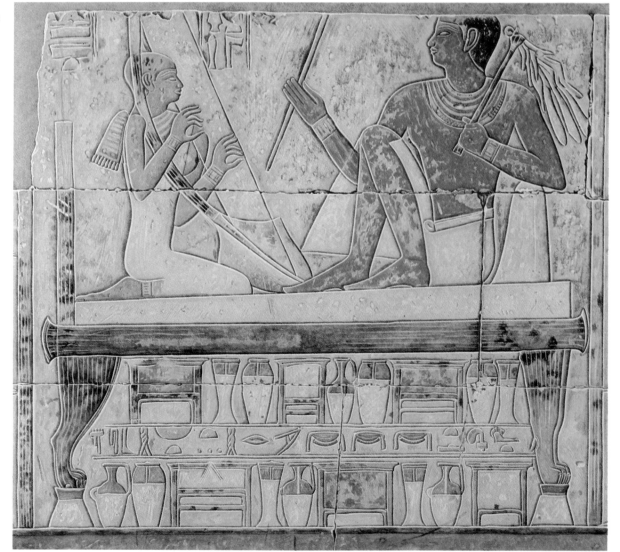

to be widowed several times. A Middle Kingdom deed illustrates the complexity of inheritance. A man retires and hands over his office to his son while disinheriting the son's mother and leaving his remaining property to his children (who may not yet be born) by another woman; it seems that neither woman is his wife.

Very little is known of the social background to marriage. It was possible to marry quite close blood relatives, including on occasion half-siblings, but the precise definition of permitted and prohibited partners is not known. In the royal family there was some brother–sister marriage, but this practice may be in intentional contrast with that of ordinary people. In Greco-Roman Egypt such marriages are well attested among the Greek population. Our chief difficulty in understanding the framework lies in Egyptian kinship terms, of which there were very few. A single word could mean brother, mother's brother or brother's son (and no doubt more besides); others will have had similarly extended meanings. This means that reconstructed genealogies can seldom be verified.

The age of either partner at marriage is unknown. Some family trees show that men on occasion had children well before they were 20, but the clearest cases are in the royal family, which may be untypical here too. At first marriage women were no doubt younger than their husbands, but this may not have been true of subsequent marriages.

Sexuality and fertility

Men, who produced our evidence, will have been concerned to enhance women's sexuality for their own ends – which were religious as well as pleasurable – but not to promote it as an independent and subversive force. Their attitude to it was ambivalent. In stories the evil seductress is a common motif, and love poetry of the New Kingdom is often written in the words of the ardent woman, in this case without the same moralistic overtones. Although the stories have religious elements, both these sources give a secular view of the matter. In religious terms, however, sexuality was important because of its relationship with creation, and, by association, with rebirth in the hereafter. It was also significant for the character of certain deities – Hathor among goddesses and Min among gods. In a funerary context the covert erotic references in tomb scenes could have two purposes: to ensure rebirth through potency in the next life, or to enable the deceased to lead an enjoyable existence. Scenes with an erotic content include ones of hunting in the marshes, where the deceased is accompanied by his wife, who is somewhat implausibly dressed in her most elaborate costume, wears a heavy wig and carries two symbols of Hathor. Heavy wigs, especially when associated with nudity, could be erotic signals. In a New Kingdom story the evil wife accuses her husband's brother of attempting to seduce her by reporting him as saying, "Come, let us spend an hour lying. Put on your wig."

Motifs like this are rarer in earlier periods, the best example being a scene in the 6th-Dynasty tomb of Mereruka at Saqqara, where the owner and his wife sit facing each other on a bed and she plays the harp to him. Such a scene was intended partly to ensure an erotic ambiance for him in the next life. A spell or a female statuette placed in a tomb could

Right Hunting in the marshes. Nebamun and his wife and daughter are on a papyrus boat, all elaborately dressed. The duck on the front of the boat has erotic associations, as do the wife's wig and the counterpoise and sistrum she holds in her left hand. Nevertheless, the text refers simply to "having pleasure, seeing good things, trapping birds as a work of Sekhet [the marsh goddess] . . ." Reign of Tuthmosis IV. London, British Museum.

Below Copulating couple. One of a number of positions of intercourse shown in a humorous obscene papyrus of the late New Kingdom. As in one other scene, the woman appears to be indifferent to the man. Turin, Museo Egizio.

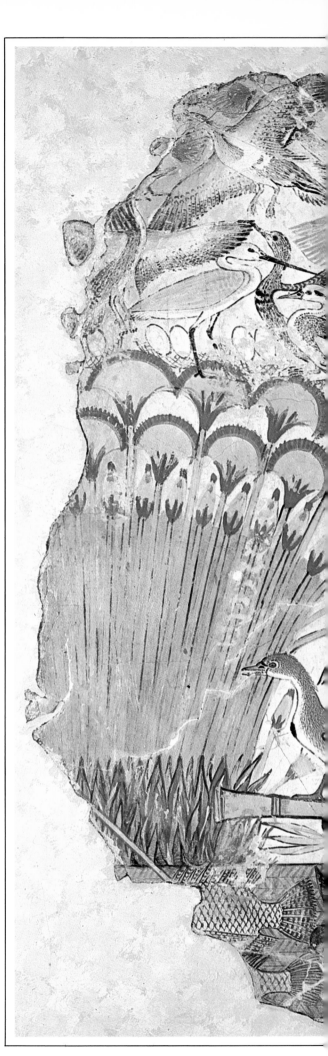

have a similar purpose, but was less conjugal in its reference. A Middle Kingdom spell in the Coffin Texts has the simple beginning, "Copulating by a man in the necropolis." On a mythological plane the same concerns are seen in the Book of the Dead, where Osiris complains to the creator god Atum that after the end of the world "There will be no [sexual] gratification there," to which Atum replies, "I have given transfiguration in place of water, air and gratification" – here held to be the three preconditions of life – "and peace of heart in place of bread and beer."

There is only one obscene document of any size, which dates to the late New Kingdom. This is a set of drawings with brief captions on a papyrus, which shows a variety of sexual encounters between a fat, priapic man (or perhaps men) and a woman (or women) who is dressed in a wig, necklace, armlets, bracelets and a belt. The papyrus also contains humorous sketches of animals in human roles – a well-known motif – suggesting that the obscene part may be humorous too. From about the same time there is a case of prudery, where paintings of nude dancing girls and lightly clothed women in an 18th-Dynasty tomb were covered in drapery by a later owner. On Late Period dwelling sites obscene objects, mostly statuettes of men with enormous penises, are often found. These did exist earlier, but

are mostly lost because of the scarcity of settlement material. They were probably charms intended to increase men's potency.

If potency was a man's worry, where the death rate was so high fertility was inevitably important to women – as well as to men. In all but the wealthiest families children would be vital to contribute their labor, particularly in agriculture, and on another plane to carry on the family line, whose most obvious feature was the common practice of giving a son the name of his grandfather. Gynecological texts are known, including prescriptions for reproductive disorders, birth prognoses, contraception and abortion, but it is unlikely that any of these, except perhaps those for abortion, were very effective. From shrines of Hathor as well as dwelling sites and tombs we have numerous clay figurines of women whose forms emphasize the genitals. The most likely explanation of these is that they were offered by women for their own fertility. It is noteworthy that they do not conform to the norms of Egyptian representation. They may come from a different class of the population from most representational works, or have been considered to be outside the canon for some other reason. Until modern times the gift of such offerings was probably as effective a way of helping to produce a child as visiting a doctor.

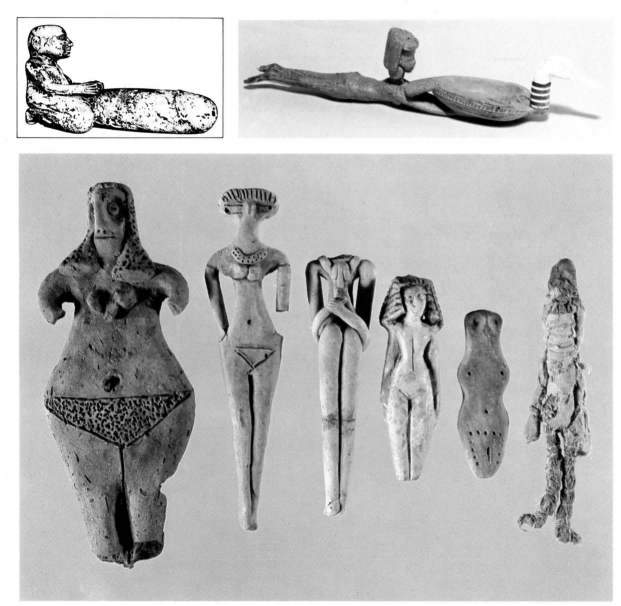

Far left Limestone statuette of a squatting man with an enormous erect penis; probably a fertility or potency charm. Late New Kingdom, from Deir el-Medina. Turin, Museo Egizio.

Left Decorated spoon, perhaps a ritual ointment container, in the form of a swimming girl holding out a duck. The girl has an elaborate wig, heavy earrings and a necklace, but is clothed only in a belt with a diagonal strap on the back. The motif of a girl presenting an animal to her lover in order to attract him is known from love poetry. Wood and bone. 18th Dynasty. Length c. 30 cm. Paris, Musée du Louvre.

Left Fertility statuettes of naked women in clay and faience, with a "doll" of reed and linen. The forms of all except the faience figure (3rd from right) emphasize the genitals. The 4th figure from the right (photographed from the back) holds a child, and has an "Isis-knot" amulet, which is associated with life and sexual fertility, hanging around its neck. Middle-New Kingdom. Height 15–20 cm. London, Petrie Collection (University College).

RELIGION

Wooden figure of a ram-headed demon, probably originally holding a pair of snakes. Like a number of mortuary objects, it was covered in black resin. One of a group from the Valley of the Kings that have parallels in New Kingdom underworld books and mythological papyri; this type was not found in the tomb of Tut'ankhamun. Height 45·7 cm. London, British Museum.

Egyptian culture was pervaded by religion, and the official version of Egyptian history was a religious one. In later periods the economy itself was organized around the temples – which does not necessarily mean that it became more religious, since temples were probably not very different from other landlords. However this may be, it is clear that the pattern of secularization, which we tend to take for granted in the development of societies, was absent. The central institution of the kingship ended by losing its charisma, but in other respects society became if anything more religious. Religion in Egypt divides sharply into the official, state aspect, about which we know a great deal, the mortuary sphere, which is also well represented, and the everyday practices of most of the population, which were largely separate from the official cult, and are very poorly known.

The king and history

In the official view society consisted of the gods, the king and mankind. But mankind is absent from most official pictorial records, which represent history and religion as the interplay of gods and the king. Part of the reason for this is a set of rules governing the compatibility of different types of figure in representation and the contexts in which they may occur; in early periods these do not permit a private individual and a god to be shown together, and they never allow normal people to be shown in temples. But in addition the king acts as a mediator – in some respects the only one – between god and man. He represents man to the gods and the gods to man. He is also the living exemplar of the creator god on earth – an idea which is defined by a terminology of great richness and complexity – and reenacts the creator god's role of setting order in place of disorder. History is a ritual in the cosmos, of which this reenactment is a principal theme.

The king is responsible for the well-being of the people, and takes their cares on himself like the "good shepherd" of the Old Testament – a formulation known from Egypt too. Kings also sought to enhance their status before the people, by identifying with gods or, in some instances, by deifying themselves, so that they could even be shown in their normal guise offering to their divine alter egos, as is attested for Amenophis III and Ramesses II. Finally, kings could be deified after death, more on the model of deified private individuals than as if they were true gods. So the king did not have a simple status as god or man. By virtue of his office he was a being apart, and his role differed according to the context in which he acted.

Official and private religion

The official religion consisted of cult and festivals in the main temples, and of the process of history in the way just mentioned. The cult was founded on reciprocity. The king (in theory, but in practice the priests) provided for the gods and cared for their cult images. In return, the gods took up residence in the images and showed their favor to the king and

hence to humanity. The almost commercial nature of the relationship is expressed quite plainly in offering formulae in the lowest register of temple decoration (see p. 64), which say "The king has come to you [the deity], bringing offerings which he has given to you, so that you may give to him all lands [or a similar gift]." The same point is made in the main areas of relief, but more discreetly. The contract between deity and mankind does not exclude other facets from the relationship, any more than a marriage contract does. The king expresses his adoration and veneration of the deity, and celebrates the deity's qualities. The deity responds with love for the king and delight in his presence. The Egyptian language has an enormous vocabulary to express these basic ideas, some of whose key elements work in unexpected ways. Man or the king cannot "love" a god, but only "respect," "adore" or "thank" him. Qualities attributed to kings or deities are often what we would consider reactions to them, so that "fear" means the capacity to arouse fear, and "love" that to inspire love. The relationships between the participants are very hierarchical, and the lower party to any grouping is an active provider of humble benefits, but a passive recipient of higher ones.

The aim of the cult is the aim of history: to maintain and enhance the established order of the world. The chief temples were dedicated to local deities, who were mostly held within their areas to be the creators, and to encompass the important aspects of the divine world. The cult was carried out by a hierarchy of priests. It did not concern the mass of the population, except for part-time priests, who served one month in four, and people who worked on temple lands. Only priests could enter the temple. The god left the temple for various festivals during which he could be approached by normal people, notably for oracular consultations, but even then the cult image was kept hidden in a shrine that was carried on a symbolic bark, so that the god was known to be present, but not seen.

Outside these festivals, the official cult was irrelevant to the private individual. It is impossible to know his attitude to it, whether he viewed it as essential but not concerning him, or as a meaningless extravagance. There are one or two passages

Left Entrance to room 31 in the temple of Ramesses III at Medinet Habu. The king holds a mace and scepter, symbols of his divine and ritual role, and says "Everybody who enters the shrine, purify four times."

Above Tubular case of gold made to contain a rolled strip of papyrus with a decree by Khons for the protection of the owner, who would wear it around his neck. The text says "Speech by Khons in Thebes, Neferhotep. He made good protection [of] Shaq, deceased." One of three similar cases. 22nd Dynasty. Height 5·2 cm. Cambridge, Fitzwilliam Museum.

Left Relief of Amenophis III offering to his deified self, in the temple of Soleb in Upper Nubia. The presentation is that of any normal temple relief. The deified king, "Nebma'atre' [Amenophis' praenomen], great god," has a lunar headdress and divine scepter, but wears the royal uraeus, headcloth and false beard.

Above Group of faience amulets from a single mummy. Above: *wedjat* eye, scarab and winged scarab pectoral, all symbols of rebirth. Below: mummiform Duamutef and Qebehsenuf, Sons of Horus; Isis and Nephthys, who mourn for Osiris; ram-headed god, probably Amun; two *djeds* and papyrus stem, symbolizing duration and freshness. From Abydos. 30th Dynasty. Width of winged scarab 8·7 cm. Oxford, Ashmolean Museum.

Below Group of animal mummies: elaborately wrapped ibis (with a figure of Thoth), cat and snake; fish in a box. Late or Greco-Roman Period. Oxford, Ashmolean Museum.

in texts that question the value of offerings, but these must be seen against the background of the general assumption that they were necessary. Whatever his attitude was, for his own religious needs he turned elsewhere. Apart from the main temples there were many local shrines to lesser deities, or to different forms of the main ones, throughout the country, rather as in European cities cathedrals coexist with smaller churches. Normal people went to these shrines, where they prayed, placed offerings or deposited oracular questions. There were also centers of pilgrimage, such as Abydos, which had its heyday in the Middle Kingdom, and Saqqara, where the animal necropolis acted as a focus in the Late and Ptolemaic periods. If we are to believe letter formulae, people would visit shrines – or possibly pray in their homes – every day in order to intercede for the welfare of the absent correspondent. Such formulae are not necessarily good evidence, but certain details suggest that there is a core of genuine practice in these ones.

Religious activities of this sort are paralleled by a host of other practices, many of which shade off into the magical. Among types of religious objects one may cite, almost at random, amulets, including divine decrees safeguarding their bearers, busts of ancestors in houses, and numerous special objects and modes of dress surrounding childbirth. From texts we know of magical cures for illness, love charms, calendars of lucky and unlucky days, the avoidance of the evil eye, divination through dreams and various rarer practices, letters written to dead relatives who were thought to hold a grudge against the living, and much else besides. Despite the multifarious forms of religious observance and

the hundreds of different deities, some important events in life were rather surprisingly secular. We have no evidence for rituals performed on the newborn child, only of ones aimed at easing the birth and removing pollution from the mother after it. Similarly, phases of life like the circumcision of boys, apparently just before puberty, or marriage, do not seem to have been ritualized.

One area of popular and official religious life that impressed foreigners in antiquity was animal worship. There had always been animals kept as sacred to particular deities – or possibly worshiped as deities in their own right – and buried ceremonially. In the Late Period these practices proliferated enormously. The species associated with the main deity of an area was often held sacred there, and either a single member of it or all members were mummified and buried. To pay for an animal's burial was a "good deed." In Memphis, whose population was no doubt very mixed, many species were buried. The most famous is the Apis bull, sacred to Ptah, which was buried in one catacomb (the Serapeum) and its mother in a second, while ibises, dogs or jackals, cats, baboons, ichneumons and rams are all attested in varying numbers. Other species, including several types of fish, snakes and crocodiles, are known from other parts of the country. A whole town sprang up in the desert at north Saqqara to cater for these needs, and ibises were farmed on an almost industrial scale, before being probably hastened to their death. These practices, whose precise understanding eludes us still, were common to all classes of society. Their public character and the decline of private tombs at the time may be related to a weakening of the belief in individual life after death.

The Egyptian Pantheon
Local Gods

It is impossible to arrange Egyptian deities into neat categories; any attempt to do so involves simplification. There are two main reasons for this: the complexity of Egyptian religious ideas and the long period over which they developed. The religious practices of ordinary people differed considerably from the official religion of the large temples.

In addition to their representations and hieroglyphic forms of their names, the following lists provide three types of information: 1. the main iconographic features by which the deity can be recognized; 2. the character and function of the deity, its relationship with other gods etc.; 3. its main places of worship.

Many of the gods and goddesses can be described as local deities because from the earliest times they were closely connected with a particular locality. Nonetheless, numerous apparently local deities are found over much of the country from early times. The gods shared the fate of their home towns, and while some of them were ultimately promoted to be Egyptian "state gods" (e.g. the Memphite Ptah, the Theban Amon-Re', and the Heliopolitan Re'-Harakhty) whose cult spread over the whole of Egypt, others fell into obscurity and oblivion and were replaced by, or more often assimilated with, the more vigorous gods of other localities. The latter could be done in two different ways: by adopting another god's attributes (e.g. Osiris took some of his iconographic characteristics from the god 'Andjety) or by the creation of a composite deity (e.g. Ptah-Sokar-Osiris), a process known as syncretism. Because of their connection with the resident god, various "guest deities" were worshiped in local temples.

Re'(Re'-Harakhty)
Sun-disk on head, hawk-headed (Re'-Harakhty)/sun god, identified with Harakhty and the primeval creator god Atum as Re'-Harakhty-Atum; often linked with other gods (Amon-Re' etc.)/Heliopolis; as a state god of the New Kingdom worshiped at many other places.

Bastet
Lioness-headed or cat-headed/ war goddess; closely connected with Mut and Sakhmet/Tell Basta.

Neith
Red crown or two crossed arrows and shield on her head (also held in hands)/goddess of war and hunting; closely connected with Sobek; guardian deity/Sa el-Hagar, also Memphis, the Faiyum and Esna.

Thoth
Ibis-headed, often with moon crescent/god of writing and counting; baboon another sacred animal/el-Ashmunein and el-Baqliya.

Harsaphes
Ram-headed or ram/gained importance during the 1st Intermediate Period when Herakleopolis was Egypt's northern capital; closely connected with Re', Osiris, and Amun/Ihnasya el-Medina.

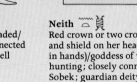

Hathor
Sun-disk, cow's horns, also cow-headed, cow, "Hathor-pillar" or sistrum etc./goddess of women, also sky goddess, tree goddess (Memphis) or necropolis goddess (Thebes)/Heliopolis, Memphis, Atfih, el-Qusiya, Dendara, Thebes, Gebelein, Abu Simbel, Sinai (Serabit el-Khadim).

Montu
Often hawk-headed, sun-disk and two plumes/war god; connected with the Buchis bull of Armant/Armant, but also Karnak, Tod, Nag' el-Madamud.

Khons ,Mut and Amun (Amon-Re')
Khons: child's side-lock of hair, sometimes with moon crescent, often mummiform; Mut: vulture headdress or crowns (white or double), also lioness-headed; Amun (head of the triad): two plumes, sometimes ithyphallic/Mut a war goddess; Amun's female counterpart Amaunet/Theban triad (Karnak, Luxor), but Amun also important at el-Ashmunein; as a state god of the New Kingdom Amon-Re' worshiped at many other places (Tanis, Memphis, the oases).

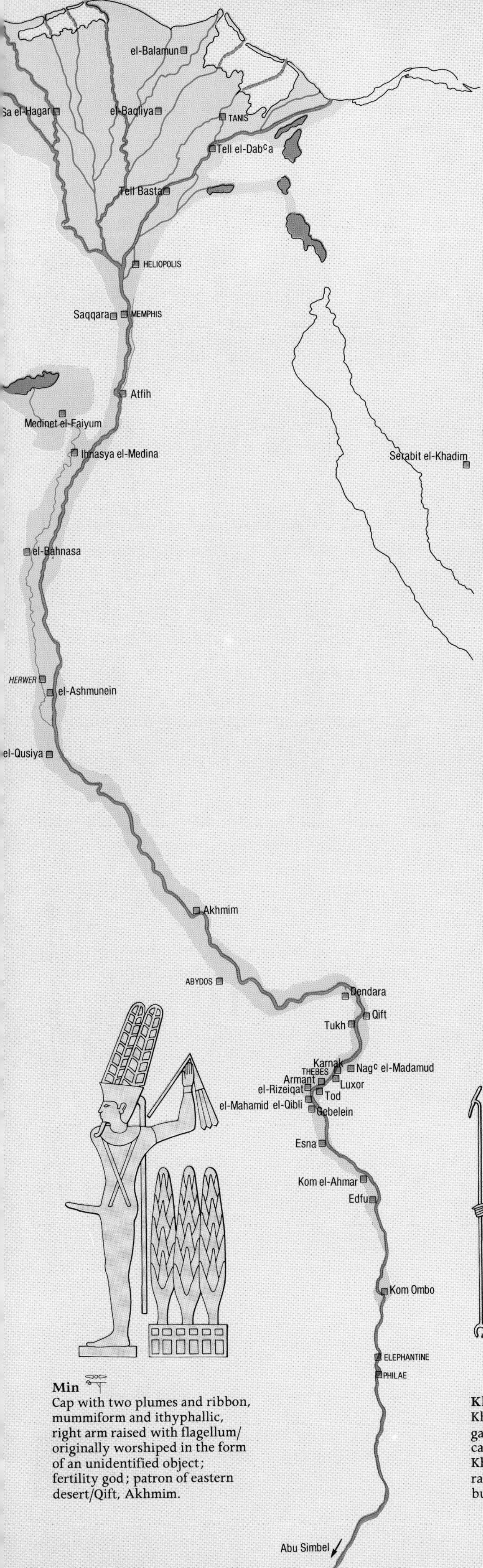

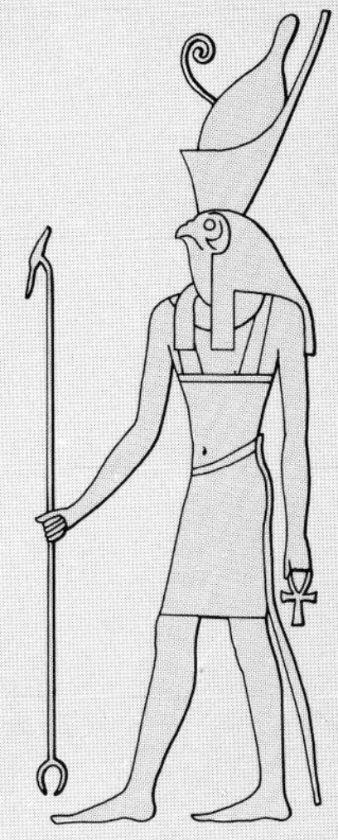

Horus (various local forms, e.g. Horus *Nekheny*)
Hawk-headed or hawk, often with double crown/sky god; the earliest state god of Egypt; closely connected with king; member of Heliopolitan ennead: son of Osiris and Isis.

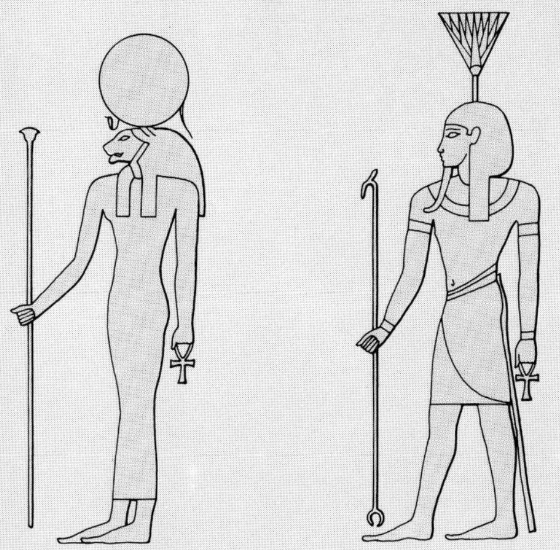

Ptah , **Sakhmet** and **Nefertem**
Ptah (*below right*): mummiform with three scepters; Sakhmet: lioness-headed; Nefertem: lotus flower on head (sometimes with two plumes), or a child on lotus flower/Ptah a creator god, patron of craftsmen, soon merged with necropolis god Sokar and Osiris into Ptah-Sokar-Osiris, connected with Apis bull; Sakhmet connected with Mut and Bastet/Memphite triad; Ptah also worshiped at Thebes and Abydos and as a state god of the New Kingdom at many other places (e.g. in Nubia).

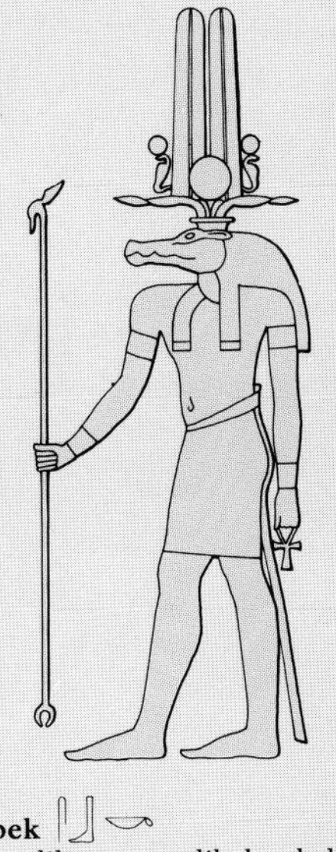

Sobek
Crocodile or crocodile-headed/the Faiyum, but also el-Mahamid el-Qibly near el-Rizeiqat (*Sumenu*), Gebelein, Esna and Kom Ombo.

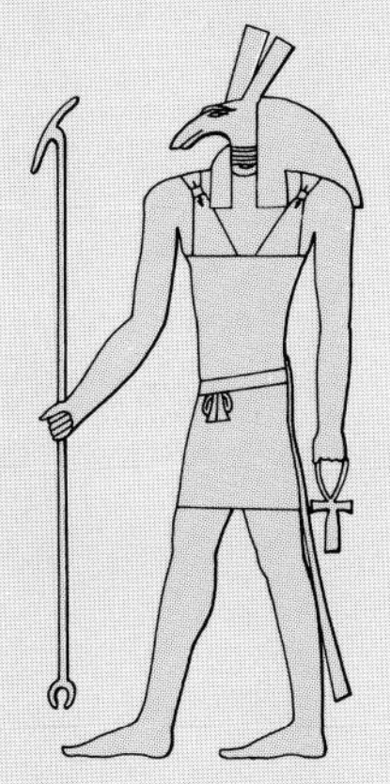

Seth
Unidentified animal or man with the head of such animal/god of disorder, deserts, storms and war; member of Heliopolitan ennead: brother of Osiris/Tukh, el-Bahnasa, Tanis, Tell el-Dabʿa (popular in the eastern delta because of his similarity to Syrian Baʿal).

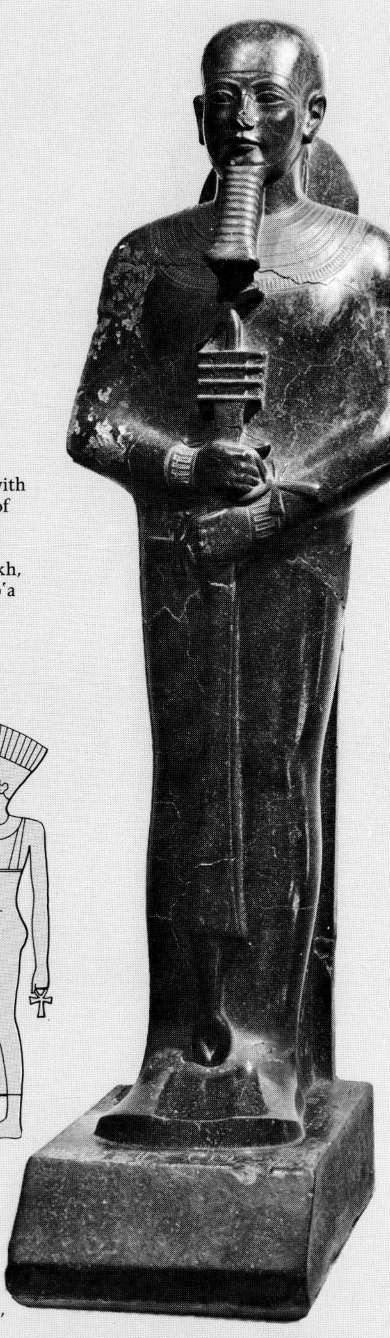

Min
Cap with two plumes and ribbon, mummiform and ithyphallic, right arm raised with flagellum/originally worshiped in the form of an unidentified object; fertility god; patron of eastern desert/Qift, Akhmim.

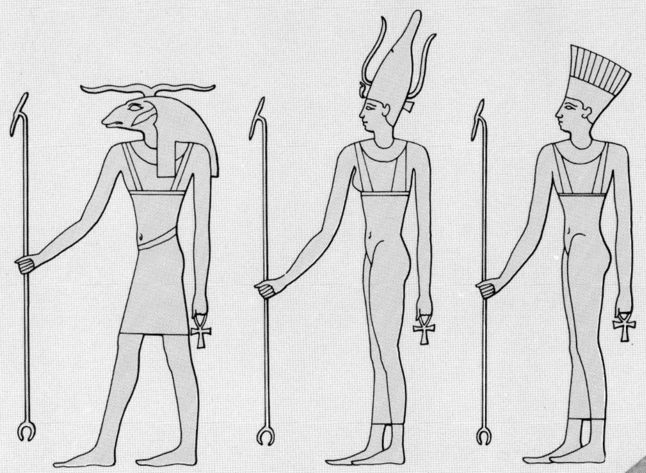

Khnum , **Anukis** and **Satis**
Khnum: ram or ram-headed; Anukis: white crown flanked by two gazelle horns; Satis: feather headdress/triad worshiped in the 1st cataract region, hence Khnum's connection with the inundation; Khnum also ancient creator god (because of procreative powers of ram), sometimes shown molding men on a potter's wheel/Elephantine, but Khnum also at Esna and *Herwer* (Hur, near el-Ashmunein).

Universal Gods etc.

Some Egyptian gods were "universal" in the sense that there was no particular place with which they were connected; this, however, did not prevent them from becoming members of local theological systems (e.g. Isis belonged to the Heliopolitan ennead) and having temples built for them (Isis was the chief deity worshiped at Philae). Conversely, some of the "universal gods" probably started as local deities (e.g. Anubis).

Isis 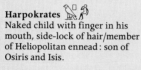 **and Harpokrates**
Woman, often hieroglyph of her name on her head/member of Heliopolitan ennead: wife of Osiris; guardian and magician.

Harpokrates
Naked child with finger in his mouth, side-lock of hair/member of Heliopolitan ennead: son of Osiris and Isis.

Below **Apis**
Bull with markings on hide and sun-disk between horns, or bull-headed/connected with Ptah; burial place at Saqqara.

Above **Geb** 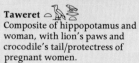 **, Shu**
and Nut
Members of Heliopolitan ennead; deities of earth (Geb), air and light (Shu) and sky (Nut).

Osiris
Mummiform, scepter and flagellum white crown with plumes and horns/dying god of vegetation; ruler of netherworld.

Anubis
Recumbent dog ("jackal") or dog-headed, black/necropolis god; connected with mummification.

Bes
Dwarf with mask-like face, often crown of feathers and lion's mane/family god; protector of pregnant women.

Imhotep
Deified official of Djoser; patron of scribes; healer, sage and magician; regarded as son of Ptah and a woman Khredu'ankh.

Nephthys
Woman with hieroglyphs of her name on her head/member of Heliopolitan ennead: sister of Isis; guardian deity.

Taweret
Composite of hippopotamus and woman, with lion's paws and crocodile's tail/protectress of pregnant women.

The priesthood

Before the New Kingdom there was no large, full-time priesthood. The growth of temples in the 18th Dynasty, accompanied by other religious changes, saw the rise of the priesthood as a class, a rise that continued with few checks into the Late Period. The basic needs of the cult could be satisfied by an officiant, a ritual specialist or lector priest, who might be the same person as the officiant, and the part-time priests who saw to the practical and less sacred functions. But at Karnak, for example, there were first to fourth priests of Amun at the head of a huge staff, which wielded considerable power. There was a constant tendency, which accorded with a basic Egyptian principle, for son to follow father in his priestly office. This was opposed by another tenet, that the king should freely appoint the best man for the job. By the end of the New Kingdom the former was triumphant, and Egyptian society was developing towards a rigid condition somewhat like that described by Herodotus in the 5th century BC, in which there was a division into various occupational types almost similar to castes. The analogy is reinforced by the restrictions priests had to observe in their diet, mode of dress, shaving, and sexual continence when they were in service – but perhaps not at other times.

The priests received income from the temples and often held sinecures at several of them. Offerings were laid before the god and, "after he had satisfied himself with them," reverted first to minor shrines and then to the priests, who consumed their less spiritual residues. The offerings themselves must, however, have been only a small proportion of the temples' income, so that much – also notionally offerings – was devoted directly to paying staff and to barter for particular products the temple lacked. Temples also had workshops and schools attached to them, which functioned in a broader context as well as supplying the needs of the institution to which they belonged.

Professional priests and bureaucrats, including those in the army, were the two basic categories of literate people. The bureaucracy seems to have lost its independence and importance in politics in the course of the Ramessid Period, being replaced by the army and the priesthood (often one and the same). Thus priests became the repository of intellectual culture. Legitimate or "white" magic had been the traditional preserve of lector priests, but in the Late Period priests assumed a wider cultural importance. Greek visitors speak frequently of them, and they influenced events, chiefly by mobilizing opinion against cuts in their revenues, at vital points in history, notably after the death of Cambyses (522) and in the reign of Teos (360). The culture of Greco-Roman Period temples was a priestly culture, of which one notable feature is the devaluation of the king's role: in earlier periods priests came before the god as deputies of the king, but now the king approached by virtue of his being a priest. The stereotype of an Egyptian society dominated by priests is not valid for earlier periods, but has some accuracy for later times.

Gods and myths

Egyptian polytheism clothes man's response to the world in a highly complex form. The gods themselves are more prominent in it than are myths about them; myth was not so striking a feature of the religion as, for example, in ancient Greece. Some gods are defined by myth, others by geographical location and by organization into groups. Most also have a basic association with an aspect of the world, such as Reʿ with the sun, Ptah with crafts, Hathor with women etc., but this does not exhaust their characteristics. In particular contexts many gods may exhibit the same features, while any god can take on virtually all the characteristics of divinity for a particular worshiper.

There are scarcely any complete native versions of Egyptian myths, and for some we have to rely on Classical authors. The form of most Egyptian religious texts excludes narrative, and it has been doubted whether there were any large-scale texts that recounted entire myths. We have versions of episodes in the conflict between Horus and Seth for the inheritance of Osiris from the Middle Kingdom, the late New Kingdom and the 4th century, but the text is not the same in any two of them, and the episodes vary. The versions have in common a rather secular tone and an unflattering portrayal of the gods. They belong as much with fiction as with religious texts, although there are mythical narratives that are comparable in tone which are embedded in religious and especially magical compositions.

Creation myths give primacy to the sun god Reʿ, who may also be called Reʿ-Harakhty or (Reʿ-)Atum. The most widespread one has the creator appearing from the watery chaos on a mound, the first solid matter, and creating a pair of deities, Shu and Tefenet, by masturbation or by spitting. Shu and Tefenet in their turn produced Geb and Nut, the earth and the sky, whose children were Osiris, Isis, Seth and Nephthys. This group of nine deities formed the ennead of Heliopolis; other centers had similar groups. Osiris and Isis are the main actors in

Right Bronze hawk's head finial, made to be attached to a staff or piece of temple furniture by the inverted T-shape projection at the back. The flange at the top probably supported a crown in a different material. Late Period. Height 12·1 cm. London, British, Museum.

the best-known Egyptian myth, which concerns Seth's murder of Osiris, Isis' conception of Horus on Osiris' dead body, and Horus' eventual defeat of Seth. This was recorded in Greek by Plutarch in the 1st century AD; most of his basic narrative appears to be authentically Egyptian.

Perhaps more typically Egyptian than these myths are ideas about the solar cycle. These use a small repertory of basic motifs, which is varied endlessly. It would be wrong to seek complete consistency in the variations; the constant meaning is the cycle itself. The sun god is born anew each morning, crosses the sky in the solar bark (boats being the normal mode of transport), ages, dies – which is never stated explicitly – and travels through the underworld during the night in a cycle of regeneration. Whereas in the creation myth the sky goddess Nut is the granddaughter of the sun god, for the purposes of the cycle she is his mother, into whose mouth he enters at night, and from whom he is born in the morning. At the rebirth she may also be Hathor, who is otherwise called the daughter of Reʿ. Possibly in allusion to these ideas creator gods, notably Amon-Reʿ, may be called "bull of his mother." These motifs are mythical situations rather than complete myths, since they are not combined to form narratives. They may, however, generate myths, and we know two complete ones, the "Destruction of Mankind" and "Isis and Reʿ," that take as their starting point the old age of the sun god, which is one of the basic features of the cosmographic cycle, and elaborate it in terms of bodily decay and of its consequences for the god's kingship at the end of the primeval age on earth.

The solar cycle gave rise to a host of linked conceptions, the most striking of which surround the crucial moment of sunrise. In his travels through the night the god is accompanied in his boat by a group of deities, most of whom are personifications of aspects of his being, with names like "magical power" and "perception"; at one point in its journey the boat is towed by a team of jackals. Both the personnel and the furniture of the boat vary in different "books," as the mixed pictorial and textual compositions about the underworld are known. When the sun god emerges from the night the whole of creation rejoices, and he may be greeted by gods and goddesses, the king, the "eastern souls," personifications of categories of humanity, and baboons that screech acclamation. It is noteworthy that, as in temples, normal humanity is excluded from the scene. All these elements seem almost to be responses to questions such as: "What are the changing aspects of the sun god's being in the night?" or "How is his appearance at dawn heralded?" The answers are more tableaux than myths.

The organization of gods into local sets is comparable in its variety and seeming arbitrariness. The commonest grouping is the triad, consisting of two "adult" deities and one youthful one. The triads are, however, only selections, and other deities may have a loose connection with the group or may interchange with members of it. Thus the Theban triad consists of Amon-Reʿ, Mut and Khons, the deities of the three main temples at Karnak. It has the form of a family group, but Mut is not the wife of Amon-Reʿ, nor is Khons their son. Rather,

Below One version of the sun god's journey through the night. The boat is towed by jackals and uraei with human heads. Seth spears Apopis; behind Reʿ-Harakhty are mummiform figures of Horus and Thoth. Papyrus of Hirweben, 21st Dynasty. Cairo, Egyptian Museum.

Above The setting sun. Center: the hieroglyph for "west" surmounted by a sun disk and placed in the desert. Top: two winged Horus eyes protect the sun. Below: adoring figures of: "subjects"; groups of deities; baboons; Isis and Nephthys; the deceased's *ba*, shown as a hawk with human head and arms. Papyrus of Anhai. 19th Dynasty. London, British Museum.

Right Bronze statuette of Wadjit with lioness's head and a uraeus above. The uraeus is the normal animal of Wadjit, while the lioness embodies her ferocious aspect in myth. Height 45 cm. Reign of Apries. Probably from Tell el-Fara'in. Bologna, Museo Civico.

Below Bronze statuette of Atum. The creator god of Heliopolis is shown in a form modified from the much commoner one for Osiris. The face is that of the aged, setting-sun god. Bronzes were dedicated in temples by private worshipers. This one has a dedication by Peteese son of Harwedja. Height 23·5 cm. Oxford, Ashmolean Museum.

Faience "pilgrim" flask with a scene of Bes with plumed headdress, wings and pendent breasts, holding a pair of *wedjat* eyes; between his face and arms are two signs of life. There are floral motifs above, below and in the corners, and sun disks (?) on either side. Height of figure 5·6 cm. Early 19th Dynasty (?). From el-Riqqa. Oxford, Ashmolean Museum.

three local deities with different origins are associated using a family model, whose lack of realism is clear from the fact that there is only one "child." The importance of the number three and a principle of economy may together account for this simplification. Amaunet, a female Amun, is another Theban deity, who is sometimes found in place of Mut, while Montu, probably the original god of the Theban nome, had his own temple complex immediately to the north of the main enclosure at Karnak. At Memphis the four chief deities, Ptah,

Sakhmet, Nefertem and Sokar (the god of the necropolis), were similarly varied in their association: the first three form a triad, while Sokar is frequently identified with Ptah. Hathor and Neith, whose cults were important in Memphis, are excluded from the main group. At Heliopolis the sun god, whose cult was split into separate ones of Reʿ and Atum, stood most naturally by himself, but acquired two female companions, Iusʿas and Hathor-Nebethetepet, who are in essence personifications of the sexual aspect of the solar creation myths.

A further important means of associating deities is called syncretism. A deity acquires a multiple name, mostly by taking on the name and character of a more important one. Amon-Reʿ is thus Amun in his aspect of Reʿ, and this can be expanded to form Amon-Reʿ-Atum, Amun as Reʿ *and* Atum, the aged aspect of the sun god. Reʿ is by far the commonest name in such groupings; this reflects the sun god's universality and his importance in early periods. In a slightly different case, at Abydos Osiris is identified, as Osiris-Khentamentiu, with a local god whose cult may have been the original one in the area. Such associations never submerge completely the identities of the deities whose names are linked.

The gods mentioned so far may be called major deities. Almost all had a cult and an area in which they were sovereign. Some cosmic deities, such as Geb, had no local cult. But there are also minor deities found only in restricted contexts. The best known of these are probably Bes and Taweret, who are "household" figures associated particularly with childbirth. Both have monstrous composite forms of a sort not found among major deities, Bes as a dwarf with an outsize mask-like face, and Taweret as a mixture of hippopotamus and crocodile, with pendent, apparently human, breasts and a huge belly. In addition, there are enormous numbers of demons, attested from magical and underworld texts, who have very diverse names and often grotesque forms. Most of them seem to be restricted to one or two contexts each – a particular text, or one hour of the night. The chief exception is Apopis, a gigantic snake, who is the sun god's enemy as he passes through the crucial phases of his cycle, and must be defeated by Seth, who spears him from the prow of the solar boat.

The world of the dead
The underworld that has been mentioned is one particular version of the realm of the dead, known mainly from New Kingdom royal tombs; as in all areas of Egyptian religion, there are many alternatives. Conceptions of the afterlife of the king, who was held to join the gods in death, were initially different from those for the rest of humanity, although they came to be diffused among more and more people. Whatever one's destiny, it was by no means assured. The afterlife was full of dangers, which were mostly to be surmounted by magical means.

The starting point for all these ideas was the tomb. The Egyptians' unparalleled expenditure of the resources of the rich on burial was evidently intended in part to enhance the tomb owner's prestige while he was alive, but this is a sideline to the ultimate purpose. The deceased might continue to exist in and around the tomb, or he could travel

through the afterworld. His aim was to identify with gods, in particular Osiris, or to join, as a transfigured spirit, in the solar cycle, as a member of the "boat of millions." The boat is never shown with its vast complement, possibly because human beings were excluded from the type of picture in which it occurs. Both these latter destinies seem to have been restricted originally to the king, and Old Kingdom private texts refer instead to "walking on the perfect ways of the west [the realm of the dead]."

Between death and incorporation in the divine world came judgment, a theme that is less prominent for kings than for the rest of humanity. The judgment is shown very often, in tombs, on papyri, coffins and shrouds. Its central motif is the weighing of the deceased's heart in a balance against Ma'at, the Egyptian conception of right order, which is mostly shown as a hieroglyph, either an ostrich feather or a figure of the personification Ma'at, a goddess with the feather inserted in a band

around her wig. Thoth, the scribe god of wisdom and justice, performs the weighing before Osiris, who presides over a judgment hall with 42 judges. If the heart and Ma'at are in equilibrium the test is successful, and the deceased is presented to Osiris in triumph. The judgment is of conformity to Ma'at, that is, correct conduct in life. Everybody naturally wished to avoid it, and the deceased had ready a declaration of innocence from all manner of sins. Both the declaration and the illustration of a successful outcome were magical ways around the judgment, just as funerary literature and other provisions in the tomb were magical aids to success in the hereafter.

Judgment scenes show a female hybrid monster called "Eater" or "Eater of the Dead." Her role was to consume those who failed the test, and a Roman Period example shows this happening. For Egyptians departure from this life was a first stage, and the second death, which brought complete annihilation, was what had to be avoided. Here,

Scene of weighing the deceased's heart in the Book of the Dead papyrus of Hunefer. On the left Anubis leads Hunefer in. A second figure of Anubis checks the balance while Thoth records the result and the "Eater" stands at the ready. Horus then presents Hunefer to Osiris, whose throne is placed on the "Lake of Natron," out of which a lotus emerges with the four "Sons of Horus" on it; behind are Isis and Nephthys.

In the small register above Hunefer adores a group of deities consisting of the Heliopolitan ennead without Seth, but with Utterance, Perception and the Southern, Northern and Western Ways (presumably in the hereafter) added. 19th Dynasty. London, British Museum.

however, the categories they used become strange to western eyes. The annihilation did not remove the victims entirely, but the "dead" – that is, second dead – are shown being punished in the lower registers of the underworld books. They entered another mode of existence, which was a threat to the ordered world, and had to be combated.

Scenes on tomb walls were part of the provision for life after death, but in many cases their relevance to survival is not clear and their superficial content secular. In addition to them, the burial contained material possessions in great variety, including (in early periods) enormous quantities of food, statues which could be inhabited by the "soul" of the deceased – as a cult statue was by a god – and the mummy itself, elaborately wrapped, protected with numerous amulets, placed in a coffin or nest of coffins, and magically brought to life in a ritual called the "opening of the mouth." Many of the possessions in the tombs repeated the motif of rebirth in symbolic form; the idea was expressed in

an enormous variety of ways. Some objects provided for particular needs in the hereafter. As many as 400 *shawabty* figures, perhaps the commonest of all Egyptian antiquities, accompanied burials. These were substitute figurines of the deceased, one of whose functions was to act as workers, who were to answer a possible call for corvée duty which involved carrying sand. This conception is obscure; it does not appear to be part of a coherent body of belief, but to be an isolated idea.

The accent in mortuary beliefs changed, but few disappeared. Instead, objects corresponding to a number of different conceptions were used in tombs. No overall consistency need be sought in them, except insofar as they relate to the hope for rebirth and continued life after death. The most extensive and varied provision preserved is that for Tut'ankhamun, but his funerary equipment was, no doubt, modest in comparison with that for Amenophis III or Ramesses II.

Burial Customs

Mummification

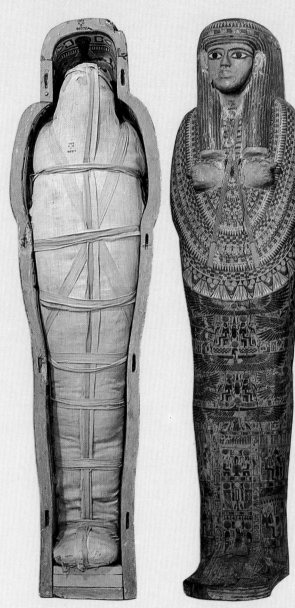

Mummification is a method of preserving artificially the bodies of deceased people and animals. Ancient Egyptian civilization is not the only one in the world to have practiced this custom, but Egyptian mummies are the best known and often, to the chagrin of professional Egyptologists, tend to be regarded as the embodiment of ancient Egypt itself and the main object of interest for those who study it. Mummies can contribute to our knowledge in various ways, in particular by providing information on such subjects as illnesses and conditions of ancient Egyptians, their diet etc. In the case of royal mummies, we can add to our understanding of Egyptian chronology by helping to establish the age of a king at the time of his death; family relationships can also be discovered from examination of mummies.

Development
Like many other practices, mummification was introduced as a result of man's interaction with his natural environment. It was an attempt to preserve an element of it by artificial means when his own action started threatening it.

For most of the Predynastic Period burials were very simple. Bodies were placed in shallow graves dug on the edge of the desert and covered with sand. In the dry atmosphere the contact with hot sand produced dehydration (desiccation) very quickly, often before the tissues decomposed, so that bodies were sometimes preserved by entirely natural means. This did not escape attention because such "mummies" were from time to time accidentally uncovered, and a belief developed that the preservation of the body was essential for man's continued existence after death. When at the end of the Predynastic Period some of the graves turned into larger tombs and coffins were introduced, these natural conditions were altered, in particular the contact with sand. It became necessary to look for methods which would achieve by artificial means what nature had previously accomplished unaided, and thus the custom of mummification was introduced. Its history is one of a continuous struggle between two approaches to the problem. The first aimed at a genuine preservation of the body, while the other, more formalistic, concentrated on the mummy's wrappings and packing. The peak of the craft of mummification was reached at the end of the New Kingdom and in the period immediately following; from then on, there was a sharp decline, as if in recognition of the impossibility of the task, and the formalistic approach prevailed.

Procedure
Mummification was carried out in workshops attached to the necropolis; these also supplied most of the funerary equipment. Methods varied according to the period and the wealth of the deceased's family. Although there is no detailed ancient Egyptian description of the procedure, its steps can be reconstructed from the examination of mummies.

The method described here was used at the end of the New Kingdom and during the 3rd Intermediate Period; it took some 70 days, and its most important part was dehydration of the body by burying it in natron, a naturally occurring dehydrating agent (a mixture of carbonate, bicarbonate, chloride and sulphate of sodium):

1. Extraction of the brain.
2. Removal of the viscera

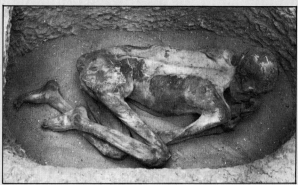

through an incision made in the left flank.
3. Sterilization of the body cavities and the viscera.
4. Treatment of the viscera: removal of their contents, dehydration by natron, drying, anointing, and application of molten resin.
5. Temporary packing of the body with natron and fragrant resins.
6. Covering the body with natron for some 40 days.
7. Removal of the temporary packing materials.
8. Subcutaneous packing of the limbs with sand, clay etc.
9. Packing the body cavities with resin-soaked linen and bags of fragrant materials, such as myrrh and cinnamon, but also sawdust etc.
10. Anointing the body with unguents.
11. Treatment of the body surfaces with molten resin.
12. Bandaging and inclusion of amulets, jewelry etc.

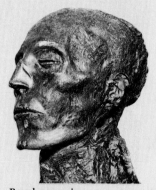

Royal mummies
Egyptologists have the unparalleled advantage of being face to face with the protagonists of their subject. The cache of royal mummies, discovered at Deir el-Bahri in 1881, contained the bodies of some of the most important rulers of the New Kingdom, including Sethos I (*above*) and Ramesses II (*below*).

Canopic Jars

The term canopic jars was devised by early Egyptologists, who mistakenly associated them with Kanopos, the pilot of Menelaos of the Trojan war. He was said to have died tragically and been buried at Kanopos (Egyptian *Per-gwati*, present Abu Qir) in the northwestern delta, and was worshiped there in the form of a jar.

The jars were usually made of calcite ("alabaster"), but also of limestone, pottery or faience, and contained the viscera removed from the cavities of the body during mummification. They were placed in the burial chamber of the tomb, close to the coffin. Simple lids became human-headed in the Middle Kingdom, and from the Ramessid Period they began to be made in the form of the heads of the four Sons of Horus. Texts on the jars placed each one under the protection of a goddess. Although reliable evidence is scarce, jars probably contained particular organs.

	head	goddess	contents
Imset	man	Isis	liver
Ha'py	baboon	Nephthys	lungs
Duamutef	jackal	Neith	stomach
Qebehsenuf	hawk	Selkis	intestines

Periods, was *cartonnage* (the term is also conveniently used in the same way as "coffin" or "sarcophagus"). This was made by successive application of linen (papyrus in the Greco-Roman Period), glue and gesso around a "model mummy," and painting it with bright watercolors.

Coffins and sarcophagi are of two basic forms: *rectangular* and *anthropoid* ("mummiform"), but only the latter is known in cartonnage. Anthropoid coffins appeared in the Middle Kingdom as a natural extension of the earlier mummy-masks covering the upper part of the mummy.

Decoration varies according to date. Some of the coffins of the Early Dynastic Period have a "palace facade," as do sarcophagi of the Old Kingdom. In the 1st Intermediate Period and the Middle Kingdom the interior of the Herakleopolitan type of rectangular coffin was often inscribed with the Coffin Texts, and there were also representations of various items of funerary equipment and an offering-list. Anthropoid *rishi*-coffins (named for the decoration imitating feathered wings) are characteristic of the 17th Dynasty, while white coffins with bands suggesting mummy bandages were common in the 18th Dynasty. For the rest of the New Kingdom and later the tendency was to increase the amount of decoration by adding small scenes with various deities and texts. Rectangular coffins and sarcophagi became rare, and were only partly revived towards the end of the Late Period. The perfection of workmanship and finish of anthropoid sarcophagi of the Late Period are justly famous. They were made of a dark hard stone, usually basalt, but there were also imitations in wood. The decoration and inscriptions on coffins and sarcophagi of the Late and Greco-Roman Periods drew their inspiration from religious texts and their vignettes, including the Book of the Dead, the Pyramid Texts and underworld books. The outside of the lid was often inscribed with Chapter 72 of the Book of the Dead, the "spell for going forth by day and penetrating the netherworld."

Coffins and Sarcophagi

Most of our material for the study of ancient Egypt derives from tombs. Coffins and sarcophagi are thus among the commonest antiquities, though this somewhat somber aspect of Egyptology is brightened by their often very attractive appearance. Dating into broader periods presents no problems, but only exceptionally have a more detailed typology and chronology been worked out.

The terms *coffin* and *sarcophagus* are used by some as though they were interchangeable; here they denote chests made of wood and stone (limestone, granite, basalt etc.) respectively, regardless of shape. Each consists of the lid and the lower part ("case"). Coffins were often placed inside a sarcophagus, and we find whole sets of them (inner and outer, or 1st, 2nd and 3rd), though sometimes only a *mummy board* (another "lid") was placed on top of the mummy. A third type of material, particularly common during the 3rd Intermediate and Greco-Roman

Funerary Statuettes

From the end of the Middle Kingdom one or more funerary statuettes (the Egyptian terms vary between *shabty*, *shawabty* and *ushebty*) formed an important part of the funerary equipment. In the 18th Dynasty the statuettes started to combine, in a somewhat incongruous fashion, a likeness of the mummified body

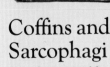

of the deceased with agricultural or other implements. This was a reflection of the two main ideas connected with these objects: a body substitute and a worker who acted as the deceased's deputy when he was called upon to perform various corvée tasks in the netherworld. The formula inscribed on the statuettes (Chapter 6 of the Book of the Dead) contained appropriate instructions, but reflected a similar ambiguity concerning the statuette's identity. An increase in the number of funerary statuettes can be detected in the Ramessid Period; in the Late Period there were often several hundreds of them in the tomb of one person.

The following are some of the more important clues to the dating of funerary statuettes:
made of dark hard stone probably Middle Kingdom or 25th Dynasty, certainly not later than 26th Dynasty;
made of wood if very crude, end of 17th and early 18th Dynasties; at any rate not later than New Kingdom;
tools mid-18th Dynasty or later (statuettes without tools also continued to be made);
baskets held at front, 18th Dynasty; on the back, 19th Dynasty and later;
polychrome (red, blue/green, yellow, black) decoration on white background end of 18th Dynasty or Ramessid Period;
flat back and/or head fillet 3rd Intermediate Period;
small pedestal and back pillar mid-26th Dynasty and later.

EGYPT IN WESTERN ART

Although Egyptian culture had influenced various peoples around the Mediterranean since the second millennium, the Romans were the first to show interest in Egyptian objects for their very Egyptian-ness – an interest colored, as later, by the Greek view of Egypt as the repository of esoteric wisdom, and manifested in a superficial imitation of Egyptian art without comprehension of its basic character.

The appeal of things Egyptian was linked to the worship of the Alexandrian deities Isis and Sarapis, whose cults were established at Rome by the late Republic (1st century BC). The conquest of Egypt in 30 BC opened the way for the importation of antiquities to serve as public monuments, to adorn houses and gardens, or to decorate the temples of the Egyptian gods, like this baboon in gray granite, one of a pair from the Iseum Campense, Rome. Roman taste favored the exotic rather than the intrinsically Egyptian. With the creation of

The monuments exported to Rome and her empire constituted the west's only visual source of Egyptian art until the 18th century. Some remained visible throughout the Dark Ages, like the lions and sphinxes copied in 13th-century Roman sculpture. This one is from the Duomo at Città Castellana. The reemergence of others, and the discovery of Classical texts which included accounts of Egypt, aroused the interest of the humanists of the Renaissance.

Egyptianizing pieces, like this double-headed herm made for the Nilotic garden, or Canopus, of Hadrian's villa at Tivoli, the bizarre aspect became more pronounced. By the mid-4th century, Rome boasted numerous obelisks, two pyramids and a variety of sculpture.

By Classical authors they were told that hieroglyphs embodied abstract concepts in a symbolic, universally intelligible form. Leon Battista Alberti's (1404–72) device symbolizing divine omniscience (*above*) is an early example of the application of this idea.

The allegorical use of ''hieroglyphs'' flourished, perfected in the work of Dürer and trivialized in the 16th-century literature devoted to emblems. The major technical feat of the century was the reerection of the Vatican obelisk in front of St Peter's in 1586, illustrated here by Domenico Fontana; the resurrection of others followed, and the obelisk entered the repertory of European architecture, where it

soon shed its specifically Egyptian character. More important was the serious interest in Egypt which the event excited; in the following century the hieroglyphs were subjected to fresh examination and the first scholarly publications of Egyptian antiquities appeared, culminating in the great encyclopedic works of the 18th century, where Egyptian objects figured beside Classical. From such sources, and from the first

well-illustrated travelers' accounts published around the mid-century, came the inspiration for Egyptianizing works like Dinglinger's gem-studded Apis Altar (1731) or the exuberant decor created for the Caffè Inglese, Rome (1760), by Piranesi. His championship of the majestic Egyptian style was echoed in the work of French and British architects towards the close of the century.

Alongside this new appreciation of Egypt, the mystic tradition continued. The field of *arcana* already prospected by the Rosicrucians was exploited by Freemasonry, and the brotherhood's newly adopted Egyptian rites supplied Schikaneder, librettist of Mozart (himself a Freemason), with some of the ideas expressed in *The Magic Flute*. This frontispiece to the 1791 edition is full of occult gloom.

The French invasion of Egypt seven years later brought with it scholars as well as soldiers, outstanding among them Vivant Denon; his medal cabinet was designed after the picture of a pylon in his own book on Egypt which, together with the expedition's official publication, the *Description de l'Égypte*, provided a wealth of illustrations.

the decorative arts sometimes entailed no more than a playfully ornamental use of motifs, as in Wedgwood's "hieroglyphic" tea service of about 1810 (*bottom*).

Other designs represent a more straightforward imitation of the form of Egyptian objects, as in Holman Hunt's chairs of 1855, the furniture produced later by Liberty, or the occasional pieces of silver plate based on the shape of ancient vessels, like the claret jug below. The decipherment of hieroglyphs, the growth of Egyptology as a scholarly discipline and the formation of large collections of antiquities in the museums of Europe and America ensured a continuing popular interest in Egypt; from time to time the fashion for Egyptianizing designs received fresh impetus from events like

The detailed drawings of the great Egyptian temples, in particular the Greco-Roman with their exaggerated cornices and ornate column capitals, served as models for architecture of a more soberly imitative kind than that advocated by Piranesi. The Egyptian style was considered

The elegant designs of Napoleon's interior decorators, Percier and Fontaine, were the forerunners in the fashion for *Egyptiennerie* on the continent

appropriate for the massive, the monumental and the funereal. In Europe and America courthouses, jails, factories, railway stations, bridges, churches and, especially, cemeteries, like this one at Alberobello, south Italy, received Egyptian treatment.

during the three decades following the French campaign, paralleled by the work of Thomas Hope (1807) and others in England. The Egyptian style in

the opening of the Egyptian Court in the Crystal Palace in 1854. This much-admired extravaganza, replete with replicas of the most famous monuments of Egypt, is probably the inspiration behind the later Egyptian garden at Biddulph Grange (*top right*) with its stone sphinxes and topiary pyramid, a trim Victorian descendant of Hadrian's Canopus, Angelo Querini's Egyptian garden at the Villa Altichiero in 18th-century Padua, and Canina's charming Egyptian Portico in the Borghese Gardens, Rome (1827).

The discovery of Tut'ankhamun's tomb in 1922 generated a new wave of Egyptianizing trivia in the decorative arts, but the monumental building style has been employed in this century only in the fantasy architecture of the cinema; the pharaonic splendors of Grauman's Egyptian Theater, Hollywood (1922), are reflected in some less grandiose creations in England, like the 1930 Carlton in Islington (*above*).

Appreciation of modern art has helped towards an understanding of the different representational principles of the ancient Egyptians, and their sculpture in particular has influenced contemporary artists. David Hockney's 1978 sets for *The Magic Flute* (*below*) present a starker vision of Egypt than Schinkel's elaborate compositions for the 1815 production, but a sense of majestic spaciousness is common to both.

MUSEUMS WITH EGYPTIAN COLLECTIONS

Although collections of ancient Egyptian antiquities, consisting of curiosities and tourist mementos, had been formed earlier, it was mainly in the first half of the 19th century that museums which displayed Egyptian objects for the delectation and edification of the general public came into existence. Nowadays over 500 of these, scattered over five continents, hold Egyptian objects of importance, and in thousands of others ancient Egypt is represented to some degree. Trained Egyptologists are on the staff of many of these establishments, and museums have also become important centers for the research and study of ancient Egypt. "Excavation" in museum storerooms and basements in order to make available the treasures kept there both to the specialist and to the layman is one of the most urgent tasks of the discipline.

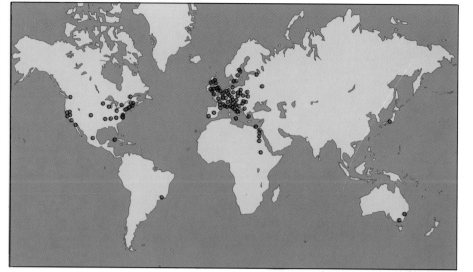

Australia
Melbourne
National Gallery of Victoria
Sydney
Australian Museum
Nicholson Museum of Antiquities

Austria
Vienna
Kunsthistorisches Museum

Belgium
Antwerp
Museum Vleeshuis
Brussels
Musées Royaux d'Art et d'Histoire
Liège
Musée Curtius
Mariemont
Musée de Mariemont

Brazil
Rio de Janeiro
Museu Nacional

Canada
Montreal
McGill University, Ethnological Museum
Museum of Fine Arts
Toronto
Royal Ontario Museum

Cuba
Havana
Museo Nacional

Czechoslovakia
Prague
Náprstkovo Muzeum

Denmark
Copenhagen
Nationalmuseet
Ny Carlsberg Glyptotek
Thorwaldsen Museum

East Germany
Berlin
Staatliche Museen, Ägyptisches Museum
Staatliche Museen, Papyrussammlung
Dresden
Albertinum
Leipzig
Ägyptisches Museum

Egypt
Alexandria
Greco-Roman Museum
Aswan
Museum on the island of Elephantine
Cairo
Egyptian Museum
Luxor
Luxor Museum
Mallawi
Mallawi Museum
Minya
Minya Museum

Limestone tomb stela of Wadj, from the king's tomb at Abydos. Paris, Louvre, E.11007.

France
Avignon
Musée Calvet
Grenoble
Musée de Peinture et de Sculpture
Limoges
Musée Municipal
Lyons
Musée des Beaux-Arts
Musée Guimet
Marseilles
Musée d'Archéologie
Nantes
Musée des Arts Décoratifs
Orléans
Musée Historique et d'Archéologie de l'Orléanais
Paris
Bibliothèque Nationale
Louvre
Musée du Petit Palais

Musée Rodin
Strasbourg
Institut d'Egyptologie
Toulouse
Musée Georges Labit

Greece
Athens
National Museum

Hungary
Budapest
Szépmüvészeti Múzeum

Ireland
Dublin
National Museum of Ireland

Italy
Bologna
Museo Civico
Florence
Museo Archeologico
Mantua
Museo del Palazzo Ducale
Milan
Museo Archeologico
Naples
Museo Nazionale
Parma
Museo Nazionale di Antichità
Palermo
Museo Nazionale
Rome
Museo Barracco
Museo Capitolino
Museo Nazionale Romano delle Terme Diocleziane

Limestone relief showing a blind harpist, from the Saqqara tomb of the Royal Butler Patenemhab of the end of the 18th Dynasty. Leiden, Inv. AMT.1–35.

Rovigo
Museo dell'Accademia dei Concordi
Trieste
Civico Museo di Storia ed Arte
Turin
Museo Egizio
Vatican
Museo Gregoriano Egizio
Venice
Museo Archeologico del Palazzo Reale di Venezia

Relief with Negro captives, from the Saqqara tomb of Haremhab, probably of the reign of Tut'ankhamun. Bologna, 1887(1869).

Brown quartzite head of a princess, from the so-called sculptor's studio of Thutmose at el-'Amarna. East Berlin, 21223.

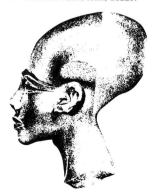

Diorite-gneiss statue of seated Khephren, with Horus-falcon perched on the back of the throne, from Giza. Cairo, CG 14.

Granite statue of Senwosret III, from Deir el-Bahri. London, British Museum, 684.

Japan
Kyoto
University Archaeological Museum

Mexico
Mexico City
Museo Nacional de Antropologia

Netherlands
Amsterdam
Allard Pierson Museum
Leiden
Rijksmuseum van Oudheden
Otterlo
Rijksmuseum Kröller-Müller

Poland
Kraków
Muzeum Narodowe
Warsaw
Muzeum Narodowe

Portugal
Lisbon
Fundação Calouste Gulbenkian

Spain
Madrid
Museo Arqueológico Nacional

Sudan
Khartum
Sudan Museum

Sweden
Linköping
Östergöttlands Museum
Lund
Kulturhistoriska Museet
Stockholm
Medelhavsmuseet
Uppsala
Victoriamuseum

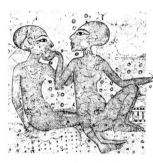

Wall painting of two daughters of Queen Nefertiti, from a palace at el-ʿAmarna. Oxford, Ashmolean, 1893. 1–41(267).

Switzerland
Basel
Museum für Völkerkunde
Geneva
Musée d'Art et d'Histoire
Lausanne
Musée Cantonal d'Archéologie et d'Histoire
Musée Cantonal des Beaux-Arts
Neuchâtel
Musée d'Ethnographie
Riggisberg
Abegg-Stiftung

United Kingdom
Bristol
City Museum
Cambridge
Fitzwilliam Museum
Dundee
Museum and Art Gallery
Durham
Gulbenkian Museum of Oriental Art and Archaeology
Edinburgh
Royal Scottish Museum

Glasgow
Art Gallery and Museum
Burrell Collection
Hunterian Museum
Leicester
Museums and Art Gallery
Liverpool
Merseyside County Museums
School of Archaeology and Oriental Studies
London
British Museum
Horniman Museum
Petrie Collection (University College)
Victoria and Albert Museum
Manchester
University Museum
Norwich
Castle Museum
Oxford
Ashmolean Museum
Pitt Rivers Museum

United States of America
Baltimore (Md.)
Walters Art Gallery
Berkeley (Ca.)
Robert H. Lowie Museum of Anthropology
Boston (Mass.)
Museum of Fine Arts
Brooklyn (N.Y.)
Brooklyn Museum
Cambridge (Mass.)
Fogg Art Museum, Harvard University
Semitic Museum, Harvard University
Chicago (Ill.)
Field Museum of Natural History
Oriental Institute Museum

Below Colossal diorite head of Amenophis III. Brooklyn, 59.19.

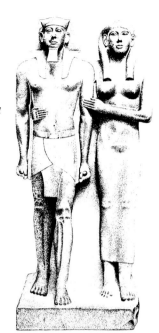

Left Blue faience sphinx of Amenophis III. New York, M.M.A. 1972.125.

Graywacke pair-statue of Menkaureʿ and Queen Khaʿ merernebty II, from the king's valley temple at Giza. Boston, 11.1738.

Cincinnati (Ohio)
Art Museum
Cleveland (Ohio)
Museum of Art
Denver (Col.)
Art Museum
Detroit (Mich.)
Detroit Institute of Arts
Kansas City (Miss.)
William Rockhill Nelson Gallery of Art
Los Angeles (Ca.)
County Museum of Art
Minneapolis (Minn.)
Institute of Arts Museum
New Haven (Conn.)
Yale University Art Gallery
New York
Metropolitan Museum of Art
Palo Alto (Ca.)
Stanford University Museum
Philadelphia (Pa.)
Pennsylvania University Museum
Pittsburgh (Pa.)
Museum of Art, Carnegie Institute
Princeton (N.J.)
University Art Museum
Providence (R.I.)
Rhode Island School of Design
Richmond (Va.)
Museum of Fine Arts
St Louis (Miss.)
Art Museum
San Diego (Ca.)
Museum of Man
San Francisco (Ca.)
M. H. De Young Memorial Museum
San José (Ca.)
Rosicrucian Museum
Seattle (Wash.)
Art Museum
Toledo (Ohio)
Museum of Art
Washington D.C.
Smithsonian Institution
Worcester (Mass.)
Art Museum

U.S.S.R.
Leningrad
State Hermitage Museum
Moscow
State Pushkin Museum of Fine Arts

West Germany
Berlin
Staatliche Museen Preussischer Kulturbesitz, Ägyptisches Museum
Essen
Folkwang Museum
Frankfurt-am-Main
Liebieghaus
Hamburg
Museum für Kunst und Gewerbe
Museum für Völkerkunde
Hanover
Kestner-Museum
Heidelberg
Ägyptologisches Institut der Universität
Hildesheim
Roemer-Pelizaeus-Museum
Karlsruhe
Badisches Landesmuseum
Munich
Staatliche Sammlung Ägyptischer Kunst
Tübingen
Ägyptologisches Institut der Universität
Würzburg
Martin von Wagner Museum der Universität

Yugoslavia
Zagreb
Archeološki Muzej

Painted limestone head of Queen Nefertiti, from the so-called sculptor's studio of Thutmose at el-ʿAmarna. West Berlin, 21300.

225

GLOSSARY

Wherever possible in this book we have avoided using specialized terms. A certain number, for which there was not sufficent space in the text for an explanation, are treated in this Glossary, and supplementary information is given, especially for administrative and priestly titles. Any terms that are not covered can be found easily in appropriate works listed in the Bibliography. Cross-references within the Glossary are underlined.

abacus Rectangular block placed on top of a column capital in order to support the architrave.

ambulatory Roofed colonnaded walkway, often running around the outside of small New Kingdom temples and bark stations, and of Greco-Roman birth houses.

architrave Horizontal stone beam between columns, or between a column and a wall, which supports a ceiling.

ba One of many Egyptian words for aspects of the personality, often translated "soul." The ba is associated with divinity and with power; gods have many bas. It also describes the ability to take on different manifestations, which are themselves bas, as the Apis bull is of Ptah. The ba of the deceased is able to move freely in the underworld and return to earth. See also ka.

Badarian From el-Badari, the type site of the earliest certainly identified Neolithic culture of the Nile valley (c. 4500 BC).

bark shrine Deities were carried in model barks when they went out from temples in procession at festivals; larger divine barks were used on the river. The model barks were kept in shrines in the temples; those at Karnak and Luxor are sizable structures.

birth house Special type of small temple (also called mammisi), attached to the main temples of the Late and Greco-Roman Periods. These were where the god of the main temple was born, or, if the main temple was dedicated to a goddess, where she bore her child. The birth scenes derive from earlier cycles depicting the birth of kings.

Book of the Dead A collection of spells mostly written on papyrus and placed with the mummy in a burial, attested from the New Kingdom to the Greco-Roman Period. The texts continue the tradition of the Pyramid Texts and Coffin Texts. The choice of spells, of which about 200 are known, some very long, varies from copy to copy.

cartouche Circle with a horizontal bar at the bottom, elongated into an oval within which kings' names are written from the 4th Dynasty on. Detailed examples show that the sign represents a knot of rope, looped so that it is never-ending; it thus symbolizes cyclical return, probably with solar reference. Kings had two cartouche names, the first a statement about the god Re' (praenomen) and the second their birth name.

cataract Stretch of rapids interrupting the flow of the Nile, caused by areas of granite interspersed in the Nubian sandstone belt. There are six numbered and several minor cataracts between Aswan and Khartum. All are hazards to navigation. The 2nd Cataract, the most formidable, was impassable except during the annual inundation. Cataracts 1–4 and the Dal Cataract were political frontiers at different times.

cavetto cornice Crowning element of walls, doorways, flat-topped stelae and false doors, consisting of a semicircular forward flaring, with a scalloped decoration, often with a winged disk in its middle; probably derived from reed or other plant architectural forms. It was much imitated outside Egypt.

cenotaph Symbolic tombs or mortuary cult places additional to the owner's burial place. The south tomb of the Step Pyramid of Djoser is a cenotaph, as are probably the subsidiary pyramids of the 4th–6th Dynasties. At Abydos cenotaph chapels for private individuals are characteristic of the Middle Kingdom, and there are royal cenotaph temples of the Middle and New Kingdoms. Other sites with cenotaphs are Gebel el-Silsila and Qasr Ibrim.

Chief Steward New Kingdom and Late Period title of the administrator of an estate of the temple of a god, the king or his mortuary temple, of a member of the royal family (e.g. a Divine Adoratrice) or even a private individual. Because of the economic importance of the function, Chief Stewards were very influential, e.g. Senenmut, who combined the offices of Chief Steward of Amun, of Queen Hatshepsut and of Princess Nefrure'; or Amenhotpe Huy, the brother of the vizier Ra'mose, who was Chief Steward of Memphis in the reign of Amenophis III.

Coffin Texts Texts written inside coffins of the Middle Kingdom that are intended to aid the deceased in his passage to the hereafter. The texts continue and develop the tradition of the Pyramid Texts, but are used by private individuals. More than 1,000 spells are known.

colossus Over-lifesize statue, usually of a king, but also of private individuals and gods; typically set up outside the gates or pylons of temples, and often receiving some sort of cult or acting as intermediaries between men and gods.

contrapposto The depiction in sculpture in the round of the organic adjustment of the human body to asymmetrical poses; very rare in Egyptian art.

count Conventional translation of a ranking title of the Old and Middle Kingdoms. As with many titles, the word lost its original meaning, and modern translations are therefore conventional rather than precise. In the New Kingdom the same title was used for a local administrative function and is better rendered "mayor."

cuneiform The Mesopotamian script, written with a stylus on clay tablets, with characteristic wedge-shaped (cuneiform) strokes. The script wrote many different languages, the most widespread being Akkadian, which was the diplomatic language of the late second millennium BC. Cuneiform texts have been found in Egypt at el-'Amarna, and on various objects of the Persian Period. In the Near East cuneiform tablets from Egypt have been found at Boğazköy in Anatolia and Kamid el-Loz in Syria.

cursive Rapid, handwritten forms of the script, chiefly hieratic and demotic. Cursive hieroglyphs are special simplified sign forms, similar to hieratic, written in ink and used for religious texts and for the initial training of scribes; the form died out in the first millennium BC.

demotic From Greek "popular," a further elaboration of hieratic, developed in northern Egypt in the 7th century BC; the normal everyday script of the Late and Greco-Roman Periods. Latest dated text 452 AD.

Divine Adoratrice Chief priestess of Amun in Thebes, an office known from the New Kingdom–Late Period. The priestess was celibate. In the 23rd–26th Dynasties princesses held it, notionally "adopting" their successors, and acting as important vehicles of political control.

ennead Group of 9 deities. Enneads are associated with several major cult centers. The number 9 embodies a plurality (3) of pluralities (3, i.e. 3 × 3), and so stands for large numbers in general; hence some enneads have more than 9 members. The best-known, the great ennead of Heliopolis, embodies two myths within its composition. It consists of Re'-Atum, Shu, Tefenet, Geb, Nut, Osiris, Isis, Seth and Nephthys.

Fan-Bearer on the Right of the King Court title, probably purely honorific or ranking, of high officials of the New Kingdom. The right was the prestigious side.

fecundity figure Type of offering bearer shown at the base of temple walls bringing offerings into the temple; mostly personifications of geographical areas, the inundation, or abstract concepts. The male figures have heavy pendulous breasts and bulging stomachs, their fatness symbolizing the abundance they bring with them.

funerary cones Pottery cones found mostly in Theban tombs of the Middle Kingdom to Late Period, with a flat circular or rectangular base bearing an impression of a stamp with the titles and name of the tomb owner. The cones, some 30 cm long, were originally inserted in the brick-built tomb facade or tomb pyramid to form horizontal rows.

God's Father Common priestly title of the New Kingdom and later, usually further extended by the name of a god (e.g. God's Father of Amun). God's Fathers mostly ranked above ordinary wa'eb-priests ("the pure ones") but below "prophets."

Herald Middle and New Kingdom title borne by an official whose function was probably to report to the king and make his commands known, both at court and, for example, on the battlefield.

hieratic From Greek "sacred," the normal form of the script, mostly written on papyrus or ostraca, and used throughout Egyptian history. In later periods hieratic was restricted to religious texts, hence its name. Hieratic signs lost the pictorial character of hieroglyphs, and are often joined together.

hieroglyph Sign in the Egyptian script, from Greek "sacred carving"; used only for the monumental form of the script, in which most signs are identifiable pictures, and no signs are joined together.

High Priest Conventional translation of the title of the head of the local priesthood. The Egyptian forms of the most important among them were as follows:
Amun (Thebes): "The First Prophet of Amun"
Ptah (Memphis): "Greatest of the Directors of Craftsmen"
Re' (Heliopolis): "Greatest of the Seers"
Thoth (el-Ashmunein): "Greatest of the Five."

Horus name The first name in a king's titulary, normally written inside a serekh, and consisting of an epithet that identifies the king as a manifestation of an aspect of Horus.

hypostyle hall Term for columned halls, from the Greek for "bearing pillars." The halls are the outermost, and grandest, parts of the main structures of temples, frequently added after the rest, and exhibit an elaborate symbolism. Many temples have two hypostyle halls.

ichneumon A small rodent that kills snakes and destroys crocodile eggs, akin to the Indian mongoose. The ichneumon and the shrewmouse formed a pair of animals associated with the sun god. Ichneumons in particular were often buried in the Late and Greco-Roman Periods; many bronze statuettes of them are known.

ithyphallic With erect penis (from the Greek). Various gods were shown in this form, such as Min, Amun (especially at Luxor) and the revitalized Osiris.

ka Obscure conception of an aspect of the personality, perhaps associated originally with sexual fertility. The ka was born as a "double" of the living person, but came into its own in the afterlife, when it received mortuary offerings and ensured the deceased's survival. See also ba.

kiosk Small, open temple structure used as a way station for statues of gods during festivals when they left their main temples, or in the sed festival.

Lector Priest Priest (literally "One who bears the ritual book") whose function was to declaim the ritual texts in funerary and temple cult. He wore a distinctive broad white sash diagonally across the chest. "Chief Lector Priest" was a higher rank.

logogram Sign in the script that writes an entire word, often with the addition of a stroke and/or the feminine ending -t.

mastaba Arabic word for bench, used as the term for free-standing tombs of the Early Dynastic Period and Old Kingdom (and some later ones). The basic form of a mastaba's superstructure is a rectangle with flat roof and vertical (mud-brick) or slightly inclined (stone) walls.

Mistress of the House Housewife, title given to married ladies from the Middle Kingdom onwards.

naos Shrine in which divine statues were kept, especially in temple sanctuaries. A small wooden naos was normally placed inside a monolithic one in hard stone; the latter are typical of the Late Period, and sometimes elaborately decorated. Also used as a term for temple sanctuary.

necropolis Greek word for cemetery. "Necropolis" normally describes large and important burial areas that were in use for long periods, "cemetery" smaller and more homogeneous sites; cemeteries may also be subdivisions of a necropolis.

Nilometer Staircase descending into the Nile and marked with levels above low water; used for measuring, and in some cases recording, inundation levels. The most famous are on Elephantine island and on Roda island in Cairo.

nomarch The chief official of a nome. In the late Old Kingdom–early Middle Kingdom nomarchs became local, hereditary rulers, who governed their nomes more or less independently of the central authority; the kings of the 11th Dynasty began in this way. During the 12th Dynasty the office ceased to have political importance.

nome Administrative province of Egypt, from Greek *nomos*; the ancient Egyptian term was *sepat*. The nome system seems to have been elaborated in the Early Dynastic Period, but did not reach final form until the Ptolemies. During some periods of highly centralized administration (e.g. late Middle Kingdom) the nomes had little real importance.

obelisk Monolithic tapering shaft, mostly in pink granite, with a pyramidion at the top; from a Greek word for a spit. Obelisks are solar symbols, probably similar in meaning to pyramids, and associated with an ancient stone called *benben* in Heliopolis. They were set up in pairs outside the entrances to some Old Kingdom tombs, and outside temples; a single obelisk in east Karnak was the object of a cult.

ogdoad Term describing the group of 8 deities (four male-female pairs) associated with Hermopolis, who symbolize the state of the world before creation. The group's composition varies, but its classic form is: Nun and Naunet, the primeval waters; Huh and Hauhet, endless space; Kuk and Kauket, darkness; Amun and Amaunet, what is hidden.

orthogram Sign in the script whose function is to elucidate the function of another sign or to write a dual or plural.

Osirid pillar Pillar, mostly in an open court or portico, with a colossal statue of a king forming its front part; unlike caryatids in Classical architecture, the statues are not weight-bearing elements. Most are mummiform, but not all; the connection with Osiris is doubtful.

ostracon Flake of limestone or potsherd used for writing (from the Greek for potsherd); also fragment from an inscribed jar (e.g. a wine jar inscribed with the details of a vintage). Ostraca are known from all periods, but 19th- and 20th-Dynasty examples are commonest (up to 20,000 have been found). Most texts are in hieratic or demotic, but there are also cursive hieroglyphic texts and numerous pictures, including drafts of hieroglyphic inscriptions.

Overseer of Sealers Typical administrative title of the 12th Dynasty borne by a high official of the Treasury. The "Overseer of Sealers" was responsible to the head of the Treasury ("The Overseer of the Seal") and his deputies. The term derives from the fact that most containers of produce and goods were sealed when entering or leaving the Treasury magazines. Clay impressions of seals are common finds.

papyrus The chief Egyptian writing material, and an important export. The earliest papyrus (blank) dates to the 1st Dynasty, the latest to the Islamic Period, when the plant died out in Egypt. Sheets were made by cutting the pith of the plant into strips laid in rows horizontally and vertically, which were then beaten together, activating the plant's natural starch to form an adhesive. Separate sheets were gummed together to form rolls. The better surface of a papyrus (the normal recto) had the fibers running horizontally, but letters were normally begun on strips inscribed across the fibers.

peristyle court Court with a roof around the sides supported by rows of columns (from Greek *peristylon*) and an open space in the center.

phonogram Sign in the script that records a sound. Only consonants are precisely recorded, and phonograms may write 1–4 consonants.

praenomen A king's first cartouche name, which he adopted on his accession; also called "throne name." It consists of a statement about the god Re', later with additional epithets, e.g. Menkheprure' (Tuthmosis IV)

"Re' is enduring of manifestations."

pronaos Room in front of the sanctuary (naos) of a temple, whose exact location varies with the design of individual temples; sometimes used as a term for hypostyle hall.

Prophet Priestly title (literally "God's Servant"), ranking above *wa'eb*-priests and God's Fathers, usually extended by the name of a god (e.g. "Prophet of Montu"). The head of the local priesthood, particularly in the provinces, was often called "Overseer of Prophets." The high priest of Amun at Thebes was "The First Prophet of Amun"; below him were the Second, Third and Fourth Prophets.

propylon Gateway that stands in front of a pylon.

pylon Monumental entrance wall of a temple, from the Greek for gate; consists of a pair of massifs with an opening between, mostly elaborated into a doorway. All the wall faces are inclined; the corners are completed with a torus molding and the top with torus and cavetto cornice. Pylons are the largest and least essential parts of a temple, mostly built last. Some temples have series of them (e.g. 10 at Karnak, on two axes).

pyramidion Capstone of a pyramid or top of an obelisk. The pyramidion was decorated and became a symbolic object in its own right, being used also as the most striking feature of the small brick pyramids of private tombs of the New Kingdom (Deir el-Medina, Saqqara) and Late Period (Abydos).

Pyramid Texts Texts on the walls of the internal rooms of pyramids of the end of the 5th and 6th–8th Dynasties, later used by private individuals for most of Egyptian history. Some texts may relate to the king's burial ceremonies, but others are concerned with temple ritual and many other matters.

ranking title Title that indicates status but does not go with any specific function; very important in the Old and to a lesser extent the Middle Kingdom. The typical sequence of titles, in ascending order, is "Royal Acquaintance," "Sole Companion," "Count," "Hereditary Prince."

reserve heads Old Kingdom tomb sculptures in the round, aiming at a realistic representation of the head of the deceased (hence the alternate term "portrait heads"), and acting as its substitute. Some 30 have been found, mainly at Giza.

revetment Cladding of a wall surface or bastion; may be ornamental, e.g. stone covering mud brick, or structural, and intended to give stability to a core of rubble.

sabbakhin Arabic word for diggers of *sabbakh*, nitrogenous earth from ancient sites used as fertilizer; *sabbakh* may be mud brick or remains of organic refuse. *Sabbakhin* are among the chief agents of destruction of ancient sites.

saff tomb Arabic word for row, describing rock-cut tombs of the early 11th Dynasty that consist of a row of openings – or colonnade – in the hillside.

sea peoples Invaders of Egypt in the late 19th and early 20th Dynasties, probably associated with a wave of destruction on Near Eastern sites and more remotely with the fall of Mycenaean Greece and the Hittite empire. Their precise identity and origin are much disputed by scholars.

sed festival Ritual of royal regeneration, almost always celebrated after 30 years of a king's reign, and thereafter at three-yearly intervals, but very occasionally performed earlier; features prominently in the decoration of royal mortuary temples, reflecting the king's wish to rule long in the next world.

semogram Sign in the script that conveys meaning, not sound. Subcategories are logograms, taxograms and orthograms. Also called ideograms.

serekh Image of a brick facade to a palace or enclosure, with a rectangular space above; the facade is in the style of the beginning of the Early Dynastic Period. A falcon (the sign for Horus) perches on the top horizontal of the rectangle, which encloses a king's Horus name.

sistrum Musical instrument – a kind of rattle – sacred to Hathor. Two types are common: (a) a naos shape above a Hathor head, with ornamental loops on the sides (the rattle was inside the box of the naos); (b) a simple loop with loose cross bars of metal above a smaller Hathor head; both had long handles. (a) was used from the New Kingdom on as a type of column capital, making play with the association between the rustle of aquatic plants and the joyful sound of the sistrum (plant and sistrum forms are occasionally combined). At Dendara the sistrum (mostly type (a)) was an important sacred object.

Standard Bearer of the Lord of the Two Lands Military title of the New Kingdom, borne by an officer of the infantry, chariotry, or one attached to a ship, who was in charge of a company of some 250 men. Companies of the Egyptian army had distinguishing "standards."

stela Slab of stone or sometimes wood with texts, reliefs or paintings. Commemorative or votive stelae are placed in temples; tomb stelae function within the decoration of a tomb.

talatat Arabic word for three (handbreadths), describing the length of the typical small stone building blocks of temples of Amenophis IV/Akhenaten. They are found reused at a number of sites (some 30,000 at Karnak), and are decorated with scenes in the 'Amarna style. Some complete walls have been reassembled from scattered blocks.

Tasian From Deir Tasa, a Predynastic site in Upper Egypt; name of a Predynastic culture that may not be distinct from Badarian.

taxogram Sign in the script that is placed after the phonograms in the writing of a word, and indicates the class or area of meaning to which it belongs.

torus molding Semicircular or cylindrical band forming the edge of a stela or the corner of a stone wall. Detailed examples are decorated with a pattern that suggests lashings around a pole or reed bundle, almost certainly indicating that the form derives from architecture in flimsy materials.

tree goddess A goddess associated with a sacred tree and represented as a tree with arms or a woman emerging from a tree. Hathor, Isis and Nut are found as tree goddesses, all in the context of mortuary cult.

underworld books Mixed pictorial and textual compositions inscribed in New Kingdom royal tombs that describe the passage of the sun god through the underworld and the sky; taken over by private individuals in the Late Period.

uraeus The most characteristic symbol of kingship, a rearing cobra worn on the king's forehead or crown. The cobra is associated with the goddess Wadjit or with the sun, whose "eye" it is held to be. It is an agent of destruction and protection of the king, spitting out fire.

Viceroy of Kush Administrator of Nubia during the New Kingdom, at first called "King's Son," from the mid-18th Dynasty "King's Son of Kush." Despite the form of the title, its holder was not a real son of the king. The area governed by the viceroy extended as far north as Kom el-Ahmar (Hierakonpolis). His two deputies, one for Lower Nubia (Wawat), the other for Upper Nubia (Kush), resided at 'Aniba and 'Amara respectively.

vizier The highest official in the administration, whose post is found already in the Early Dynastic Period. In the New Kingdom there were two viziers, at Memphis and Thebes; from this period on, the most important individuals were often not viziers, and the office was less important in the Late Period. There are texts that describe the installation of a vizier and detail his functions.

winged disk A sun disk with an outspread pair of wings attached. The earliest possible example of the motif is of the 1st Dynasty. It is associated with Horus of Behdet (Edfu), and symbolizes the sun, especially in architecture on ceilings, cornices and stelae. It was often copied outside Egypt.

zodiac The Babylonian and Greek signs of the zodiac were introduced into Egypt in the Greco-Roman Period, "translated" into Egyptian representational forms, and used in the decoration of astronomical ceilings of tombs and temples, and on coffin lids.

LIST OF ILLUSTRATIONS

BIBLIOGRAPHY

Much of the work of Egyptologists is published in specialist journals, of which a dozen are devoted exclusively to the subject. These are listed in the *Lexikon der Ägyptologie* (see below). The presentation in this book is often based on material in journals, and may differ from that in other books. This applies especially to "The Historical Setting."

*Has been translated into other languages.

General and Reference Works
British Museum, *An Introduction to Ancient Egypt*. London 1979.
F. Daumas, *La Civilisation de l'Égypte pharaonique*. Paris 1965.
A. Erman and H. Ranke, *Ägypten and ägyptisches Leben im Altertum*. 2nd ed. Tübingen 1923.*
W. C. Hayes, *The Scepter of Egypt*, i–ii. New York 1953, Cambridge (Mass.) 1959.
W. Helck and E. Otto, *Kleines Wörterbuch der Ägyptologie*. 2nd ed. Wiesbaden 1970.
W. Helck *et al.* (eds.), *Lexikon der Ägyptologie* (6 vols. planned). Wiesbaden 1972–.
E. Hornung, *Einführung in die Ägyptologie*. Darmstadt 1967.
H. Kees, *Ägypten*. Munich 1933.
S. Moscati (ed.), *L'alba della civiltà*, i–iii. Turin 1976.
C. F. Nims, *Thebes of the Pharaohs*. London 1965.
E. Otto, *Wesen und Wandel der ägyptischen Kultur*. Berlin etc. 1969.
G. Posener *et al.*, *Dictionnaire de la civilisation égyptienne*. Paris 1959.*
J. A. Wilson, *The Burden of Egypt/The Culture of Ancient Egypt*. Chicago (Ill.) 1951.*

Part One: The Cultural Setting
The geography of ancient Egypt
W. Y. Adams, *Nubia: Corridor to Africa*. London 1977.
K. W. Butzer, *Early Hydraulic Civilization in Egypt*. Chicago (Ill.) and London 1976.
H. Kees, *Das alte Ägypten, eine kleine Landeskunde*. 2nd ed. Berlin 1958.*
A. Lucas and J. R. Harris, *Ancient Egyptian Materials and Industries*. 4th ed. London 1962.
P. Montet, *Géographie de l'Égypte ancienne*, i–ii. Paris 1957–61.
B. Trigger, *Nubia under the Pharaohs*. London 1976.

The study of ancient Egypt
W. R. Dawson and E. P. Uphill, *Who was who in Egyptology*. 2nd ed. London 1972.
L. Greener, *The Discovery of Egypt*. London 1966.
Works of travellers to Egypt are also available; many are collected in "Voyageurs occidentaux en Égypte," Cairo 1970–.

The historical setting
E. Bevan, *A History of Egypt under the Ptolemaic Dynasty*. London 1927.
J. H. Breasted, *A History of Egypt*. 2nd ed. New York 1909.*
Cambridge Ancient History, i–iv. 3rd ed. Cambridge 1970–.
A. H. Gardiner, *Egypt of the Pharaohs*. Oxford 1961.*
W. Helck, *Geschichte des alten Ägypten*. Leiden and Cologne 1968.
E. Hornung, *Grundzüge der ägyptischen Geschichte*. 2nd ed. Darmstadt 1978.
F. K. Kienitz, *Die politische Geschichte Ägyptens vom 7. bis zum 4. Jahrhundert vor der Zeitwende*. Berlin 1953.
K. A. Kitchen, *The Third Intermediate Period in Egypt (1100–650 B.C.)*. Warminster 1973.
J. G. Milne, *A History of Egypt under Roman Rule*. 3rd ed. London 1924.

Principles of art and architecture
A. Badawy, *A History of Egyptian Architecture*, i–iii. Giza 1954, Berkeley (Cal.) 1966–68.
S. Clarke and R. Engelbach, *Ancient Egyptian Masonry*. London 1930.
J.-L. de Cenival, *Égypte. Époque pharaonique*. Fribourg 1964.*
E. Iversen, *Canon and Proportions in Egyptian Art*. 2nd ed. Warminster 1975.

K. Lange and M. Hirmer, *Ägypten*. 4th ed. Munich 1967.*
H. Schäfer, *Von ägyptischer Kunst*. 4th ed. Wiesbaden 1963.*
W. S. Smith, *The Art and Architecture of Ancient Egypt*. Harmondsworth 1958.
—— *A History of Egyptian Sculpture and Painting in the Old Kingdom*. 2nd ed. London and Boston (Mass.) 1949.
C. Vandersleyen *et al.*, *Das alte Ägypten*. Berlin 1975.

Stelae
J. Vandier, *Manuel d'archéologie égyptienne*, ii(1). Paris 1954.

Part Two: A Journey down the Nile
For most sites we have faced the almost impossible task of limiting the selection of publications to one or two items. We have chosen those which give the best idea of the present state of knowledge of the area in question, either by presenting general information or by illustrating a particular feature. Complete bibliographical data are given by B. Porter and R. L. B. Moss, *Topographical Bibliography of Ancient Egyptian Hieroglyphical Texts, Reliefs, and Paintings*, i–vii, i² (Oxford 1927–), quoted here as PM. Regular reports on current archaeological work in Egypt and Nubia are published by J. Leclant in *Orientalia* (since 1950).

Elephantine and Aswan (PM v.221–44)
E. Bresciani and S. Pernigotti, *Assuan. Il tempio tolemaico di Isi. I blocchi decorati e iscritti*. Pisa 1978.
E. Edel, *Die Felsengräber der Qubbet el-Hawa bei Assuan*, i–. Wiesbaden 1967–.

Philae (PM vi.203–56)
H. Junker and E. Winter, *Philä*, i–. Vienna 1958–.
H. G. Lyons, *A Report on the Island and Temples of Philae*. [London 1897].
S. Sauneron and H. Stierlin, *Die letzten Tempel Ägyptens. Edfu und Philae*. Zürich 1978.*

Kom Ombo (PM vi.179–203)
J. de Morgan *et al.*, *Kom Ombos*, i–ii. Vienna 1909.

Gebel el-Silsila (PM v.208–18, 220–21)
R. A. Caminos and T. G. H. James, *Gebel es-Silsilah*, i–. London 1963–.

Edfu (PM v.200–05; vi.119–77)
M. de Rochemonteix and É. Chassinat, *Le Temple d'Edfou*, i–xiv. Paris 1892, Cairo 1918–.

Kom el-Ahmar (PM v.191–200)
B. Adams, *Ancient Hierakonpolis*, with *Supplement*. Warminster 1974.
W. A. Fairservis, Jr. *et al.*, "Preliminary Report on the First Two Seasons at Hierakonpolis," *Journal of the American Research Center in Egypt*, ix (1971–72), 7–68.
J. E. Quibell (vol.ii with F. W. Green), *Hierakonpolis*, i–ii. London 1900, 1902.

el-Kab (PM v.171–91)
P. Derchain, *Elkab*, i. *Les Monuments religieux à l'entrée de l'Ouady Hellal*. Brussels 1971.
Fouilles de el Kab, i–iii. Brussels, 1940–54.

Esna (PM v.165–67; vi.110–19)
D. Downes, *The Excavations at Esna 1905–1906*. Warminster 1974.
S. Sauneron, *Esna*, i–. Cairo 1959–.

el-Mo'alla (PM v.170)
J. Vandier, *Mo'alla, la tombe d'Ankhtifi et la tombe de Sébekhotep*. Cairo 1950.

Gebelein (PM v.162–64)

Tod (PM v.167–69)
F. Bisson de la Roque, *Tôd (1934 à 1936)*. Cairo 1937.

Armant (PM v.151–61)
R. Mond and O. H. Myers, *Temples of Armant. A Preliminary Survey*. London 1940.
—— *The Bucheum*, i–iii. London 1934.

Luxor (PM ii.²301–39)
H. Brunner, *Die südlichen Räume des Tempels von Luxor*. Mainz 1977.
A. Gayet, *Le Temple de Louxor*. Cairo 1894.

Karnak (PM ii.²1–301)
P. Barguet, *Le Temple d'Amon-Rê à Karnak. Essai d'exégèse*. Cairo 1962.

Reliefs and Inscriptions at Karnak, i–, by the Epigraphic Survey. Chicago (Ill.) 1936–.

The West Bank (PM i² and ii.²339–537)
H. Carter and A. C. Mace, *The Tomb of Tut.ankh.amen*, i–iii. London etc. 1923–33.
E. Hornung and F. Teichmann, *Das Grab des Haremhab im Tal der Könige*. Bern 1971.
Medinet Habu, i–viii, by the Epigraphic Survey. Chicago (Ill.) 1930–70.
E. Naville, *The Temple of Deir el Bahari*, Introductory Memoir and i–vi. London 1894–1908.
J. Osing, *Der Tempel Sethos' I. in Gurna. Die Reliefs und Inschriften*, i–. Mainz 1977–.
G. Thausing and H. Goedicke, *Nofretari. Eine Dokumentation der Wandgemälde ihres Grabes*. Graz 1971.

Nag' el-Madamud (PM v.137–50)
F. Bisson de la Roque, J. J. Clère *et al.*, *Rapport sur les fouilles de Medamoud (1925–32)*. Cairo 1926–36.

Naqada and Tukh (PM v.117–19)
J. de Morgan, *Recherches sur les origines de l'Égypte*, ii, 147–202. Paris 1897.

Qus (PM v.135–6)

Qift (PM v.123–34)
W. M. F. Petrie, *Koptos*. London 1896.

Dendara (PM v.109–16; vi.41–110)
É. Chassinat and F. Daumas, *Le Temple de Dendara*, i–. Cairo 1934–.
F. Daumas, *Dendara et le temple d'Hathor*. Cairo 1969.
A. Mariette, *Denderah*, i–iv. Paris 1870–73.

el-Qasr wa-' l-Saiyad (PM v.119–22)

Hiw (PM v.107–09)
W. M. F. Petrie, *Diospolis Parva: the Cemeteries of Abadiyeh and Hu, 1898–9*. London 1901.

Abydos (PM v.39–105; vi. 1–41)
A. M. Calverley *et al.*, *The Temple of King Sethos I at Abydos*, i–. London and Chicago (Ill.) 1933–.
A. Mariette, *Abydos*, i–ii, Paris 1869–80.
W. M. F. Petrie, *The Royal Tombs of the First Dynasty/Earliest Dynasties*. London 1900–01.

Beit Khallaf (PM v.37)
J. Garstang, *Mahâsna and Bêt Khallâf*. London 1903.

Akhmim (PM v.17–26)

Wannina (PM v.31–34)
W. M. F. Petrie, *Athribis*. London 1908.

Qaw el-Kebir (PM v.9–16)
H. Steckeweh, *Die Fürstengräber von Qaw*. Leipzig 1936.

Asyut (PM iv.259–70)
F. L. Griffith, *The Inscriptions of Siut and Der Rifeh*. London 1889.

Deir el-Gabrawi (PM iv.242–46)
N. de G. Davies, *The Rock Tombs of Deir el Gebrawi*, i–ii. London 1902.

Meir (PM iv.247–58)
A. M. Blackman, *The Rock Tombs of Meir*, i–vi. London 1914–53.

el-'Amarna (PM iv.192–237)
N. de G. Davies, *The Rock Tombs of El Amarna*, i–vi. London 1903–08.
G. T. Martin, *The Royal Tomb at el-'Amarna*, i–. London 1974–.
T. E. Peet, C. L. Woolley, J. D. S. Pendlebury *et al.*, *The City of Akhenaten*, i–iii. London 1923, 1933, 1951

el-Sheikh Sa'id (PM iv.187–92)
N. de G. Davies, *The Rock Tombs of Sheikh Saïd*. London 1901.

Deir el-Bersha (PM iv.177–87)
P. E. Newberry and F. L. Griffith, *El Bersheh*, i–ii. London 1892.

el-Ashmunein (PM iv.165–69)
G. Roeder, *Hermopolis 1929–1939*. Hildesheim 1959.

Tuna el-Gebel (PM iv.169–75)
S. Gabra and E. Drioton, *Peintures à fresques et scènes peintes à Hermoupolis ouest (Touna el-Gebel)*. Cairo 1954.
G. Lefebvre, *Le Tombeau de Petosiris*, i–iii. Cairo 1923–24.

el-Sheikh 'Ibada (PM iv.175–77)
Antinoe (1965–1968). Missione archeologica in Egitto dell' Università di Roma. Rome 1974.

Beni Hasan with Speos Artemidos (PM iv.140–65)
P. E. Newberry, F. L. Griffith *et al.*, *Beni Hasan*, i–iv. London 1893–1900.

Zawyet el-Amwat (PM iv.134–39)
A. Varille, *La Tombe de Ni-Ankh-Pepi à Zâouyet el-Mayetîn*. Cairo 1938.

Tihna el-Gebel (PM iv.127–33)
R. Holthoer and R. Ahlqvist, ''The 'Roman Temple' at Tehna el-Gebel, *Studia Orientalia*, xliii.7 (1974).

el-Bahnasa (PM iv.124)
W. M. F. Petrie, *Tombs of the Courtiers and Oxyrhynkhos*. London 1925.
The Oxyrhynchus Papyri, i–. London 1898–.

el-Hiba (PM iv. 124–25)
H. Ranke, *Koptische Friedhöfe bei Karâra und der Amontempel Scheschonks I bei el Hibe*. Berlin and Leipzig 1926.

Dishasha (PM iv.121–23)
W. M. F. Petrie, *Deshasheh 1897*. London 1898.

Ihnasya el-Medina (PM iv.118–21)
E. Naville, *Ahnas el Medineh (Heracleopolis Magna)*. London 1894.
W. M. F. Petrie, *Ehnasya 1904*. London 1905.

Kom Medinet Ghurab (PM iv.112–15)
L. Borchardt, *Der Porträtkopf der Königin Teje*. Leipzig 1911.

el-Lahun (PM iv.107–12)
W. M. F. Petrie, *Kahun, Gurob, and Hawara*. London 1890.
—— *Illahun, Kahun and Gurob 1889–90*. London 1891.

The Faiyum (PM iv.96–104)
E. Bresciani, *Rapporto preliminare delle campagne di scavo 1966 e 1967*. Milan and Varese 1968.
A. Vogliano, *Rapporto degli scavi … Madînet Mâdi*, i–ii. Milan 1936–37.

Maidum (PM iv.89–96)
W. M. F. Petrie, *Medum*. London 1892.

el-Lisht (PM iv.77–85)
H. Goedicke, *Re-used Blocks from the Pyramid of Amenemhet I at Lisht*. New York 1971.

Mit Rahina (PM iii.217–27)
R. Anthes *et al.*, *Mit Rahineh 1955* and *1956*. Philadelphia (Pa.) 1959 and 1965.
W. M. F. Petrie *et al.*, *Memphis*, i–v. London 1909–13.

Dahshur (PM iii.228–40)
J. de Morgan, *Fouilles à Dahchour*, i–ii. Vienna 1895–1903.
A. Fakhry, *The Monuments of Sneferu at Dahshur*, i–ii. Cairo 1959–61.

Saqqara (PM iii.83–215 and iii.²393–776)
P. Duell *et al.*, *The Mastaba of Mereruka*, i–ii. Chicago (Ill.) 1938.
M. Z. Goneim, *Horus Sekhem-khet. The Unfinished Step Pyramid at Saqqara*, i: Cairo 1957.
J.-P. Lauer, *Saqqara. The Royal Cemetery of Memphis*. London 1976.★
Le Tombeau de Ti, i–iii (i by L. Epron and F. Daumas, ii and iii by H. Wild). Cairo 1939–66.
A. M. Moussa and H. Altenmüller, *Das Grab des Nianchchnum und Chnumhotep*. Mainz 1977.

Abusir (PM iii.²324–50)
L. Borchardt, *Das Grabdenkmal des Königs Śa3hu-rē'*, i–ii. Leipzig 1910–13.
H. Ricke *et al.*, *Das Sonnenheiligtum des Königs Userkaf*, i–ii. Cairo 1965, Wiesbaden 1969.

Abu Ghurab (PM iii.²314–24)
E. Edel and S. Wenig, *Die Jahreszeitenreliefs aus dem Sonnenheiligtum des Königs Ne-user-Re*. Berlin 1974.

Zawyet el-'Aryan (PM iii.²312–14)
D. Dunham, *Zawiyet el-Aryan. The Cemeteries Adjacent to the Layer Pyramid*. Boston (Mass.) 1978.

Giza (PM iii.²10–312)
D. Dunham and W. K. Simpson, *The Mastaba of Queen Mersyankh III*. Boston (Mass.) 1974.
H. Junker, *Gîza*, i–xii. Vienna and Leipzig 1929–55.
G. A. Reisner, *Mycerinus. The Temples of the Third*

Pyramid at Giza. Cambridge (Mass.) 1931.
—— *A History of the Giza Necropolis*, i–ii. Cambridge (Mass.) 1942–55.
W. K. Simpson, *The Mastabas of Kawab, Khafkhufu I and II*. Boston (Mass.) 1978.
C. M. Zivie, *Giza au deuxième millénaire*. Cairo 1976.

Abu Rawash (PM iii.²1–10)
F. Bisson de la Roque, *Rapport sur les fouilles d'Abou-Roasch (1922–1923)* and *(1924)*. Cairo 1924–25.

Ausim (PM iv.68)

Kom Abu Billo (PM iv.67–68)

Kom el-Hisn (PM iv.51–52)

Naukratis (PM iv.50)
D. G. Hogarth, H. L. Lorimer and C. C. Edgar, ''Naukratis, 1903,''*Journal of Hellenic Studies*, xxv (1905), 105–36.

Alexandria (PM iv.2–6)
A. Adriani, *Repertorio d'arte dell'Egitto greco-romano*, series C, i–ii. Palermo 1966.
P. M. Fraser, *Ptolemaic Alexandria*, i–iii. Oxford 1972.

Sa el-Hagar (PM iv.46–49)
R. el-Sayed, *Documents relatifs à Saïs et ses divinités*. Cairo 1975.

Tell el-Fara'in (PM iv.45)

Behbeit el-Hagar (PM iv.40–42)

Tell Atrib (PM iv.65–67)
P. Vernus, *Athribis*. Cairo 1978.

Tell el-Muqdam (PM iv.37–39)
E. Naville, *Ahnas el Medineh (Heracleopolis Magna)*. London 1894, 27–31.

Samannud (PM iv.43–44)
G. Steindorff, ''Reliefs from the Temples of Sebennytos and Iseion in American Collections,'' *Journal of the Walters Art Gallery*, vii–viii (1944–45), 38–59.

el–Baqliya (PM iv.39–40)
A.-P. Zivie, *Hermopolis et le nome de l'Ibis*. Cairo 1975.

Tell el-Rub'a and Tell el-Timai (PM iv.35–37)
H. De Meulenaere and P. MacKay, *Mendes II*. Warminster 1976.

Heliopolis (PM iv.59–65)
W. M. F. Petrie and E. Mackay, *Heliopolis, Kafr Ammar and Shurafa*. London 1915.
H. Ricke, ''Eine Inventartafel aus Heliopolis im Turiner Museum,'' *Zeitschrift für ägyptische Sprache und Altertumskunde*, lxxi (1935), 111–33.

Tell el-Yahudiya (PM iv.56–58)
E. Naville, *The Mound of the Jew and the City of Onias*. London 1890.
G. R. H. Wright, ''Tell el-Yehūdīyah and the Glacis,'' *Zeitschrift des Deutschen Palästina-Vereins*, lxxxiv (1968), 1–17.

Tell Basta (PM iv.27–35)
Labib Habachi, *Tell Basta*. Cairo 1957.

Saft el-Hinna (PM iv.10–11)
E. Naville, *The Shrine of Saft el Henneh and the Land of Goshen 1885*. London 1887.

District of el-Khata'na and Qantir (PM iv.9–10)
M. Bietak, *Tell el-Dab'a I*. Vienna 1975.

Tell Nabasha (PM iv.7–9)
W. M. F. Petrie, *Tanis II, Nebesheh (Am) and Defenneh (Tahpanhes)*. London 1888.

San el-Hagar (PM iv.13–26)
P. Montet, *La Nécropole royale de Tanis*, i–iii. Paris 1947–60.
—— *Les Énigmes de Tanis*. Paris 1952.

Tell el-Maskhuta (PM iv.53–55)
E. Naville, *The Store City of Pithom and the Route of the Exodus*. London 1903.

el-Dakka (PM vii.40–50)
G. Roeder and W. Ruppel, *Der Tempel von Dakke*, i–iii. Cairo 1913–30.

Quban (PM vii.82–83)

'Amada (PM vii.65–73)
H. Gauthier, *Le Temple d'Amada*. Cairo 1913–26.

el-Sebu'a (PM vii.53–64)
H. Gauthier, *Le Temple de Ouadi es-Sebouâ*. Cairo 1912.

el-Derr (PM vii.84–89)
A. M. Blackman, *The Temple of Derr*. Cairo 1913.

el-Lessiya (PM vii.90–91)
S.Curto, *Il tempio di Ellesija*. Turin 1970.

Qasr Ibrim (PM vii.92–94)
R. A. Caminos, *The Shrines and Rock-inscriptions of Ibrim*. London 1968.

Dabod (PM vii.1–5)
M. Almagro, *El templo de Debod*. Madrid 1971.

Tafa (PM vii.8–10)
H. D. Schneider, *Taffeh. Rond de wederopbouw van een Nubische tempel*. The Hague 1979.

Beit el-Wali (PM vii. 21–27)
H. Ricke, G. R. Hughes and E. F. Wente, *The Beit el-Wali Temple of Ramesses II*. Chicago (Ill.) 1967.

Kalabsha (PM vii.10–21)
K. G. Siegler, *Kalabsha. Architektur und Baugeschichte des Tempels*. Berlin 1970.

Dendur (PM vii.27–33)
C. Aldred, ''The Temple of Dendur,'' *Metropolitan Museum of Art Bulletin*, xxxvi (1) (Summer 1978).

Gerf Hussein (PM vii.33–37)

'Aniba (PM vii.75–81)
G. Steindorff, *Aniba*, i–ii. Glückstadt etc. 1935–37.

Abu Simbel (PM vii.95–119)
C. Desroches-Noblecourt and C. Kuentz, *Le Petit Temple d'Abou Simbel*, i–ii. Cairo 1968.
W. MacQuitty, *Abu Simbel*. London 1965.

Sinai
A. H. Gardiner, T. E. Peet and J. Černý, *The Inscriptions of Sinai*, i–ii. London 1952–55.

Boats
B. Landström, *Ships of the Pharaohs. 4000 Years of Egyptian Shipbuilding*. London 1970.
M. Z. Nour *et al.*, *The Cheops Boats*, i. Cairo 1960.

Pyramids
I. E. S. Edwards, *The Pyramids of Egypt*. London. Various editions.★
A. Fakhry, *The Pyramids*. Chicago (Ill.) and London 1969.
J.-P. Lauer, *Le Mystère des pyramides*. Paris 1974.

Part Three: Aspects of Egyptian Society
Women in society
P. W. Pestman, *Marriage and Matrimonial Property in Ancient Egypt*. Leiden 1961.
S. Wenig, *Die Frau im alten Ägypten*. Leipzig 1967.

Scribes and writing
There are grammars of different stages of the language by: J. B. Callender; J. Černý and S. I. Groll; E. Edel; A. H. Gardiner; H. Junker; G. Lefebvre; F. Lexa; W. Spiegelberg; and dictionaries by: W. Erichsen; A. Erman and H. Grapow; R. O. Faulkner. The terminology used in the description of the script is that of W. Schenkel.

The army
A. R. Schulman, *Military Rank, Title, and Organization in the Egyptian New Kingdom*. Berlin 1964.
W. Wolf, *Die Bewaffnung des altägyptischen Heeres*. Leipzig 1926.
Y. Yadin, *The Art of Warfare in Biblical Lands in the Light of Archaeological Discovery*. London 1963.

Religion
H. Frankfort, *Ancient Egyptian Religion*. New York 1948.★
E. Hornung, *Der Eine und die Vielen*. Darmstadt 1971.
S. Morenz, *Ägyptische Religion*. Stuttgart 1960.★
E. Otto, *Osiris und Amun. Kult und heilige Stätten*. Munich 1966.★

Burial customs
J.-F. and L. Aubert, *Statuettes égyptiennes, chaouabtis, ouchebtis*. Paris 1974.
M.-L. Buhl, *The Late Egyptian Anthropoid Stone Sarcophagi*. Copenhagen 1959.
W. R. Dawson and P. H. K. Gray, *Mummies and Human Remains*. London 1968.
A. M. Donadoni Roveri, *I sarcofagi egizi dalle origini alla fine dell'Antico Regno*. Rome 1969.
J. Hamilton-Paterson and C. Andrews, *Mummies: Death and Life in Ancient Egypt*. London 1978.
H. Schneider, *Shabtis*, i–iii. Leiden 1977.

GAZETTEER

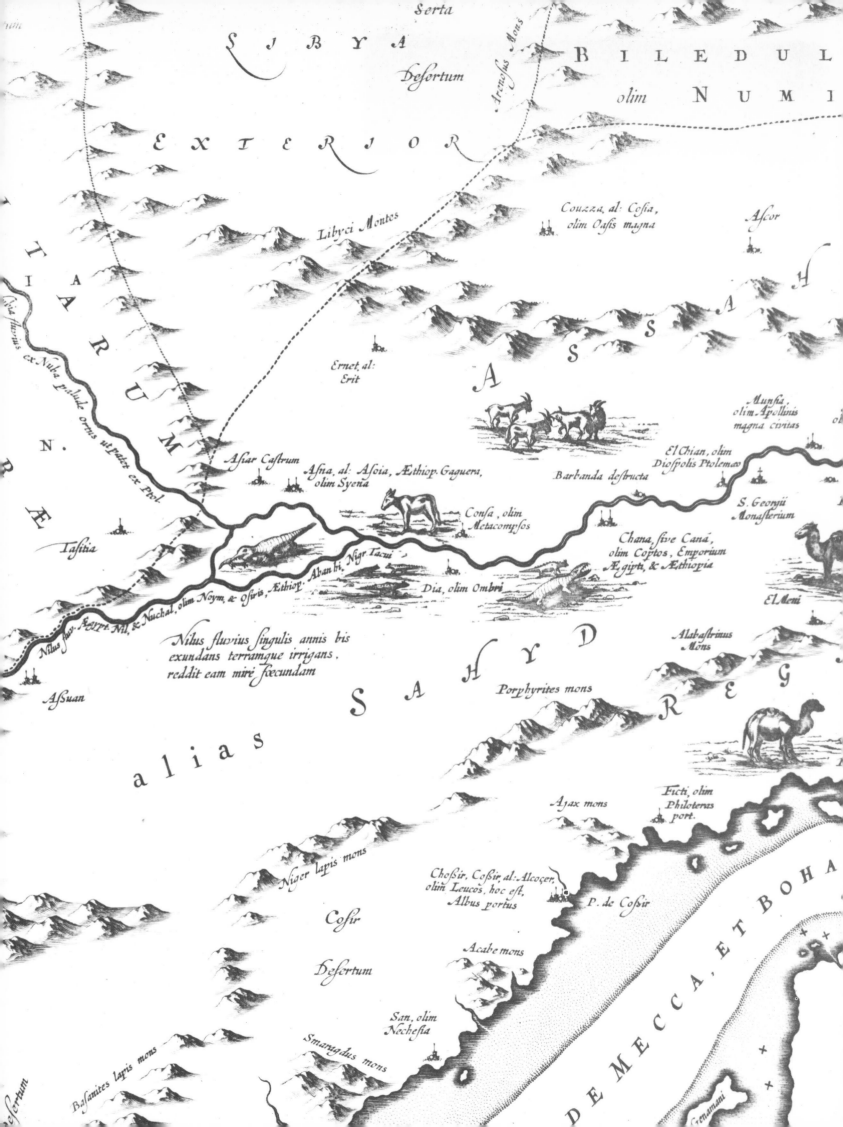

Serta

S I B Y A

EXTERIOR

Desertum

BILEDUL

olim NUMI

Arenosus mons

Libyci Montes

Couzza, al: Cosia,
olim Oasis magna

Ascor

ASSA

Ernet, al:
Erit

Munsia,
olim Apollinis
magna civitas

Assar Castrum

Asna, al: Asoia, Æthiop. Gaguera,
olim Syena

Barbanda destructa

El Chian, olim
Diospolis Ptolemæo

S. Georgii
Monasterium

Tafitia

Consa, olim
Metacompsos

Chana, sive Cana,
olim Coptos, Emporium
Ægipti, & Æthiopia

Abanhi, Nigr. Tacui

Dia, olim Ombri

El Meni

Nilus fluv. Ægypt. Nil, & Nuchal, olim Noym, & Osiris, Æthiop.

Nilus fluvius singulis annis bis
exundans terramque irrigans,
reddit eam miré fœcundam

Alabastrinus
Mons

SAHYD

REG

Assuan

Porphyrites mons

alias

Ajax mons

Ficti, olim
Philoteras
port.

Niger lapis mons

Chossir, Cossir, al: Alcoçer,
olim Leucos, hoc est,
Albus portus

P. de Cossir

Cossir

Acabe mons

Desertum

San, olim
Nechesia

Smaragdus mons

Basanites lapis mons

DE MECCA ET BOHA